Interpreting the PSALMS
for Teaching & Preaching

Interpreting the PSALMS
for Teaching & Preaching

Herbert W. Bateman IV
D. Brent Sandy, EDS.

CHALICE
PRESS
ST. LOUIS, MISSOURI

Cover image: Crosiers
Cover and interior design: Elizabeth Wright

Visit Chalice Press on the World Wide Web at **www.chalicepress.com**

10 9 8 7 6 5 4 3 2 1   10   11   12   13   14   15

EPUB: 978-08272-16365   EPDF: 978-08272-16372

Library of Congress Cataloging-in-Publication Data

Interpreting the Psalms for teaching & preaching / general editors, Herbert W. Bateman IV, D. Brent Sandy.
  p. cm.
Includes bibliographical references (p.   ).
ISBN 978-0-8272-1635-8 (pbk.)
1. Bible. O.T. Psalms–Criticism, interpretation, etc. 2. Bible. O.T. Psalms–Study and teaching. 3. Bible. O.T. Psalms–Homiletical use.
I. Bateman, Herbert W., 1955- II. Sandy, D. Brent, 1947-
BS1430.52.I57 2010
223'.20601–dc22   2010030169

Printed in the United States of America

Contents

Contributors

Martin G. Abegg Jr. is professor of relgious studies and co-director of the Dead Sea Scrolls Institute, Trinity Western University in Langley, British Columbia, Canada.

Richard E. Averbeck is professor of Old Testament and Semitic Languages, Trinity Evangelical Divinity School in Deerfield, Illinois.

William D. Barrick is professor of Old Testament and director of doctoral studies, The Master's Seminary in Sun Valley, California.

Herbert W. Bateman IV is professor of New Testament Studies, Southwestern Baptist Theological Seminary, Fort Worth, Texas.

Kenneth Bickel is a professor of pastoral Ministries, Grace College and Seminary, Winnoa Lake, Indiana.

Robert B. Chisholm Jr. is professor and chair of Old Testament Studies, Dallas Theological Seminary, Dallas, Texas.

David C. Deuel is academic director, The Master's Academy International, Valencia, California.

David S. Dockery is president of Union University, Jackson, Tennessee.

Walter C. Kaiser Jr. is distinguished professor emeritus of Old Testament and president emeritus, Gordon-Conwell Theological Seminary.

Bernon P. Lee is professor of Old Testament, Bethel University, St. Paul, Minnesota.

Eugene H. Merrill is distinguished professor of Old Testament, Dallas Theological Seminary, Dallas, Texas.

Richard D. Patterson is distinguished professor emeritus, Liberty University, Lynchburg, Virginia.

Timothy J. Ralston is professor of pastoral ministries, Dallas Theological Seminary, Dallas, Texas.

Tiberius Rata is professor of Old Testament Studies, Grace College and Seminary, Winnoa Lake, Indiana.

D. Brent Sandy is manuscript curator and researcher at Grace College, Winnoa Lake, Indiana.

Andrew J. Schmutzer is professor of Bible (Old Testament), Moody Bible Institute, Chicago, Illinois.

Julius W. L. Sing is a professor of Bible, Moody Bible Institute, Chicago, Illinois.

David Talley is professor of Old Testament, Biola University, LaMirada, California.

J. Glen Taylor is professor of Old Testament, Wycliffe College and the School of Graduate Studies, The University of Toronto, Canada.

Marion Ann Taylor is professor of Old Testament, Wycliffe College, The University of Toronto, Canada.

Preface

Most Evangelical Christians believe that if the body of Christ is going to mature as it should, and if the members of the community are going to grow spiritually as they should, they need to correctly interpret, conscientiously apply, and faithfully heed God's Word. It is the staple in a healthy diet for all believers, offering everything from milk to meat.

Rightly dividing the Word of truth is foundational to the Christian life. Unfortunately, most people are dependent on the commitment and skill of teachers and preachers in local churches for biblical interpretation and application because fewer and fewer Christians study the Bible on their own.

This book is designed for the church to enable teachers and preachers to offer informed teaching and faithful preaching of the psalms. The guiding questions behind each of the chapters have been: What are the most important things Christians need to know to understand and be transformed by the psalms? How can the psalms best be taught and preached? This book also attempts to help preachers and teachers correct what Walter Kaiser observes to be "a distressing absence of the Old Testament in the church. It is possible to attend some churches for months without ever hearing a sermon from the older testament... [T]his vacuum is unconscionable..."

This does not mean, however, that contributors have ignored the world of scholarship. The authors are well-informed in scholarly matters, and carefully drew together biblically valid insights in ways that enable scholarship to contribute to the church.

Part 1 opens the book with three introductory chapters, laying a foundation for interpreting and proclaiming the psalms. Part 2 considers fifteen representative psalms from the five books of the Psalter, providing models of interpretation along with suggestions for how to teach and preach the psalms. Interpretation is never complete without application, so Part 3 closes the book with four chapters on how the psalms apply to the Christian life, in regard to devotional reading, to incorporating the psalms into worship services, and to teaching and preaching the psalms.

Several features of the psalms are emphasized in the chapters that follow. (1) The psalms are designed for transformation. We should walk away from an encounter with the psalms as changed people. (2) The psalms are poetry. They speak with deep emotion and with picturesque language, seeking to touch our emotions. (3) The collection of 150 psalms was intentionally arranged into five books and into special groupings. This work of the collectors assists readers in understanding the meaning of the psalms.

A model of careful interpretation and of teaching and preaching the psalms is John J. Davis, to whom this book is dedicated. Dr. Davis has a B.A. from Trinity College (Florida); M.Div., Th.M., and Th.D. degrees from Grace Theological Seminary; and a D.D. from Trinity College. Across many years, classrooms, churches, and continents, John has been a scholar, professor, and preacher of the Old Testament. He served at Grace College and Seminary as professor of Old Testament and Hebrew studies for forty years and, for six years, was the institution's president. He has pastored churches in Florida and Indiana. He has authored sixteen books. He has participated in numerous archaeological expeditions in Palestine and elsewhere, specializing in tombs. He is a multitalented person who constantly develops and shares the gifts God has given him. He has been writing the column "Outdoor Scene" for a local newspaper for over twenty-five years. He has conducted fishing clinics throughout the United States. He has released several musical CDs. He has served on community boards. His circle of influence has reached far and wide.

This book on teaching and preaching the psalms is dedicated to John Davis because it reflects one of his passions: to help people to know God through the text of Scripture. The editors and contributors, assembled from friends, former students, and colleagues, wish to honor John for his lifetime devoted to the study, application, and proclamation of God's Word. This one's for you, John!

Herbert W. Bateman IV
D. Brent Sandy

Abbreviations
Bibles, Reference, and Series

AB   Anchor Bible
ABD   *Anchor Bible Dictionary.* Edited by D. D. Freedman. 6 vols. New York, 1992.
ANE   Ancient Near East
ANET   *Ancient Near Eastern Texts Relating to the Old Testament.*
Ant   Josephus, *Jewish Antiquities,* ca. 90 c.e.
ASV   American Standard Bible, 1901
b.c.e.   Before the Common Era (equivalent to b.c.)
BDB   Brown, F., S. R. Driver, and C. A. Briggs. *A Hebrew and English Lexicon of the Old Testament.* Oxford: Oxford University Press, 1907.
BJSUCSD   Biblical and Judaic Studies from the University of California, San Diego. Eisenbrauns.
BST   *The Bible Speaks Today,* ed. J. Stott and J. A. Motyer
c.e.   Common Era (equivalent to a.d.)
ESV   English Standard Version
FOTL   The Forms of the Old Testament Literature
GKC   *Gesenius' Hebrew Grammar,* ed. E. Kautzsch. Trans. A. E. Cowley. 2nd ed., 1910.
HOTE   Handbook for Old Testament Exegesis
HBS   Herders biblische Studien
HCSB   The Holman Christian Standard Bible, 2003
JPCS   The John Phillips Commentary Series
JSOTSup   Journal for the Study of the Old Testament Supplement Series
HALOT   *The Hebrew Aramaic Lexicon of the Old Testament.* L. Koehler, W. Baumgartner, and J. J. Stamm. Trans. and ed. M. E. J. Richardson. 5 vols, 1994–2000.
KJV   King James Version
LXX   Septuagint or earliest Greek translation of Old Testament
NASB   New American Standard Bible, 1977
NASB95 New American Standard Bible, 1995
NCBC   New Century Bible Commentary
NEB   New English Bible, 1970
NET   New English Translation, 2001
NICOT New International Commentary on the Old Testament, Eerdmans
NIDOTTE   *New International Dictionary of Old Testament Theology and Exegesis.* Ed. W. A. VanGemeren. 5 vols. Grand Rapids: Zondervan, 1997.
NIV   New International Version, 1984
NIVAC NIV Application Commentary, Zondervan
NKJV   New King James Version, 1982

NJB   New Jerome Bible, Catholic Bible Press, 1985
NLT   New Living Translation, 1996
NRSV   New Revised Standard Version, 1989
NTSI   The New Testament and the Scriptures of Israel
OBT   Overtures to Biblical Theology
REB   Revised English Bible, 1989
RSV   Revised Standard Version, 1952
SBL   Society of Biblical Literature
SBLDS   Society of Biblical Literature Dissertation Series
SHS   Scripture and Hermeneutics Series, Zondervan
TDOT   *Theological Dictionary of the Old Testament.* Ed. G. J. Botterweck and
         H. Ringgren. Trans. J. T. Willis, G. W. Bromiley, and D. E. Green.
         8 vols. 1974–2006. German orig. 1970–1995.
TEV   Today's English Version, 1976, 1992
TLOT   *Theological Lexicon of the Old Testament.* Ed. E. Jenni assisted by
         C. Westermann. Trans. M. E. Biddle. 3 vols. Peabody, Mass.:
         Hendrickson, 1997. German orig. 1971, 1976.
TOTC   Tyndale Old Testament Commentaries
TWOT   *Theological Wordbook of the Old Testament.* Ed. R. L. Harris and G. L.
         Archer Jr. 2 vols. Chicago: The Moody Bible Institute, 1980.
WBC   Word Biblical Commentary

Periodicals

BASOR   *Bulletin of the American Schools of Oriental Research*
Bib   *Biblica*
B.Sac   *Bibliotheca Sacra*
ChrT   *Christianity Today*
ExpTim *Expository Times*
Int   *Interpretation: A Journal of Bible and Theology*
JBL   Journal of Biblical Literature
JETS   *Journal of the Evangelical Theological Society*
JGPPS   *Journal of Group Psychotherapy, Psychodrama & Sociometry*
JNSL   *Journal of Northwest Semitic Languages*
JR   *Journal of Religion*
PBA   *Proceedings of the Bible Association*
RBL   *Review of Biblical Literature*
StudBib *Studia Biblica*
TS   *Theological Studies*
TynBul *Tyndale Bulletin*
VT   *Vetus Testamentum*
WTJ   *Westminster Theological Journal*
ZAW   *Zeitschrift für die alttestamentliche Wissenschaft*

PART 1

Introducing
the
Psalms

CHAPTER 1

Approaching the Psalms

Key Insights

D. Brent Sandy and Tiberius Rata

The book of Psalms reaches heavenward. Each psalm was carefully crafted in elegant poetry seeking in form and style to be worthy of addressing God. With more chapters than any book in the Bible–including the longest and shortest chapters–Psalms devotes a majority of its words to prayer and is the greatest book of poetry and prayers ever assembled. In its concentration on prayer, Psalms joins the brief book of Lamentations in standing unique among the books in Scripture (see Ps. 72:20).

The Dead Sea Scrolls contained more Psalms manuscripts than those of any other Old Testament book, suggesting how much devout Jews valued the psalms. Similarly, the New Testament quotes the psalms more often than any Old Testament book, underscoring their significance for the faith of Christians. Thus it is not surprising that these poems are the favorite of many. They have been sung and prayed in churches and synagogues for centuries. Psalm 23 is arguably the most beloved chapter in the whole Bible.

The beauty of the psalms is that they say things we feel, only better than we can express those feelings. They take the words right out of our mouths, or, perhaps more accurately, they put the right words into our mouths. The psalms are inward reaching. Praise is proclaimed, worship is experienced, sins are confessed, fears are expressed, doubts are exposed, frustrations are dumped, anger is unloaded. On our own we are reluctant to express our feelings to God so freely. We would barely give birth to words of praise so high and seldom, if ever, shout out complaint so deep.

The *modus operandi* of the psalms is to reach inward and then heavenward, to wrestle honestly with our feelings and then to talk freely with God. It is the methodology of communication. Written by a variety of authors, the psalms provide a striking cross-section of believers wrestling with various aspects of faith. "In its chorus of voices, we hear every intonation of what getting along with God might involve."[1]

Yet, the book of Psalms is primarily about God. It belongs on the shelf marked "theology."[2] It presents a different kind of theology. Rather than lining up a systematic arrangement of propositional truths about God, Psalms invites readers to listen in on a conversation. Humble souls sort out how the God-life applies to human life. We hear a lot about God and his relationship with his followers, but discover no simple six-step program, no one-size-fits-all procedure. Life is too complex. Answers are more intuitive than explicit. The playing field is the covenant relationship with God, and the players take the heavenly coach's game plan and seek to work out God's instructions in the ebb and flow of life.

Whereas the prophets are covenant enforcers, the psalmists are covenant appliers. They enlighten the path of pilgrims, whether hearts are filled with thanksgiving and praise or emptied by sorrow and suffering. For both ancient Israelite and modern Christian, these ancient Hebrew poems nourish the life of faith. They are indispensable for healthy living. Study them carefully, and proclaim them faithfully. For people who are committed to teaching and preaching the whole counsel of God, the spirituality of the psalms is our bread and butter.

The objective of the present chapter is to present key insights for understanding the psalms. The next chapter will lay out a method for study; here the focus is foundational concepts: The psalms are from another world where people thought differently. They originated in real-life situations. In the worship experiences of the ancient Israelites, the psalms served both as personal response to these life situations and as official acts of the community at large. They record the authors' and audiences' faith experiences. They speak to people's emotions. As poetry, the psalms speak with intense emotions, which means they must be read with heart and not just head. The language of metaphor gives a heightened sense to the profound meaning of ongoing dialogue with God. The psalms reflect an up-close-and-personal encounter with God Almighty.[3]

The Psalms Are from Another World

Some Christians err in reading the Bible as if it were the morning newspaper. They almost forget that the document in their hands was written two to three thousand years ago, its contents gradually collected and arranged by pre-Christian editors. Such readers expect to understand the psalms with little effort.

Unintentionally, our Bibles may give false impressions: the psalms are formatted in verse, precisely the way we are accustomed to find poetry; contemporary translations use language that we hear day-in-and-day-out; and, if we have read the psalms frequently in the past, nothing appears too out-of-place as we read them again. Oblivious to the antiquity of the psalms, we lose sight of the dissimilarities between the world of the Bible and the world of the daily news.

Fundamentally, modern readers need to beware of reading back onto the biblical text current ways of thinking. Since the Enlightenment—with scientists and explorers discovering explanations for all kinds of phenomena—people of modernity have become very confident in the explosion of knowledge. We think we can explain everything, and if we cannot, we turn to an expert whom, we assume, can. Our tendency is to downplay the ambiguities of life. To do so, we may unwittingly cross over into oversimplification. The ancients, however, assumed that much of life is incomprehensible. The scientific revolution was light years away, and for them, living with paradox was not a liability. They were more inclined to embrace and appreciate ambiguity. In studying the psalms, one finds mystery in many places, and we will do well to accept that mystery, rather than to reduce it to easy formulations.

One way ancients dealt with paradox was to speak to opposite sides of a coin. When a solution for complexity was not evident, one recourse was to give credence to various perspectives on the issue. Modern readers may decide that biblical authors came close to being inconsistent because they stated seemingly opposing points of view. Yet, generally, both statements were true in some sense, though just how the tension should be resolved is not clear. Desiring to speak with more precision, many Bible interpreters, when encountering ideas expressed in black and white, are inclined to look for the exact shade of gray between the two poles. The starkness of black and white may seem too close to overstatement. However, we must accept the validity of equivocation in biblical authors' statements. What appears to be inconsistency only reflects complexity.

The world of the Bible was primarily oral, while our world is full of printed pages and digitized forms of communication. The psalms were composed for oral presentation. Particularly for the psalms, the authors' intent was performance as part of the temple worship. For example, the "songs of ascent" (Pss. 120–134) were procession hymns that the community of worshipers sang as they made their way up to Jerusalem and the temple. When the value of the psalms for future worshipers was recognized, the psalms were collected so they could continue to be performed. This oral nature of the Book of Psalms has an important implication for interpretation: it is possible for moderns to err in overanalyzing and dissecting the psalms. They are poetry to be performed. To understand them, we need to approach them in the spirit in which they were first sung and then written.

A common form of thinking and expression in the psalms we might refer to as "rules of thumb," known as maxims, axioms, or proverbs. They are found in many cultures. "The ancient Israelite was on the whole more interested in generalizations about human life and conduct, and his proverbial literature is full of them. The Bible could well be regarded as the text book of his working hypotheses, revised in the light of subsequent experience and insight."[4] Allowing biblical authors to articulate truths as if they are always true, though in fact there are exceptions, is key to correct interpretation.

Fuller discussion of ancient culture, noting differences and similarities between the world of the Bible and the modern world, can be found in a variety of sources, including books on life in biblical times, Bible background commentaries, and numerous Bible dictionaries and encyclopedias.[5]

The Psalms Speak to Emotions

Do the psalms speak to the left or to the right side of the brain? Are psalms more cerebral, rational, and propositional (left-brained); or more heartfelt, emotive, and poignant (right-brained)? Are they more like an encyclopedia packed with information, or more like a personal journal of life's ups and downs? Answering this question will set the tone for preaching and teaching the psalms. We need to know whether the psalms are making direct theological statements, or whether they are speaking poetically in figures of speech. Actually, the answer is yes to both sides of the question. Psalms refuse to be reduced to either/or. Both sides of the brain need to embrace the psalms. Though the psalms are characterized more by poetry than by proposition, the eternal truths of God are never far away. "Though we can learn a great deal from Biblical poetry, its primary purpose is not so much to teach us but to *reach* us."[6]

Poetry was a preferred form of expression in the Bible. Turning the pages of the Old Testament, this striking fact jumps out at you. More than half is poetry, including Job, Psalms, Proverbs, Ecclesiastes, Song of Songs, and the majority of the prophets. Poetry is generally considered the most beautiful form of human expression. It "says more and says it more intensely than does ordinary language."[7] It allows authors to speak from the heart, with figures of speech that underscore the depth of their feelings. Concepts that are difficult to grasp can be described with imagery, adding richness to the expression. It is fair to say that the ancient Hebrews "thought with their heart."[8]

In contrast, most Christians would prefer to read about God's attributes in an encyclopedia rather than in a poem. Poetry seems slippery and lacking precision. The current generation prefers language that is rational, precise, scientific, and is wary of mystery and inexplicable realities. "We seek a language that behaves, one in which there is a strict, one-to-one correspondence between each word and the meaning that word is meant to convey."[9] God revealed truth in the genre of poetry for good reason. Poetry is a powerful form of literature when used to communicate the greatness and incomprehensibility of God and the divine ways.

A comparison with spirituals will help us understand the poetry of the psalms. Both the psalms and the soulful songs of American slavery are plaintive cries of the human heart, most often from a context of adversity and despair. While spirituals may seem simplistic in melody and naïve in theology, they, *like the psalms,* communicate profound truths in powerful ways.[10]

Remarkably, the oppressed adopted the religion of the oppressors and with unabashed faith turned to God for help. Even though their masters—many of whom claimed to be Christians—rarely demonstrated divine love, the slaves trusted in a loving God. Their freedom to express pain yet not to give up hope is one of the most compelling features of their faith, especially in light of the incredible hardships of slavery. The subtext of the spirituals is encouragement to the community of servants that God has not forgotten them, that faith in God is the only way to survive, and that they may only escape slavery in the eternal state: "Steal away, steal away; steal away to Jesus. / Steal away, steal away home, I ain't got long to stay here." The more vivid (and more audacious) the imagery the better: "Rock o' my soul in the bosom of Abraham."

These characteristics of spirituals apply to the psalms as well. Almost everything that can be said about one can be said about the other. The point is that the emotional language of poetry is effective. It creates more energy and greater impact on the hearer who knows what is meant and feels what was experienced. Such poetry obviously is not meant to be deceptive by its use of non-literal imagery. Though poetry may seem too slippery for the revelation of God's truth, it has the potential to be more complete and exact in its intended communication. Biblical poetry entails language that is pregnant with meaning. It is language with the volume turned up.

"The power of Psalms lies first and foremost in its evocative use of language. The psalms at once caress and assault the soul. They orient, disorient, and reorient; they scale the heights of praise as well as plumb the depths of despair."[11] Reducing an artist's full-color rendering of an October mountainside in Vermont to a black and white pencil sketch loses much of what the Creator designed for our benefit.

If poetry works in this way, we must learn to see the psalms, hear them, and feel them. We must read with imagination and put ourselves into the psalmists' experiences. "We must have *lived* in the hamlets of human existence before the Psalms can speak to us in all their power."[12] We must empathize with the feelings of the poet, carefully balancing head and heart to understand their depths. We must look through the poem, not just look at it.[13] "Performative by nature, the psalms find their relevance in what they *evoke* rather than in the countless ways they can be dissected and categorized."[14] When the poetry of the psalms is most successful at penetrating our souls, the measuring rod is not knowledge, but insight…not facts, but feelings…not head, but heart.

The implications for interpretation are challenging. The implications for preaching and teaching are mind-bending. "What has been written with imagination, must also be read with imagination, provided the individual has imagination and it is in working order."[15] We must relearn how to interpret the psalms, and we must discover ways to engage our listeners with the pilgrimage of faith in the psalms.

The Psalms Originated in Real-Life Situations

From peasant to king, the authors of the psalms represent a wide range of life experiences. Equally wide-ranging were the types of psalms the ancient Israelites composed and the time periods when they were written. The unifying features are the covenant relationship with God, the honesty of the poets, and the artistry of the poetry. Despite the difficulties of life on this earth, the psalmists believed that seeking God's face was the path to healing. Or, on the other hand, delighted with the rich blessings of life, the psalmists turned to God and gave him glory.

Some prayer-psalms were crafted to speak to God on behalf of the individual and some on behalf of the community of worshipers. Some arose from a setting of pain and ill fortune and some from a setting of praise and great fortune. Some originated in the monarchy, when Israel was ruled by King David or one of his successors. Some were written in exile, when Israel suffered under the evil hand of gentile rulers in foreign lands. Apparently some were composed after the exile. All the psalms resulted from the work of poets who invested energy and skill in crafting the most beautiful poetry they could. The psalms represent the heartfelt expressions of those who sought to understand life from God's perspective.

Who composed the psalms is clearer for some psalms than for others. Thirty-four psalms are anonymous, while one hundred and sixteen have titles that may suggest who wrote them. Whether the titles were original to these psalms or were added later cannot be determined with certainty, thus we cannot be sure of their accuracy.[16] In most cases they probably represent early reliable tradition. Of those with titles, seventy-three mention David, but which ones were dedicated to David, or written for him, or written by him is open to question. The translation of the Hebrew preposition preceding the name David is indecisive. Does it mean *of, to, by, under the direction of,* or *for?* Other titles mention Solomon (Pss. 72 and 127), Moses (Ps. 90), Asaph (Pss. 50 and 73–83), and the Sons of Korah (Pss. 42; 44–49; 84; 85; 87; and 88).[17] Other biblical books provide evidence supporting David as author of certain psalms. Jesus and Peter attest to David's writing three psalms (Mk. 12:35–37 [=Lk. 20:42] and Acts 2:24–36). Other biblical passages refer to David as a writer of sacred poetry (2 Sam. 1:17; 22:1; 23:1).

Identifying the time of writing is partly tied to the question of authorship and partly to the content of the psalms. If David (and maybe even Moses) can be credited with composing some of the psalms, some were written before 1000 B.C.E. At the other end of the spectrum, it is clear from the content of certain psalms (for example, Pss. 74, 79, 137), that they were written at least five hundred years later, during or after the Babylonian exile.

The audience of the psalms are as diverse as the authors. Psalm 2, apparently spoken by a Davidic king, encouraged the faithful Israelites to trust in God, to worship him, and to rejoice in him—even though the wicked were plotting against God and his chosen king. Most psalms were aimed at Israelites who lived in a monarchy-led community and were in a covenant relationship with Yahweh. In contrast, Psalm 90 offers a poetic account of the Israelites who experienced distress while going through "the wilderness." They pled with God to return to them (Ps. 90:13) and to give them joy after he afflicted them (Ps. 90:15).

Though the psalms reflect historical situations from thousands of years ago, their significance for readers across the centuries is unending. The well-known words in Psalm 23:4, "Yea, though I walk through the valley of the shadow of death, I will fear no evil" (KJV), reflected the real-life experiences of its author. As a figure of speech it may not have meant that the author was near death—any more than we are near death when we are tired and say, "I'm dead." Yet hundreds of readers have identified with the emotions of the psalmist's struggles. As originally penned, the meaning of the "valley of death" was likely tied to a historical event or to a series of events in the author's life, yet its significance lies in encouraging millions of people since who have joined the audience facing life's darkest hours.

While the psalms are widely used today for devotional, liturgical, and pastoral purposes, they had specific functions in the religious life of the Israelites. Rabbinic tradition, probably reflecting Jewish life before the advent of Jesus, affirmed that the psalms were sung by the Levites after the daily libation of wine. Each liturgical psalm was sung in three parts, and during the intervals between the parts, the sons of Aaron blew three different blasts on the trumpet. While many of the psalms are devoid of specific liturgical structure or character, the message of some psalms and their superscriptions point to the use of those psalms in worship. Psalm 92 is designated "For the Sabbath," indicating that it was used liturgically. Psalm 100 is designated "For thanksgiving," suggesting that this Psalm was associated with the offering of thanksgiving sacrifices in the temple. Psalms 38 and 70 are designated "To bring to remembrance," possibly situating them with memorial sacrifices. Psalm 30 was designated "For the dedication of the Temple/House." While scholars do not agree whether this refers to the Jerusalem temple or someone's house, it seems to have had a religious function. The Psalms of Ascent (120–134) were sung by the pilgrims who were going up to the Jerusalem temple to worship.

Alongside the use of psalms in worship, many psalms had a didactic function (Pss. 1, 17, 49, 75, 121), even though only Psalm 60 is specified "For instruction." Other psalms fit in the realm of devotional poetry. The psalms were used both in public and private worship in ordinary Israelite life and can be a teaching and encouragement tool for all hearers under distress in all ages.

Collecting the Psalms as a Book

To a casual reader the psalms may appear randomly arranged. Internal evidence, however, suggests that the psalms were arranged in an organized fashion.[18] Five books of psalms are specifically indicated.

- Book I (Pss. 1–41) emphasizes God's covenant with David. Psalms 1–2 introduce the whole Psalter, meditating on the path of obedience to the Law of the Lord, on God's sovereignty, and on God's appointed king.[19]
- Book II (Pss. 42–72) shows that God will be faithful to the Davidic covenant through David's descendants. The climax comes in Psalm 72 with David's prayer for his son Solomon in view of the young king's ascension to the throne.

- Book III (Pss. 73–89) offers a detailed treatment of the Davidic covenant. Although the covenant seems to have been broken, Psalm 89 expresses confident hope that in his loyal love God will remember his covenant made with his servant David.
- In Book IV (Pss. 90–106) thirteen out of the seventeen psalms are untitled. Partly answering questions raised at the end of Book III, Book IV affirms that Yahweh is King, that he has been Israel's refuge, that he will continue to be his people's refuge, and that the ones who trust in him will be blessed.
- Book V (Pss. 107–150) is marked by detailed editorial organization. Psalms 108–110 and 138–145 are Davidic; Psalms 111–118, 135, 146–150 are hallelujah psalms; while Psalms 120–134 are songs of ascent (or pilgrim psalms).[20]

Editorial work throughout the Psalter can be seen in the way each of the five books end. The first three conclude with doxology formulae; Book V ends with a series of hallelujah psalms; and Book IV combines doxology with hallelujah psalms. Books IV and V seem to shift in emphasis from the Davidic king to Yahweh as King, the one who reigns forever. It is likely that the editor(s) of the psalms depended on the content of the psalms in systematizing them into this coherent framework.

The Psalms Are a Tent of Meeting

The Bible records a number of people who had up-close-and-personal encounters with God. Sometimes these were pleasant experiences, and sometimes not. Adam and Eve had an unwanted meeting with God as he showed them the exit door to the garden of Eden (Gen. 3:8–24). Though he suffered a hip injury in the process, Jacob was honored to realize that the stranger with whom he had wrestled all night was God himself (Gen. 32:22–32). Job was speechless as God asked him a question repeatedly–though in different ways: "Where were you when I created the world?" (Job 38:1–40:5). Seeing the brilliance of God's holiness, Isaiah could only say, "Woe is me!... I am a man of unclean lips" (Isa. 6:1–5, KJV). For Christians today, who long for these kinds of personal encounters with God, the book of Psalms may be the answer.

In their poems or in the experiences that led to the writing of these poems, the psalmists experience God in various ways. They are nearly speechless when they come face-to-face with how awesome the Holy One is. They wrestle with the Almighty about all the evil in the world. They are shamed when they discover the Deity's convicting finger pointing at them. The psalms give us a renewed appreciation of how close God is to those who draw near to the One in heaven. It is possible to live on a sinful planet and yet be in God's presence. Our world may be awash in a hurricane of buffeting winds and crashing waves, but our faith is anchored securely in the God who is the Master of the winds and the waves. "The Psalms infuse us with strength beyond our human powers because the God of the psalmists–and of us–hovers over them in love and mercy. They are his dwelling place, and there we meet him."[21]

For modern readers such encounters need not be secondhand. If we turn our hearts loose as we meditate on the psalms, we can have similar meetings with God. We will feel rebuke, stand in awe, wrestle, be transformed, and feel unworthy.

The psalms underscore important truths about God, often recounting the Saving God's great acts. The psalms confess God is creator and sustainer. God rescued the chosen people from bondage in Egypt. The Lord placed servants God anointed on the throne. God is provider, protector, revealer, guide, helper, judge, counselor, redeemer, ruler, warrior, king. The Holy One of Israel is loving, merciful, compassionate, faithful, forgiving, patient, righteous, eternal, holy, omniscient, omnipotent, omnipresent, majestic, and glorious. And he chooses to meet us in the Psalms, just as he met Moses and Joshua in the tent of meeting.

The Psalms Are Pre-Christian

The New Testament frequently quotes the book of Psalms, suggesting how important the collection was to the early Christian community. In particular, Christians mined the psalms for apologetics, because they were seeking ways to defend their revolutionary belief in Jesus as the Messiah. Among the Psalms they found great texts to support their cause: "What is involved is the attempt in debates with the Jews to demonstrate that Jesus of Nazareth lived, suffered, and rose from the dead according to the Old Testament promises, prayers, and experiences of trouble and deliverance, and that he brought them to completion and fulfillment."[22] For example, Acts 4 records the arrest of Peter and John. When brought before the top religious leaders, Peter boldly quotes Psalm 118:22 and states, "Jesus is *the stone that was rejected by* you, *the builders, that has become the cornerstone*" (Acts 4:11 NET; cf. Mt. 21:42).

In marshaling as much evidence as possible for how Jesus fulfilled the Old Testament, Christians moved quickly to application, often bypassing the original setting of the psalm. We should not be surprised by this, especially when the Christians were acting in line with commonly accepted interpretive practices of their day.[23] For example, Psalm 118 was composed as a hymn of thanksgiving to celebrate God's goodness. A typical feature in thanksgiving psalms was a description of distress from which the worshiper had been rescued. Going to one of the lowest points in life and experiencing God's aid heightened the response of praise. Underscoring that point, the psalmist employed a metaphor of a stone mason discarding useless stones in favor of better choices. In the eye of the poet, however, he sees the mason retrieve what first appeared to be a useless stone and, of all things, place it in the most important and prominent location. "The stone which the builders discarded has become the cornerstone" (118:22 NET). In ancient Israel, this kind of robust imagery and analogy called forth resounding praise. God does amazing things! Later, Jesus would underscore the same idea: "The one who is least among you all is the one who is great" (Lk. 9:48 NET). Thus early Christians found the psalmist's words a beautiful description of Jesus' own rejection and supremacy.

Correct interpretation of the Psalms depends on recognizing a three-phased trajectory of meaning.

- First, a psalm was composed in response to the circumstances and needs of the Israelite community. When we interact with the original situation, the author's intent, and the theological principle that is applicable across time, we are reading a psalm for its *contextual* meaning.
- Second, the book of Psalms is the result of compilers selecting one hundred and fifty psalms from many choices and placing them in a particular order in light of their ongoing value for the religious life of the community. When we interact with the significance of a psalm for the overall message of the Old Testament, the covenant relationship, and the redemptive movement of revelation, we are reading a psalm for its *canonical* meaning.
- Third, the early Christian community appropriated certain psalms for their messianic importance, in effect pouring new truth into old wineskins. When we recognize psalms that foreshadowed the life of Jesus, we are reading the psalms for their christological meaning. This last point may be referred to as typology.[24] Scholars frequently use *typology* to refer to cases in which passages in the Old Testament foreshadowed what Christ much later fulfilled—though not in a specific prediction-fulfillment scheme. These scholars commonly refer to the correspondence between the Old Testament event, person, or institution and Christ as a *type*.

While the Old Testament as a whole foreshadowed the coming of the Messiah, it is ill-advised to hypothesize regarding random verses in the Old Testament that may have christological meaning. The only cases that we can proclaim with certainty are those cited in the New Testament as messianic. "Typology is fundamentally retrospective; there is no attempt to assert that the original text had any forward-looking element at all."[25]

All this may leave us with a nagging question: Are modern interpreters at liberty to ignore the original setting of the Psalms and apply them freely to situations faced today? While the issue is too complex to address in full, in general the answer is no.[26] Applying the psalms in the twenty-first century is very different from applying them to the life and ministry of Jesus. We *do* need to understand the original circumstances that evoked the psalm and how the author was responding to those circumstances, for there we find the human and divine authors' original intent. There we find important spiritual principles we should apply to our lives.

The citation of psalms in the New Testament goes beyond the contextual and canonical meaning to the christological meaning. These we call "*messianic* psalms," *messiah* bing the transliterattion of the Hebrew word for "the anointed one." Christ is the Greek equivalent. Messiah in the Old Testament points to a new king who will be anointed as ruler over Israel and eventually over the world. New Testament authors took psalms that pointed to the new king and connected them in a natural way to Jesus in at least two primary ways.

a. Some psalms Christians have adopted and applied to Jesus may be explained as poetic language that foreshadowed Jesus' life. This is the case with Psalm 118 mentioned above. Another example is Psalm 22. "They pierced my hands and my feet" (v. 16, KJV) was originally composed as one of the psalmist's ways of describing the extreme pain and agony experienced in life's dark valleys. The psalmist used hyperbolic language in line with other verses in the psalm. In one saying from the cross, Jesus identified himself with the psalmist's troubles by quoting the first line of this psalm: "My God, my God, why have you forsaken me?" (Mt. 27:46; Mk. 15:34). Significantly, Jesus' hands and feet *were* pierced. In God's sovereign superintendence of inspiration, he guided the human author to speak more than he knew.

b. By extension, New Testament authors considered some psalms messianic, particularly those focusing on an anointed kingship. References to the king marked some psalms as royal psalms. In some cases, God is described in terms of royalty, for he is the King of the universe. In other cases, psalmists wrote about the ruler of Israel—for example, David or Solomon. The human kings were vice-regents for God and played a significant role in God's relationship with his people. They could even be referred to as servants or sons of God. Psalm 2, for example, was apparently a coronation psalm for one of Israel's anointed kings. This close relationship between human kings and the divine King and the similarities in terminology and concept are remarkable. For these reasons, early Christians were inclined to extend the meaning of royal psalms to refer to the divine Messiah.

All psalms have significance for Jesus in the sense that he is the second person of the Godhead, but interpreters are ill-advised to look for christological significance in every verse.[27] To proclaim that all of Jesus' bones were out of joint as he hung on the cross–based on Psalm 22:14–is misguided. That was poetic language expressing the psalmist's lamentation, not a prediction about Jesus' death.

Some psalms are clearly messianic, affirmed in New Testament references as messianic, pointing to Jesus as the present Messiah or the coming Messiah. No psalms were exclusively messianic–that is, pointing only to the distant future and having no meaning in their original setting for their original audience. Peter quoted Psalm 16, for example (Acts 2:25–28), but in its original form the psalm served simply as a psalm of trust. In this manner psalms, like some prophecy, have two or three tiers of meaning: the psalmist's original situation, the relationship to a time of fulfillment, and possibly beyond time to the permanent fulfillment in eternity.

We urge caution here. The psalms were composed in the context of ancient Israel and the author's personal observations and experiences. Even if a psalm is cited in the New Testament, the author's original intent is the starting point for interpretation. Only after we understand the original situation and the spiritual principle is it appropriate to move toward the significance in the New Testament. The clearly messianic psalms to be applied to Jesus are those quoted or referred to in the New Testament.

Conclusion

The psalms are a mapping of faith for the thirsty and hungry, for those longing for a dynamic relationship with God. Like a deer panting for a chance to quench its thirst, so these poets desired to know God more intimately (Ps. 42:1). Life drove them to seek God's face.

In contrast to modern prayers often characterized by superficial clichés and formulas–uttered to meet a certain standard of politeness and polish–the great collection of prayer psalms express in the boldest and baldest terms the whole range of human experience. You can never predict what the psalmist may say next. The psalms are emotive, poetic records of believers expressing all ends of life's spectrum, from glorious praise to gloomy despair. Their honesty can be shocking, their faith uplifting. This is the kind of genuine relationship that God longs to have with those who love him. The psalmists generally did not beg for material blessings, for favorable weather, for perfect health, for smooth sailing. Though Jesus had not yet said to seek the kingdom of God first, the psalmists already understood the point.

The book of Psalms is essentially an ancient journal, reflecting the emotions before and after meditating in the presence of God. Sometimes the psalmists descend into the valley of death. Other times they ascend the mountain of delight. Sometimes they enter into the darkness of silence where a divine word of comfort was slow in coming. Other times they approach the throne of God where divine glory was on display.

The psalmists confide in their listeners how difficult life is when we try to go on alone, and they encourage us with how helpful it is to see things as God sees them. The powerful images of poetry become like mirrors to hearers, evoking similarities of emotion and offering insight from someone who has been down the path before. Appreciating the poetry of the psalms means joining the psalmists on their introspective journey. Regardless of our own faith experiences, the psalmists have been there. The trails that they have blazed make it easier for us. Be it spiritual achievement or failure, new faith or mature faith, "we can find ourselves somewhere in this book."[28] As Calvin noted, "I have been wont to call this book not inappropriately, an anatomy of all parts of the soul; for there is not an emotion of which anyone can be conscious that is not here represented as in a mirror."[29]

CHAPTER 2

Interpreting the Psalms

Basic Methods

Robert B. Chisholm Jr.

The raw human emotion expressed in these ancient prayers, praise songs, and hymns strikes us as we read the psalms. The heartfelt cries of the lament psalms resonate with those who are suffering. The praise songs excite those who have experienced God's intervention in fresh ways. With their striking descriptions of God's majesty and goodness, the hymns inspire worshipers to anticipate the day when God's kingdom arrives on earth in full force.

Because the psalms reach the human heart and soul at so many levels, they provide an especially fertile seedbed for the preacher. Through the mystery of divine inspiration the psalms, though human words directed to God, are also God's word to us (2 Tim. 3:16). These inspired psalms, which arose out of ancient Israel's relationship with God, teach us much about God's character and how he relates to his people. They do far more than feed the intellect and supply proof texts for theologians. Through the Psalter, God invites us to express our joy and pain, our faith and even our doubts to him. As we identify with these ancient worshipers and reflect on their expressions of faith, we draw closer to God and experience in new and profound ways the vibrant relationship he desires to have with each of us. Because the psalms are vital to the life of the church, teachers and preachers have a responsibility to proclaim them in an accurate, gripping, and relevant way that will motivate God's people to turn to him with their pain, to praise him for his salvation, and to worship him for his greatness and goodness.

The challenge is great. As we read the psalms, we become aware of the chasm between the psalmists and us. The psalmists worshiped the one true God in a different historical-cultural context than the one in which modern Christians live. To bridge that chasm, we must have a strategy that successfully links the psalmists' horizon with our own. We must not simply describe how the psalmists spoke to God, as a history teacher might. Nor can we rip the psalms from their original context and read a meaning into them that is foreign to God's intention, for such readings lack authority. We must take seriously the meaning of the psalms in their original context and, building on this foundation, demonstrate how they are significant for us.

The strategy suggested in this book for interpreting the Psalms is straightforward. When interpreting a psalm in preparation for a sermon or lesson, it is helpful to ask a series of questions: (1) Why did the author compose the psalm? (2) How did the author express his ideas? (3) What are the important interpretive issues? (4) What was the author seeking to communicate? (5) What is the significance of the psalm for preaching and teaching?

Why Did the Author Compose the Psalm?

Occasionally, a psalm's heading can provide valuable background information. For example, the heading to Psalm 51 informs us that David offered this confession of sin after Nathan confronted him with his dual capital crime of adultery and murder. The content of the psalm certainly fits this scenario. However, the final two verses (vv. 18–19) look forward to the walls of Jerusalem being rebuilt, suggesting that they are an exilic/postexilic inspired addition to the psalm in which the community applies David's ancient prayer to their own circumstances. Like David, they too needed spiritual restoration, for they, like him, had blatantly violated God's law.

Unfortunately, most psalms do not provide such specific background information. In such cases we must first examine the internal evidence of the psalm against the background of what we generally know about ancient Israelite culture and then attempt to reconstruct what the author's intention appears to be. Toward this end the interpreter should determine the literary type of the psalm, for the literary form provides clues as to the psalmist's situation and intention. The Psalter contains a variety of prayer types, but most psalms fall into one of three formal categories: laments, songs of thanks, and hymns.[1]

In a lament, the psalmist asks God to intervene and to deliver him from the crisis in which he finds himself. Laments typically contain a lament proper, in which the psalmist describes his crisis, combined with a petition for help (cf. Ps. 6:1–7). Often laments conclude with a statement of confidence (cf. Ps. 6:8–10), apparently in response to an assuring divine promise (cf. Ps. 6:9).

When the Lord actually intervened to fulfill a promise, the recipient of divine deliverance would typically compose a song of thanks, rehearsing the past crisis and God's deliverance (cf. Ps. 30:1–3, 6–12). These songs may also contain calls to praise and general theological principles the psalmist learned through the experience (cf. Ps. 30:4–5).

The Psalter also contains many hymns in which the psalmist praises God in a more general manner for beneficent rule (cf. Ps. 104) and for mighty acts in history (cf. Ps. 105). The hymns typically begin with a call to praise (cf. Ps. 29:1–2), followed by reasons why God is praiseworthy (cf. Ps. 29:3–11).

In addition to these three major types, other genres appear, including songs of confidence (for example, Pss. 11, 23), royal psalms (for example, Pss. 2, 45, 89), enthronement psalms (for example, Pss. 96–100), and wisdom psalms (for example, Pss. 1, 49, 73).[2] A song of confidence resembles the confidence section of a lament. The psalmist affirms trust in God's protective power in the midst of a crisis. Royal, enthronement, and wisdom psalms do not have a specific literary structure that sets them apart. Rather they are distinguished on the basis of their themes. Royal psalms focus on the Lord's relationship with the Davidic king (Pss. 2, 18, 110); enthronement psalms, a subcategory of the hymns, celebrate God's just kingship (Pss. 47, 93, 99); wisdom psalms address issues of theodicy and contrast the behavior and destiny of the righteous and wicked (Pss. 1, 119).

How Did the Author Express His Ideas?

As the preceding chapter explains, the psalms are written in a poetic form and style.[3] Responsible interpretation is sensitive to this poetic dimension, asking the following interrelated questions: (a) What metaphors does the psalmist use, and how do they contribute to the psalm? (b) What is the psalmist's mood? (c) What emotions does he express? (d) What past and present relationship with God is described?

Metaphors convey the psalmist's message in powerful ways, for they grip the imagination and appeal to the senses.[4] For example, the author of Psalm 1 compares the godly to a tree that is well watered and flourishes (v. 3). This pleasant image suggests vitality and stability. By way of contrast, he pictures the wicked as straw driven away by the wind (v. 4). This image vividly portrays the instability of the wicked as they face God's justice, which is as relentless as a strong wind. The images support the psalmist's thesis that genuine joy is found in a godly lifestyle (vv. 1–3). Divine judgment will come, and only those deeply rooted in righteousness are insulated from its destructive effects (vv. 5–6).

The most famous psalm of all, Psalm 23, entails an extended metaphor expressing absolute trust in God. Picturing the Lord as a shepherd and himself as a sheep, the psalmist describes how God provides for the psalmist's needs; guides him down the paths that lead to food, water, and safety; and protects him when it is necessary to travel through potentially dangerous dark ravines (vv. 1–4). Though most modern readers will not be able to fully appreciate the pastoral imagery, the portrait vividly portrays God as one who provides for and protects his own because his very own reputation is at stake (v. 3). The metaphor changes in verses 5–6, where the psalmist pictures himself as an honored guest at a royal banquet and a permanent resident of God's royal palace. Enemies are lurking nearby (v. 5), but God's goodness and faithfulness, not his enemies, will "pursue" the psalmist. This creative use of irony, in which a verb normally connoting hostility is used of God's favor, emphasizes the psalmist's confidence in God's protection.

Attention to the psalmist's mood(s) and emotions enables one to capture the pathos of the psalm and reflect it in the sermon, where it is important to reach the emotions, as well as the intellect, of the audience. As much as possible, the expositor should recreate the psalmist's emotions in his or her own audience to facilitate their application of the psalm's message to their own experiences.

As an example, Psalm 6 is a lament in which the psalmist desperately begs for God's mercy. He feels as if he is an object of God's anger and so expresses his helplessness and fear. With a touch of hyperbole he describes his bones as shaking and speaks of drenching his bed in tears as he groans in sorrow. The psalmist is obviously seeking to move God emotionally so that God will take pity on him and intervene in his circumstances. In proclaiming the psalm, the preacher should help the audience connect with the psalmist at an emotional level, perhaps by asking them to recall a time in their lives when they may have felt the depth of emotion expressed by the psalmist.

Of course, the psalm does not end on a negative note. Apparently the Lord responded to the psalmist through an oracle of assurance (v. 9; cf. Ps. 12:5), for the psalmist's mood changes drastically from fear to confidence as he affirms that the Lord has heard his petition and will destroy his enemies. To highlight the reversal that God's intervention brings, the psalmist anticipates his enemies being "terrified" (v. 10; Hebrew *bâhal*), the same verb he used earlier to describe his own fear (v. 3).[5] Again the expositor will want to help the audience connect with the psalmist, perhaps by asking them to recall a time when they experienced God's intervention in a powerful way that transformed fear and sorrow into confidence and joy.

Considering the psalm at this poetic level, where the psalmist's emotions are on full display, has important theological and practical ramifications. Since this is an inspired psalm, one can reasonably assume that pouring out one's heart before God in such a manner is not inappropriate, let alone wrong, as some Christian stoics and fatalists have argued. On the contrary, honestly expressing one's fears to God may well be one of the ways in which we cast all our cares on him and express our faith (cf. 1 Pet. 5:7). The psalmist appeals to God's mercy, faithfulness, and desire for praise in an effort to motivate a positive response to his petition (cf. vv. 2, 4–5). He does not approach God as if the Deity is impersonal and dispassionate, but instead appeals to and reasons with a Heavenly Parent, as if he believes his words can be the catalyst for divine intervention. The psalmist was not disappointed, for the Lord assured him of heavenly help and instilled him with confidence. The psalmist's example reminds us that even in the darkest times we can look to the Lord for a resolution to our crises because he responds to the heartfelt cries of his needy people.

What Are the Important Interpretive Issues?

In dealing with the meaning of any ancient text, one must address three basic, interrelated questions that are the focus of biblical interpretation: (1) What is the text? (2) What does the text say? (3) What did the text mean in its original context?[6] Those trained in the Hebrew language will have an advantage when doing biblical interpretation; those limited to an English Bible may utilize basic Bible study methods and take advantage of the many translations and commentaries that are available.[7]

The psalms were written thousands of years ago; they were copied by scribes for centuries and translated into many languages. Though God has superintended the transmission of the inspired Word, this has not insulated the psalms from some degree of textual corruption due to the human element in the transmission process. An examination of the evidence sometimes reveals competing textual traditions and readings.[8] Thankfully, this involves a relatively small percentage of words and phrases. The work of dedicated scribes and later generations of biblical scholars has put us in a position to make well-reasoned decisions concerning the identity of the original text for most passages where variant readings occur.[9]

Once the text is established, the next step in interpretation is to determine what the text says. This is the task of translation, which involves a whole array of decisions regarding the meaning of words and phrases and the significance of various grammatical constructions. Many modern, up-to-date translations are available, so the interpreter does not need to reinvent the wheel. When studying the text, it is beneficial and enlightening to compare and contrast various translations. Such an analysis will surface interpretive trouble spots and issues.[10] Word studies of key terms will assist in evaluating the text at a syntactical level. All interpreters should take full advantage of commentaries and word study books, though facility in Hebrew will enable one to utilize such tools more efficiently and confidently.[11]

With the text established and translated, the interpreter is now ready to tackle the third question, "What did the text mean?" In the process the following questions are helpful: (a) What is the psalm's logical structure? (b) What theological theme(s) does the psalmist develop? (c) Which divine characteristics and roles does the psalmist highlight? (d) Does the psalmist give any indications or hints as to how the reader is to respond to his prayer or song? (We illustrate the process below with Psalm 30.)

What Was the Author Seeking to Communicate?

Once the literary analysis and interpretive spadework are completed, one is ready to build a bridge from the psalm to the modern context of the interpreter and his or her readers or listeners. The first stage in this process is to determine the primary theological theme(s) of the psalm. I have found the following steps to be a helpful and practical way to do this:

1. Develop a *descriptive* outline that reflects the psalmist's mood(s) and the psalm's literary structure.
2. Turn this outline into an *interpretive* outline that reflects the psalmist's underlying assumptions and the psalm's logical development.
3. Convert the interpretive outline to a *theological* outline that reflects the theological principles underlying the psalmist's words. Then construct a theological summary statement that expresses the main theological idea(s) of the psalm.

To illustrate this process, we will consider Psalm 30, a thanksgiving song in which the psalmist expresses gratitude for God's forgiveness and salvation.

Descriptive Outline

(This outline merely describes the psalmist's mood and reports what he says.)

I. Thanksgiving: The psalmist thanks the Lord for delivering him from the clutches of death (vv. 1–3).
II. Call to praise: The psalmist urges the Lord's faithful followers to praise God because God's discipline is short-lived, but divine favor lasts a lifetime (vv. 4–5).

III. Narrative: The psalmist recalls his crisis, his prayer, and God's positive response (vv. 6–11).
   A. The psalmist recalls that he had been smugly self-confident (v. 6).
   B. The psalmist recalls the fear he experienced when the Lord removed divine security and favor (v. 7).
   C. The psalmist recalls that he desperately begged for God's mercy, arguing that his death would separate him from the worshiping community and prevent him from giving God the praise God deserves (vv. 8–10).
   D. The psalmist recalls the joy experienced when the Lord delivered him (v. 11).
IV. Vow of praise: The psalmist promises to thank God continually (v. 12).

Synthetic and Interpretive Outline

(This outline attempts to reflect the psalmist's underlying assumptions and the psalm's logical connections.)

   I. The Lord is praiseworthy because God delivered the psalmist from death (vv. 1–3).
  II. The Lord's followers should join the psalmist in praise, for the psalmist's experience demonstrates that God is favorably disposed to God's people, even when the Lord must discipline them for a brief time (vv. 4–5).
 III. The Lord disciplined the psalmist when he became self-sufficient, but the Lord saved him when he begged for mercy (vv. 6–11).
 IV. Because the Lord delivered him, the psalmist is compelled to express his gratitude through praise (v. 12).

Theological Outline

(This outline attempts to derive theological principles from the psalmist's experience and words.)

   I. The Lord deserves praise because God delivers the people of God from danger (vv. 1–3).
  II. Divine discipline is sometimes necessary, but God is predisposed to show the people divine favor (vv. 4–5).
 III. Self-sufficient pride brings divine discipline, but God responds positively when those under discipline humbly ask for mercy (vv. 6–11).
 IV. The Lord deserves praise for showing the people mercy (v. 12).

Regardless of which outline you use, the main idea is the same: God deserves praise because, even when God has had to discipline them for their self-sufficient pride, God still responds to the people's cries for mercy and restores them to a position of lasting favor.

What Is the Significance of the Psalm for Preaching and Teaching?

Having stated the main theological idea(s) of a psalm, the interpreter is in a position to move toward application. Making this move involves an important intermediate step. One should filter the theological outline through the grid of *New Testament theology* and modify the theological principles in light of progressive revelation. In this step it is important to develop a christological angle to the main idea, explaining how Christ's redemptive work impacts the main theological idea. This christological dimension is important, for without it our preaching and teaching will be mere moralizing that is not truly Christian.

One is now in a position to transform the theological outline and main idea into an *applicational* outline and main idea geared to a contemporary audience. This outline will be more hortatory in tone and can be easily converted or adapted into a full-fledged homiletical outline. Again, we use Psalm 30 to illustrate the procedure.

First, New Testament theology warrants consideration when preaching the psalms as part of God's big picture. According to the New Testament, God disciplines his people when they rebel against him, just as a loving father disciplines his disobedient children (Heb. 12:5–13). This discipline, which can be painful, is designed for our benefit and is intended to make us holy. Because of Jesus' redemptive work and advocacy on our behalf, we can confess our sins to God and receive immediate and complete cleansing and restoration (1 Jn. 1:7–2:2). Thus in light of New Testament theology the following applicational outline is suggested for Psalm 30. It applies the psalm's theological message to our situation.

 I. We should praise the Lord when God delivers us from the effects of sin (vv. 1–3).
 II. We should praise the Lord because God is predisposed to bestow eternal blessings on us, even though God must occasionally discipline us for a time (vv. 4–5).
III. We should avoid self-sufficient pride, which leads to sin and discipline (vv. 6–7), but when we do experience divine discipline, we should seek God's mercy extended to us in Christ (vv. 8–11).
IV. We should express our unending gratitude to God for divine mercy and forgiveness (v. 12).

This thanksgiving song contains a narrative of the psalmist's experience. For this reason one may choose an alternative model that reflects the chronology of events and the plot structure of the psalmist's experience. The following applicational outline reflects this approach.[12]

I. "Oops!": We can develop a self-sufficient attitude when we forget that God's favor is our source of security (vv. 6–7a).

II. "Ugh!": Self-sufficient pride prompts God to discipline us, which can be a very terrifying experience (v. 7b).

III. "Aha!": We should seek God's mercy when we are being disciplined (vv. 8–10).

IV. "Whee!": God responds positively to our cries for mercy because God is predisposed to show God's people lasting favor (vv. 1–3, 5, 11) on the basis of Christ's redemptive work.

V. "Celebrate": God's merciful forgiveness should prompt praise and gratitude (vv. 4, 12).

Regardless of which applicational outline you chose to use, the main idea remains the same: the Lord is praiseworthy because, even though he must discipline us when we grow self-sufficient, he forgives our sin because of Christ's redemptive work, delivers us from the effects of sin, and restores us to his good favor when we cry to him for mercy.

Psalm 12: A Lament for Divine Justice

The suggested strategy used for interpreting Psalm 30, a thanksgiving psalm, addressed a series of questions: (1) Why did the author compose the psalm? (2) How did the author express his ideas? (3) What are the important interpretive issues? (4) What was the author seeking to communicate? (5) What is the significance of the psalm for preaching and teaching? Yet these same questions are equally appropriate for a lament psalm. The following demonstrates the same strategy for Psalm 12.

Why did the author compose the psalm?

The psalmist was overwhelmed by what was happening in his society. Evil men were deceiving and destroying the godly, prompting the psalmist to cry out to God for justice and deliverance (vv. 1–4). The Lord responded to his cry for help (v. 5), moving the psalmist to express his confidence in God and his word of promise (vv. 6–8).

How did the author express his ideas?

The psalmist is desperate as he abruptly cries out, "Deliver, LORD!" With a touch of hyperbole he laments that the righteous have vanished, or so it seems, and the only people left are guilty of lies and flattery. He feels like his is the lone voice crying out to God (vv. 1–2). His longing for God to correct these wrongs is so intense that he asks God to cut off the lips and cut out the tongues of the arrogant (vv. 3–4). This "curse," in which he calls down judgment on his persecutors, conveys harsh and violent images, but effectively expresses the psalmist's sense of urgency and concern for justice. After receiving an assuring promise from the Lord (v. 5), the psalmist uses a metallurgical metaphor to affirm his belief in God's faithfulness. He compares the Lord's word of promise to silver that is refined multiple times to remove all impurities (v. 6). In contrast to the deceitful enemies whose words cannot be trusted (v. 2), the Lord's promise is untainted and completely reliable.

What are the important interpretive issues?

Like most psalms, Psalm 12 presents some text-critical and translational challenges, including, among others:

(1) the meaning of the verb in verse 1b ("disappeared" in NET),

(2) the meaning of "double heart" (NASB95. NAB), literally in the idiomatic Hebrew "with a heart and a heart" in verse 2b,

(3) the meaning and syntax of verse 4a, which appears to read literally, "who say (or "said"): 'to (by) our tongue we make strong',"

(4) the meaning of the statement in verse 4b "our lips are our own" (HCSB), which reads literally in the Hebrew, "our lips [are] with us,"

(5) the meaning of the final verb in verse 5: "I will put the one who longs for it in a safe place." (HCSB), which is variously interpreted to mean, "to witness," "to rage," "to blow on," "to sigh," to "gasp after," to "testify against,"

(6) identification of the antecedents of the pronouns "them" and "him" in the first line of verse 7, "You, O LORD, will keep them; You will preserve him from this generation forever (the very literal reading of NASB95), and

(7) the syntactical and conceptual relationship of verse 8 to verse 7.

For discussion of these issues, see the NET Bible study notes, as well as the standard commentaries cited above.

Once these basic, technical matters are resolved, one is in a position to address the meaning of the psalm in its original context and to bring to the surface its interpretive theological issues. We suggested earlier that one should ask several leading questions at this point in the process, including:

a. What is the psalm's logical structure?

As is typical with lament psalms, the psalm moves from petition (vv. 1–4) to confidence (vv. 6–8), with the divine response to the petition serving as the hinge or turning point (v. 5). Certainly this suggests something about the power of the divine word to transform the perspective of God's people when they are facing severe trials.

b. What theological theme(s) does the psalmist develop?

At least three interrelated themes emerge from the psalm: God's justice, his concern for the persecuted, and the reliability of his promises. Because God is just, he is predisposed to intervene on behalf of his oppressed people, and one can trust his promises to do so.

c. Which divine characteristics and roles does the psalmist highlight?

As noted above, God's just character is highlighted here, but his compassion is also apparent, for the psalmist states that the "painful cries" of the oppressed get his attention and prompt him to act on their behalf.

d. Does the psalmist give any indications or hints as to how the reader is to respond to his prayer or song?

Though the psalmist does not directly address his audience or urge them to act in some specific way, it seems apparent from his confession of trust (vv. 6–7) that he wants them to know that God is faithful and will vindicate and protect his persecuted people.

What is the author seeking to communicate?

Now that the interpretive spadework is completed, we are ready to build a bridge from the psalm to the modern context of the interpreter and his/her readers by summarizing the psalm's message through descriptive, synthetic-interpretive, and theological outlines.

Descriptive Outline

I. Prayer:
   A. Petition: The psalmist prays for the Lord's deliverance because godly people are vanishing and society is overrun by deceitful people (vv. 1–2).
   B. Curse: The psalmist asks the Lord to judge those who speak deceitfully and arrogantly (vv. 3–4).
II. Oracle: The Lord announces that he will provide safety for the needy, because they are suffering terribly at the hands of their oppressors (v. 5).
III. Response:
   A. The psalmist affirms that the Lord's words are completely reliable (v. 6).

B. The psalmist expresses his confidence that the Lord will protect the helpless, even though evil people have overrun society and promote evil (vv. 7–8).

Interpretive Outline

I. Because the godly are being persecuted and deceitful people are overrunning society, the psalmist appeals to the Lord's just character, asking him to deliver the needy and to judge the deceitful and arrogant (vv. 1–4).

II. Because the Lord is moved by the plight of the needy, he promises to intervene on their behalf (v. 5).

III. Because the Lord's promises are reliable, the psalmist is confident the Lord will protect the needy, despite how bad society has become (vv. 6–8).

Theological Outline

I. Because the Lord is the just king of the world, he is the ultimate source of relief and vindication for his persecuted people (vv. 1–4).

II. Because the Lord is committed to justice and has compassion for the needy, he has guaranteed that he will intervene on their behalf (v. 5).

III. The Lord's reliable promise should instill his persecuted people with confidence, no matter how prevalent evil may be (vv. 6–8).

Once again, regardless of which outline is used, the main idea remains the same: because the promise of the Lord, the just King of the world, is reliable, his people can have confidence they will be vindicated.

What is the significance of the psalm for preaching and teaching?

We are now in a position to move toward modern application. First, we filter our theological observations through the grid of New Testament theology and modify them in light of progressive revelation and Christ's redemptive work. Then we transform our theological outline and main idea into an applicational outline and main idea geared to a contemporary audience.

a. New Testament believers living in a sinful world are just as helpless as the psalmist and may face the same kind of persecution he did. In fact, Christ warned that we would face persecution because we are his followers. Yet Christians are told by Jesus and Paul not to call curses down on their enemies (cf. Mt. 5:44; Lk. 6:27–28; Rom. 12:14, 17–21; 1 Cor. 4:12–13). Though we may long for and anticipate the outworking of divine justice (cf. 2 Thess. 1:6–9; 2 Tim. 4:4), we should not expect or formally seek immediate justice from the Lord. The psalmist's faith in God's justice prompted him to pray for it; our faith in God's justice enables us to wait patiently for it in obedience to his wishes.

b. The Lord does not necessarily promise persecuted believers physical protection in the present era. In fact, he did not always provide such protection in the Old Testament era. Yet Paul does assure us that nothing, not even persecution and death, can separate us from God's love in Christ Jesus (Rom. 8:31–39). True, we do sometimes see the outworking of divine justice in the present era. However, it will not be perfectly revealed until the end of the present age.

c. Paul does assure persecuted believers that the Lord will eventually vindicate his people, but this awaits the second coming of Christ (2 Thess. 1:5–10).

Taking into consideration these New Testament theological realities, the following applicational outline may be appropriate for Psalm 12.

I. When persecuted and overwhelmed by the sinful world around us, we should remember that our king is just (vv. 1–4).

II. We should remember that our compassionate and just king is aware of our suffering and has promised that he will vindicate us (v. 5).

III. No matter how dark the situation may be, we may confidently anticipate the day of vindication, for our just king's promises are reliable. This confidence insulates us from despair and motivates us to remain faithful and to carry out the king's will (vv. 6–8).

Thus the main idea for Psalm 12 is that in the face of spiritual opposition we can be confident of ultimate vindication, for the promise of our sovereign and just God is reliable and will be fulfilled through the Lord Jesus Christ when he comes to judge the world and establish his kingdom.

Conclusion

Although a variety of psalms exist in the Psalter, the same interpretive strategy may be used for each as it was evidenced with the thanksgiving psalm (Ps. 30) and the lament psalm (Ps. 12). As you later move through "Part Two: Interpreting the Psalms," these five questions will be addressed: (1) Why did the author compose the psalm? (2) How did the author express his ideas? (3) What are the important interpretive issues? (4) What was the author seeking to communicate? (5) What is the significance of the psalm for preaching and teaching? Yet not every author will employ every outline suggested in this chapter. Some will limit their outlines to either a descriptive, synthetic, or theological outline. Some may offer an applicational outline for their respective psalm. Nevertheless, it is helpful to be able to distinguish between the varieties of outlines used throughout this book. Before moving on to these interpretations of various psalms, Timothy Ralston offers some helpful insights on preaching and teaching the psalms.

CHAPTER 3

Preaching the Psalms[1]

Sermonic Forms

Timothy J. Ralston

God's people have always cherished the Psalter. Its poetry adorned Israel's celebrations of God's grace toward them and captured their moments of frustration in a broken world. Like their Jewish forbears, the early Christians found that the Psalter's inspired passages spoke so eloquently of their own faith and hope that many psalms became beloved standards within worship, whether in the *Troparions* of Chrysostom, the *Venite* of Cranmer, the metrics of Calvin's Psalter, or the paraphrases of Watts' hymnody. Monks sang the entire Psalter each week, if not each day, and contemporary Christian music would be poorer without its quotations and paraphrases.

This ancient genre endures in worship because its language captures the common experience of God's people and evokes deep feelings. Yet comparatively few sermons on the psalms have survived from antiquity.[2] One church father even classified them as a separate form of Christian preaching.[3] The uniqueness of these poems suggests that we must modify our methods to accomplish an effective exposition.

The psalms present us with special challenges. Their form follows ancient poetic conventions. A modern reader who does not intuitively know the form will struggle to maintain emotional engagement.[4] The psalms also employ symbols and images that are increasingly foreign to modern readers. This distance makes the meaning more difficult to recover accurately and to experience emotionally.

Problems Preaching the Psalms

We all want to teach and preach the psalms well, but not all preachers have treated them with equal care. Some believe that Bible exposition requires a verse-by-verse explanation of the passage, slavishly following the biblical text. This ensures that the preacher addresses the entire passage, but such sermons often become bogged-down with word studies or syntactical analyses. Sermonic rabbit trails produce imaginative flights of allegorical fantasy, fueled by the comparison of Old and New Testament theologies—a nosegay of ideas. Such homiletic tragedies occur anytime textual details become the focus of exposition. The effect is acute if the passage's thought does not develop in an uncluttered straight line from first verse to last.

Unfortunately, few psalms possess a linear framework in which a verse-by-verse approach will capture the flow of thought. Instead of a simple psychological structure (such as problem-solution, cause-effect, past-present, or condition-result), we encounter complex Ancient Near Eastern songs. A typical lament psalm begins with a summary cry of distress to God, then expresses confidence in God's ability to address the situation, requests God's intervention, and finally offers a promise of public praise for the expected deliverance. The thanksgiving/acknowledgment psalm answers the lament: the psalmist states his plan to offer praise now, rehearses the original problem, reports the deliverance received, and concludes with a restatement of the praise. A descriptive praise psalm exhorts us to honor God with a call to praise at both beginning and end, bracketing the reason for praise in the middle. Acrostic psalms begin each line set with the artificial mechanism of an alphabet letter or key word.

These structures help us to appreciate a psalm's message and how its parts contribute to the whole. But this knowledge tempts us to make another mistake: to make these patterns the focus of our message and organize our sermon around them. By so doing, we transform the pulpit into a lectern and a worshiping community into a seminary class.

Some preachers try to avoid this pitfall by making the psalm's exegesis the first main point of the message, followed by the application as the second main point. But this introduces new dangers.

First, even if the preacher excels in charismatic delivery and story-telling skill, the audience must endure the exegetical analysis before hearing anything of practical significance. Application may have a chance, but only if the listeners can survive long enough to hear it.

A second problem occurs by the structural separation of exegesis and application. Such separation logically disconnects application from exegesis. The listener must believe that the preacher's call for life change represents a legitimate logical extension of the ancient text to the modern context. By formally separating exegesis from application, the preacher may forget to validate this move.

Finally, this structural division of the sermon into exegesis, then application often degenerates into a communication error: the audience hears the sermon's main points focusing on exegesis. Application is heard as the conclusion, simply summarizing the previous points. Application should be the sermon's focus, main points coming from application, not from the exegetical notes. Leaving application to the conclusion denies listeners sufficient time to complete the process of hearing, absorbing, processing, integrating, believing, and then visualizing the new truth in their experience. The very reason for preaching has been lost.

The natural press of pastoral duties and the weekly-sermon-sausage-grinder creates another pitfall for the preacher. Analyzing and synthesizing the complexities of Old Testament poetry, language, and theology with specific, valid application takes time. So each Sunday the tired preacher looks to the psalmist's behavior and fervently exhorts his audience to imitate the psalmist. "Discouraged? Trust God!" "Guilty? Confess it!" "Blessed? Praise Him!" Application by imitation is not wrong, but biblical protagonists do many things that cannot—or should not—be imitated. Every preacher knows this intuitively. That is why we do not urge congregations to raise the dead or supernaturally increase the size of our potluck provisions.

Sometimes the problem of imitation drives us in directions opposed to the psalmist. When dealing with Old Testament imprecations, should the preacher exhort us to imitate the psalmist's prayer for God's destruction of our enemies? The modern preacher usually tells us to abhor such vindictive behavior and forgive our enemies instead (usually validated by an appeal to the New Covenant values of love and mercy that are viewed as correcting the misplaced Old Testament emphasis on judgment). Something similar happens in wisdom psalms that seem to promise temporal reward for spiritual faithfulness. Some naively follow the text with an American individualism that associates possession with permission for self-consumption. If we do the right thing, God gives us more stuff with which to make our lives more comfortable, and prosperity theology results. Others will argue that the reward was temporal under the Old Testament but eschatological under the New. Both positions overlook the Old Testament paradigm of responsibility within covenant community that offers faithful stewardship the reward of additional responsibility. This paradigm lies behind the New Testament teaching concerning reward for faithful stewardship in both Jesus' parables and the apostolic teaching. Accurate exposition flounders on the preacher's ignorance.

Application by imitation must reflect the specifics of the passage and integrate the theological framework of the action imitated. Most preachers, however, limit imitation to broad generalizations that can be validated easily by reference to other biblical passages or commands. When one approaches preaching the Psalter through this lens, individual psalms blur together under broad exhortations and each psalm's unique contribution to biblical theology and personal holiness is lost.

No wonder modern pulpits avoid the psalms! Maybe a preacher dips into the psalms occasionally, sometimes only for a verse or two on which to base a message or develop a theological assertion. More often, we are satisfied with a devotional thought, something suggested by an expression and congruent with our prejudice. When we find it, we convince ourselves that the psalms have worked their magic again.

Step 1: Discover the Purpose

God's design for his Word is not merely information, but ethics—the molding of his people's beliefs and behaviors so that they may reflect the holy character of the triune God. Therefore, our purpose as teachers and preachers of God's Word must not be just to communicate ideas, but to persuade to godly action.

To persuade, good preaching must be effective communication, where the message sender and recipient share the same understanding. We study the biblical text to understand what God said in history. We study our audience to understand how to reframe God's message. We want them to hear it with the same meaning and force as originally spoken, to be persuaded of its continuing validity, and to know how to perform its demands on their circumstances. Every audience listens for this argument, first to the preacher's explanation, then to the biblical, theological, and sociological evidence that validates the interpretation, and finally to the application the preacher proposes.[5] A lesson or sermon that resembles a nosegay of unrelated textual observations, exegetical explanations, or emotional connections has failed this most basic test of communication.

Persuasion occurs when what we believe (belief) and how we believe it (reason) are in harmony (emotion). A good teacher will explain the text's meaning but also demonstrate that meaning's validity and seek the listener's empathy. The sermon's strategy is molded for the specific audience and is driven by a single purpose (to which all other purposes are subordinate). Such strategy is summarized in a single statement or main idea (to which all other assertions are subordinate)[6] and provides evidence consistent with the receiver's values and reasoning.

Step 2: Define the Journey

Once we have our purpose, main idea, and argument, we must take the next step. Every effective speaker and argument takes an audience on a psychological journey—from evidence to conclusion, cause to effect, or problem to solution. The speaker begins by defining the listener's current circumstance and by exposing the deficiencies that indicate the need for a change. The speaker then proposes a solution by which the audience will benefit, and unpacks it for them, describing and defending it. Finally the speaker concludes by summarizing how to achieve it and receive its benefits.

The main idea of the sermon defines the journey, both its path and destination.[7] Its subject defines the path, framing the explicit question asked by the *modern* audience that drives them to this text for an answer. Its complement is the destination, the answer as developed from this passage. The appropriate subject framed as a question will possess sufficient emotional force to engage the interest and the passions of the listeners.

Standardized forms arouse an audience's expectations of meaning and significance, inform the audience's intuition, and define its expectation. "Once upon a time" announces a magical plot that promises the joyful triumph of good over evil despite insurmountable odds. An awareness of sonnet or haiku form intuitively shapes our expectation and informs our understanding. Similarly, the psalms' ancient audience listened to them with an awareness of the structures and an innate appreciation of the associated emotion. The modern preacher's challenge is to re-present and recreate the intellectual and emotional significance of a written text whose ancient forms are not intuitively appreciated by the modern audience.

Cultures employ poetry for its unique capacity to evoke emotional empathy for the subject at hand. Therefore, the proper interpretation and communication of a psalm's message to any listener ought to include the same emotional force with which the original audience heard it. This emotional dimension, therefore, must also assume a prominent role in its exposition. As Brueggemann observes, "Most of the psalms can only be appropriately prayed by people who are living at the edges of their life, sensitive to the raw hurts, the primitive passions, and the naïve elations that are at the bottom of life."[8]

Whether looking at an image, reading an essay, or hearing a song, our understanding of the art and empathy toward the message grows as we learn of and appreciate the artist's circumstance. People love stories about people.[9] (Every preacher has stepped down from the pulpit to discover that the audience remembers only a powerful story used to illustrate a major point.) Such stories of faith amidst profound personal loss, loneliness, and tragedy have informed the poetry of many beloved hymns, evoking profound empathy from generations of Christians who might otherwise have relegated their rhyming meters to history's dustbin.

An astute preacher must develop a storyteller's skill with which to describe the human canvas of the psalm.

Thankfully, some psalms include superscriptions that suggest the circumstance to which the psalm responds. These brief summaries provide an interpretive framework that controls the historical referents behind the metaphors employed. Superscriptions are not the only historical clues. Literary parallels with Ancient Near Eastern counterparts imply historical contexts. All these various indicators provide a good foundation for telling the story behind these psalms and are sources of emotional connection and empathy for the message.

Unfortunately, most psalms provide no explicit clues by which to reconstruct their historical context (although some older commentators hypothesized specific events for every one of them[10]). Even here it is possible to find the human face behind the text. If every psalm can be summarized by a single main idea, we can identify the specific question (subject) for which each psalm proposes an answer (complement). Human longings, struggles, and triumphs have changed little over the millennia.

Once we discover the subject, we can recast these two elements into the language of the modern listeners and the question (subject) becomes the point of contact between the psalmist and our audience. Exploring the intellectual and emotional implications of the question (subject) pours the foundations for the bridge between the ancient writer and modern listener. The complement captures the psalmist's answer, laying down the arch across the chasm of time. Understanding the ancient images employed by the psalmist and communicating their emotional force through modern counterparts completes the emotional paving of the roadway between the two worlds.

Step 3: Design the Sermon

Once we have a clear main idea, we need an effective delivery system, a communication strategy that fosters an accurate and persuasive communication of the psalmist's message and also preserves its associated emotional power. Simply proceeding through the psalm may be accurate and can be persuasive, but will not suffice to transport our listeners into the emotional world of the original writer. For that to occur, we need to look to a familiar form we have known since childhood, one in which we found ourselves drawn into other worlds where we have laughed and cried with empathy for the experience of others. Think of the sermon as a form of story, and preaching as the act of storytelling.

Lowry argues, "A sermon is not a doctrinal lecture. It is an *event-in-time,* a narrative art form more akin to a play or novel in shape than to a book."[11] Life does not come in sterile packaging with a foolproof instruction manual that shows us the conclusion and how to get there. Life occurs as a succession of moments, minutes, hours, and days, its pages filled with mistakes, wrong turns, regrets, happiness, and occasionally a triumph or two. The narratives accumulate into the chapters and volumes of life's wisdom. We live and learn and grow as a story. Implicitly every sermon we hear comes to us in narrative as we listen to its argument develop, feel our agreement grow, and experience our passion increase. Sermons are by nature stories.

The psalms were intended to be memorized, recited, heard, and experienced. Psalms are by nature stories to be retold and experienced in their own right, the testimony of individuals consumed by a passion for God's glory in the midst of their human pilgrimage. They express a life of faith, flowing naturally from a position of security, through painful disorientation, to renewed security.[12] Therefore, approaching the psalms as narratives to be told provides the modern lens by which to experience them.

Similarly, every story starts in a state of equilibrium, with a well-defined landscape of characters and events around the hero. Then something enters to upset this equilibrium. The hero struggles against the intruder's effects to understand them and to solve the ensuing problem. Suddenly, a key insight or event provides an invaluable clue to reach the goal. The hero grasps the clue, solves the problem, and restores the equilibrium. By following the narrative, we are engaged at both intellectual and emotional levels. The slower speed of the storytelling allows our feelings to keep pace with our understanding so that, along with the characters, we experience peace, confusion, anger, struggle, triumph, and satisfaction.

To capture this journey on a Sunday morning, we must assume that our listeners exist in a general state of equilibrium. Our first task is to disturb this calm. So we begin with an illustration by which we capture the listeners' attention and arouse their empathy for the subject of the sermon yet to come. Then we identify the story element (or key issue) and draw an analogy between this and the main idea of our message. Finally, we provide the passage context to demonstrate how this is the appropriate biblical text from which to address the issue we have identified, state the main idea, and, after reading the passage, move into the exposition. To be effective, this process leading up to exposition takes time, usually between 15 and 20 percent of the entire message. Unfortunately, an average Sunday morning message scarcely gives listeners enough time to absorb the personal significance of the message or to develop any emotional empathy for the characters in its story.

To arouse our listeners to the emotional power of the original psalm, we should develop our message in a storytelling style through two strategies. The first strategy focuses on structuring the sermon. To sustain narrative tension and foster emotional engagement, we must decide where in the sermon the listener initially hears the main idea of the message. Here we should develop the main idea inductively, rather than deductively.

In deductive sermon development, listeners hear the complete main idea (subject and complement) stated explicitly in the introduction. The message body elaborates on it. The conclusion reviews it. This enhances the clarity of the message, since the listeners hear the conclusion as the message begins. But this clarity comes with a price: knowing the end eliminates the mental and emotional pilgrimage to the conclusion. Deductive structure and presentation can hinder the development of emotional empathy during the suspense of the journey. The listener will not identify with the journey's disappointment over lost dreams, frustration over blind alleys, and joy of triumphant struggles.[13]

By contrast, inductive sermon development only reveals the narrowed message subject in the introduction. The sermon body becomes the search for the answer. The complete answer is only revealed as the last major point of the message body. Then the sermon conclusion reviews the answer (one that the listener has already heard in the message body) and the journey to it. Consequently the answer develops naturally, sustaining the listeners' suspense about the destination and improving the potential for developing our emotional empathy with the issue and its answer. Inductive sermons foster the preacher's storytelling stance toward the message, sustaining narrative tension and ensuring presentation of a resolution of that tension.

A second strategy for narrative development of the psalm addresses how one presents the biblical text in the message. One essential facet of biblical exposition is the presentation of the biblical text to the listener. Although preachers often present each verse of the passage in its biblical sequence, many passages develop their argument deductively or include significant digressions of thought. Preachers may struggle to sustain the listener's involvement in the sermon's narrative tension for the entire exposition.

Biblical audiences possessed specific pre-understandings and prejudices concerning the subject. These influenced the sequence in which biblical authors ordered the argument. Therefore, the order in which the text presents itself to its first audience should not necessarily confine us to follow the same sequence. Once we have determined the main idea, we should identify the psychological starting point in the text from which the trail began. The expository sermon begins at that spot in the passage and then takes the listener on the pilgrimage to the conclusion by revealing the trail of logic the biblical author used. When skillfully employed, such a strategy will enhance the listeners' understanding of the biblical truth and their emotional empathy for it.

A narrative approach to biblical exposition will result in one of three approaches toward preaching a psalm (see below). Each structure can be delivered inductively, thereby increasing the narrative quality of the message. Each allows the audience to follow the psychological path necessary to understand and engage with the psalm at its emotional level. These structures also prevent the outline from emerging as an academic analysis of an ancient form. They don't, however, *guarantee* that the sermon will sustain the emotional force of the original text. That depends on the preacher's ability to speak clearly, fluently, and connect the ancient flow of thought with contemporary equivalents that carry similar emotional force. These structures do give the creative preacher differing ways to maintain narrative interest, emotional involvement, and personal identification with the sermon's major topic.

Option 1: A Linear Development

Some psalms develop their argument in a direct psychological sequence from opening line to the final verse. Consider Psalm 121, a psalm of ascent. The writer opens with a question, provides the answer, and then defends the answer. The psalm has two parts. In the first section (vv. 1–2), the pilgrim anticipates the danger of a Jerusalem journey made to fulfill God's requirements. The pilgrim does this by expressing his concern over the journey's dangers (v. 1) and yet affirming his confidence in God (v. 2). The second section (vv. 3–8) confirms the psalmist's faith. God shows consistent concern for his people's needs (vv. 3–4) by promising protection (vv. 5, 6) at all times (vv. 7–8). The psalm's main idea, therefore, is that God, the guardian of Israel, will protect his people at all times as they travel to Jerusalem in obedience to celebrate one of his festivals.

The question (subject) of the psalm can be rephrased to fit a general audience: "Who will protect us [God's people] as we follow God's direction?" The sermon introduction should address the problems that confront people who struggle to live God's way. The introduction needs to address the debilitating effect on us as we face the unresolved struggle of the world's lack of perception of God's presence and goodness and of our faithful endurance.

This first major point of the message echoes the question and then answers it with an unqualified affirmation of faith in God's protection. The second major point adds the qualifiers from the psalm. (These qualifiers may be split into additional major points to allow for adequate development and clarity.) The simplicity of following the text's movement from problem to confident solution makes this an easy passage to preach and develop emotionally. The sermon outline might take this form:

> When obedience leads to the threshold of danger, trust God completely (vv. 1–2).
>
> Obeying God can lead us into danger (v. 1).
>
> When obedience leads us face to face with danger, trust God completely (v. 2).
>
> When obedience leads to danger, trust God completely because he will always care and protect (vv. 3–8). [*main idea*]
>
> Trust God in danger because he cares for you (vv. 3–4).
>
> Trust God in danger because he will protect you (vv. 4–5).
>
> Trust God in danger because he'll always be there for you (vv. 7–8).

The same outline could become even more narrative by following the sub-point structure, making each specific addition to the argument the focus of the main points (noted by the italics):

> Obeying God can lead us into danger (v. 1).
>
> When obedience leads us into danger, *trust God completely* (v. 2).
>
> When obedience leads to danger, trust God completely *because he will care for you* (vv. 3–4).
>
> When obedience leads to danger, trust God completely will care *and protect* (vv. 5–6).
>
> When obedience leads to danger, trust God completely because he will *always* care and protect (vv. 7–8). [*main idea*]

Option 2: The Event in Biblical History

As noted earlier, the easiest avenue to emotional empathy is human interest. We dress the ancient story to let the modern listener glimpse a human face. In days past a preacher could make this connection quickly in the sermon's introduction with a brief allusion to the background event. He could assume the audience would draw on a lifetime of biblical knowledge and emotional associations. Unfortunately, as biblical literacy declines, modern listeners have less knowledge of the Bible's basic stories (much less episodes at its fringes). Even worse, a listener's awareness of the event has been so corrupted by modern representations that a passing reminder or allusion evokes a distorted mental image or an inappropriate emotional association.[14]

Therefore, historical references provide a second option for a narrative sermon structure: present the original biblical story as the psychological starting point for the journey. The sermon will develop in much the same fashion as the first option, but now the question is framed by the crisis of the original story, the event, and its emotional implication.

Consider Psalm 57. The superscription identifies it as written while David hid from Saul in the cave, an allusion to the series of hiding places when David fled from Saul (1 Sam. 22–24). David speaks of physical jeopardy and employs figures of speech for his enemies suggesting their damaging slander of David at Saul's court (vv. 4–5). David relies on God's covenant promise that God will be faithful to deliver his people (vv. 3, 11). David grieves that his absence prevents any defense or vindication. Therefore, he commits himself to God's faithfulness to accomplish what God has promised (vv. 2, 3, 6, 8–12). The psalm is an individual lament with a two-part structure. In the first section (vv. 1–5), David describes his predicament with formal lament elements, including an introductory petition (v. 1), description of the cause (v. 4), and confessions of trust (vv. 2, 3, 5). The tone escalates in the second section (vv. 6–11), where he expresses his unequivocal confidence in God's vindication of his covenant faithfulness.

The issue for the psalmist is not much different from a common circumstance today when we ask, "How do we [God's people] deal with unjust–and unanswerable–criticism of the righteous?" The sermon introduction paints the image of criticism that's unfair, made worse by circumstances that prevent any defense. The first major point of the message restates this problem with reference to the psalm and tells David's circumstance (vv. 4–5). The psalmist's tension, however, must remain unresolved at this point. The second major point of the message resolves the tension by describing the response of God's people to unanswerable criticism, intimated in the first section but unpacked completely in the second. The sermon outline might take this form:

> Sometimes you're helpless when unfair attacks come (superscription, vv. 4b–5).
> When unfair attacks come, *make God's promise your defense* (vv. 1–3).
> When unfair attacks come, make God's promise your defense *because God will vindicate his glory* (vv. 5–6, 7–11). [*main idea*]

When a psalm refers to background events, the expositor should skillfully repaint the circumstances of these historical allusions, retaining their emotional and interpretive significance. Structurally, this retelling of the original event (and its emotional effect on the psalmist) forms the first main point of the sermon (and may include a specific element of detail of exposition within the psalm itself). The remainder of the exposition can follow the resolution offered within the psalm.

Option 3: The Author's Implied Need

For those psalms without an associated historical context, we must look at the psalm as the *answer* to a question implied by the contents of the psalm itself. Consider the message taught by two of the most popular psalms. In Psalm 23 the psalmist identifies God as his complete sufficiency (v. 1). The psalmist defends his confidence by describing God as his provider, leader, healer, defender, and deliverer (vv. 2–5). In God the psalmist knows the security of covenant fellowship (v. 6). The psalm answers the implied question: "Whom can I trust to meet all my needs abundantly?" The preacher must now ask the antithesis: "What are my needs? Where have I often tried–and failed–to fulfill them?" This implied question forms the core of the introduction–or can be expanded to the first main point of the message, if the audience needs time to identify and develop an understanding of their own faulty search strategies. The subsequent exposition follows the biblical sequence of the psalmist's argument–whether as a single main point or separate main points for his assertions–and it follows then each of the reasons offered in the psalm. The sermon outline might look like this:

> From the moment we're born, our needs are more than we can meet ourselves.
> The Lord can meet every need abundantly (vv. 1–5).
> Find all you need in the Lord (v. 6). [*main idea*]

Our second example, Psalm 100, answers the implicit question, "Why does God deserve our praise?" The psalm provides two major answers corresponding to its two movements. The psalmist begins with a call to universal praise (vv. 1–2), reasoning that God's power alone has created the covenant community (v. 3). Second, he calls his readers to praise again (v. 4), reasoning that God's covenant faithfulness is unending (v. 5). The preacher should now ask the antithesis: "Why would I think that God doesn't deserve my praise?" We live in a damaged and hurting world where God often seems absent and is often blamed for the damaging effects of his absence. This issue forms the core of the introduction–and possibly of the first major point of the message. The next major movement of the message provides the answer, either a single major point summarizing the two reasons or separating them into individual main points that add together to form the answer. The sermon outline might take this form:

Some folks can't find a reason to thank God.

Everyone can thank God (vv. 1–2, 4).
Everyone can thank God *because he gave us life* (v. 3).
Everyone can thank God because he gave us life *and he'll never leave
us* (v. 5). [*main idea*]

From these brief examples one can see that the message for a
particular psalm might be constructed to fit one or more of these narrative
options.

Step 4: Translate the Images

Once we have determined the most effective communication
strategy for a given psalm, we can return to an earlier focus of interest in
our exegesis: the figures of speech the psalmist employed. An inductive
message development forms the primary psychological framework within
which to engage the listener emotionally. Now the figures of speech can
assume a significant role within the message structure to illuminate the
story as concrete emotional illustrations of the psalmist's message.

Art, imagination, and passion form a powerful triad for persuasion.
Passion reflects one's capacity to imagine vividly. Imagination is fueled
by the aesthetics of image and associations. To appreciate art well, one
must understand its use of symbols, patterns of structure, and laws of
composition. Structure and composition limit the significance of the
symbols employed by the artist within a body of work.

Figures of speech give language its color. They allude to a concrete
experience and present a simple path to intellectual understanding and
its emotional significance. Images and their associations are always
context-specific. Like all skilful art, the significance of a psalmist's
symbol is determined by its original context. Unfortunately, listeners
who lack firsthand experience with the referent of the figure may import
an experience not assumed by the image and thereby misinterpret the
message and/or its associated emotion.

Modern listeners know little of life in the Ancient Near East (or even
a farm down the road). They have no experience with seasonal sowing
and winnowing, weaving cloth, or driving a cart. Their lives are not
built around a lifetime of religious pilgrimage and festivals. Their bills
are paid invisibly with credit cards, not shekels carefully counted from
a pouch. Our emotional associations with the biblical images are only
secondhand, cultivated in us by others with varying degrees of historical
accuracy and emotional sentiment.

Our strategy for using the psalmist's images must be twofold. First,
using simple, concrete language, an effective teacher must describe the

image, unpacking the referent and meaning of the original expression. Often a vivid, accurate description of the situation invoked by the image may arouse a listener to feelings of empathy for the psalmist. But we must not think that this is sufficient. We want the listener to understand the personal significance of the image with the same emotional power as intended by the psalmist.

The second step, therefore, is to translate the image into the same (or similar) emotional life experience of our audience. The effective teacher will create a corresponding image for the audience by describing a concrete image rooted in the modern listeners' experience, one that places the listeners in the same position as the psalmist and that possesses a similar emotional association to the biblical image.[15] The search for appropriate analogies is the hardest work the preacher will assume in preparation, but the preacher will find it the most engaging emotionally for the audience.

These image translations function as illustrations within the message. But we must avoid thinking that each figure of speech within a psalm requires this same translation process. (Otherwise, our sermons would become endless to the listener!) Instead, we should recognize where individual images contribute to a larger metaphor. Sometimes this may be the subparts of one image, such as a nocturnal, hunting animal (Ps. 7:2,5). Sometimes several different images may combine to make the same point, as in Psalm 58:6–9, where each image (broken teeth, rain runoff, dull arrows, snail tracks, miscarriage, whirlwind) makes the same point (the impotence of his enemies), but takes the import of the image to a higher intellectual and emotional level! Sometimes different images are combined in unusual ways to make a larger point—as in Psalm 57, where David's enemies are described as stalking lions (v. 4a) who wield words as deadly, human weapons (v. 4b).

In summary, the effective translation of these images supports the message developed around the main idea. The images should not be the focus of exposition or emotional engagement, but should provide both exegetical assistance and emotional connection for the listeners within the context of the broader argument.

Conclusion

The psalms express magnificent theology accompanied by deep feelings, yet our preaching and teaching has often treated them academ—ically with less emotion than they deserve. One reason may be that our understanding of what Bible exposition requires has been too limiting. We've often focused too much on the emotional connections of the images or on unpacking an ancient form in its presentation sequence. To ensure our audience engages a psalm's truth with its emotional packaging intact, we have two strategies. First, our messages must be designed inductively with a storyteller's heart. Second, the text's images must be translated accurately into the listener's world. Where the psalm emerges from a biblical narrative or an event in the life of God's people, we can bridge the original and modern listeners with that human face and color its question. Where there is no event to invoke, we should seek the question within the words of the psalm itself. When we preach the message, the question raised in the original should be the starting point for the psychological and emotional journey, the engine that drives the search for the answer that is only found in the main idea.

If we can invite our listeners to join us on the journey, with all of its spiritual, psychological, and emotional dimensions intact, we will find that, then, the psalms–and the Spirit–can do their greatest work.

PART 2

Interpreting the Psalms

Book One: Psalms 1–41

Book I of the Psalter is a wonderful collection of insights into the pathways of life. Two themes receive particular attention: the path of life under the guidance of God's law and the path of life King David followed. The themes are interrelated, for David was a model of living in light of a covenant relationship with God. Psalm 1 introduces the theme in the very first verse, encouraging hearers not to walk in the paths of the wicked.

Comprising forty-one psalms, Book I contains a wide variety of psalm types, though 40 percent are laments. Note in particular the following examples: lament psalms (3, 5, 6, 7, 10, 13, 14, 17, 22, 25, 26, 27, 28, 31, 35, 38, 39, 40); royal psalms (2, 18, 20, 21); declarative praise psalms (23, 30, 32, 34, 41); descriptive praise psalms (8, 29, 33); enthronement psalm (24); wisdom psalms (1, 19, 37). As is true for each section of the Psalter, Book I closes with a clear doxological formula: "The Lord God of Israel deserves praise in the future and forevermore. We agree! We agree!" (Ps. 41:13 NET).

The featured psalms for Book I are two psalms of wisdom (Pss. 1, 19) that praise the eternal king's glory for his perfect law and a royal psalm (Ps. 2) that celebrates the divine choice of an anointed king. Glen Taylor introduces Psalms 1–2 as a literary unit that serves as a signpost for preaching a psalm in light of its placement in the Psalter.

CHAPTER 4

Psalms 1 and 2

A Gateway into the Psalter and Messianic Images of Restoration for David's Dynasty

J. Glen Taylor

My family and I live in a Victorian house in downtown Toronto. One of the things that drew us to buy this old home was the entrance, which consists of two nicely sculpted wooden doors with stained-glass panels that make up the upper half of each door. The first door is attractive, but mostly utilitarian. It has such aesthetic features as square wooden panels, but mostly it just keeps out old man winter. The second door is especially lovely. People often comment on the beveled glass and especially on the round, ruby-like glass buttons that form an inner frame to a cluster of diamond- and square-shaped glass pieces. It provides visitors with the same favorable impression of the house that it provided my wife and me when we first saw it. Perhaps more than any other feature of the house, this entrance captured our interest and sparked our imaginations as to the potential the whole house had to become our home. (Otherwise, the house, formerly a rental property, was a bit run down.) The rest is history. We packed up our belongings and made this red-brick Eastlake-type house into our home, a place that we prayed might become a haven for our three kids and two dogs, along with four boarders and a stream of guests.

Over the past twenty-five years, Old Testament scholars have come to reflect on the beauty and significance of a similar set of double doors that leads to a haven of spiritual refreshment and solace within the Bible itself. This spiritual home is the book of Psalms, and the two doors that elegantly lead into it are Psalms 1 and 2. Simply put, Psalms 1 and 2, in addition to having their own discrete exegetical roles, are also "The Introduction" to the Psalms by virtue of their placement at the beginning of the book (more on this below).

The point of this essay is not to describe Psalms 1 and 2 in detail but to explore their role as introduction(s) to the psalms. This is important because, as with any other introduction to a book, Psalms 1 and 2 provide important clues about how the psalms as a whole are to be read, prayed, and also preached. It is important also because the rediscovery[1] that an initial psalm (or psalms) could play an introductory role is relatively recent. Finally, as I hope to show, the role Psalm 2 plays as introductory "opens a door" for a way of reading the whole book of Psalms as a book about God's Messiah. This will lead quite naturally to a quest to see how well (if at all) Jesus fulfills that expectation.

Let us assume for now that Psalms 1 and 2 may be an introduction to the Psalter and that Psalm 2 introduces us to a messianic theme of the book of Psalms. This leaves us with Psalm 1. What introductory role might it play? What is its distinctive message? Psalm 1 concerns the value of meditating on God's law. To what does "the law" in Psalm 1:2 (NAB, NASB95) refer?

The context of Psalm 1, including its placement at the beginning of the Psalms, may provide an answer. It might not be too far a reach to argue that "law" could refer to the five-book structure of the book of Psalms as a whole (Pss. 1–41, 42–72, 73–89, 90–106, 107–150), if one considers this structure an echoing of the five-book Torah (or law book) of Moses, the Pentateuch. This would suggest that the psalms are, like the Pentateuch, a sort of law book, but of a different form, on which one can meditate for spiritual benefit.[2] Psalm 1 is thus like a sign hanging on the first entryway door. It says something like: "Ponder the things in this house to your joy and benefit; neglect them to your peril." This role is somewhat analogous to the more conventional introduction to the book of Proverbs (Prov. 1:1–7), which also has the theme of deriving benefit from studying that poetic book.

I hope that by now readers will have begun to see some of the significance that Psalms 1 and 2 have for understanding the psalms as a whole. Before exploring more of the riches these psalms offer, I will provide some background to this new perspective that will help the reader to understand what we have explored so far, and to prepare the reader for what lies ahead. Two background issues merit consideration.

I. What Evidence Exists That Psalms 1 and 2 Are Introductory? Are There Other Psalms That Signal That They Are a Conclusion or Climax to the Collection?

What then (briefly and summarily) is the evidence that Psalms 1 and 2 have a role to play as the introduction to the Psalms? More generally, what is the evidence that the various psalms in the Psalter have consciously been organized to form a sort of booklike "argument"?

The introductory essay to this volume has already referred to the phenomenon of a purposeful ordering of many of the psalms.[3] While not all scholars conclude that the psalms have been intentionally ordered, most agree on the following evidence:

1. The demarcation of the psalms into a collection of five books implies that some thought has been given to organizing the psalms into a coherent (Pentateuch-like) whole. In other words, the book of Psalms has likely been shaped to echo the Pentateuch, the five-volume Law of Moses.

2. Books I–III (i.e., Psalms 1–89) of the Psalter place more emphasis on the role of human (i.e., Davidic) kingship in God's plans, whereas Books IV–V (i.e., Psalms 90–150) place relatively more emphasis on divine kingship. (An important corollary to this point is that psalms attributed to King David, including many of the so-called messianic psalms, occur more frequently in Books I–III than in IV–V.)[4] Indeed, historically speaking, the order of Books I–III became authoritatively fixed prior to Books IV–V.[5]

3. In general, the book of Psalms shows a spiritual-psychological progression. In other words, psalms of hurtful complaint (often called lament psalms) eventually give way to psalms of praise as one progresses through the book.[6]

4. Several "Hallelujah" psalms (i.e., Pss. 146–50) cluster at the end of the book, as if to conclude it. Since Psalms 146–150 conclude the book, Psalm 73 is near the midpoint of the Psalter. This psalm seems appropriate as a midway psalm, reflecting on the perspective of Psalm 1.[7]

5. A detailed study of a collection of temple hymns from ancient Sumer and of other pertinent data offer corroborative evidence for believing that the Psalms were purposefully arranged.[8]

We come now to our initial, more specific, background question: What evidence do we have that Psalms 1 and 2 are implicitly the introduction to the book of psalms? Several lines of evidence are outlined below:

1. Unlike almost every other psalm within Books I–III, Psalms 1 and 2 bear no title or superscription (for example, "to the choir director. A psalm of David.").[9] The intended effect appears to be that Psalms 1 and 2 are *themselves* the heading, superscription, or introduction to the Psalter.[10]

2. Although they differ in subject matter, Psalms 1 and 2 have several features in common. The word translated "meditates" in Psalm 1:2 is the same word in Hebrew translated as "plots" in Psalm 2:1.[11] Both psalms contrast a pious individual with a godless mob. Both

contrast the fixed nature of the godly individual with the fleeting mobility (and ultimate demise) of the wicked.[12] Also, both psalms in the final verse have the Hebrew words '*abad*, "perish," and *derek*, "way" but used in different ways. Thus NRSV reads in 1:6: "way of the wicked will perish" and in 2:12: "you will perish in the way."

Most importantly, Psalm 2 ends in the same "happy" way that Psalm 1 begins.. The second Psalm ends: "Happy are all who find refuge in him!" (REB), while Psalm 1 begins: "How happy is the man who does not follow the advice of the wicked" (HCSB).

Although the word translated "happy" is in itself important,[13] its significance here is that the Old Testament often marks a coherent unified literary unit through the repetition of the same word at both the beginning and end of that unit. In short, this framing device implies that Psalms 1 and 2 can also be understood as a single entity.[14] This factor alone likely accounts for numerous cases in history where Psalms 1 and 2 have been interpreted as a single psalm, including one manuscript tradition of Acts 13:33 in which Psalm 2 is referred to as Psalm 1, which can easily be explained if Psalm 2 was thought to be the continuation of Psalm 1.

3. Psalm 2 bears a number of clear similarities to the second-to-last psalm, Psalm 149 (cf. Ps. 149:2, 7–9). This suggests that neither the second nor the penultimate psalm has been placed coincidentally, but rather with reference to the other.

4. Psalm 1 has several grammatical features that are more characteristic of prose than of poetry.[15] Why is this important? Since we don't normally think of hymn collections (which the book of Psalms is) as introductory, the profusion of proselike features in Psalm 1 might well be a clue that it plays the double role of hymn (poetic) and introduction (normally prosaic). In other words, the proselike traits of Psalm 1 signal its added role as an introduction to the book.

To summarize, ample evidence supports the premise that Psalms 1 and 2 have intentionally been placed at the beginning of the book to introduce it. To fully understand the importance of these psalms, one needs to do more than an exegesis of each in its own (original) historical-grammatical context. It is this other "canonical" understanding that we are exploring in this essay.

II. Can a Psalm Have Valid Meanings in Addition to the Meaning Intended by the Original Author?

What we have learned about the importance of the editorial placement of Psalms 1–2 presents a challenge to a commonly held rule of thumb (at least within some circles of biblical interpretation) that a text can properly mean today only what its author intended it to mean when he wrote it. The challenge with both Psalms 1 and 2, however, is that *two* divinely led people have strongly affected the meaning of each psalm. First is the person who in each case wrote the psalm (meriting the sort of grammatical-historical exegesis that is modeled elsewhere in this volume). Second is the person who, likely at a much later time, decided that each psalm should be placed at (or, in the case of Psalm 2, near) the beginning of the Psalter (meriting the canonical/positional approach that is followed in this essay). In situations such as this, where editorial placement is relevant, the traditional interpretive focus on authorial intent must be adapted to reckon also with the meaning of the later–but clearly intentional, important, and inspired–work of the person(s) who put the finishing touches on the book of Psalms by arranging the order of psalms such as 1 and 2 (as introduction), 73 (as midpoint), and 146–50 (as conclusion), and likely others as well.

I have implicitly invoked this mode of interpretation. An example of this slightly different (or supplementary) approach to grammatical-historical exegesis can be found in the argument made earlier in this essay that "law" (NASB95) in Psalm 1 now has as an additional reference: the five-book collection that comprises the book of Psalms as a whole.[16] This interpretation gives credence to what seems likely to have been the intended meaning, *not of the original author*, but rather of an inspired compiler of this part of the book of Psalms. The intended meaning of the original author is not ruled out or deemed irrelevant; it contributes to the overall sense that the psalm conveys. Given the important role Psalm 1 plays as partly introductory to the psalms as a whole, the latter meaning *in its context of placement as introduction* adds to that of the original writer. Thus, the "law" to which Psalm 1 perhaps *now* refers is the five-book Pentateuch-like collection that is the book of Psalms. Sometimes, as here, the question of an author's original intent requires a split focus between the intent of the one who originally wrote the poem and the intent of the one who later assigned it a particular place and role within a biblical book.

To my mind another issue of seeking the meaning of a text is addressed by asking a different interpretive question: *not* "What is the original intention of the author?" but rather, *"How does the text in its present context want the reader to interpret it?"* This question nicely handles the problem of a split focus between the intent of an author and that of a later compiler, but we cannot always be sure what the intent of the original author was.

To ask this different interpretive question is not as radical or different an approach as some might judge. For one thing, this question seeks to moor the quest for meaning in a similarly objective way to authorial intent. For another, it avoids the impression that the Bible, often not divulging authorial intent, might be deficient by not providing the all-important clue to its own interpretation. For still another, it leaves room for God as the ultimate Author of scripture to reveal through his Word subtleties of meaning that transcend the limited perspective (and intention) of the human biblical writer. [17]

Another homey illustration will underscore this point. As often as our family can, we escape from the summer heat and humidity of Toronto by going to a cottage at a place called Eagle Lake, a three-hour drive north of the city. In this cottage there hangs from the ceiling a wagon wheel that has been converted into a chandelier. The old wagon wheel hangs flat and has three anchored chains attached to the rim. The chains extend upward to converge at the ceiling. Light sockets sit on the upper edge of the rim, and wiring runs inconspicuously through the links of the chain up into the housing of the ceiling fixture that now provides the light for our cottage.

To my mind, Psalm 1 is a lot like this chandelier. Just as the chandelier was originally a wagon wheel with its own original purpose in relation to the wagon to which it belonged, so Psalm 1 had a purpose intended by its original author. So, just as the form or shape of the wheel betrays its original role as part of a wooden wagon of yesteryear, so the method of form criticism has helped biblical scholars to identify the form of Psalm 1 as a wisdom psalm and to identify its original role as a poem that functioned within wisdom circles in ancient Israel, perhaps within a context of training scribes for service within the royal administration and temple (this is the work of historical-grammatical exegesis). As it now hangs from our ceiling, the wagon wheel has been adapted for an entirely different purpose—to be a chandelier. Moving beyond its original purpose, Psalm 1 is a wagon wheel cum chandelier that now serves to shed light on the purpose of the psalms as a whole.

The same analogy can be applied to Psalm 2. In its earlier wagon-wheel incarnation, Psalm 2 may have been part of the liturgy for a coronation ceremony for a king of Judah. On this understanding the ceremony was a dramatic affair that visualized (and perhaps ritually enacted) such things as the implications the king's rule would have for nations foolish enough to oppose the Lord's anointed. A key focus would also have been on ritually confirming the Lord's adoption of the king as his appointed ruler and son, in keeping with God's covenant with David in 2 Samuel 7.

As dramatic as that wagon-wheel phase in the life of Psalm 2 may have been, it can hardly be compared to the chandelier phase. That phase came long after the time when God's judgment fell on Judah, resulting in the demise of Davidic kingship in Judah. This coronation hymn for a king, like the wagon wheel, fell out of service for a long time. The theology of the hymn remained true, and its hyperbole came more and more to reflect the God-given, historical hope in another and even greater messiah who would bring God's rule to Judah and who would judge the nations. In its chandelier phase as introduction, Psalm 2 now casts a bright and powerful beam that sends messianic shimmers throughout the Psalter as a whole.

III. Psalms 1 and 2 in Their Role(s) as Introduction to the Psalms

With a summary of the evidence behind us showing single versus multiple meanings in a text, we may ponder further what this double-introduction is trying to reveal about the message of the psalms as a whole. Here I will simply quote a few representative views in keeping with how Psalms 1 and 2 want to be heard. First, though, a clarification is needed. As introduction(s), Psalms 1 and 2 can each be heard *independently* of the other, but also *together*. In light of this I will first offer views on the meaning of Psalm 1 independently. Views on Psalm 2 as an independent introduction shall follow. Finally shall come views on the message of Psalms 1 and 2 *together*–a double-barreled introductory message.

Category A: Psalm 1 (Alone)

"Israel reflects on the psalms…to learn the 'way of righteousness' which comes from obeying the divine law and is now communicated through the prayers of Israel."[18]

"Psalm 1…sets the tone of the collection in terms of the choice between the life of the righteous and the wicked. In addition, with its reference to Yahweh's instruction (v. 2), it directs the community to view the Psalter as teaching about the life of faith."[19]

"Psalms 1 and 2 both show that a way to security and blessing is through submission to the rule of God."[20]

"Psalms 1 and 2 may be read as an introduction to the story of the Psalter. Psalm 1 urges the reader to meditate on the Torah as the path to right living, and Psalm 2 states that, regardless of the useless plotting of earthly rulers, the God who sits in the heavens is sovereign over the created order."[21]

"Here at the threshold of the Psalter we are asked to consider the teaching that the way life is lived is decisive for how it turns out… This first beatitude prompts the reader to think of the entire book as instruction for life and commends a kind of conduct that uses the Psalter in that way."[22]

Category B: Psalm 2 (Alone)

"Psalm 2 addresses the question of the community of faith faced with the problems of a history made by nations contending for power; its word to faith is the announcement of the messiah into whose power God will deliver the nations."[23]

"As a result [of placing Psalms 1 and 2 as introduction] the theme of how Yhwh's *mashiah* will conquer all opposition and rule the world from Zion must be considered as one of the broad, overarching themes of the Psalms, in whose light all the ensuing lyrics, including the royal psalms, should be interpreted."[24]

Category C: Psalms 1 and 2 Together

"[W]e…learn that this book will speak to us of individuals and their way and destiny but also of kings and nations and their conduct and fate… Psalm 1 may be a word of instruction to the king or other rulers and leaders even as Psalm 2 is a word of assurance to the individual member of the community of faith… The way of the Lord's instruction and the rule of the Lord's anointed are the chief clues to what matters in all of this."[25]

"Those who engage in such meditation [as in Psalm 1] will find joy in so doing, and will be well nourished and productive, like trees planted by the riverside. But this theological reflection is not done in isolation. It takes place in the context of a world where nations plot and engage in war, a world, nevertheless, ruled by the Lord and where those who are hurting can find refuge in God."[26]

"Just as Psalm 1 and 2 call our attention to the main idioms within the subject matter of Jewish Scripture—the Torah (Psalm 1:2), the prophetic promise and judgment of God (Psalm 2:6–12), and the wisdom of God (Psalm 1:1, 2–6)—so this phrase [i.e., 'happy are all who take refuge in him' (NRSV) at the end of Psalm 2 is an editorial effort to demarcate a specific sub-theme for the laments that predominate in the first half of the Psalms."[27]

To my mind the interpretations in each category above resonate with how these texts as introduction want to be heard. As for my assessment of these, I would like to return to the analogy of the two doors with which I began this essay.

First, as illustrated in categories A and B above, we ought to think of entering the two front doors of the Psalter *independently*, as if entering one of two doors that stand side by side. In this understanding, the double introduction provides the reader with the option of reading the psalms from the perspective of either Psalm 1 or Psalm 2. The person who enters through Psalm 1 (as in category A) is to faithfully meditate on the book of Psalms for the purpose of growing into a deeply rooted and spiritually productive person who follows the way of life and avoids the path of evildoers. Alternatively, the one who enters through Psalm 2 (as in category B) is invited to read the Psalter as a book that deals with God's plan to exercise sovereignty over the entire world through his begotten Davidic son, the messiah who would restore David's dynasty. In either case, the Christian reader stands to benefit immensely from meditating on the psalms.

Second, though not as in category C, we ought also to think of entering these two doors as if they existed *in relation to each other*, as if one led to the other in a single narrow hallway such that one must first go through one door *and then* the next. From this perspective the reader cannot encounter one psalm without the other; in other words, the type of understanding reflected in *both* categories A and B above must be invoked. To read the psalms for the purpose of personal spiritual growth (the way of Psalm 1) is to be told in the very next psalm that the messiah's reign is the means by which God executes his plan to bring salvation or judgment. So, too, to read the psalms as messianic (the way of Psalm 2), one must first "sign on" to the plan of personal growth and the avoidance of evil advocated by Psalm 1. Indeed, given the placement of Psalm 1 prior to Psalm 2, the messiah cannot be the subject matter of the entire Psalter independently of the call of Psalm 1 for dedication to God's law. This concept merits elaboration briefly.

To this point we have been thinking of Psalm 1 as non-messianic, relating as it does to the importance of meditating on God's instruction or "law." The real messianic psalm, so we have seen, is its next-door neighbor, Psalm 2. In one sense Psalm 2 casts a messianic shadow over Psalm 1 so that it too can be seen to address the messiah. The shadow I am referring to can best be seen and understood by recalling Deuteronomy 17 and its discussion of God's plan to allow Israel to have a king. God ordains that a king not amass wealth, horses, and wives. Deuteronomy 17 provides the king a surprising job description:

> When he sits on his royal throne he must make a copy of this law on a scroll given to him by the Levitical priests. It must be with him constantly and *he must read it as long as he lives, so that he may learn to revere the Lord his God and observe all the words of this law*

and these statutes and carry them out. Then he will not exalt himself above his fellow citizens or turn from the commandments to the right or left, and he and his descendants will enjoy many years ruling over his kingdom in Israel. (Deut. 17:18–20, NET, emphasis added)

God's anointed king is not above the law. The law applies as much to him (or more so) than to anyone. My point: given that Psalm 2 already establishes the introduction as indisputably messianic, Psalm 1 might also have been placed at the beginning to emphasize this royal mandate on the messiah.[28] In this way, then, Psalm 1 might be not only a chandelier inviting the ordinary person to prosper through meditation on God's law, as we saw in category A above, but also a chandelier that complements the messianic chandelier of Psalm 2 by inviting the messiah to take up his divinely appointed role to meditate on the law (Ps. 1; cf. Deut. 17:17–19).

Third, as in category C above, which integrates both psalms into a single message, we can think of entering these two doors as if they were *bound together as one,* much as a screen door is adjoined at the frame to the main door.[29] This understanding sees an implied connection between the righteous individuals in both psalms (the one obedient to Torah in Ps. 1 and to the Davidic king of Ps. 2) and between the wicked (the anonymous chaff in Ps. 1 and the conspiring nations of Ps. 2). Implicitly as well, the happy *both* avoid the influence of the godless (Ps. 1:1) and take refuge in the Lord (Ps. 2:12). (NRSV)

IV. How to Read the Psalter Messianically

Reading the book of Psalms as a whole from a messianic perspective (the way of Psalm 2) than from a devotional perspective (the way of Psalm 1) calls for hard work and deep thinking. In light of such difficulty, I want to share a few *general* insights on seeing the Messiah (for Christians, that is Christ Jesus) in the Psalter.

One of the most helpful discussions on reading the Psalms messianically comes from the nineteenth-century Anglican scholar J. J. Stewart Perowne, whose Psalms commentary still draws the attention of reprint publishers.[30] Perowne advocates reading the psalms as "typologically prophetic."[31] Reading the psalms typologically allows one to read the psalms as any other type in Scripture, namely, with a view to focusing on that which corresponds to Christ Jesus and to overlooking that which does not. Take Psalm 41:9—"one who ate my bread has raised his heel against me" (HCSB). In John 13:18 Jesus applied the words in present tense, not past, to Judas: "The one who eats My bread has raised his heel against Me." Psalm 41 can be interpreted to echo the agony of Jesus despite the fact that the psalm also contains a confession of personal guilt from sin which cannot easily refer to Jesus (see v. 4). Perowne suggests verse 4 simply be overlooked as part of the type that does not apply (much in the same way, I would add, that, in seeing the typological application to Christ Jesus of the serpent lifted on the pole in Numbers 21, we instinctively know not to equate Christ with the serpent, a symbol of sin and evil.) This sort of "picking and choosing" what applies to Jesus and what does not will not do much to convince a skeptic that the psalms apply to Christ Jesus. But, as Psalm 1 reminds us, our purpose in reading the psalms is not primarily apologetic (in the sense of defending the faith), but devotional and, as Psalm 2 reminds us, messianic.

Other general ways to see Christ Jesus in the psalms include being open to different ways in which the psalms (or parts thereof) might apply to Christ Jesus. For example, most of Psalm 22 may be read christologically as words said *by* Jesus himself, whereas psalms such as 72 are best read as words *about* an anticipated messiah and his kingdom. Even the parts of psalms that contain cries for vengeance can be read messianically (a) as part of the type that does not apply to Jesus, (b) as a legitimate prerogative that Jesus thankfully chose not to exercise, or (c) as awaiting fulfillment at the return of Jesus as judge.[32]

You can see Christ Jesus in the psalms in other general ways. For example, it is helpful to take seriously the inseparability of the experience of the individual psalmist and that (typologically and prophetically) of the later Christ, and to see that inseparability as testimony to Christ's solidarity with human suffering and to the Christian's with his. It is also helpful to understand the messianic character of the psalms not too narrowly. Note, for example, what one scholar says about Martin Luther's later, more mature understanding of how the psalms relate to Christ Jesus:

> Luther's approach to the psalms is notable, particularly because it is Christ centered. For him, all aspects of Christian life, including the psalms, relate to Christ. Even the psalmists' down-to-earth requests for protection and thanks for deliverance Luther applied to his own circumstances and life as a Christian. The psalmists asked for blessing and gave thanks for blessings as members of the covenant people of God, relying on God's grace, trusting his promises, worshiping in his temple, receiving his forgiveness. Yet all of these—covenant, grace, promise, temple, and forgiveness—found their fulfillment in Jesus Christ. Christ "is himself the God whom we are exhorted to worship." When the psalmist exults that God's "love endures forever," Luther responds that *Christ* "stands hidden" in that phrase.[33]

As this reference to Luther illustrates, present-day Christians have a lot to learn from believers in times past who quite naturally saw Christ Jesus reflected in most psalms.

V. Is It Really Appropriate to Read the Whole Psalter Messianically?

You may think I am giving too much weight and influence to Psalm 2 to suggest, as I am, that this one psalm casts so long a shadow (or, better, light) over the book of Psalms such that the whole book can be read messianically.[34] However, evidence from early Jewish and Christian history indicates that the book of Psalms was read in this full-blown sort of way. For instance, the Septuagint, a prominent Greek translation of the Old Testament, came into use in the third century B.C.E. and was broadly influential throughout the time of Jesus and the early church. Interestingly, the words found at the head of many superscriptions, "for the choir director" were translated into Greek as *eis to telos,* which means, "pertaining to the end," "concerning fulfillment," or the like.[35] Since this notation is very often followed by the words "of David," readers of the psalms in Greek would read "of David" in conjunction with "concerning fulfillment." I think it very likely that this influenced readers of the psalms to understand the psalms of David to be read no longer simply as hymns but as *prophecies.* Prophecies about what? Most likely: "of [the] David" who is yet to come, God's messiah, the one to resurrect David's dynasty (Am. 9, Jer. 31, and Zech. 6).

Furthermore, the Dead Sea Scrolls witness at least five different arrangements of the Psalter and include David's last words from 2 Samuel 23:1–7, Psalm 151 known from the Septuagint, Psalms 154 and 155, ben Sirach 51, a list of David's compositions, a hymn to the Creator, a plea for deliverance, an apostrophe to Zion, an apostrophe to Judah, an eschatological hymn, and four Psalms against demons including Psalm 91. David's list of compositions credits him with 3,600 psalms and 446 songs for special occasions. The final line of the list says David spoke these psalms and songs through prophecy from the Most High.[36]

Interestingly, the passage from Samuel is one of only a few texts in the Old Testament that refers to David as a prophet. An implication arising from the Dead Sea additions to the Psalter is they bear witness to an element within Judaism (roughly at the time of Christ) that understood at least some of the psalms of David to be "prophecies." As with the Septuagint cases, it is easy to imagine that the fulfillment of these Davidic prophecies was thought to lie with a son of David who was yet to come.

Finally, the apostle Peter in Acts 2 interprets Pentecost for the bewildered crowd who had just witnessed it. Peter first cites the prophet Joel. What often goes unnoticed is that Peter, without batting an eyelash, goes right on in verses 25–35 to cite another prophet, king David (v. 30), and then cites from two psalms (Psalm 16:10 and 110:1) as if they were prophecies.

To reiterate, my point has not only been that Psalm 2 can be read as a messianic psalm, but that through its introductory role, it may paint the entire book of Psalms with a messianic brush. This broad messianic brushing was implicitly condoned by the apostle Peter and continued by Christians throughout history. They instinctively knew to read the psalms as if they ultimately had to do with the expected messiah or Christ. Given this ancient historical tradition first within Judaism and then in early Christianity of reading the psalms messianically, Christians cannot rightly be accused of misreading the psalms by reading "Christ" (the messiah) back into the book.[37] Rather, the earliest Christians were continuing a practice of messianic exegesis begun within Judaism long before Jesus.

VI. How Does Jesus Fare in Reading the Psalter Messianically?

We have seen evidence that the book of Psalms was organized to be read as testimony concerning Israel's expected messiah. This leads to an important question: What kind of messiah might the book of Psalms as a whole expect? At least for Christians the question becomes more specific: How well does Jesus live up to those expectations? Here then is a selective walk through the book, with a view partially to answering that question.[38]

Psalm 1 is a doorway through which the messiah must first successfully pass. The king must diligently study God's law (v. 2; compare Deut. 17:18–20). Such a king would perhaps from his youth be found in the temple, listening to the teachers and asking them questions. The teachers in turn would be "astonished at His understanding and answers."[39] He might even offer his own version of the beatitudes of Psalm 1, proclaiming such things as, "Happy are those who…"[40] His teachings might reflect such strength and maturity that common people would recognize his teaching as uniquely authoritative.[41]

Psalm 2 expects the messiah to be one whom rulers would oppose and be glad to be free of (vv. 1–2). He is, after all, according to God's own declaration, "my son" (v. 7). He is well pleasing to God. By placing his only begotten son as king of the Jews in Zion (v. 7), God has put the destiny of all nations in his hands (v. 8). All authority in heaven and earth is given to him (v. 8). Lords of the nations are told to put their trust in him (v. 12b), to revere him with trembling joy (v. 11), or else to face his wrath and perish (v. 12a).

Immediately following is Psalm 3, and after it dozens of others that speak of the Davidic king suffering (3–7; 12; 13; 22; 25–28; 35; 38–40; 42–44; 51; 54–57). So prominent is this theme of suffering that present-day scholars categorize these psalms as lament psalms.[42] These laments are too many to list. Perhaps the best way to illustrate the flavor of these laments in relation to Davidic kingship is to note that one of the main schools of scholarly interpretation understands them originally to have been prayers made by the king, often on behalf of his people, and ritually reenacted within the temple. The prominent scholar of the psalms, John Eaton, a proponent of this view, summarizes the content of the lament psalms as follows:

> In symbol the king was beset by enemies from all quarters and brought to the realm of death; his humble fidelity was thus proved and Yahweh answered his prayer, exalting him above all dangers and foes. While the order of the ceremonies and texts remains uncertain, the chief elements of the royal suffering and exaltation are strongly attested, as is also the close relation to the assertion of Yahweh's own kingship.[43]

Psalm 72 celebrates the majesty, eternality, and universality of the reign of the son of David. Psalm 89 does this also, but, significantly, includes a rude interruption in which God rejects his anointed one. Enemies and other passersby shame and dishonor the king, casting his crown and throne to the dust (vv. 39, 44). The psalmist asks why God has seemingly forsaken his covenant with David (v. 49). This is clearly a moment of profound disillusionment. Hopes for a promised eternal reign of the messiah have been dashed by an unexpected tragedy.

After the shocking disclosure of the messiah's suffering, Moses appears on the scene (Ps. 90).[44] The psalms that follow Psalm 90 (especially Ps. 91) give assurance that all is well. Moreover, Psalms 110 and 132 resurrect the notion of the messiah just as God had promised he would in Jeremiah and Zechariah. Messiah reappears despite the seeming finality of Psalm 89.

True, all is well (including hope in the messiah), but something has changed. From Psalm 90 onward, a change in emphasis moves away from the kingly rule of the son of David towards a focus on the king as Yahweh himself. This change comes soon after the messiah's downfall.

Thus, Psalms 93; 95; 96; and 97 all proclaim: "Yahweh reigns!" It is as though something happened subsequently to Psalm 89 to instill belief in the kingly rule of God not so much through his Son, but as himself. Note, however: by making this transition from human to divine kingship, the Psalter has created a seemingly impossible challenge for any king who would aspire to fulfill the messianic hope that Psalm 2 sets up for the whole book.

We draw our portrait of the messiah of the psalms to a close by adding a postscript that brings us to Jesus' own day. So far as we know, Judaism in Jesus' day did not expect a messiah who would be both human and divine. Were such a messiah to appear at this time, as Christians believe he did, he would almost inevitably be in a clash with the religious authorities. He would have to spend a lot of time defending his unexpectedly divine identity, perhaps by alluding to psalms such as Psalm 110, which implies that the son of David would be David's "Lord" who occupies a place at God's right hand. More so—and ironically—were the true Messiah to appear at this time, something else would have happened that the psalms further speak about, but that the Jewish establishment expected no more than the messiah's divinity: the messiah would suffer. Any claimant to something so unexpected as a divine messiah would very likely face persecution and perhaps even death at the hands of his own people (and others), which of course was the fate of Jesus.

Wolfhart Pannenberg, Reinhold Niebuhr, and others have observed that Jesus could not have appeared as a messiah to the Jews if the Jewish people were not in turn looking for such a figure.[45] This is true. But what happens when a messiah comes whose understanding of the nature of the messiah differs from that of his Jewish contemporaries? This would be a recipe for conflict and would pose a problem for the acceptance of the true messiah. Were he to be the true messiah of God despite this different expectation by the Jews, something would need to happen to confirm the identity of that messiah for the Jews and for others. This is precisely what Christians affirm that God did through the resurrection of Jesus. Luke puts it eloquently when he quotes from the sermon of Simon Peter after Pentecost:

> This Jesus God raised up, and we are all witnesses of it. So then, exalted to the right hand of God, and having received the promise of the Holy Spirit from the Father, he has poured out what you both see and hear. For David did not ascend into heaven, but he himself says,

> "The Lord said to my lord, 'Sit at my right hand until I make your enemies your footstool for your feet.'"

Therefore let all the house of Israel know beyond a doubt that God has made this Jesus whom you crucified both Lord and Christ. (Acts 2:32–36, NET)

What a privilege for Christians to proclaim the good news of a Messiah who was both a son of David and David's Lord.

CHAPTER 5

Psalm 19

Proclaim the King's Glory, for His Law Is Perfect

David C. Deuel

A masterpiece of poetry remarkable for its beauty and power, Psalm 19 marvels at God's glorious handiwork and ponders God's precious precepts. The poem points earthlings' gaze heavenward while summoning the entire universe to bow in worship. It evokes the gifted few to express its truths artfully. From the illustrator of St. Albans Psalter (England, twelfth century), who depicted the Psalm with a bridegroom coming out of his marriage chamber, to the contemporary artist Moshé Tzvi Berger, who merged God's sun and law into a single image, the psalm has inspired some of the world's best art and music. The composer Haydn (1732–1809) penned the opening measure of his majestic work, *Creation,* with "The heavens are telling the glory of God." Ambrose of Milan (340–397) drew on the imagery of Psalm 19:1–6 when he composed a hymn about the earthly mission of Jesus:

> Forth from His chambers cometh He,
> The court and bower of chastity;
> Henceforth in two-fold substance one,
> A giant glad His course to run.
> From God the Father He proceeds,
> To God the Father back He speeds;
> Runs out His course to death and hell,
> Returns to God's high throne to dwell.

Even in its artful applications, the psalm invites readers to meditate deeply. It bids preachers to proclaim its message eloquently. It calls for theological reflection on the nature of God's revelation and the basis for man's responsibility. It speaks volumes worth reading, teaching, and preaching over and over again.

Why Did the Author Compose the Psalm?

Psalm 19 was written to elevate the hearts of God's people toward him in worship, whether in joyful song, deep study, or simple and quiet heartfelt prayer. Considering how God's greatness is written across his skies and inscribed in his law, the psalmist responds with emotional language exalting God as Creator of the universe and Revealer of wisdom. True worshipers cannot sit on their hands or mumble along lethargically when they read this psalm. By putting his message in the mouths of celestial heralds, the psalmist first lifts fellow worshipers up to God's heavenly royal court in responsive praise (vv. 1–6). The poet then invites God's people to enter into the sanctuary of the heart, where God reigns as king and where his law is perfect instruction (vv. 7–14).

The psalm's title, "For the music director; a psalm of David" signals its use in worship and reminds us that the Psalter has played a critical role in Israel and the church's liturgy.[1] Fifty-four of the one hundred and fifty canonical psalms claim this title.[2] Psalms 1, 19, and 119, with similar structure and content focusing on God's instruction, have been identified as Torah psalms. Torah training nurtures righteous character that responds to God contritely in prayer and praise. Its essential commitments are to trust in the reign of the king and to devote oneself to the Lord's instruction. It shows concern for wickedness in self and society, as well as for the arrogance and power of the wicked. God's people demonstrate faithfulness to their king through study and obedience. They find hope through prayer and waiting. This is the essential core of the Torah psalms and the Psalter as a whole.[3]

Classifying Psalm 19 as a Torah psalm does not preclude other emphases. God's kingship is a crucial theme, particularly regarding his governance and administration, an emphasis that may unite the entire Psalter.[4] "Behind all the elements of psalmic praise is the conviction that Yahweh reigns."[5] No literary axiom forces us to choose exclusively between the Torah theme's *law of the Lord* or the kingship theme's *Lord of the law*. Rather, the psalmist worships the king *for* his perfect law.

How Did the Author Express His Ideas?

The psalmist wove together a beautiful tapestry of images exalting God through hymnic praise and prayer. Engaging his creative and poetic spirit in worship, the author underscored creation's role in revealing God by imagining the sky speaking and its voice echoing throughout the earth–without words. The poet pictured a tent pitched in the sky for the sun, a bridegroom emerging from his chamber, and an athlete who enjoys running a course. The result is a colorful array of literary devices. In the tradition of Torah wisdom instruction, the psalmist modeled worship as he meditated about God in three closely related ways.

He practiced imaginative listening. By using ear-gate imagery to simulate the sensory process of listening (cf. Isa. 55:1–5), the psalmist invites us to join the celestial bodies in telling the glory of God. The heavens are *speaking* through visual perception, and we should be *listening* (vv. 1–6) by observing their method of praise and then following their example.

He worshiped God as king. "The LORD has established his throne in heaven" (Ps. 103:19). The psalmist introduces the divine king's court, where heralds make royal proclamations for the Lord's central administration (vv. 1–6).[6] Following a highly symbolic transition (v. 6), the poet marvels at the divine king's law, exalting its virtues and God's rule through compassionate administration in the lives of his subjects (vv. 7–14). The author employs the imagery of royal distance to create movement in the psalm from transcendence to immanence. Starting out, the psalmist points to the Lord reigning high and lofty in his heavenly palace, as in Psalms 18 and 20. God uses heralds to make his royal proclamations. By the end of the psalm, the psalmist speaks directly to the divine king, praising him for his magnificent Torah instruction.[7]

He praised God for his incomparability. God's kingship is without equal, as evident in the recurrent cry in Israel, "Who is like you, O LORD, among the gods?" (Ex. 15:11, NET). On this the first commandment was clear: worshiping foreign gods and idols is strictly forbidden lest something compete for the hearts of God's people (Ex. 21:3). In the same spirit, the psalmist uses terminology and imagery to demonstrate God's superiority (vv. 1–6). The effect is to draw comparisons between God and pagan deities and belief systems. The claim that "God is greater" is an invitation to revere him, even as another psalmist personalized the praise lyrics: "I will give you thanks with all my heart; before the heavenly assembly I will sing praises to you." (Ps. 138:1, NET). God's incomparability is an appealing invitation to worship.[8]

In an Assyrian relief called the Black Obelisk[9] (see figure on page 66) the captors of Jehu, king of Israel, followed normal ritual protocol for defeat by demanding that Jehu bow before their Assyrian king Shalmaneser III and worship their sun god Shamash. Passages such as Psalm 19 call Jehu back, as they did others, such as Daniel, Esther, and the three youths standing before the fiery furnace. The captors' attempt to coerce the worship of foreign gods must be resisted.

The incomparability message carries over into verses 7–14, in which the psalmist exalts God's law as the source of wisdom. There may be

Jehu, King of Israel (or his agent) bows in humble submission as the Assyrian King Shamaneser III and his functionaries worship Shamash, the sun god, symbolized by a winged disc.[10]

an implicit contrast here with the tree that was "desirable for making one wise" (Gen. 3:6). The tree is no longer available. God's law is the replacement. On a different plane, most of Israel's neighbors had some form of law that was often little more than monumental propaganda.[11] The psalmist extols the virtues of God's law, the ideal administration: "The law of the LORD is perfect" (v. 7). It even warns and rewards (v. 11).

What Are the Important Interpretive Issues?

Many studies of Psalm 19 argue for a complex history of textual development with editorial stages.[12] They question the psalm's unity based on thematic change between verses 6 and 7 marked by transitional abruptness.[13] But because the psalmist alludes to Genesis 1–3 throughout the psalm, we can make a strong argument for a cohesive text. In fact, the thematic transition that occurs between Genesis 1 and chapters 2–3, the passage the psalmist alludes to, may account for the thematic change in Psalm 19 between verses 6–7, the alleged rough spot. What is more, a connection between a royal theme of justice emblematic of the sun's role (vv. 4–6) and the law's excellence introduced in verse 7 might best explain that transitional abruptness.[14]

Several New Testament connections to Psalm 19 stand out. The message of the psalm may lie behind the apostle Paul's argument for human inexcusability in Romans 1:18ff. Paul probably uses the reflex argument from Romans 1:18ff (and imagery of Psalm 19) when he writes, "The god of this world has blinded the minds of the unbelieving *so that they might not see the light of the gospel of the glory* of Christ" (2 Cor. 4:4, NASB95, emphasis added). In Romans 10:18, Paul's message brims with the terminology and imagery of messengers and proclamations as he quotes the psalm to develop his discussion of preaching in Israel's experience. Of great significance to this study, Paul's interpretation argues, along with citations from Ambrose (supra) and other Early Church interpreters (infra), that the royal proclamation metaphor passes like a thread through Psalm 19:1–6. Despite these interpretive issues, we must not lose sight of the author's message.

What Was the Author Seeking to Communicate?

Placed in a series of royal psalms offering a candid picture of a troubled Davidic kingdom, Psalm 19 portrays a cosmic drama depicting two things: the scope of God's universal rule as revealed from one end of the heavens to the other and the significance of his perfect law as it governs the life of a model subject. Celestial voices call us to forsake our terrestrial allegiances, bow before the king, and embrace his rule for our lives. Worship is, at once, like entering his royal courts and returning to the garden of Eden, a spiritual journey from heaven to earth where fellowship finds its perfect rest in the presence of God. His *Torah* is like the tree that bears the fruit of the knowledge of good and evil. A descriptive outline for Psalm 19 follows. The chiastic structure for verses 1–6 also marks the textual unit for the extended metaphor of the herald and his proclamation.

1. Praise God, the king like a herald in his universal kingdom (vv. 1–6):

   (A) The heavenly heralds proclaim the king's glory (v. 1).

     (B) The king's proclamation never ceases (v. 2).

       (C) The king's proclamation is not heard (v. 3).

     (B') The king's proclamation reaches to the ends of the earth (vv. 4a-b).

   (A') The sun is envoy of the king's proclamation (vv. 19:4c–6).

2. Embrace Yahweh's perfect law like one of his subjects (vv. 7–14):

   A. Yahweh's servant recognizes the advantages of the king's law (vv. 7–11).

   B. Yahweh's servant responds in true humility to the king's law (v. 12a).

   C. Yahweh's servant requests solutions prescribed in the king's law (vv. 12b–14).

Let us look at this outline in more detail.

1. Praise God, the king like a herald in his universal kingdom.

All the king's works worship his majesty (Ps. 145:5–10). In Psalm 19:1 the psalmist does not focus on the finished product, but rather on the creative process. In photographic terms, he took a video not a still shot. The psalmist selects two heavenly messengers, "heavens" and "firmament" (NRSV) to stir our memory of Genesis 1 and to set the historical stage. In a mighty act, God created and named the firmament "heavens" as a divine demonstration of his perfect wisdom, a significant theme in this passage. The two verbs, "declare" and "tell" (NASB95) regularly occur in the Psalms for public declaration of praise. Although they describe acts of royal proclamation, the specific content of the heralds' message in Psalm 19 is not given–it is only described for us in one word, "glory."

What is the nature of God's glory? In our passage, a chiastic structure parallels the "glory of God" with "the work of his hands" (NASB95). The psalmist makes this connection in Psalm 96, another passage exalting God's kingship, when he says, "Tell the nations about his splendor! Tell all the nations about his amazing deeds!" (Ps. 96:3; see also 1 Chr. 16:24). In other passages, specific aspects of God's character are proclaimed: God's power (Ex. 9:16), righteousness (Ps. 22:30–31), faithfulness (Ps. 30:9), steadfast love (Ps. 92:2), wisdom (Ps. 104:24), and his name or reputation (Ex. 9:16). God's glory can encompass these and other attributes, as well as God's wonderful deeds/mighty acts (Ps. 71:17). In short, we can understand God's glory as the "majesty that envelops all those qualities which call forth worship and praise."[15]

In other passages, the heavens shout proclamations of God's glory and righteousness (Pss. 97:6; 50:6; 97:6), but these spotlight his kingship.[16] That God's creation exalts his royalty may seem strange to modern ears. Why not his deity? Although the precise reasoning may not be obvious, one explanation seems clear. The personified creation mimics Israel's role as a people of praise to remind them satirically of their fitting response to their creator and king. Israel's priestly function, in part, was to offer testimony for God to each other and to the nations (Ps. 67), a message applied by analogy to a struggling church in 1 Peter 2:9ff, and by application, to all faltering churches.

To underscore the ongoing nature of the proclamation, the psalmist uses participles (19:1) and finite imperfect verbs (19:2) in addition to the "day after day…night after night" imagery. Even after the celestial heralds' long journey, they exuberantly "bubble forth" their speech, a verb that paints an image of perpetual springs (Prov. 18:4). The term "knowledge"

(19:2) has in view a "message," (NAB) for this is drama in spectacular display, not a dry lecture. With blue-sky backdrop, the king's greatness is revealed from heaven in all of its grandeur. The cosmic stage lights up and lives with actors who witness to God's magnificence by public proclamation, the sun giving testimony by day; the moon and the stars by night. The imagery calls to mind the messenger relay of which the prophet spoke: "One runner after another will come to the king of Babylon. One messenger after another will come bringing news" (Jer. 51:31).

The psalmist marks the structural turning point of the section (vv. 1–6) when he says, "Their voice is not heard" (19:3) (HCSB). The shortest line in the chiastic pattern and its conceptual center, this stands out with striking emphasis. It underscores the uniqueness of the heralds' message. It cannot be heard! A herald delivered proclamations by projecting his voice. In Nebuchadnezzar's Babylon, "the herald made a loud proclamation" (Dan. 3:4). In stark contrast to the heralds of the ancient world whose voice must be strong, the heavenly heralds' voices in Psalm 19 are not audible. Yet, though silent, they blast forth a message from their high position in the sky that reverberates to all corners of creation.

The scene changes suddenly. From the celestial council emerges a solitary figure, known in the ancient Near Eastern world for its messenger prowess. The sun is reputed to be bright, permanent, and strong (Song 6:10; Ps. 89:36; Judg. 5:31). Its unrivaled brightness and reputation for traversing the firmament makes it the best qualified messenger for this incredible mission. What is more, the sun witnesses everything as it runs its course across the sky. It is best informed to tell the story of God's mighty acts, the proto-act being creation. Its unique radiance in the form of heat distinguishes it from the cool light of the other planetary council members (v. 6).

When the psalmist says that God pitches a tent for the solar herald, he reminds us that God has the power to realign celestial objects. Tents are emblematic of the heavens (see also Isa. 40:22; Ps. 104:2). From its heavenly pavilion, the sun emerges each morning. The imagery of God providing the sun's shelter may serve less as a staunch refutation of sun worship and more as an affirmation of YHWH's incomparability (Ezek. 8:16). As with most polemic themes, the intent is to glorify God.[17]

The poet uses two similes to portray the sun's fervor to run its course. The first, "as a bridegroom goes forth" (19:5) paints a picture of vigorous joy by focusing on the zeal with which the sun runs the road to herald the proclamation. The second simile, "It rejoices as a strong one," (19:5) builds on the bridegroom imagery in an "and what's more" fashion. A strong one is often a warrior in the Old Testament. Warriors endure battles. "They run like warriors. They climb walls like soldiers" (Joel 2:7, God's Word).

An extra-biblical passage, 1 Esdras 4:34, describes the fleet-footedness of the sun: "the sun is swift in its course, for it makes the circuit of the heavens and returns to its place in one day" (NRSV). The herald's extended metaphor ends with verse 6. The phrase "its circuit" for a messenger's path is applied to the moon in Ecclesiasticus (ben Sirach) 43:7: "From the moon comes the sign for festal days, / a light that wanes when it completes its course" (NRSV). The psalmist's reference to the route of a celestial body makes significant play on words for the journey of the sun-herald. Heralds ran circuits or courses in much the same manner as our paperboys deliver newspapers. This blending of images is the work of a master wordsmith. Although no one can hear the message, all can see the message of the sun-herald. Often, the heat of the sun is emblematic of a destructive force against which God promises to protect (Ps. 121:6; Isa. 49:10). Here it presents a positive image pointing back to the larger message of verses 1–6. You cannot hear the herald's proclamation, but neither can you miss it. Creation praise never ceases. It reaches the outer limits of the cosmos as a model of worship for us (vv. 2–6).

Verse 7 introduces a new section that carries over the praise of the first. Although studies suggest many explanations for uniting the two sections of the psalm with different themes, the extended metaphor for creation-kingship offers a thematically consistent solution. R. J. Clifford explains: "In Psalm 19, the 'fine-tuned regularity of the universe' (vv. 2–7) witnesses to God's power to ensure in turn a well-ordered and beneficent human community through the *Torah*, observed faithfully by those who are wise and loyal subjects (vv. 8–15)."[18] The attributes that make God a wise and powerful creator-king also present him as a qualified lawgiver worthy of his subjects' worship. In several other psalms, God's creative wisdom and power form the basis for his tender rule in his people's lives (Pss. 135; 136; 146; 147). They embrace his law-instruction in response.

2. Embrace Yahweh's perfect law like one of his subjects.

God's servant recognizes the advantages of his king's law (vv. 7–11). In the psalmist's world, law and instruction went hand in glove. Although the celestial heralds use neither speech nor words (v. 3), our king, the perfect law and wisdom teacher, has not left his people without clear instruction.[19] The psalmist boasts, "The law of the LORD is perfect" (Ps. 19:7). Another Torah Psalm echoes, "O how I love your law" (Ps. 119:97).

In Psalm 19, the psalmist shows us God's rule through his law in two specific ways. First, we see his administrative prowess in the terms for law. We can read in any number of ways the names for God's law in this rare six-part Hebrew poetic structure set off by an absence of conjunctions. These legal terms each have an instruction-related meaning (Torah, testimony, precept, commandment, fear, and ordinance). Other Torah Psalms (Pss. 1, 119) and wisdom books have similar lists, though the order here is unique. A thread of royal administration runs through the six titles for the king's law with a secondary set of correlate meanings:

> 19:7 Yahweh's Law... Yahweh's covenant stipulations
>
> 19:8 Yahweh's administrative orders... Yahweh's decrees
>
> 19:9 The commands to fear (serve) Yahweh... the judgments (verdicts) Yahweh renders

A poetic word play aligns this set of meanings,[20] all reflecting God's rule through his law and drawing on the kingship metaphor. The addition of meanings through word plays does not cancel out the instructional meaning.

The second way that we see the king's praiseworthy administration is in the descriptions that follow each title for law. These are ways that the king's law affects his subjects. They cut deeper than what we might identify as the civil and social impact of legislation. Without a hint of the harsh taskmaster image, the psalmist describes the ways that the law graciously protects from sin that threatens to rule us (v. 13).

The qualifiers that serve as the effects of God's instruction (vv. 7–9) might be explained as follows: Yahweh's Law "preserves one's life" (NET). It renews spiritual vitality to trial-tested and weary souls. This is the language of struggle and overcoming (v. 7). Yahweh's Covenant (with its stipulations) is intended to "impart wisdom to the inexperienced," (NET) that is, it prevents decision disaster–in a word, it helps to keep us from acting the fool (v. 7; but compare 2 Tim. 3:15). Yahweh's Administrative Order is to "make one joyful"(NET), causing the joy that comes from God and his prescribed ways, not ephemeral experiences (v. 8, NET). Yahweh's Decree is to "give insight for life," meaning it offers us the right perspective for decision-making rooted in righteous motives and goals that produce outcomes in kind (v. 8, NET). The Commands to fear (serve) Yahweh are "right and endure forever." Because they are true, they are without end (v. 9). The judgments (verdicts) Yahweh renders are "trustworthy and absolutely just." Because they can be relied on, they are rooted in the just character of God (v. 9, NET).

The descriptions of the law contain allusions to the tree of knowledge taken from Genesis 2–3, a composite literary device by which the psalmist demonstrates the similarity to or perhaps the superiority of God's law over the knowledge tree.[21] In Genesis, the tree is "desirable for making one wise" (Gen. 3:6), meaning it appealed as a source of wisdom. Here, the law is likened to honey and gold, the two most precious commodities in their respective categories: honey, the choicest food due to its scarcity and its natural sweetness; gold, the most precious metal due to its scarcity and indestructibility. The adjectival qualifiers that follow the terms gold and honey emphasize that God's law instruction is more desirable than the finest of our most precious possessions. Nothing should be more desirable. The King lavishes his instruction on us! Yahweh is God of gods *because* he is King of kings and his law is incomparable.

The shift to address God directly in verse 11 brings the worshiper into the prayer presence of the king previously proclaimed from afar (vv. 1–6). "Servant," a term cleverly selected, can apply either to a royal subject or a worshiper. The poet's ambiguity leaves the imagination to play with images. The king's servant who hears the heavenly proclamation now embraces the king's law as his rule. The worshiper who brings the sacrifice of his lips, an offering of praise, will be concerned about his acceptability before God (see v. 14). The term "reward" applies to the blessings for obeying the law, an example of which is "the reward for humility" (Prov. 22:4, NET).

God's servant responds in true humility to the king's law (v. 12a). By asking the rhetorical question, "Who can discern his errors?" (NIV), the psalmist begs the resounding and unspoken answer, "Only You, God!"[22] With this critical structure comes a prelude for a series of petitions and their details ("acquit...keep back...let them not rule...let the words" NASB95). This contrite response shows the amazing impact God's gracious instruction has on his servants. The question is critical for the psalmist because it becomes the point of reaction, and, as questions go, it now becomes the reader's own question. The law heightens the psalmist's sensitivity even for unintended sin (see Lev. 4–5), but especially for avoiding presumptuous sin(ners), a term used almost exclusively in the Old Testament of persons (see the Torah psalm Ps. 119:21, 51, 69, 78, 85, 122).

3. God's servant seeks spiritual help from the heavenly king's law.

God's servant seeks spiritual help from the heavenly king's law (vv. 12b–14). The request to "acquit" (NASB95) is an appeal to a judge, a key role of kingship. It is followed by an assurance of acquittal if Yahweh engages his resources, even for "great transgression" (v. 13, NASB95). The word translated as "rule" (NASB95), with obvious correlations for kingship, is also found in Genesis 1:18; 3:16; and 4:7. It may be a subtle reminder that either we enjoy God's loving administration or suffer a viciously tyrannical alternative.[23]

The psalmist's term translated "acceptable" (v. 14, NET; NASB95) is used in sacrificial contexts to describe the validity of a sacrifice (Lev. 1:3; compare Ex. 28:38; Lev. 19:5; 22:19–21, 29; 23:11). In other passages it describes people and their approachability before God (e.g., Deut. 33:23). Are they acceptable to him? That is because worship, a sacred process that begins in the heart, can be rejected like sacrifices.[24] The psalmist asks God to help him offer the acceptable sacrifice of his lips, the meditations of a pure heart. Torah study characterizes the righteous and helps them make their worship acceptable.[25] God's servant now boldly addresses the king by an affectionate nickname: "Oh Yahweh, my Rock and Redeemer." The psalmist uses this title pair in Psalm 78:35 to describe God's sentence of death on a group of his people for sinning presumptuously at the Manna feeding. In Psalm 78:1–5 he emphasizes the response of the faithful to Torah instruction. This is Torah wisdom education at work.

The progressively lengthening lines of verses 12–14 finish the psalm with the signature brushstroke of an artist. Something is accomplished, but what? With our model David, we have moved from heaven's transcendence, standing from afar with worshipful wonder (v. 1) to covenant immanence, enjoying the intimacy of individual worship with God. We who have joined with the psalmist in worship find ourselves at the feet of our king in humble petition for acceptance (v. 14). And our hearts long for his royal instruction (Ps. 32:8).

What Is the Significance of the Psalm for Preaching and Teaching?

1. Follow the Davidic example of worship in Psalm 19. This means that we should praise God as King by heralding his glory (vv. 1–6) and embracing his perfect law like one of his subjects (vv. 7–14). Doing the latter means that we will recognize the advantages of the king's law (vv. 7–11), respond in true humility (v. 12a), and request solutions prescribed by his gracious instruction (vv. 12b–14). The result will be that "praise in the world is united with praise above the world."[26] Our meditation leads to exaltation.

2. Call others to worship with you. The preacher or teacher who invites others, "Let us exalt his name together" (Ps. 34:3, NASB95; NRSV; NIV), will capture the herald spirit of Psalm 19.

3. Teach and preach Bible exposition with doxological passion. In unflinching terms, the psalmist proclaims, "the law of the LORD is perfect" (19:7). He shows us his confidence in God's Word when he alludes to Genesis 1–4 while penning Psalm 19. The psalm models expositional instruction.

4. Disagree with others in a way that commends the Savior. In its message about God's incomparability, our psalm models a ministry form that begs our imitation, one often lacking in this age. In our teaching and preaching, the way that we disagree with others for what they believe and teach must be consistent with our Gospel message. F. F. Bruce once wrote,

> But in every form of Christian witness, including apologetic and polemic, the object must always be to commend the Savior to others. A victory in debate is a barren thing compared with the winning of men and women to the cause of Christ. If at times we are inclined to forget this, the Christians of the first century will refresh our memories.[27]

All creation stands waiting as a ready source of messengers. Another psalm says, "He makes the winds his messengers" (Ps. 104:4). The Savior once told a group of antagonists that even if they could silence him and those with him, the stones would cry out (see Lk. 19:39–40). The impact of Psalm 19 is clearly felt in the Early Church. Origen (182–251 C.E.) beautifully passed down the Psalm 19 imagery including the polemic force when he wrote,

> Nay, even if sun, and moon, and stars were able to prophesy better things than rain, not even then shall we worship them, but the Father of the prophecies which are in them, and the Word of God, their minister. But grant that they are his heralds, and truly messengers of heaven, why, even then ought we not to worship the God whom they only proclaim and announce, rather than those who are the heralds and messengers?[28]

One cosmic herald stands out. Ancient hymn writer, Ephraem the Syrian (306–373 C.E.), drew on Psalm 19 when he wrote of the heralding Bethlehem star: "The whole creation proclaims, the Magi proclaim, the star proclaims: 'Behold, the king's son is here.'"[29]

Book Two: Psalms 42–72

Book II of the Psalter offers encouragement for people faced with difficult circumstances. The special focus of these psalms is the nation of Israel and David their king. The psalms provide assurance of God's faithfulness regardless of the problems encountered with the surrounding nations. While some of the psalms are national and some personal, the psalms basically follow the career of David, particularly Psalms 51–65, with references to specific events in his life. David's confession in Psalm 51 is especially meaningful.

More than half of the psalms in Book II are laments. There are two royal psalms, several declarative praise psalms, two descriptive praise psalms of Zion, and one wisdom psalm. (See "Classification of the Psalms by Category" at the end of the book.) The climax comes in Psalm 72, in which David's rule comes to an end and he prays for his son Solomon in view of the young king's ascension to the throne. He asks that the new king may rule with justice, that the surrounding nations may respect him, and that he may have a long reign. A doxological formula in 72:19 concludes the book: "His glorious name deserves praise forevermore! May his majestic splendor fill the whole earth! We agree! We agree!" (NET).

The two psalms selected for study in this section are Psalm 46, a praise psalm of Zion, and Psalm 63, an individual's psalm of thanksgiving.

CHAPTER 6

Psalm 46

A Psalm of Confidence

Herbert W. Bateman IV

Early Tuesday morning I lay in bed half asleep, barely noticing my two-year-old little girl, Leah, straining to climb into bed with me as we both waited for Mommy to finish her shower. In my somewhat stuporous state, it occurred to me that Leah was no longer in pursuit of her daily endeavor. Silence boomed in the room! Not a good sign. Where did she go? As I meandered out of bed, I noticed Leah lying on the floor next to the bed, motionless. When I rolled her over on her back, she lay there lifeless. No evidence of breathing, white as our bed sheets, and her lips a light shade of blue.

After yelling out to Cindy (my wife) that something was wrong with Leah, I ran to the phone fumbling to dial those three simple numbers 9-1-1. Within ten minutes an ambulance arrived, and yet no change was apparent in Leah's condition. After climbing into the ambulance, I sat next to her weeping at the thought that I might never get to play with her again. In the midst of my grief, I remembered something I had written on a three-by-five card the day she was born. In fact, I had placed it in her *Baby's Book* under "Wishes and Messages for Baby." It was a prayer, a threefold prayer I had written and prayed regularly since that day: "Lord, I pray that Leah might grow into a godly woman who loves and lives for you, that she might meet a godly man who will love her as Christ loves the church, and that I might let go when the time comes."

Suddenly, a terrifying thought flashed across my mind, "Maybe God is asking me to let go now." With absolutely no ability to fix or change the events unfolding before me, with panic overwhelming me, and fear overpowering me, I stopped and said, "Lord, when I asked you for the ability to let go, I was thinking of marriage. But if you want me to let her go now, I want to thank you for the two years we have had with Leah. I hand her and this situation over to you." Within seconds, an awareness of God's protection covered me like a blanket. A warm sensation of peace ran through me like a shot of Wild Turkey.[1] I was able to let Leah go and trust God.

As it turned out, Leah had fallen on her head. In her attempt to cry she experienced a "breath-holding spell." For the next year, whenever Leah fell and banged her head, she had one of these spells. Leah is now a teenager. She has long since outgrown those breath-holding spells. I now experience them, every time she talks about the boys she meets at school. Yet that event in 1993 turned out to be a confidence booster for me. It was one of those totally-trust-in-God situations. Like my story, which resulted in my renewed sense of confidence in God, Psalm 46 echoes a similar story of renewed confidence. Yet the psalmist sang his song long ago, expressed it in poetic prose, and contextualized it according to his Ancient Near Eastern setting.

Why Did the Author Write the Psalm?

As it is with many psalms, Psalm 46 provides no explicit evidence identifying the situation that inspired the psalmist's poetized lyrics. We ponder the question, "Why did the psalmist pen Psalm 46?" The superscription of Psalm 46 identifies it as a psalm "for the music director: a psalm of the sons of Korah." Naturally, a community sang the song. The psalmist makes it clear that the subject is God (vv. 1, 5, 7) and the place is Jerusalem, "the city of God" (v. 4). Thus it seems that Psalm 46 is a descriptive praise psalm of Zion intended to lift up God's name.[2] The historical occasion remains elusive for contemporary readers. The psalmist has presented us with several pointed literary clues that tie Psalm 46 with Isaiah. For instance, the confidence expressed in God as "protector" in Psalm 46:1 parallels Isaiah 25:4, the streams in Psalm 46:4 parallel Isaiah 33:21, and the exalted in Psalm 46:10 parallels Isaiah 33:10. Thus Psalm 46 may have been written sometime during Isaiah's ministry.[3]

The prophet Isaiah began his ministry *circa* 740 B.C.E. when Uzziah was king over Judah (Isa. 1:1; 6:1), and ministered into the latter years of Hezekiah's reign, which ended in 686 B.C.E. (1:1; 39:1–8). For nearly fifty-four years, Isaiah availed himself to the royal house of David, presented God's message to kings Jotham, Ahaz, and Hezekiah, and experienced both the joys and disappointments of ministry. During Isaiah's ministry, people throughout the Ancient Near East lived in fear of the military threat from Assyria, an empire once again maneuvering its military forces to strengthen and expand its control over western territories. Isaiah and the kings of Judah watched as the Northern Kingdom of Israel fell to the Assyrian kings: Tiglath-pileser in 732 B.C.E., Shalmaneser V and Sargon II in 722 B.C.E. Yet God spared Jerusalem from Sennacherib's assault in 701 B.C.E. because King Hezekiah of Judah heeded Isaiah's warnings.[4] Thus it seems reasonable to assume that the rejuvenated Assyrian Empire was the military menace alluded to in this poem.

If Psalm 46 was composed during the time of Isaiah's ministry under the shadow of Assyrian intimidation and exploitation, is it reasonable to place Psalm 46 during the reign of King Hezekiah and his successful stand against King Sennacherib's army in 701 B.C.E.? Perhaps! Obviously, Psalm 46 first summons the people of Jerusalem to express their confidence in God's efficacious protection: "God is our strong refuge" (46:1–7). It then offers an invitation to worship God: "Come! See the works of God" (46:8). Thus Psalm 46 may be considered a descriptive praise psalm of Zion whereby the psalmist proclaims the security the people of Jerusalem feel knowing that God, who dwells in Jerusalem, is the city's great warrior-king who protects them.[5] As we address the interpretive issues for Psalm 46, historical and literary clues will present reasonable evidence to suggest that Psalm 46 is a celebration of God's military protection of Jerusalem against the foreboding Assyrians during the days of king Hezekiah, an event that is well documented in Isaiah 36:1–38:20 and 2 Kings 18:13–19:36.[6]

What Are the Interpretive Issues?

We have two types of interpretive issues to consider: cultural behavior in war and poetic imagery in writing. The first is a set of cultural issues. Whereas we live in a democratic society, whereby people govern themselves, the psalmist did not. Psalm 46 was composed during a period of time when kings (i.e., *suzerain*) and people (i.e., vassals) entered into covenant relationships with one another. Kings promised to protect people provided those same people pledged their allegiance to serve the kings. Thus, whenever a group of people came under attack, they would cry out to their king for help. Their king, in turn, would protect them and provide a place of refuge for his people. Naturally a person's protective shelter was dependent on the king's ability to deliver. For the people of Israel, their king is Yahweh. He is the God of Jacob with whom they as a nation entered into this sort of covenant relationship (Ex. 19:5–8; 24:3–8). Thus when the psalmist speaks of the God of Jacob as Israel's protector (vv. 7, 11), that triggers in the mind of a Jew of Isaiah's day their unique covenantal relationship between God (i.e., *suzerain*) and the nation (i.e., vassals).

Similarly, Davidic kings, God's vicegerents, were to depend on their divine king for protection. Judah was a theocratic state whereby the

Davidic king ruled as God's agent. As the Davidic king went, so went the nation. Whenever terrorized, the king of Judah was to call on Yahweh for protection. Unfortunately, not all kings turned to God when harassed by foreign nations. When the Northern Kingdom of Israel and Damascus frightened King Ahaz of Judah with war, Ahaz failed to look to God for support (2 Kings 16:5–9; Isa. 7:1–12). Yet later when King Sennacherib of Assyria attempted to intimidate King Hezekiah and the city of Jerusalem, Hezekiah, unlike his father, King Ahaz, turned to his divine suzerain for protection. Judah's overwhelming panic over the encroachment of Assyria and God's intervention is a major factor behind this psalm.

The Assyrian nation was a militaristic state. The heart and soul of the empire was keeping military forces, executing military maneuvers, and exerting military control. The Assyrians implemented at least two well-known strategies, one of which will strike twenty-first–century readers as brutally inhumane and barbaric. The first method of warfare was psychological, in which they surrounded the city, sent a messenger to stand and address the entire city, and promised lenient treatment if they surrendered (cp. Isa. 36:1–21). If the city refused, the second method of warfare was employed. It involved a pitched battle or siege, and the consequences of defeat were notably gruesome. Once victory was secured, houses were pillaged and set aflame. Vanquished people of the city became victims of rape, mutilation, murder, and, if you were fortunate, slavery. Those selected for mutilation had their skin flayed. Their mutilated corpses were hung on stakes surrounding the city while the city burned to the ground. Thus, when Sennacherib surrounded the city of Jerusalem, summoned the city to surrender, and strutted his military might before God's people, King Hezekiah and his people had absolutely no ability to change or control the events unfolding before them. Panic overwhelmed them, and fear overpowered them (Isa. 36:22–37:3). Yet the psalmist offers relief for Jerusalem's overpowering fear through the use of poetic imagery and contrasts. Thus, the second set of interpretive issues addresses Psalm 46's poetic language.

Poetic Imagery of Contrast

Psalm 46 begins with a description of turbulence in the world (vv. 2–3), which is then contrasted with the peace of Jerusalem (vv. 4–5). Several figures of speech identify a military threat via natural elements. First is a series of concrete actions in verse 3 (NASB95): "they foam," "they roar," "they quake." These descriptive terms describe natural turbulences of the earth that imply a comparison (the technical term is *hypocatastasis*) with the nations in verse 6. This sort of comparison is not unusual and is clearly observed in Isaiah 17:12 when Isaiah writes: "The many *nations* massing together are as good as dead, those who *make a commotion as loud as the roaring of the sea's waves.* The *people* making such an uproar are as good as dead, those who *make an uproar as loud as the roaring of powerful waves*" (emphasis mine).[7] Thus the psalmist uses concrete terms to describe the instability in his world where powerful foreign nations rule. Naturally the militaristic Assyrians were a menace to more than one nation.

Despite the instability of the psalmist's world, Jerusalem, the city where God dwells, is quite stable. Verse 4 presents Jerusalem with a river whose channels bring joy to the city of God. Naturally, "the city of God" is Jerusalem (Pss. 48:1–2; 87:2–3). The holy city is personified with the human emotion of joy. Furthermore, the psalmist may be exchanging one idea of a river with streams flowing through Jerusalem with another associated idea of a river whose streams flowed out of the garden of Eden (Gen. 2:10). If so, this word-picture (the technical term is *synecdoche*), borrowed from the garden paradise impresses on the reader that as God was in the garden of Eden, so he is in Zion.[8] Similar references to streams and rivers occur in Isaiah 33:21, in which they tie the prophet's confidence to the Lord.[9] However we identify this river, it certainly offers a picture of serenity. The condition of the nations of the world is associated with turbulent waters, due to the menacing military threat of the Assyrians, but Jerusalem is depicted as a city of peace. The psalmist's picture presented about God's city is serene, where streams of a river freely flow. Peace reigns where God, the Most High God, dwells.[10]

Poetic Images of Rescue

Psalm 46:6–8 is a clear description of divine rescue. Naturally, God's deliverance of his people involves a holy war tradition in which Yahweh fights for Israel as a warrior or literally a "man of war" (Exod. 15:3, ESV).[11] Thus God is presented as Jerusalem's warrior-king. Verse 5 makes this clearly evident. The psalmist employs a particularly pointed phrase overflowing with significance. He muses, "God rescues it [i.e., Jerusalem] *at the break of dawn,*" or, more literally, "at the turning of morning." This phrase is also found in Exodus 14:27: "So Moses extended his hand toward the sea, and the sea returned to its normal state when the sun began to rise" (NET; literally, "*at the break of dawn,*" author's translation). Standing at God's disposal, the sea dramatically overcame Pharaoh's army, and they were no more. "So the LORD saved Israel on that day from the power of the Egyptians, and Israel saw *the Egyptians dead on the shore* of the sea" (14:30, emphasis added).

In a similar way, "The LORD's messenger went out and killed 185,000 troops in the Assyrian camp. When they [the Assyrian army] got up *early the next morning, there were all the corpses!* So King Sennacherib of Assyria broke camp and went on his way. He went home and stayed in

Nineveh" (Isa. 37:36–37, emphasis added). The incidents associated with Pharaoh's army and Sennacherib's army are both revealed as miraculous events that celebrate God as Israel's warrior-king. The Jewish people are mere spectators (cf. Ps. 46:9), and the evidence is unmistakable. The international scene is perilous: nations in turmoil and losing all power. Suddenly the spectators hear the powerful divine voice. At God's voice, the nations/earth melts or dissolves like wax (Ps. 46:6; cf. Ps. 97:5; Mic. 1:4). The nations of the world are no match for Jerusalem's warrior-king (cf. Ps. 2:1–6). Thus, the psalmist reminds worshipers, "The LORD who commands armies is on our side!" (Ps. 46:7a, 11a).

Poetic Images to Support Worship

Psalm 46:9–10 is a clear invitation to worship. The psalmist exhorts, "Come – See." Similar terminology occurs in Psalm 66:5 when he writes, "Come see the works of God, who is awesome in his deeds toward the sons of men." Then he lists those works as being: "He turned the sea to dry land," "he rules by his might," "his eyes keep watch on the nations." If our psalmist has witnessed one hundred eighty five thousand dead men sprawled around the city of Jerusalem, I can only imagine the excitement. Certainly it would be more than Gomer Pile's "Gol–ly!" God, Jerusalem's warrior-king, has caused the war with Assyria to cease.

Simple statements in Psalm 46 about the destruction of instruments customarily used for war stand as figures symbolizing victory (the technical term is synecdoche): "He shatters the bow and breaks the spear; he burns the shields with fire" (v. 9). This list, in which all the weapons are emphasized, illuminates the extent of victory (the technical term is *merism*). Thus the author's poetic referencing of God's victorious intervention as Jerusalem's warrior-king provides reason to support Jerusalem's worship of God. Now these cultural and poetic figures can serve to point us to the central truth of the psalm.

What Is the Central Truth the Author Was Seeking to Communicate?

Psalm 46 communicates both a theological and a practical message. Thus the central truth communicated in Psalm 46 is twofold. Theologically, the psalm boasts in the fact that confidence is found in God. Practically speaking, the psalm first invites all people to worship the one who protects and supports those who depend on him. It then draws attention to God's expectation that the people trust him. Thus the psalm is about trusting and praising God.

On the one hand, the author expressed confidence in God with a timeless theological fact, a fact that transcends all cultures, a fact that is applicable to all people groups, a fact that is true for all of us today:

God protects and supports his people (vv. 1–7). This timeless truth is enhanced through two latchkey phrases that unlock the central theological emphasis of the psalm. The first occurs in verse 1: "God is our refuge and strength" (NASB95, NIV). The ancient hearers would intuitively discern the composer's comparison between "refuge" (*hsh*) and "strength" (*'zrh*). Of the twelve times the term translated as "refuge" occurs in the Psalms, Yahweh is always the subject. Naturally, God is not a literal shelter that one seeks during a rainstorm (cf. Isa. 4:6), but rather in the Psalms' use of the term for "refuge" is figurative language for protection (the technical term is *metaphor*). People (i.e., vassals) find protection in God (i.e., suzerain). Scripture typically describes God figuratively with terms such as "rock" (Deut. 32:37), a "shield" (Ps. 144:2), a "refuge" (Ps. 62:6), and as a mothering bird with outstretched wings (Ps. 57:1), all of which convey the same notion: we can rely on God. We can place our trust, our confidence, our reliance in him. When "refuge" is joined with the term "strength," they emphasize a single idea (the technical term is *hendiadys*) that may be rendered, "God is our strong refuge," or, "God is our source of strength" (NET; cf. Ps. 71:7). Thus the statement is both personal and powerful.

The second latchkey phrase occurs in verse 7 and again in verse 11: "the God of Jacob is our refuge" (KJV, NASV), or "the God of Jacob is our stronghold" (NASB), "the God of Jacob is our fortress" (NIV), and "The God of Jacob is our protector!" (NET). Naturally, protection is the overriding perception. Yet the Hebrew term in verses 7 and 11 (*'sgb*) is different from the one used in verse one (*hsh*). The term in verses 7 and 11 literally means "our elevated place." All twelve usages in the Psalms envision God as the ultimate source of protection (cf. Ps. 9:9; 18:2; 59:16–17; 62:2, 6). Nevertheless, the variety of terminology throughout this brief psalm reinforces the deeply felt perception of God who protects his people. Again the statements are both personal and powerful.

For those of Hezekiah's day, confidence in God manifested itself when God served as Jerusalem's protector and military support in times of military threat, invasion, and siege (v. 1). This confidence eventually resulted in the lack of emotional fear and the people of Jerusalem living in peace (vv. 3–5). Jerusalem is God's city, which God rescued from Assyria (v. 6). God is more powerful than any of Jerusalem's neighbors (v. 7) and willingly provides for all of Jerusalem's military protection (v. 8).

On the other hand, the psalmist extends an invitation. It, too, is timeless, an invitation to worship God, Jerusalem's warrior-king (vv. 8–11). The psalmist says, "Come! Witness the exploits of the LORD…" (v. 8). The invitation to "come" is not without a basis. The psalmist's invitation to worship God is based on what God has done. In the case of Hezekiah, the call was to witness the 185,000 dead Assyrian soldiers sprawled around the city of Jerusalem. Despite the fact that Josephus attributes this massive death to God having visited a pestilential sickness on the army (*Ant* 10.1.4–5 § 20–22), Isaiah attributes the massive killing to the Lord sending his angel out, killing members of Sennacherib's army (37:36). In either case, God had intervened by killing a significant portion of Sennacherib's army and subsequently forcing Sennacherib to retreat back to Nineveh (Isa. 37:37).[12]

The psalmist directs the reader's attention to God's expectation. God commands silence so that he might be recognized, that he might be exalted (v. 10). The term translated "be still" (*hr*) is not a summons to quiet meditation or a spiritual pause. Rather, it is an expectation to cease from independent actions for self-help and preservation (cp. Ps. 37:8). It is an authoritative command to contentious people to "shut up," or "stop it." Furthermore, the expectation to "recognize that I am God" calls people to recognize God's position as suzerain and submit to his Lordship.[13]

Thus, Psalm 46 is a psalm that teaches a timeless fact about the confidence we can have in God. When we are forced to face the challenges of life and we look to God for both safety and support in the midst of those challenges, a confidence in God will occur. The outcome will be one of worship.

What Is the Significance of the Psalm for Preaching and Teaching?

Well-written poetic lyrics celebrating military victory against threatening military forces are intentionally emotive, especially if we feel the fear of the assault and the relief of triumph the author felt at the time. Reading the lyrics for the "Star-Spangled Banner" exemplifies what I mean:

> Oh, say, can you see, by the dawn's early light,
> What so proudly we hail'd at the twilight's last gleaming?
> Whose broad stripes and bright stars, thro' the perilous fight,
> O'er the ramparts we watch'd, were so gallantly streaming?
> And the rockets' red glare, the bombs bursting in air,
> Gave proof thro' the night that our flag was still there.
> O say, does that star-spangled banner yet wave
> O'er the land of the free and the home of the brave?

These lyrics, composed by Francis Scott Key in September 1814, are but a small portion of a larger poem entitled "In Defense of Fort McHenry." Though they remain stirring words, the words in-and-of-themselves merely echo the author's story.

The story behind the lyrics recalls a specific day in the life of the author. British forces had just raided and burned most of Washington, D.C. (August 24, 1814). Frances Scott Key was visiting a British fleet in the Baltimore Harbor in Maryland on September 13th to secure the release of Dr. William Beanes, a man who had been captured during the Washington invasion. However, both men were detained on a British ship so as not to warn the Americans about the Royal Navy bombardment of Fort McHenry. Key and Beanes watched in fear as the British fleet opened fire on Fort McHenry. The assault, which began at dusk, lasted twenty-five hours. Throughout the entire night, Britain's Royal Navy repeatedly hammered Fort McHenry with cannonball.

At early dawn on September 14, Key witnessed a huge American flag waving above the fort. The flag was fluttering high before the barrage of cannonball began, and it had not been removed in defeat. All emotional fear about Fort McHenry's ability to endure Britain's steady shelling was relieved when Key saw our American flag soaring high above Fort McHenry. That sight, that moment of pride, inspired him to write "In Defense of Fort McHenry," of which a portion of the words were later recontextualized into music format. In 1917, it was sung during the World Series baseball game between the New York Giants and Chicago White Sox as a way to honor those fighting in the Great War. In 1931, Congress proclaimed this inspiring song the national anthem of the United States of America. Knowing the historical events behind the poem and the various ways in which it has been reapplied provides a heightened sense of appreciation.

In a similar way, Psalm 46 captures an historical event in the life of the psalmist. It is important to capture the emotive force of being overwhelmed with panic and overcome with fear and being totally dependent on God. In an attempt to capitalize on the suzerain king–vassal concept, a sermon might emphasize that God's protection is both personal and powerful (v. 1), God's promised rescue is secure (vv. 2–7), and God's expectations are clear (vv. 8–11).

Naturally, God, creator-king of the universe, our suzerain, is capable of delivering his promise of protection. The fact that God is our refuge and strength is a timeless one. At one point in Old Testament times, Assyria was the external enemy, an enemy that threatened Hezekiah and the people of Jerusalem. During the reformation period, Martin Luther recognized the threat to be a select few people within the Roman Catholic Church, whom he frequently associated with Satan's instruments. Based on Psalm 46, he composed the words to "A Mighty Fortress Is Our God."[14] Even today, God provides protection and support in everyday struggles of life. My wife and I experienced this protection firsthand when our daughter Leah suffered from breath-holding spells. God's protection covered us like a blanket, and a sense of divine peace ran through us.

Those familiar with eyewitness testimony about Jesus' life and work know of his battle against the enemies of Yahweh, namely Satan and his demonic hordes (Mt. 4:1–11, Mk. 1:21–28; 5:1–20) who afflicted God's chosen people (Mk. 9:14–27; cf. *Sib Or* 3.63–74). This imagery is also reminiscent of first-century Jewish expectations of the Messiah's victory over demonic forces.[15] Jesus, the Messiah, successfully battled Satan, "the lord of death," and thereby reinforced the presence of God's kingdom (Mt. 12:22–27). Although death or the lord of death has not been annihilated (that is yet to be accomplished: Rev. 12:7–12; 20:10, 14), Satan's tyranny and the subsequent fear of death are "condemned to inactivity or ineffectiveness."[16] Thus, the Son has rendered Satan powerless (Rev. 20:14) and thereby "liberated" (Heb. 2:15) those who have had a lifelong fear of death (cf. 1 Cor. 15:53–55). Thus God's rescue has been secured. He is our victorious warrior-king. His protection is both personal and powerful and our response ought to be one of worship.

CHAPTER 7

Psalm 63

Finding Satisfaction in God

Eugene H. Merrill

To find satisfaction in life is a persistent and unending quest of the human soul. Whether health, marriage, family, education, employment, or material prosperity, people long for fulfillment and success. Inwardly we yearn for tranquility, for an absence of stress and turmoil, for freedom from the pressures of human existence that rob the spirit of joy and contentment.

The Bible makes clear that these noble aspirations are possible in the final and fullest sense only when people know God personally through his redemptive grace. Only when they enter into unbroken fellowship with him can they find genuine satisfaction, a state of being grounded in that relationship and issuing from it to every aspect of human existence. As Augustine said, "Thou hast created us unto Thyself, and our heart finds no rest until it rests in Thee."[1] Psalm 63 speaks to that sentiment in terms and tones as resonant to us today as to the composer of the sacred text 3,000 years ago. The psalm provides a beautiful path to tranquility and rest.

Why Did the Author Compose the Psalm?

The superscription of Psalm 63 identifies it as a work of David "when he was in the desert of Judah" (NIV). Whether psalm superscriptions in general are deemed to be part of the inspired text or not, no grounds exist either internally or externally to doubt the authorial and historical credibility of this one.[2]

Addressing first the geographic setting of the composition, we note that the Hebrew word for "desert" (*midbar*) is only one (though by far the most common) of a number of terms occurring in the Old Testament to describe such locales. The full name "desert of Judah" occurs in only one other place, referring to a region of the upper Negev "south of Arad" (Judg. 1:16 NASB95). In any event, the desert here is associated with territory to the south and/or east of Jerusalem, the place from which David had become alienated (v. 2).

As for the specific historical circumstances that resulted in the lamentable situation in which David found himself, it is possible to rule out all the occasions when he was in flight from Saul, as likely as those might seem at first blush. The clearest clue that those do not qualify is David's reference to himself as king (v. 11), an office he did not hold officially until after Saul's demise and his own succession to the throne, first over Judah alone at Hebron (2 Sam. 2:4) and then over all the nation at Jerusalem (2 Sam. 5:3, 7). His exile thus took place sometime during his own kingship.

Careful reading of the entire Davidic narrative yields only one such involuntary retreat by David from Jerusalem. That came on the heels of Absalom's rebellion against his father in the aftermath of their falling out over Amnon's rape of Tamar (2 Sam. 15:1–37; cf. 13:1–39). Having crossed over the Kidron Valley, David headed for "the way of the desert" (2 Sam. 15:23). Once there, he camped near the Jordan at the desert crossing (v. 28) but was told by his advisers not to stay there because of Absalom's approaching troops (2 Sam. 17:16). David therefore passed over the Jordan to Mahanaim, another desert area. There he and his followers were said to be "hungry, tired, and thirsty in the desert" (*midbar*) (2 Sam. 17:29 NET). Two of these descriptive words occur in Psalm 63 where David says he "thirsts" (*same'a*) in a "dry and weary (*siyya weayep*) land" (v. 1 NRSV), thus adding to the likelihood that his exile to the Transjordan through the *midbar* of Judah provides the background to the psalm.

The importance of establishing the life situation of a psalm (or any other biblical text) lies in the insight it provides into the particular circumstances that generated the composition in the first place.[3] It is helpful to know, if possible, who wrote the piece and when and where so that the reader can both interpret it with greater precision and draw more apt conclusions and applications from it. Should the reader find himself or herself in a similar life situation, the relevance and thus helpfulness of the psalm is more readily apparent. On the other hand, such background information is not critical to the usefulness of a given text because the human condition is so trans-historical and universally shared that the tragedies and triumphs of any individual at any time and place can resonate with anyone else, other differences notwithstanding.

How Did the Author Express His Ideas?

The psalmist uses picturesque language to express his ideas. The most prominent in the psalm is the use of physical imagery to speak of spiritual realities and of anthropomorphism to describe God's person and actions. The psalmist describes himself as *nepeš*, commonly rendered "soul," and says that that immaterial part of him thirsts after God as, in fact, does his very body (v. 1). His desire for God, particularly absent as he is from God's dwelling-place, the temple, can only be compared to physical thirst. He is not only in a literal desert "where there is no water" but in a desert of spiritual drought that threatens to overwhelm him. God's response will result in a lavish banquet of fat (*ḥeleb*) and fatness (*desen*), a hendiadys of similar terms emphasizing the bountiful nourishment of soul that David can expect once his restoration has been completed (v. 5).[4]

In common with Old Testament imagery elsewhere, the psalmist speaks of God anthropomorphically—that is, in human terms. Such a resort is necessary in light of God's absolute transcendence that admits of no physical or material reality. David therefore speaks of seeing God in the sanctuary (v. 2) and of rejoicing in the shadow of his wings (v. 7; cf. Ex. 19:4; Ruth 2:12; Pss. 17:8; 36:7; 57:1; 61:4; 91:4). Referring to God's omnipotence, he employs the familiar metaphor of God's "right hand," which holds him up when he would otherwise be faint and unable to stand (v. 8; cf. Ex. 15:6, 12; Pss. 17:7; 18:35; 20:6; 73:23; Isa. 48:13; Hab. 2:16). God's protection and power—both described metaphorically—were as real to David as were literal wings and hands.

What Are the Important Interpretive Issues?

In addition to the insights to be gained by understanding the setting of a psalm, other considerations also must come to bear on its interpretation. First among these is the determination of its literary classification or genre. Psalms of different types are susceptible to different ways of analysis and thus to different interpretations. Psalm 63 begins as an individual lament or complaint, but quickly transmutes into a song of confidence and thanksgiving.[5] David finds himself in the difficult straits of desert exile (v. 1), but he is able at the same time to view God as he who inhabits the sanctuary (v. 2) and who even from that distance is able to provide him complete satisfaction (vv. 3–8). As for his enemies, David is confident that God will defeat them (vv. 9–10) and that he, the king, will eventually be exonerated and restored (v. 11).

Of special interest and theological significance is that precisely when David was most distressed, he looked beyond himself to God. In fact, the Hebrew particle translated "so" in verse 2 (*ken*) suggests in strong terms that the natural thing for David to do after recounting his complaint was to look to God. As Gerstenberger puts it, the particle "expresses trust based in real spiritual experience."[6] David was in such a desperate situation that looking to God was part and parcel of the situation. Built into the complaint was an awareness that David's plight would not continue forever. It contained the seeds of its own resolution that would turn everything around and, indeed, make everything better than it had ever been before.

Books II and III of the Psalter (Pss. 42–72; 73–106 respectively) are "Elohistic." That is, except for the Korah psalms (42; 44–49; 84–85; 87–88) they prefer to refer to God as Elohim rather than Yahweh. This is not invariable because Yahweh occurs a few times in the Elohistic psalms (44 times compared to 200 for Elohim), whereas Elohim, though rare in Book I (15 times compared to 278 uses of Yahweh) and even more uncommon in Books IV and V (9 times as opposed to 339 times for Yahweh), is attested in so-called "Yahwistic" psalms. Psalm 63 obviously falls within the category of "Elohistic" psalms; indeed, only the name Elohim occurs there.

While it is possible to account for this phenomenon in the Psalter generally (and Psalm 63 in particular) from many angles, the most reasonable and satisfying suggestion is that the various divine names here–and throughout the Old Testament for that matter–are employed for theological reasons. At the risk of being overly simplistic, it is correct to say that the epithet Elohim generally connotes the idea of God's transcendent glory, power, and remoteness. Yahweh, on the other hand, describes God's condescending immanence, his willingness to bridge the gap between his awesome "otherness" and lowly, sinful humankind, especially in covenant contexts.[7]

Lament psalms are particularly inclined to the use of Yahweh (of forty-two such psalms, twenty-eight are in the "Yahwistic" books), no doubt because they were uttered by God's covenant people and appealed to that relationship as the basis for his favor toward them. Its absence in Psalm 63 clearly cannot reflect the fact that David saw himself as standing outside that relationship, for, by itself, his self-identification as king of the chosen nation precludes that possibility.[8] More likely, David appeals to God as Elohim because his situation dictates not so much a testimony of assurance of God's covenant faithfulness as it does the hopelessness of his condition. He has been alienated from family and friend and driven off to a foreign land, far from his seat of power, and, more tragically, from the sanctuary where God dwelt among his people in a unique and powerful way. What he needs is not only the assurance of God's presence with him but of God's power to restore him to his place and position of royal responsibility.

David's appeal to God as "my God" (v. 1) hints at a personal relationship otherwise connoted by the covenant name Yahweh.[9] His desperate situation demands that God be near him and not just as a theological principle. He is not just God to David in an abstract sense, but one whom David can claim as his own and to whom he can turn in times like these. The powerful verbs the psalmist employs in fleshing out the urgency of his appeal more than compensate for any lack of reference to God as Yahweh. He seeks him, thirsts for him, and longs for him (v. 1), all of which presupposes an intensely personal relationship. Sadly, the relationship has become interrupted, at least geographically, because of the dire circumstances in which the author finds himself.

The saint of God need not depend on proximity to sacred places, however, to find solace and strength in time of need. Thus, David can say that he (like Isaiah later on) has already gazed on God's strength and glory in the holy place (v. 2). That is, his relationship to God is unimpeded by distance from the sanctuary at Jerusalem. The basis for his confidence in this assertion is God's covenant loyalty (*hesed*) to him, a fact more precious to him than life itself and for which David offers praise even in his perilous state (v. 3).

This confidence in God's faithfulness enables David to turn from lament to praise. The verbs of longing employed in verses 1–2 give way to verbs of profound satisfaction in verses 3–8. He will praise God, he will bless him as long as he lives, he will lift up his hands to him, he will be satisfied in him, and he will offer praises to him (vv. 3–5b, NASB95). Though the verbs may suggest a pledge of future response to God's deliverance, neither the grammar of the passage nor its overall tenor demands such an idea. Whatever lament David may have expressed concerning his present situation (v. 1), it is more than matched by the comfort he finds even in the midst of it.[10] His confidence in the presence of God more than compensates for his absence from the sacred temple precincts, as painful as that may be. Thus David is able to praise and glorify his God as though his exile were already over and his position as king had already been restored.

The psalmist's confidence in God rests not only in a propositional theological tenet, as important as that was (and is), but in an intensely internal and experiential relationship with him. He remembers God (v. 6a) and meditates on him in the night hours. The intellectual or cognitive apprehension of divine relationship and the power it avails is buttressed by a sense of communion, of a dynamic intercourse between the man in need and the living God who is there to succor him and see him through. By means of a chiastic structure the poet articulates this sense of nearness and help:

A) The LORD is his helper (7a)
  B) He rejoices in His protection (7b)
  B) He seeks after Him (8a)
A) The LORD upholds him (8b)

Such reliance on God is not a psychological whistling-in-the-dark prop for a person at his wits' end, but a settled conviction rooted in God's revelation of himself as the sovereign One able to save. It is the testimony of a man who through a lifetime of walking with God has found him to be trustworthy through thick and thin.

The reverse side of God's deliverance of his saints is his judgment on those who put them in jeopardy. As painful as it must have been for David to do so under these special circumstances, he uttered an imprecation against his enemies, in this case his own son Absalom, if our understanding of the psalm's setting is correct. In a devastating display of poetic justice, God will do to David's foes what they had intended to do to him—consign them to the depths of Sheol (v. 9) and deliver them over to the sword and to the beasts of prey (v. 10). In sum, David and those who allied themselves with him will achieve a glorious victory, whereas those who brought him to such a low point will suffer humiliating defeat (v. 11).

The book of Psalms appears among the Writings (the Kethubim) in the Hebrew canon, the last section of the Old Testament. In this section it comes first, suggesting perhaps its didactic and theological significance to Israel's religious and cultic life. The book elaborates on the great covenant themes of Torah and the Prophets, interpreting and celebrating them from the vantage point of the personal experience and reflection of its various human authors, most notably David. Psalm 63, by virtue of its inclusion in the Psalter, not only provides an account of a personal struggle by a man of God—the king no less—but makes its own contribution to the theology of ancient Israel, in this case certainly in the context of the temple and cultus.

More specifically, Psalm 63 is part of the Davidic corpus embracing Psalms 51 to 71, and within that collection it appears to be linked closely to Psalms 61, 62, and 64. Tate observes that with them it forms an ABBA arrangement, with 61 and 64 consisting of individual laments and 62 and 63 individual psalms of thanksgiving.[11] Sensitivity to such patterns can often afford exegetical and theological insight otherwise difficult to discern.

What Is the Central Truth the Author Was Seeking to Communicate?

Of many purposes intended by Psalm 63 and lessons to be learned from it, the overriding, dominant idea is that the child of God can have confidence in God's covenant faithfulness no matter the circumstances in which he or she may be caught. Moreover, this confidence can be so well-founded that one can praise God in the midst of the crisis as surely as if the crisis were over and full deliverance had already come to pass. With respect to the issues of authorship and perspective, though David most likely penned the words of Psalm 63 years after the events he describes, there is no reason to think that his reactions–both negative and positive–were inspired only from the favorable position of hindsight and therefore were not reflective of his actual thoughts and feelings at the time they took place. His was not a faith formulated only after he witnessed God's mighty acts on his behalf; rather, it was faith already existent if still maturing, one based on still earlier experiences in and out of which God had delivered him.

Confidence based on wishful thinking is doomed to disappointment, but, when it is rooted in God's revelatory self-disclosure coupled with one's own experience with God, it has an authenticity that commends itself to others weak in faith. Psalm 63 is designed, therefore, not just to testify to the power of trust exhibited by one man, but to declare that the God who honored that trust is well able to act on behalf of all who call on him. As the psalm found its way into the liturgy of ancient Israel's worshiping community, the "I" of the poem became a "we," collective testimony recognizing the covenant faithfulness of Israel's God and instilling in the collective people of God a historical and eschatological hope that God can be trusted and in the end will prevail.[12]

A corollary to this central theme is the importance of thanksgiving to God for his unfailing loyalty to his saints, a loyalty expressed in daily experiences no matter how painful and perilous and in his promises about the future. From the point of view of the psalm itself, David was in the midst of trouble with no visible means of escape. He sought God and thirsted and longed for him but apparently in vain, at least at the moment. Reflection on God's power and glory and remembrance of his gracious interventions in the past enabled David not only to rest in him in quiet confidence but to anticipate a day when his present evil circumstances would give way to glorious triumph. He would at last achieve vindication as God's chosen one, and those who had conspired to bring him low would themselves sink into abysmal ruin.

What Is the Significance of the Psalm for Preaching and Teaching?

The differences of 3,000 years and thousands of miles between the ancient text and today's world are monumental, in some respects insuperable. How can a composition such as Psalm 63–written about an utterly foreign world, addressing a situation only the bare elements of which can be determined, and written in a language still fraught with difficulties of translation–have practical relevance to the believer of this generation? This is especially true when we are confronted with all manner of problems and perils, many of which could not have been imagined in the day of the sacred penman? Can we enter into the experiences of the psalmists?

In some respects, the task seems hopeless, for the chasm between then and now is so impassable that only a measure of understanding can be achieved. On the other hand, ancients and moderns share a common humanity and, presumably, a commonality of rationality, emotion, values, and even experience. These commonalities offer some hope that the past can be at least partially recovered, correctly interpreted, and put to use in the modern world.[13] Proper historical and archaeological research in association with rigorous attention to language and linguistics has already opened vistas of understanding unknown to earlier generations and bodes well for the future.

More important and in another dimension altogether: the word of God was designed not only to communicate revelation to its human authors and their respective communities but also to speak to every generation of believers, including our own. It therefore follows that its message transcends the encumbrances to be expected in ordinary discourse because of time and space limitations. What God said to and through David must and can be understood by moderns, if not perfectly, then at least sufficiently enough to be relevant and instructive to all who care to make the effort. In a very real sense, David's experience can be our own. The way he responded to its challenges can model how we must encounter the problems of alienation and despair. With steadfast hope in the God of the ages, we can stand triumphantly in the face of adversity.

This said, we must underscore once more the significant differences between David's times and circumstances and our own lest too facile a use of the psalm (or any biblical text) be made. He was king of a theocratic state ruling at God's behest and as such epitomized the whole nation. His exile and tribulation was not his alone to suffer but symbolized the plight of the covenant community as well. His success or failure with respect to the outcome of his ordeal would have ramifications far beyond the small compass of his private and even family life. As David the king went, so would go the nation.

Moreover, the locus of God's presence in that era was decidedly geographic–specifically, in the Jerusalem temple. Deuteronomy 12:5 declares of the nation yet to come, "You must seek only the place he chooses from all your tribes to establish his name as his place of residence, and you must go there." The Lord's revelation to David at the threshing floor of Araunah certified that this central sanctuary would be at Jerusalem (1 Chr. 21:18–22:1). When the time came for Solomon to build a temple, its location at Jerusalem was a foregone conclusion (1 Chr. 28:1–10). David's exile in the Transjordan was therefore an exile from the presence of God, not in an ontological sense, of course, but certainly in terms of his access to the temple and cultus that marked God's dwelling among his people. As late as New Testament times, the localizing of God in the sacred precincts was commonly understood and accepted. Jesus' instruction to the Samaritan woman that "a time is coming when you will worship the Father neither on this mountain nor in Jerusalem" because "the true worshipers will worship the Father in spirit and truth" (Jn. 4:21, 23) anticipated an end to the temple and a cessation of the notion of a central sanctuary where the Lord was particularly to be found.

Finally, the imprecation (vv. 9–10)–as mild as it is–must remain a feature of the times and ethos of the Old Testament economy in which the wrath and judgment of God was linked to the present world as an aspect of the antagonism between the theocratic state of Israel and the hostile powers that threatened it with destruction. When David invokes punishment of his personal enemies and with satisfaction anticipates their demise, he does so not out of personal animosity but as a representative of the kingdom of God. It is that Kingdom and its Sovereign that are under attack and that must be defended and vindicated. The New Testament view (and that of the Church) is that the just deserts of the foes of the Kingdom are not annulled, but they are postponed to a day when God will judge evil, wrong will be made right, and the kingdom of Heaven will be all in all (Rom. 2:1–11; Heb. 9:27–28; 2 Pet. 3:5–7; Rev. 20:11–14).[14]

How then can Psalm 63 speak to our time and condition? What teachings can we legitimately derive from it without ignoring the contextual issues and other constraints just elaborated? The answer, we submit, lies in the abstraction of principles that are a-contextual, timeless, and unchanging. The God with whom we have to do today is the God of David and the fathers of the faith. We share with them a common humanity with all the pleasures and perils to which all flesh is heir. The hurts and longings of the alienated king are not foreign at their core to those experienced by all of God's people of all the ages. Their remedy is precisely the same as that for which David pleaded–a restoration of fellowship with the sovereign God whose fidelity to his covenant promises is so unimpeachable that one can praise him for deliverance before it has actually occurred. When all the incidentals of a contextually bound composition such as Psalm 63 are stripped away, there remains a bedrock body of truth that knows no limits and that is sufficient for whatever trials and tribulations the pilgrim en route to glory may encounter. In this case, the central truth of Psalm 63 is that the believer, no matter his or her circumstances, can not only endure but rejoice in the midst of life's reversals, knowing that the God of eternity works out all things well in history and in the human condition.

What Is the Significance for Preaching and Teaching?

Psalm 63, like all biblical texts, is more than a simple sample of ancient Israelite literature that at worst merely exemplifies poetic style of a bygone era and at best provides insight into the struggles of a troubled man of another place and time. As a constituent element of the written word of God, it has importance, meaning, and relevance for all generations of men and women who confess David's God as their own, including our own generation. But how can that message be understood? What, indeed, is its relevance for today? We suggest the following four steps as a means of access to the intended truth of the psalm.

Uncover Its Setting and Background

As we have already suggested, the psalm appears to reflect a time in David's life when he was king (v. 11), but he found himself in a desert place far from the sanctuary and all it represented. Apart from the possibility that a narrative detailing the circumstances of his plight is lacking in the canonical record, the extant historical texts available must be examined to see if any of them provides a likely environment against which the poet's message best fits. As we have suggested above, the most obvious choice is the rebellion of Absalom, which forced his father David into exile (2 Sam. 14:1–18:33), particularly the pericope recounting David's sojourn in the Judean and Transjordanian deserts (2 Sam. 17:15–29).

Analyze Its Structure and Content

Though the author of the psalm is beset by all manner of difficulty, his focus is not so much on the present but on God's past goodness to him (v. 2) and especially on his anticipated deliverance and vindication, as the imperfect verbal constructions suggest. He is in present peril (v. 1), but can recall God's past favor (v. 2), and is fully confident for the future (vv. 3–11). Major turning points otherwise are marked by the adverbial conjunction *ken*, which provides the rationale for David's confidence in his present predicament (v. 3) and hope for relief in the future (v. 5).

Develop an Outline

People vary in their approach to the construction of Psalm 63, the only point of near concensus being the isolation of verses 9–11 as an independent unit. Otherwise, Delitzsch suggests a three-fold division: verses 1–3, 4–8, 9–11;[15] Gerstenberger[16] and Kraus,[17] four parts: verses 1, 2–4, 5–8, 9–11; 1–2, 3–5, 6–8, 9–11, respectively; Tate finds three parts: verses 1–4, 5–8, 9–11;[18] and VanGemeren only two: verses 1–5, 6–11.[19] Our own suggestion (with apologies for "preachers' alliteration") is as follows:

1. The Psalmist's Thirst (vv. 1–2)
   a. His condition (v. 1)
   b. His confidence (v. 2)
2. The Psalmist's Trust (vv. 3–8)
   a. Because of God's *ḥesed* (vv. 3–4)
   b. Because of God's help (vv. 5–8)
3. The Psalmist's Triumph (vv. 9–11)
   a. The elimination of his enemies (vv. 9–10)
   b. The exaltation of his God (v. 11)

Make Application

We have already suggested appropriate applications of Psalm 63 to modern life. We conclude by underscoring the point that ancient texts like this, whose setting and situation are far removed from our own, must not be subjected to the kind of application that reads into and out of it one-to-one correspondences between the "then" of the text and the "now" of the present. We are not David, and his unique set of problems is not ours. But God is God, and he who addressed the needs of the king of Israel long ago can meet ours as well. Psalm 63 helps show us how.

Conclusion

This world is no friend of grace, and the saints of God who inhabit it are never free from the troubles and pain it visits on the righteous and wicked alike. However, Psalm 63, a testimony of King David to his times, teaches that the Sovereign God who permits such tribulation within the framework of his mysterious design is more than sufficient to provide solace, strength, and ultimate victory to those who call on him.

Book III: Psalms 73–89

Book III of the Psalter reflects on what could have been if only the people had obeyed the Lord. The disobedience of God's chosen nation led to a divided kingdom and almost endless examples of unfaithfulness to the covenant. Arrogance, idolatry, injustice, and empty worship characterized kings and subjects. Book III ends with the capitals of the Northern and Southern Kingdoms in ruin and the people in exile. These psalms reflect bleak events and provide lessons in how *not* to live in God's favor. The point is to call people back to God and to recognize that true blessedness comes in a faithful covenant relationship.

As with Books I and II, lament psalms dominate Book III, with nearly 60 percent representation. Nevertheless, this collection includes one royal psalm, two communal declarative praise psalms, two descriptive praise psalms of Zion, and two wisdom psalms. (See "Classification of the Psalms by Category" at the end of the book.) The concluding doxological formula for Book III reads like the previous two in that the book closes with "The LORD deserves praise forevermore! We agree! We agree! (Ps. 89:52).

As was the case in Book I, we will once again study both a wisdom and a royal psalm. Once again, both psalms play pivotal roles in the structure of the Psalter. The first psalm studied is Psalm 73. This wisdom psalm appears at the beginning of Book III and serves as a microcosm of the Psalter's shift. It begins with lament and ends in confidence and praise. The second is the royal lament Psalm 89, which serves as a conclusion for Books I–III.

CHAPTER 8

Psalm 73

The Prosperity of the Wicked and the Perspective of the Believer

Walter C. Kaiser Jr.

"The great value of the Book of Psalms," began Martyn Lloyd-Jones in his magnificent series of messages on Psalm 73, "is that in it we have godly men stating their experience, and giving us an account of things that have happened to them in their spiritual life and warfare."[1] Psalm 73 is one of the quintessential psalms in the Psalter.[2] It addresses a common human experience–comparing ourselves with others and wanting what they have. When we observe people who seem prosperous and carefree, we wonder why we cannot have what they have. We even ask if life is fair. The psalmist fell into this trap. Instead of hiding his problem, he dealt with it openly. Then he showed the way of wisdom and what to do about the temptation. It is a solution for all of us to use in facing temptation.

The most remarkable aspect of Psalm 73 is the dramatic turning point that comes in verse 17. In the middle of a crisis of faith and doubt, wondering whether God was just and fair, the psalmist suddenly "entered the precincts of God's temple."[3] There he gained a better understanding and perspective on the final destiny of the wicked, whom up to that point he had envied. No doubt the psalmist was a devout person; nonetheless, he wrestled with the question of why the wicked prosper while the righteous have one sort of trouble and illness after another. After all, he was pure in heart and had sought to live a pure and holy life. Why was he wracked with pain while the wicked seemed to enjoy good health, enormous prosperity, and ease–despite their arrogant irreverence for God and for any of God's demands on life? Watching this seeming disparity between his situation and that of the wicked become even more unbalanced and unfair, the psalmist was vexed and bothered to the point he was losing confidence in all he held to be true in his faith in God. Suddenly a dramatic experience occurred in the temple. The experience resolved his crisis and strengthened his faith. He emerged with a story to tell about the goodness of God for all who would listen.

Why Did the Author Write the Psalm?

According to the superscription, which may be as old as the book of Psalms itself,[4] Psalm 73 is one of twelve Asaph psalms.[5] Asaph was from the Levitical line of Gershon and served King David as one of his chief musicians, as a writer of songs, and as a specialist in cymbals (1 Chr. 15:19). Often the music of the sons of Asaph was called "prophesying," as they delivered inspired musical versions of the messages of Asaph "the seer" (an old term for a prophet; see 1 Chr. 25:1–7; 2 Chr. 20:14–19; 29:30). It is unclear, however, whether the title in Psalm 73 (or in the other eleven Asaph psalms) designated Asaph as author, or referred to a special collection of related psalms (or merely to the singer[s] who used these psalms in worship).

More difficult is the literary genre of the psalm. Some see the psalm as a lament of an individual.[6] Others argue that it is a psalm of confidence, wherein trust in God was expressed in a situation of real stress.[7] The most popular suggestion is that Psalm 73 is an individual psalm of thanksgiving.[8] But the literary form that appears to fit best is a wisdom psalm.[9] Several reasons support this conclusion. The psalm deals with the problems of justice, fairness, and retribution. It contains as many as twelve words that are characteristic of wisdom materials.[10] Verses 1 and 28 have been viewed as containing partial proverbs, giving the whole psalm a figure of speech known as inclusion (a sort of bracketing the beginning and the end of the psalm). Other wisdom elements include the contrast between the wicked and the righteous, the problem of theodicy (explaining the ways of God to mortals), and a concluding statement of nearness to God–themes that are very reminiscent of the book of Job.

The structure of Psalm 73 is even more interesting. Rarely has a piece of biblical text had as many suggestions for types of structure. Allen lists eight different patterns for the structure of Psalm 73 based on what was conceived as the logic or the thought content of its poetry.[11] A much more preferred method uses the rhetorical features of the Hebrew text. Allen reviews five major contributors who used key stylistic features and the repeated use of particles to mark where the author of Psalm 73 wanted to signal the major breaks in his movement of thought.[12] Some of the key observations of the NASB95 version of Psalm 73 include: the presence of "good" (Hebrew, *ṭob*) in verses 1 and 28, which form an inclusion for the whole psalm; the presence of the dominant word "heart" (Hebrew, *lebab*) in verses 1, 7, 13, 21, and 26 (*bis*); the particle "surely" or "indeed," (Hebrew, '*ak*) in verses 1, 13, and 18; or the Hebrew particle *ki*, rendered variously as "for" (v. 3), "when" (v. 21), and untranslated in most of the English texts of verse 27. The resulting structure for preaching and teaching this psalm, using these rhetorical features to identify the various strophes in the psalm (NASB95) is as follows:

73: 1–2–"Surely" (v. 1); "Good" (v 1); "As for me" (v. 2)

73: 3–12–"For" (v. 3, 4); "wicked" (v. 12)

73: 13–17 –"Surely" (v. 13); "I am/have been (v. 14)

73: 18–20–"Surely" (v. 18)

73: 21–26–"When" (v. 21); "I was," "I was" (vv. 22, 23)

73: 27–28–["For behold"]; "As for me" (v. 28)

"Good" (v. 28)

In verses 1 and 2 the general theological truth is postulated for the whole psalm, along with the question of why the wicked have such an easy time of things. The answer comes in verses 18 to 20, while verses 3 to 12, which describe the seemingly good times of the wicked, are balanced by the new perspective that comes to the psalmist in verses 13 to 17. A major pause comes in verse 20–now that the main issue of the prosperity of the wicked has been settled–followed by a reordering of the psalmist's perspective and his advice to all who have blundered into the same trap. It is almost as if verse 21 begins anew, as the problem of the prosperity of the wicked has been settled. The realization of the final destiny of the wicked was the piece of data he had been overlooking in his envy and disgust over how successful and how free of trouble the wicked seemed to have been in his former state of thinking. Over against the grim future posed for the wicked lies the prospect of always being near the heart of God. Furthermore, "afterward you [God] will take me [the psalmist] into glory" (v. 24, NIV), which is certainly a different ending from that of the wicked.

What Are the Interpretive Issues of the Psalm?

The first interpretive issue concerns the translation of verse 1. Many wish to translate verse 1 as "surely God is good to the upright," which reads the same Hebrew consonants (*lyśr*), but merely divides the word for "to Israel" (*lyśr'l*) into two words (*lyśr*), "to the upright" and (*'el*) "God." It is true that the psalm focuses on the concerns of an individual and not those of the nation of Israel as a whole. However, despite the persuasiveness of reading "to the upright" instead of "Israel," no manuscript evidence supports this reading, and one must transfer *Elohim* (God) in the first line of the couplet to the second line. What is missed is that "Israel" is a perfectly good reading that can be explained in the second line as "those whose motives are pure"–i.e., a category of those with a particular outlook on purity within the broader concept of Israel.

This confident statement of God's goodness is followed by a problem in verse 2 that seems to be just the opposite of the proclaimed truth of the goodness of God to Israel. This verse is not only introduced with an adversative conjunction, but the prominence and persona given to the personal pronoun "I" in verses 3–13 seems to be at odds with apparently the same one who is "pure in heart" (NRSV) of verse 1. Add to this the physical metaphors of the feet almost slipping and the near loss of his foothold in verse 2, and it becomes clear that the poet is challenging the confident declaration of verse 1 based on his own experience.

As already noted, verse 17 is pivotal: "Then I entered the precincts of God's temple, and understood the destiny of the wicked" (NET). As Martin Luther observed, since God is everywhere, this verse cannot merely be about changing one's physical location. Instead, it is about the poet returning to God! Is that not where this psalm began–God is good to the pure in heart?

How can we return to God when we have suddenly felt disconnected from him? The answer the poet found was that it is not possible to gain perspective on the world while we come at it from the same world's viewpoint. We must leave the world and enter the presence of God and the divine viewpoint.

Even more troublesome for interpreters is verse 24b, which affirms, "afterward you will take me into glory" (NIV). Just as the psalmist has spoken in verse 17b of the final destiny of the wicked, so here he refers to the end of the supplicant's life with a metonymic allusion to God's presence in heaven. Furthermore, the concept of "take me" is one of taking up into glory at the end of one's earthly life, just as Enoch was "taken" (Gen. 5:24) and Elijah was also translated in a whirlwind (2 Kings 2:3, 5, 9, 10). This view is preferable to the sense of adoption, or the idea of selection by election or calling, or even being taken away from a life-threatening situation in this present life.[13]

Verse 26 goes on to use the double metaphors of "my flesh and my heart," which announce that while his heart and body are weak, and his own problem-solving abilities are limited, his solid confidence and security rest in God alone. In fact, the Hebrew literally says, "God is the rock (*ṣur*) of my heart." That is bottom-line thinking, for now Asaph realizes that no other competing values or comparisons exist by which to measure the real world with all its puzzles and enigmas, not to mention its totality. Armed with this realization, the poet concludes that happiness is found in living close to God (vv. 27–28). Departure and apostasy from God brings God's judgment, but being near to the heart of God is what goodness (cf. v. 1) and life are all about.

A second interpretive issue is the canonical placement of Psalm 73. Few have examined the "canonical shape" of the Psalter and the Old Testament as a whole more than Brevard Childs.[14] Others have followed Childs and investigated why certain psalms are placed at the "seams" of the five books in the Psalter and what is the pattern of organization, if one is to be identified at all.[15]

Walter Brueggemann and Patrick Miller note that the beginning of Book III of the Psalter stands in juxtaposition with Psalm 72, a psalm "of/by Solomon" that ends Book II.[16] The question, then, is this: Why are these two psalms placed back to back? If Psalm 73 is sapiential/wisdom type and Psalm 72 is royal, does the placement of the two psalms have more meaning and significance here than immediately meets the eye?

God invited Solomon to ask for whatever he wanted God to give him. Solomon chose a wise and discerning heart instead of a long life, riches, or the defeat of his enemies (1 Kings 3:5–12). Buber noted that the theme of the heart, which occurs six times (vv. 1, 7, 13, 21, 26 [*bis*]) in Psalm 73, is crucial to understanding the psalm.[17] The heart must be pure and kept clean, for when all is said and done, God always protects his heart (vv. 1, 13, 26). Once he got turned back to right thinking about the wicked and about God, the psalmist understood all that.

Seitz has taken the argument even further.[18] He proposes that the Davidic house and the kingship of God are portrayed in the book of Psalms (and the book of Isaiah) as being parallel to each other. As the Davidic throne recedes and finally disappears after the division of the kingdom and the fall of Jerusalem, the kingship of God rises to prominence. Thus, Psalm 72 is seen as the fading marker of the Davidic house and the completion of Books I and II in the Psalms, which contain mostly Davidic Psalms. In Book III, Psalms 73–89, a new regrouping appears as Psalms 74 and 79 lament over Jerusalem, while Psalm 89:46–51 ends with a note on the failure of kingship in Israel. According to this view, Psalm 73:3–16 presents an improper way of relating to God, as illustrated by the wicked who are at ease, well-off, rich, and arrogant in their idolatry of self, in contrast with Psalm 73:18–28, where the heart is focused on God, and nearness to God is a daily experience.[19] Just as the governance of Yahweh emerges in the latter part of Psalm 73, so God's rule and reign emerge in the enthronement psalms of Book IV (Pss. 90–106) and take the center stage for the psalmist from that point on.

What Is the Significance of the Psalm for Preaching and Teaching?

Though the modern world may seem vastly different from the biblical world, the life experiences of people in both worlds are very similar. "There is something wrong with a Christianity which rejects the Old Testament, or even a Christianity which imagines that we are essentially different from the Old Testament saints."[20]

Moreover, the psalms are poetry. While storytelling and narrative preaching may be in vogue, we have no need or reason to reduce poetry to narrative or to squeeze it into prose.[21] The psalms contain a storehouse of images, similes, metaphors, and other figures of speech that heighten our imaginative powers and aid our understanding. They are not only words *from* God, but they also contain words *to* God and words we speak *with* God. "The old saying, *lex orandi, lex credenti*, is valid: the law of prayer is the law of belief; what we pray, we believe."[22] Dietrich Bonhoeffer compared learning to pray with learning to talk: "The child learns to speak because his father speaks to him. He learns the speech of his father."[23] So it is with the psalms of the Bible.

While some preachers have purposely avoided the psalms in their preaching, others have found great power and usefulness in employing them. On July 8, 1741, at Enfield in one of the most famous sermons in American history, Jonathan Edwards preached his memorable sermon, "Sinners in the Hands of an Angry God." Hardly had he gotten into his second paragraph when he appealed to Psalm 73:18: "Surely thou didst set them in slippery places: thou castedst them down into destruction" (KJV). It is reported that many grasped hold of the pews around them as they pictured themselves on similar slippery ground and lingering over the precipice of ruin. The imaginative power of the figurative language was never more aptly illustrated.

The psalmist begins his poem triumphantly with a strong conclusion: "Certainly God is good to Israel, and to those whose motives are pure!" (73:1, NET). This may sound paradoxical, for why should the poet start with his conclusion? Surely he is not confessing how he almost slipped overboard when he was working on this problem, as if it were for exhibitionistic reasons. Rather, he wants his experience to be an illustration of the truth that God is always good to his people, to those who are pure of heart.

True, Asaph was perplexed when he tried on his own to justify the ways of God with all that was going on around him. Such perplexity was not sinful, anymore than it was for the apostle Paul who was "perplexed, but not driven to despair" (2 Cor. 4:8, NET). So how do we deal with the temptation to think that God is absent and life unfair? It is only in staying near God in pureness of heart and claiming him as the rock of our heart that we are able to say that God is always good, all the time, in all circumstances.

A sermon based on this psalm may be structured as follows. From verses 1 and 2, which we regard as the focal point of the text, comes the big idea: "Slippery thinking on the topic of the goodness of God." The sermon will need to deal with the graphic, metaphoric language and lead to the conclusion that for the upright and the pure in heart God is always good all the time.

The interrogative we have chosen from the six possible questions (who? what? why? where? when? and how?) is, "Why?" Why do we longingly compare ourselves with others and think life is unfair? Our homiletical keyword, therefore, will be *reasons.*

Having identified six strophes based on repeated rhetorical devices in the psalm, our outline for teaching and preaching could have four reasons (since the first strophe was introductory and set forth the problem (vv. 1–2), while the final strophe (vv. 27–28) sums up the argument. The flow of thought in the psalm is as follows.

I. Because we envy the wicked (vv. 3–12)
   1. Prosperity of the wicked
   2. Health of the wicked
   3. Violence of the wicked
   4. Boasts of the wicked
II. Because we think we have kept our hearts pure in vain (vv. 13–17)
   1. I am plagued all day long
   2. I don't know what to say to my children
   3. I am oppressed trying to understand it all
   4. I entered your sanctuary and I finally understood
III. Because we failed to recognize what will finally happen to the wicked (vv. 18–20)
   1. They are placed on slippery ground
   2. They are swept away by terrors
   3. They are despised
IV. Because we were ignorant and brutish until we recalled God's constant presence and guidance (vv. 21–26)
   1. Grieving hearts and embittered spirits are of no help
   2. Forgetting God's constant presence and guidance is wrong as well
   3. Desiring anything or anyone besides God and heaven is crazy
   4. Finding that God is the rock of our hearts, even as all bodily functions continue to fail

Conclusion: (vv. 27–28)

   1. Those who are spiritually far from God will perish and be destroyed

   2. The greatest good we can find is to be near God

   3. My greatest shelter and refuge is in the Sovereign Lord himself.

All of this has happened so that we may announce and boldly declare all the works of God to all generations of men and women.

The teacher or preacher must grapple with one more underlying question: can the interpreter go from poetry to principles? Do not such attempts to derive points lead to a crushing of the poetic form and to a major injustice to the psalm as it was intended by the writer and by the God who revealed it?

Some will complain: if God had wanted to say it in prose, he would have said it that way instead of in metaphoric figurative and poetic language! While the difference between the two literary forms is granted and taken seriously by what is observed above, few would want to say that the end of our exegesis and application is purely experiential, emotional, psychological, and meditative in nature. Is it not also possible to arrive at truth through the gateway of the senses and emotions so that the truths or principles that stand behind these experiences begin to take shape out of the angst of the soul and the tough experiences of life?

Others will deny that linear thinking, such as used in prose, is possible in our modern and postmodern world. People just do not think in a linear straight-line pattern anymore, it is alleged. That too is false. Watch most Westerners attend a game of baseball, football, or basketball. You will observe linear thinking, as one must keep track of the number of balls and strikes, the number of yards to go for a first down, or the amount of time left on the shot clock or game clock. With clear evidence for linear thinking, why do we announce that postmoderns are unable to do linear thinking in sermons? They can if they want to.

Therefore, the preacher and teacher must not leave his or her audience with a mere retelling of the emotional and existential description of how the psalmist felt. Retelling this psalm requires more than merely plotting the movement of the psalm. Instead, the proclaimer must go on to announce the doctrine of the restoring grace of God (even if it sounds somewhat prosaic). Did not God hold the psalmist by his right hand? Why not add God's restraining grace as well? Was it not the same right hand of God that kept the poet from falling off the edge?

Why should we be so hesitant to speak of facing the uncertainties of life with the certitude of drawing near to God and his being the rock of our heart? Of course, we must be humble and say that, at best, we only know in part; however, that is not to say nothing can be affirmed, especially if it comes with the authority and power of the God who has spoken in his word.

Thus, our work in the book of Psalms will give full attention to all the figures of speech and the poetic literary form. That must not muzzle our preaching and teaching so that no principles or truths are affirmed or taught from the passage. God has not merely entertained us; he has guided us with his word so that we may end up declaring all his deeds.[24]

CHAPTER 9

Psalm 89

A Community Lament

Bernon P. Lee

Roller coaster rides are a type of perverse pleasure. The pleasure arises, at least in part, from a sense of danger. Such rides also include a measure of discomfort. The sensations wreak havoc on the insides of bodies and minds. Many a ride has terminated with a dash to the nearest restroom. Yet for all the discomfort and trepidation, many seek the thrill of the ride. Personally, I prefer the sedate pleasures of cotton candy.

Psalm 89 is a roller coaster ride. It submits our emotional state, our feelings about God and the world, to extremes. Although Psalm 89 is a royal psalm, some have argued that the poem is a communal lament,[1] juxtaposing images inspiring awe and praise with those eliciting despair and depression. At times the movement between the highs and lows–especially in the dark night of the soul–is debilitating. Humanly speaking, the psalm leaves the impression that a tormented mind might have produced it. Perhaps its composition came from the shaking pen of one shell-shocked from the storms of life. Sometimes we discover no recourse to relief apart from writing about the turmoil and reflecting on the God of the universe.

The genius of Psalm 89 is that ancient and modern readers alike can identify with the ups and downs, the joys and sorrows of life. The poem is boldly realistic. For that reason it communicates powerfully. It is a message of encouragement to assist a community confronting its own suffering through contemplating past crises of the nation, while pondering God's promises of protection.

Why Did the Author Compose the Psalm?

The first question that comes to mind in encountering the words of anguish and disappointment in Psalm 89 concerns the historical location of the dire circumstances. Which storm in Israel's history instigated this outpouring of grief? What national tragedy inspired this desperate call for deliverance? Which king in the line of David experienced the rejection of God? Who are the enemies encountered by Israel's anointed? A survey of ancient Israel's history produces a prominent event that suits the tragic dimensions expressed by this language of lament: the sack of Jerusalem and the demise of the Southern Kingdom of Judah in 586 B.C.E.[2] Within this context, the enemies of Israel's anointed were the Babylonians, who devastated Judah and deported a majority of its population (2 Kings 25:1–21; 2 Chr. 36:15–20). The deposed Davidic monarch is thought to be Zedekiah. In light of the prominence of Judah's demise in the historical accounts, this event may be the circumstance depicted in Psalm 89.

However, the absence of any reference to the destruction of the temple and the city of Jerusalem, or to the deportation of the populace and the capture of the king in verses 38–45 of the psalm has led scholars to search elsewhere for the historical context. Rehoboam's territorial losses (1 Kings 13–15) as a consequence of Solomon's fall from divine favor have been suggested. In that context, Jeroboam and the Egyptians constitute the enemies of the Davidic king. Other proposals include the various national crises during Ahaz's reign over Judah (2 Kings 16), or the untimely demise of Josiah at the hands of the Egyptians (2 Kings 23:28–30). In the former case, for the Northern Kingdom of Israel, the Arameans and the Edomites were the enemies of the Davidic king. These proposals would account for the absence of any mention of Jerusalem's destruction and the national crises preceding the Babylonian incursion.

On the other hand, the historical situation in Psalm 89 may be impossible to pin down, precisely for the reason that the psalmist's concern is the fidelity of God and the anguish of the people across a series of historical situations. Perhaps the author presumed on the ability of those hearing the psalm to digest any historical allusion that would arise in their minds.[3] In that case, the psalm exists as a theological treatise and a piece of liturgy assisting a community meditating on Israel's present struggles against the backdrop of crises in the past. The psalm, therefore, is designed as a paradigm applicable in a host of situations. The psalmist is soliciting his readers' imagination in preparation for whatever difficult circumstances they may face.

Following the author's flow of thought through the psalm provides insight into his purpose. The psalm moves from a review of adverse circumstances to the anticipation of praise. Within this continuum stands the rehearsal of God's acts of glory in the past, which leads to the confidence of the community in seeking change by way of petition. The glorification of God through the implementation of justice and deliverance is the goal.

In paying attention to the formal features and the content of a psalm, scholars often speculate about the setting within which the poem was spoken or sung. Scholars have made several proposals regarding Psalm 89.[4] Most regard a religious and social gathering during the exile (after 586 B.C.E.), or after the exile (after 519 B.C.E.), as the most likely setting. Proposals within this general frame include exilic feasts of community lamentation, or a festival confirming the covenant with God and God's ascension as king over Israel in times of trouble. A somewhat unique proposition is a ritual of humiliation for the king. In this dramatic performance, the king suffers in the hands of enemies even as he petitions divinity for assistance. After a period of humiliation and defeat, God rescues the king from his enemies and restores his position of authority. According to this theory, the ritual is an object lesson that seeks to educate the community regarding their need to rely on God for the sustenance of their life and institutions. This element of instruction fits well with an understanding of the psalm as something between a liturgy of complaint and an instructional treatise.[5] In this case, the psalm is a call for God to live up to his promises, as well as an introduction to the problem of assigning responsibility (God's failure or Israel's failure) for the end of the line of David.

Psalm 89 may have been written to defy easy association with any one historical event or liturgical setting. It has the ability to address numerous situations and occasions. As evidenced in its formal features, the psalm is written to contemplate God's power in praise, to express the dire need for change in the present situation, and to appeal to God to bring about that change. A possible secondary function is instruction for the community on the difficulties in assigning blame for national crises.

How Did the Author Express His Ideas?

To understand the ideas expressed in Psalm 89, the reader must comprehend the rhetorical progression of the psalm. The psalm consists of various movements as the psalmist unleashed an argument with its accompanying torrent of emotion. Just like a roller coaster ride, the sensation of being at a crest just prior to a drop is quite different from that of doing a loop. Furthermore, the arrangement of these components in the design of the track would produce a different overall experience. This is why we yearn to try different rides in an amusement park, even if the next is just another roller coaster.

Westermann's comprehensive study of communal laments[6] reveals the component parts of this psalm type: address to God → lament → confession of trust in God → petition → praise.[7] The following is a brief summary for each component of the lament.

Address: The initial address acknowledges God's presence and his person as the audience to whom the poet is speaking.

Lament: The lament proper envisions adverse circumstances. Typically, three parties come to the fore: the party suffering the adversity (i.e., the party offering the lament), God, and the opposition. In its focus on the group initiating the lament, this portion of the poem rehearses the pain and the humiliation that is the plight of the oppressed party. Where the lament turns its attention to God, it often takes the form of queries concerning God's purpose in allowing the adverse circumstance (why?) and its duration (how long?). Such addresses to God tinged with outrage are themselves acknowledgements of the reality of God and his ability to reverse the present state of affairs. The questions are not accusations against God addressed to a third party, but statements of perplexity and prologues to petition for change. In the focus on the enemies, the godlessness, pride, and slander of the opposition and their abuse of God's people come into view.

Confession: The third portion of the poem is a confession of trust in God. Usually, this takes the shape of a rehearsal of God's acts of deliverance in the past.

Petition: The petition part of the communal lament is a call for God to attend to the present state of affairs, supported by appeal to divine justice, by pity, and by outrage at the insolence of the godless. This portion of the pattern may incorporate a statement expressing the expectation of a response from God.

Praise: The communal lament then concludes with the element of praise in anticipation of deliverance.

The question to consider is to what extent Psalm 89 follows the typical pattern of communal laments. In verses 2–4 the poet informs God of the intention to offer praise and to contemplate God's deeds of old. Verses 5–18, however, are an unexpected component of praise, with verses 19–37 recalling God's installation of David as king and his guarantee of support for David's line (cf. 2 Sam. 7). Verses 38–52 turn to lament, noting the discrepancy between God's promise and the current state of the kingship. Petition for God to effect change to the current state of affairs is included. Verse 52 offers a note of praise, which also functions as the conclusion to the third book of the Psalter.

Noteworthy is the change in the order of components, with the larger component of praise moved to an earlier position (immediately following the address to God), leaving a prominent lament with petition in final position. The silence following may signal an air of despondency or urgency.[8]

Looking at these component parts more closely, the introduction to the psalm (vv. 1–4) addresses God directly; the various pronouns referring to God are in the second person (*you, your*). This section announces the intention to praise God, with reference to the establishment of a covenant with David. The emphasis on God's faithfulness and the permanence of his work and his decrees is evident. Noteworthy is the twofold nature of this unit of text: verses 1–2 (with the mention of "the skies" as the location of God's "faithfulness") look toward heaven, while verses 3–4 consider the covenant with the earthly king (David). A second element of contrast occurs between verses 1–2 and 3–4: the former are the words of the psalmist, whereas the latter are the words of God quoted by the psalmist.[9] The quoted speech of God in verses 3–4 continues in verse 19.

Verses 5–18 are a hymn of praise that interrupts the quoted speech of God concerning the choice of his regent on earth (vv. 3–4 and 19–37). This hymn fulfills the promise to praise God in verse 1. The roller coaster ride that is Psalm 89 begins with a dizzying view at the top of the world: God's seat of rule in the heavens. At least two streams of logical progression appear in this hymn of praise. The contemplation of God flows from the realm of heaven (vv. 5–8) to the realm of earth (vv. 9–18). The same transition in focus had governed the flow of thought in the introduction to the psalm (vv. 1–4). The other main progression of thought through the unit of praise is a movement from question (vv. 5–8; Who is like God?) to answer (vv. 9–18, esp. vv. 9–14; no one, in view of God's qualities). The final question in verse 8 with its twofold focus on God's strength and faithfulness determines the nature of the response in verses 9–18.

Verses 9–13 dwell on the might of God as warrior, and verses 14–18 emphasize his faithfulness as the foundation of his rule. Reference to the defeat of Egypt (v. 10; "the Proud One") at the Red Sea demonstrates the strength of God. The defeat of Israel's foe is likened, through poetic expression, to God's acts in creation (the defeat/partition of the primordial waters; vv. 9–10; cf. Pss. 74:13–14, 77:16–17, 104:5–9, 114:3–6, Gen. 1:1–8). The same God who is master over the elements of chaos is supreme over those who would bring disarray on his elect.

The movement of the hymn to speak explicitly of God's acts in creation (vv. 11–12) is an apt follow-up to the poetic language pregnant with the imagery of creation as cosmic warfare (vv. 9–10). Even as the might of God expresses his supremacy over creation and Israel's enemies, the faithful quality of his rule (vv. 14–18), tempered by equity and justice (v. 14), communicates blessing on those who would rest in God's favor (vv. 15–18). In sum, the hymn portrays God's strength and faithfulness in heaven and on earth as it notes that no one is God's rival. This is Israel's confidence.

The final verse of the hymn (v. 18) mentions God's possession and sponsorship of Israel's king. This statement leads, naturally, into the concern of the next unit (vv. 19–37): the continuation (from vv. 3–4) of God's speech concerning Israel's anointed king. The text refers to the promise to David concerning the continuity of his dynastic line in 2 Samuel 7. Unlike the speech of 2 Samuel 7, which was addressed to David and communicated through the prophet Nathan, the quoted speech here in Psalm 89 is introduced as a "vision" for God's "faithful followers" (v. 19). This shift in the designation of the addressee may reflect the psalmist's understanding that the content of the speech of 2 Samuel 7, within the context of the national crisis in a subsequent period, has become the concern of the people who inherit that promise.

Verses 19–20 recount the election of David, and verse 21 confirms God's support for the king. The consequence is that no foe may stand against the king and his dominion (vv. 22–25). Verses 26–28 refer to the status of the king as God's appointed; the designation of the king as a son of God underscores the intimacy of the relationship in keeping with the royal associations of the term in its ancient Near Eastern context.[10] Verses 29–37 conclude the unit by emphasizing the efficacy of the promise, the continuation of David's dynastic line despite the moral and covenantal fallibility of David's descendants. The quoted divine speech of verses 19–37 builds on the transition of focus from the heavens to the earth in the hymn of verses 5–18 by expanding on God's dominion on earth and the flow of blessing to his faithful ones. Just as strength and faithfulness underlie the rule of God in the hymn, the same qualities characterize his support for his regent on earth. Just as God is able to vanquish his enemies and the elements of chaos (vv. 9–10), so will David be victorious over his enemies (vv. 22–25).[11] Moreover, the same faithfulness that is the object of praise in the hymn (vv. 5, 8, 14) will stand behind the continuation of David's dominion through his line (vv. 24, 28, 33–35).

The experience of elation at the crest of the ride may lead to a bout with nausea at the bottom of the drop. The components of praise (vv. 5–18) and confession of trust through the recall of promises made (vv. 19–37) have a hollow ring in light of the statements of disappointment in verses 38–51. Does the rhetoric of praise serve only to emphasize the discrepancy between expectation and reality? Do the rehearsals of divine promise and the celebration of God's faithfulness and loving-kindness only serve to exacerbate the pain of betrayal?

Verses 38–51 offer a lament for the nation's current situation with a petition for divine intervention. Many of the complaints have reference to the preceding units of praise and confession of trust in God. Verses 38–39 observe that God has rejected his king and neglected his promise to David. This action stands in contrast to the divine act of election in verses 19–20.[12] The faithfulness of God is in question! Verses 40–45 lament the collapse of the king's military might and the ascendance of the enemies of the king. The despoliation of the king (v. 41), his military impotence (v. 43), and his humiliation (v. 45) stand in sharp contrast to the psalmist's remembrance of divine guarantees of freedom from payments of tribute (v. 22) and humiliation (v. 22), and of victory over enemies (vv. 23–24). The strength and the authority of the king are in decline.

Perhaps the psalmist wonders if God himself is dethroned in heaven. Has Israel, thus, lost its advocate on earth? The thrust of the lament, therefore, is against the twofold emphasis on the faithfulness and might of God in the hymn of praise (vv. 5–18). According to the hymn and the vision, God's governance on earth through his regent is an extension of divine omnipotence in heaven. But earth is now an abandoned outpost, perhaps a casualty of bureaucratic oversight in heaven.

Verses 46–48 shift the focus to the suffering of the psalmist: the overpowering sense of God's obscurity (v. 46) and the absence of any reversal of circumstances within the foreseeable future within the psalmist's lifespan (vv. 47–51).[13] The content of the psalmist's petition, as encapsulated in verse 49, is clear: be true to your word, and bring back the good old days! Under the cloud of the lament, the concluding doxology to the third book of the Psalter in verse 52 is muted. The buoyant optimism inherent to the praise and recall of divine promise is deflated. God's omnipotence and/or his favor for Israel are in question.

What Are the Important Interpretive Issues?

Most roller coaster rides are parts of establishments offering a variety of amusements for thrill seekers. Almost certainly, it would be an error in marketing to offer only one mode of amusement to a family (or even an individual) with different tastes in entertainment. Can you imagine an amusement park featuring only houses of horror? Even within the experience of a single ride, it takes the variety of a series of vertical and horizontal sensations of motion to produce what many would consider the complete experience of the roller coaster ride. In a similar fashion, the note of despondency in the lament for the end to David's line is one movement (as variegated as that movement may be) within a longer journey. How is Psalm 89 to be understood within the context of the book of Psalms? How does this particular ride fit with the rest of the park?

B. S. Childs suggests that Psalm 89 is one in a series of psalms scattered across the Psalter that are concerned with the kingship of Israel.[14] Most of these royal psalms (Pss. 2; 72; 89; and 132) occur at the seams of the Psalter, the boundaries between the various books that comprise the book of Psalms. Psalm 2, which speaks of the establishment of God's chosen king, warns other rulers on earth to be mindful of the authority of God's regent on earth. Psalm 72, which is associated with Solomon and concludes the second book of the Psalter, is a prayer for the king to be a faithful executor of divine will. Both Psalms 89 and 132 are concerned with the promise of a perpetual reign for David's line. For Childs, this scattering of royal psalms in an arrangement wrought long after the end to the kingdom of Judah bears witness to an eschatological interpretation of God's act in establishing David's throne. Beyond the historical reference to the kingdom of David and Solomon (and successive kingdoms) in these psalms, the communities that receive the Psalter envision a reestablishment of David's kingdom in the future.

G. H. Wilson, a student of Childs, takes a similar interest in the psalms at the seams of the Psalter.[15] The sequence of Psalms 2; 41; 72; and 89 mark a movement from the establishment of the kingship of David through the sovereignty of God (Ps. 2) to its failure (Ps. 89). Psalm 41 (the end of the first book of Psalms) has David speaking of the certainty of God's protection for him in the face of his enemies. Psalm 72 (the end of the second book), as previously stated, is a petition on behalf of the king's son. The association of the psalm with Solomon fosters the impression of an historical shift in focus to a later period of the kingdom.

The common and easy association of Psalm 89 with the end of Zedekiah's reign marks a further historical movement in moving through the Psalter. Wilson considers the crisis of Psalm 89 to stand at the heart of the book of Psalms; Psalms 90–106 are the editorial center of the Psalter, in response to the crisis of Psalm 89. Psalm 90 begins the response by stating, in essence, that human iniquity is the reason for divine retribution, while Psalm 91 insists that protection is available for those who trust in God. Psalms 92–99 are a cluster of psalms celebrating the reign of God and calling on Israel to sing praises to God. Psalm 100 calls on Israel to give thanks to God, as Psalm 101 strikes a note of contrast between those who seek God and those who do not. Psalm 102 contrasts the transient quality of humanity with the permanence of divinity, even as Psalm 103 emphasizes God's pity for humanity and his willingness to forgive iniquity.[16] Psalms 104–06 are a series of praise (*halleluiah*) psalms that conclude this section, celebrating God's acts of creation (Ps. 104) and deliverance (Pss. 105–06).

The essence of the response, Wilson's editorial center of the Psalter, is as follows: (1) God is King over Israel (even if David has faltered); (2) God is Israel's refuge from the distant past (before there was a human king); (3) God will continue to be Israel's refuge; (4) Those who trust in God will be blessed. The journey through the valley of the shadow of death in Psalm 89 may be the lot of the community of faith, but God's community is not without help and hope even in the depths of its despair. The heart of the sufferer, in response to the encouraging voices of Psalms 90–106, is able to join in the litany of praise (Pss. 145–50) that concludes the book of Psalms. The disaster and the brokenness of the community in lament is not the end of the road.

Let us return to Childs' observation that later communities inheriting the various psalms must have read many of the psalms with a view beyond the common historical associations of those psalms.[17] The Christian Bible clearly shows that the New Testament writers understood the circumstances of Psalm 89 to bear significance beyond the collapse of Judah as recorded in the closing chapters of 2 Kings. God's abandonment of David and his line in Psalm 89 also points to God's rejection of Jesus at his darkest moment. Hebrews 1:5b, in proclaiming the father-son relationship between God and Jesus, cites God's confirmation of David as his son in 2 Samuel 7:14. Psalm 89, as noted already, has reference to the content of the words of promise in 2 Samuel 7. Thus, the author of Hebrews, quite clearly, understands the divine words of promise in 2 Samuel 7 (and, by extension, Ps. 89) to be applicable to Jesus. Once this interpretive link between the promise to David and the person and ministry of Jesus is established, the various details of the hymn, the confession of faith and lament of Psalm 89, become applicable to many of the situations and contexts of the New Testament. The following list provides several themes in the New Testament that have connection with those of Psalm 89:

> Jesus has authority over the sea (Mk. 4:39; cf. Ps. 89:9)
>
> Jesus suffers humiliation in the hands of enemies (Heb. 11:26; 13:13; Mt. 27:43–44; Lk. 18:22; 24:25; cf. Ps. 89:41–45)
>
> Jesus is God's firstborn (Col. 1:15–20; Heb. 1:6; cf. Ps. 89:27)
>
> Jesus is ruler over all the kings of the earth (Rev. 1:5; cf. Ps. 89:27)

In the Christian Bible the words of Psalm 89 find an echo in the stories of the life of the Christ and in the testimony concerning the impact of that life. The plight of David's scion in another time is also the experience of

Jesus. The despair of those who look on the demise of Judah is also that of those who look on the persecution and humiliation of Jesus. The Bible itself testifies to the evocative power of the psalms and the interpretive energy of communities in finding new contexts for old texts.[18]

In addressing the broader issues of interpretation for Psalm 89, one might say that lament is an integral part of faithful worship and dialogue with God. The psalms at the seams of the Psalter enact a movement from the fortitude and assurance inherent to royal installation, through the grief of defeat, and on to the jubilation and pregnant expectation intrinsic to praise. The common appeal of this progression to human experience and the witness of the New Testament to an interpretation of Psalm 89 beyond the common historical associations for that psalm encourage readers to see their own adverse circumstances through the words of the psalms. Even the Son of God, Jesus of Nazareth, was not above the experience of humiliation in the world and the accompanying sense of abandonment by God.

What Is the Significance of the Psalm for Preaching and Teaching?

Summing up the study of Psalm 89, several matters have become clear. (1) The psalm resists easy identification with any one historical situation. (2) The elements of praise and rehearsal of divine promise sharpen the intensity of pain in the concluding lament. (3) Lament is an integral part of the emotional spectrum in the book of Psalms. (4) Even Jesus became the object of God's abandonment. These four observations suggest that in the life of a community of faith the sincere expression of pain and disappointment is appropriate. Individuals and groups must be allowed to traverse the path of grief and complaint. Unfortunately, lament, in the sense of complaint leading to petition, is lacking in the life of many Christian communities. Cries for justice, especially in cases where God is perceived to be the indolent party in bringing equity to a situation, are often deemed inappropriate and even subversive. This neglect for lament may stultify the development of worshipers as responsible partners in a covenantal relationship with God.[19] Where only praise is an acceptable form of address, the Christian comes close to losing the ability to initiate change through appeal to the just attributes of divinity. The surrender of this initiative leads to an acceptance of injustice as the status quo. Accordingly, the reluctance to address God with concerns of inequity leads to a passive sponsorship for injustice in the public arena.[20]

Against this deplorable drift toward apathy stands the witness of Psalm 89. The religious community of Israel, as participants in the liturgy of communal lament, was not to stand idle in acceptance of injustice or oppression. Neither was it intended that the community be mired in depression. Israel worked out its identity in conversation with God.[21] As such, the community felt free to address God with moral outrage, screaming when its sense of judicial impropriety was violated. This covenantal relationship with God entailed the recognition that God was able to alter the lamentable state of affairs with the same potency that wrought creation. The divine word that summons creation into being is born of the volition of God: God chooses his actions. Thus, the divine will effects change in ways beyond human expectation, even as it holds on to the community through the throes of change. God's possessive grasp of Israel defines and redefines the quality of that community. Israel's God is wholly other, an essential quality on which the possibility of dialogue is predicated. Because God exists as other, Israel is able to hope, to listen with expectation, to respond with obedience, to protest the poor state of the world, and to laud the initiatives of God. To unleash the ferocity of the lament of Psalm 89 is to reckon with the reality of the living God. To exhort the community to join in the petition is to place the individual in touch with the danger and the exhilaration of knowing the God who desires us to know him.[22]

In seeking to capture the argument and the emotive impact of the psalm, it is best that a sermon retain the lexical order in the psalm. Let the ideas of the psalmist confront the person in the pew according to the design of the psalm. One might offer a meditation on the piece in two sermons. An initial message could deal with the content of verses 1–37 (address to God, hymn of praise, and confession of trust), and a second message would address verses 38–52 (lament proper and petition). In following the rhetorical design of the psalm, the people in the pew must become buoyant with the lyrics of praise, and on the other hand be deflated by the sting of disappointment. Only in perceiving the thrusts of the poet's provocative remonstrance will they see their own aspirations and disappointments. Perhaps, then, they may be roused to petition God for change and healing.[23]

Towards this end, I suggest attention to the following features of the psalm in a sermon:

- Be emphatic about the core values of God's rule in the hymn of praise: the might of God and divine faithfulness (how these values are productive of equity and justice for the faithful).
- Point to the psalm's demonstration of these core values (vv. 9–13 speak of God's victory in battle; vv. 14–18 expound on the quality of God's faithfulness); linger over, and explain, the imagery in the text that expresses these qualities (e.g., the might of God in creation

likened to a battle is the same strength that defeats the enemy in vv. 9–11).

- Point to the expectation of the psalmist that these same values characterize God's support for the reign of the king; God's rule (through the king) on earth ought to be as it is in heaven.
- Be attentive to the tone of outrage and earnestness in the lament and the petition.
- Be sure to point out that the elements of the lament stand in contrast to the various expressions of divine power and faithfulness in the hymn; the psalmist feels that God has not acted consistently.
- Provide examples from current events (personal, communal, or national) that might illustrate core values in the text; remember, one purpose of the psalm is to allow its audience to see the highs and the lows of their own journey in the words of the psalm.
- Reassure listeners that God is interested in their tribulations and perceptions of injustice; point to the repeated occurrence of the second-person pronoun in the address to God at the beginning of the psalm.
- Highlight the expectation, intrinsic to the petition, that God would respond to the cries of malcontent; the faithful are consistently in conversation with God throughout the twists and turns of their sojourn through life.

In essence, the preacher should exhort the community to maintain an open communion with God that takes stock of pain, despair, and injustice. Let us go through the turnstile and get on the ride, which is Psalm 89. God would prefer to suffer our outrage than tolerate our apathy.[24]

Book IV: Psalms 90–106

Book IV of the Psalter offers a striking change of pace. The Davidic monarchy had failed, the Israelites were in captivity, and the only hope was for God to deliver them. Partly answering questions raised at the end of Book III, Book IV affirms that God himself is their true King, that he had been Israel's refuge long before they had kings, and that he would continue to protect his people. He led the Israelites through the wilderness in Egypt, and he would lead them through the new wilderness, the exile in Babylon. The collectors structured this book to call people away from confidence in human leaders and urged them to place their complete trust in the heavenly monarch. Those who trusted in him would be truly blessed.

The nature of Book IV allows for very few laments (90; 94; 104; 106). Rather, descriptive praise psalms are prominent. Some are hymns (100; 104; 105), others are enthronement psalms (93; 96; 97; 98; 99), and still others are songs of Zion (95). A royal psalm and three individual thanksgiving or declarative praise psalms are featured. (See "Classification of the Psalms by Category" at the end of the book.) As we now anticipate, Book IV closes with a clear doxological formula (106:48), "The Lord God of Israel deserves praise, in the future and forevermore. Let all the people say, 'We agree! Praise the Lord.'"

Three significant psalms have been selected for this chapter: Psalms 99; 103; and 104. Whereas the first psalm depicts God ascending his throne to be acclaimed King, the subsequent psalms focuses on redemption, God's gracious benefits offered to unworthy people, and the beauty of God's creation and our response.

CHAPTER 10

Psalm 99

Holy Is the Lord, Our God

David Talley

This beautiful psalm powerfully shouts two seemingly contradictory points: God is transcendent beyond anything we could imagine, and he is immanent and closer than we would ever expect. He is both great and over all, as well as personal and present to all. What at first seems contradictory will actually be understood as complementary–for worship is a combination of awe, as we ponder how great he is, and remembrance, as we reflect on all he has done for us. Psalm 99 calls Israel to worship his greatness and remember his goodness. Its echo continues today as we celebrate both his magnitude and grace in our lives. God is great, and God is good.

Contemporary audiences need to hear the message of Psalm 99. In the hustle and bustle of busy lives, it is easy to marginalize and minimize God. Even in our churches, God can be "made little" as we expend our energies in "making big" our number of converts and members, our buildings and powerful ministries, and our clever plans. As a result God can be perceived as being soft, insignificant, and of little effect on most of life. People do not fear him. They cry out to him only in desperation. He becomes the last resort, taking a seat behind the idols that we have set up to bring us deliverance.

The psalmist seeks to dispel this kind of thinking on two counts. God is so big that our thoughts cannot even capture his essence or power. He is beyond understanding (cf. Isa. 40:12–26). He is an unapproachable light (cf. 1 Tim. 6:16). Nothing stands outside of his control. Recognizing how great he is and how insignificant we are strikes fear (cf. Heb. 10:31). Yet God is so near that we can live in the light of his awesome presence. We need him. In fact, he alone is what we need. He hears and answers us. All of his greatness is available to us. The Almighty One invites us into relationship. This leaves the psalmist in a posture of worship, precisely where the psalm seeks to take everyone who reads or hears these powerful truths.

Why Did the Author Compose the Psalm?

No clear reference point explains the writing of this psalm. It was probably composed when the nation of Israel was in the midst of struggle, under God's judgment for not following the covenant established at Mt. Sinai. In such times people often longed for the glorious reign of the Lord, who would restore the greatness of the nation. Thus, the psalmist celebrates God's kingship and reminds the people of his goodness. God *is* on *his* throne despite the struggles of the people. Psalm 99 remembers the past and hopes in the future, because the Lord reigns over all and has acted on behalf of his people. His majesty is unchanging, and his person (who he is) and work (what he does) must define reality, especially in times of difficulty. In the end, he will rightfully take what is already his.

The exact setting for Psalm 99 is unclear, and the original function of the psalm is difficult to establish.[1] It is a royal psalm. Common characteristics of these psalms are "references to Yahweh's ascension to the heavenly throne, general praise of his supreme authority, insistence on Israel's privileged status, expectancy of divine judgment of enemies and apostates, etc."[2] The royal psalms include Psalms 2; 18; 20–21; 45; 72; 89; 93; 95–99; 101; 110; 132; and 144. They affirm the Lord's rule over the earth, identifying God as the one who delivers his people while judging the earth.

Of these psalms, Psalms 93 and 95–99 form an interesting unit. Three of the psalms (93; 97; and 99) begin with the phrase, "the LORD reigns," while each of the psalms has a different theme. In Psalm 93, he who made the world and rules it has an everlasting throne. In Psalm 95, he is the great king above all gods. In Psalm 96, he judges righteously. Psalm 97 depicts the king in the glory of his advent as he is welcomed with joy by the people. Psalm 98 entails a call for the lands to go forth and meet the king.[3] These psalms may be a part of a coherent unit, providing a response to Psalm 94:2–3, which questions the Lord concerning the longevity of the successes of the wicked. Consequently, the unit gives assurance that the king is coming to take care of the wicked and execute justice. It is understood further that "in general, all the relevant texts (Pss. 47; 93; 95–99) carry praise elements and may be considered hymns. But each one by itself has distinct generic features."[4] The theme of Psalm 99 is that this king is *holy*, great, and to be feared–yet he loves justice and is *personal*–he responds to the voice of his people.

Scholars have proposed the use of Psalm 99 in the celebration of the Feast of Tabernacles.[5] In addition, "the reference to Yahweh's status as 'cherubim enthroned' in Psalm 99:1 may also indicate an association with the movement of the ark, which was considered to be either the throne of God or the footstool of the enthroned king, at least in pre-exilic ceremonies."[6] Considering even more regular uses of the psalm, "allowance should be made for the use of the kingship-of-Yahweh psalms in sabbath worship... And apart from the use of these psalms in the temple, we should remember their use in pious study and prayers by family groups and by individuals."[7] Obviously, this psalm has multiple potential uses because its principles apply to numerous situations. It could have been used in a corporate context such as the Feast of Tabernacles or individually in private meditation. "The emphasis of the whole psalm is on God's gracious actions towards his people: his guidance of them through the revelation of his will, his answer to their prayer, and his provision of the means of pardon."[8] The psalm provides an enduring principle for the Lord's people, which needs to be maintained as we seek to interpret the psalm for contemporary audiences.

How Did the Author Express His Ideas?

The flow of thought in this psalm may be understood in two ways: a threefold division (vv. 1–3, 4–5, 6–9; note the repetition of "he is holy") or a twofold division (vv. 1–5, 6–9; note the repetition of "Praise the LORD"). In a twofold division, the first part focuses on holiness enthroned, while the second deals with holiness encountered.[9] In a threefold division the emphases are exaltation of the Lord in Israel (vv. 1–5), the revelation of the Lord to Israel (vv. 3, 6–7), and the exaltation of the Lord in Israel (vv. 8–9).[10]

The twofold division is preferred, since the psalmist expressed two basic ideas, each theological truth followed by a similar refrain. First, God is transcendent. He is the mighty initiator, who is over his creation. Second, God is immanent. He is the gracious relater, who is with his people. Both parts provide theological explanation for who God is. He is great, and no one compares to him. He is good and does great things for his people, acting on their behalf.

Verses 1–3 form a powerful doctrine-response refrain. First, a doctrine is exclaimed, followed by a response of praise:

DOCTRINE	RESPONSE
the LORD reigns	the nations tremble
he is enthroned	the earth shakes

the LORD is exalted over all the nations	let them praise your great and awesome name
he is holy	[at this point the people would pause and consider his greatness, his otherness, his majesty, and his grandeur]

Verses 4–5 demonstrate that the greatness of the Lord's justice can be seen in what he does for his people. The lines are a crescendo of worship, building on verses 1–3 and creating an explosion of praise among the people. The teaching is short. The psalmist quickly breaks into praise and calls the people to praise. Verses 4–5 emphasize the Lord's greatness with respect to the standard of his statutes and testimonies, which he establishes and executes in the world. He is the King, so in his strength and greatness he alone establishes justice and determines what is right. His majesty is described in sequential movement: character–he *loves* justice; sovereignty–he *establishes* equity; and authority–he *executes* justice/righteousness. In other words, he loves it; therefore, he establishes it; therefore, he executes it. The connection between the two points in this first part is the emphasis on his holiness found at the end of each. He is wholly other and above all things.

The concept of otherness is underscored by referring to God's holiness. "When the Bible calls God holy, it means primarily that God is transcendentally separate. He is so far above and beyond us that He seems almost totally foreign to us. To be holy is to be 'other,' to be different in a special way."[11] Further, "But when the word *holy* is applied to God, it does not signify one single attribute. On the contrary, God is called holy in a general sense. The word is used as a synonym for his deity. That is, the word *holy* calls attention to all that God is."[12] Nothing in God is not holy. Everything that God is is holy.

Verses 4–5, which conclude the first part of the psalm, also act as a bridge to what follows. Both transcendence and immanence emerge in these verses. Having demonstrated that the Lord is above all (vv. 1–3), in verses 6–9 the poet demonstrates that the Lord is also with humanity, in that he acts for their good, not harm. Verses 4–5 bridge these two concepts by demonstrating that this above-ness is not aloof, but rather is directed toward humanity. The Lord's greatness is *for* people. He executes justice in a manner that benefits people and that brings about equity and right living. Psalm 103:6 reminds us that this benefit is especially for the oppressed (cf. Ps. 146:7). This greatness is to be both feared (vv. 1–3) and embraced (vv. 4–5 along with vv. 6–8).

The psalmist utilizes a grammatical pattern when describing transcendence and immanence.[13] He begins with the third person, providing instruction about the Lord. This is followed with the second person, ascribing personal praise to the Lord. He concludes with the third person, calling the people to praise the Lord corporately.

PERSON	FOCUS	VERSES 1–3	VERSES 4–5	VERSES 6–9
3rd person: "the LORD"	instruction about the LORD	*the LORD reigns, the nations tremble *he sits enthroned above the winged angels, the earth shakes *the LORD is elevated in Zion *and he is exalted over all the nations	*the king is strong, he loves justice	*they prayed to the LORD and he answered them *he spoke to them
2nd person: "you"	automatic response of praise by the psalmist	*let them praise your great and awesome name	*you insure that decisions will be made fairly *you promote justice and righteousness	*you answered them *they found you to be a forgiving God *one who punished their sinful deeds
3rd person: "the LORD"	call to the congregation to offer praise to the LORD	*he is holy	*praise the LORD our God *worship before his footstool *he is holy	*praise the LORD *worship on his holy hill *for the LORD our God is holy

Within this pattern, an obvious break occurs with the insertion of "He is holy!" concluding verse 3 and the brief return to the third person in verse 4, which is in the middle of the automatic response of praise by the psalmist to the Lord. This break is one of the most powerful parts of the psalm. This anomaly occasions two observations. First, as the psalmist makes mention of the awesome and great name of the Lord, he breaks forth into a shout of "He is holy!" (there is none like this great God, praise be to his name!). His soul is overwhelmed with the greatness of the Lord, so much so that he cannot contain it. So he pauses in praise.

Second, as he continues in his automatic response of praise, he reverts to the third person to offer additional instruction. It is as if he is reminded of another powerful teaching about the Lord. This powerful king, as great as he is, does not wield his power in an abusive manner. He is not aloof. He is concerned with justice. He is concerned with his creation–those who are subject to his power. He does not exercise his power and authority arbitrarily against people, but rather he exercises them with equity. The possibility of relationship with this great and awesome God is unthinkable, yet it is possible. One can come before him on his terms. He responds to those who seek him in his greatness. The psalmist will build on this in the second refrain, so this initial reference functions as a bridge.

What Are the Interpretive Issues?

This psalm offers several important challenges to any who would correctly interpret it. Particularly important are the understanding and translation of the Hebrew conjunction *waw* at the beginning of verse 4 and and how to translate the last phrase of verse 8.[14]

Regarding the Hebrew conjunction–the Hebrew conjunction *waw* has a much broader meaning than does *and*, the nearest equivalent in English. Most Hebrew sentences begin with *waw* which is quite frequently left untranslated in English. (See the NRSV to understand the discussion that follows.)

Regarding *waw,* because the refrain "he is holy" precedes the conjunction, verse 4 seems to have no connection to the flow of the psalm. However, the proposal provided above is to understand this refrain as an "interruption," resulting from the praise that must come forth from the psalmist in the midst of the great truths he is proclaiming. It is also structurally significant since it provides the "center" of the first part of the psalm (see discussion below). The refrain is carefully inserted with the conjunction to emphasize the emotive response of praise. After this outburst, the psalmist continues with his focus on ascribing praise to the Lord.

An additional reason to maintain a unity to the flow of these verses is the lexical chiasm of verses 1–4, binding the verses together. "Chiasm" is often used in Hebrew literature, especially in poetry, to express unity of thought and to highlight the focus of the message. A "lexical chiasm" is evidenced by the choice of words. Consider the following:

> verse 1: (is) king
> verse 2: great
> verse 3: great
> verse 4: king

The choice of words creates a unity of thought and brings a focus to these verses. The king is great; great is the king. If this chiasm is indeed what the writer intended, then the verses form a unit allowing a translation of the phrase beginning in verse 4 as "and the strength," which would be a second object for the verb, "let them praise," in verse 3. It would read: "Let them praise your great and awesome name... *And* let them praise the strength of a king who loves justice." This seems to be the clearest way to explain the use of the Hebrew conjunction at the beginning of verse 4.[15] The phrase, "and the strength of a king, one who loves justice," then creates both a continuity with the initial phrase of the poem, "the LORD reigns (is king,") and an ambiguity concerning to whom/what the phrase is actually making reference. The rest of the verse clarifies this by pointing to the Lord as the intended king. The Lord is the one whose acts show he is the one loving justice. The psalm heightens the majesty of the Lord in every way.

Second, the last phrase in verse 8 is difficult to understand in light of the context of the psalm.[16] A literal reading of the verse is: "Yahweh, our God [*'elohim*] you answered them; a god [*'el*] who carries you were to them, and one who takes vengeance on their actions." The NET translates the last line as "but also one who punished their sinful deeds."[17] At first glance, this translation seemingly detracts from the overall positive emphasis of the psalm. "Dissatisfaction with the phrase arises from the fact that it is inconsistent with the context which rather expresses the indulgent and forgiving attitude of Yahweh to his people."[18] This understanding leads to translating the phrase as "and he cleanseth them from their evil deeds," based on one study of Hebrew morphology.[19] The translation seemingly brings the phrase into better agreement with the overall teaching of the psalm. Another translation proposal is, "But also an avenger, on account of the evil deeds done to them."[20] In this proposal the argument seeks to maintain a consistency with the compassion of the Lord toward his people, rather than the emphasis, which the natural reading of the text seems to bring, on discipline for their deeds. However, rather than present clever options, the simple reading of the text should be maintained. The foundational theology for this phrase is Exodus 34:6–7, which functions as a creedal statement throughout the Old Testament.[21] The psalmist is not only seeking to emphasize the compassion of the Lord, he is seeking also to emphasize that this great God is great in totality. He is "The LORD, the LORD God, compassionate and gracious, slow to anger, and abounding in loving-kindness and truth; who keeps loving-kindness for thousands, who forgives iniquity, transgression and sin; yet he will by no means leave the guilty unpunished, visiting the iniquity of fathers on the children and on the grandchildren to the third and fourth generations" (Ex. 34:6–7, NASB95). He is great, compassionate, and just–all in one! Even as "avenger of deeds," he is great and greatly to be praised. Holy is he! When one is pursuing, loving, and exalting him, then he is trustworthy even when one sins. In every way he is like no other.

What Was the Author Seeking to Communicate?

The structure of a psalm can clearly highlight the theological point the author was making. Sometimes, even counting words can assist in understanding the points of emphasis. This psalm has an uncanny middle point to each part of the psalm and to the psalm as a whole.

Point of Stanza #1	Conclusion of Stanza #1	Focal Point of Poem	Point of Stanza #2	Conclusion of Stanza #2
middle words of stanza #1	final phrase of stanza #1	middle word of poem	middle word of stanza #2	final phrase of the poem
he is holy	he is holy	he	the LORD our God	for the LORD our God is holy

The center of the first half of the psalm is found in verse 3, "he is holy." Every aspect of the first part of the psalm is directed toward this theological point. God is like no other. No other can be compared to him. He is wholly separate from every created thing. Nothing compares to his majesty and greatness. Therefore, the first part concludes with a repetition of these exact words, "he is holy."

In the conclusion to the first half of the psalm, we also have the middle word for the psalm, "he." This is clearly the subject matter of the psalm. It is all about the Lord, who he is, and how he relates to his created world.

The center of the second part of the psalm is found in verse 8, "O LORD our God." He is not only great, but he is also personal with his creation. He answers those who seek him and call out to him. He is not so far *above* that he is not involved with the ones he has created. He is not only *other*, he is also *our*. Again, each word of the second half brings emphasis to this point. He answers, forgives, and avenges. He gives direction for his created beings to follow. He is good. He is indeed "our" God.

The second part of the psalm concludes with a refrain that pulls the whole psalm together and unifies the two main points. In his transcendence…in that he is like no other…in his immanence…in that he acts on behalf of his people–this is a God worthy to be exalted and worshiped. It is a profound equation: "he"–the middle word of the psalm and the point of the whole psalm–"is holy"–the middle phrase of the psalm and the point of the first part of the psalm. The "LORD our God," the middle word and the point of the second part of the psalm, relates well with his people. In other words, he is the Lord (above all), and he is our God (very near). This theology led the psalmist to exuberant praise. Let the people praise him with heart and soul!

The emphasis of the psalm on the distance between the Lord and his creation, as well as on the close relationship between the two, is expressed in numerous ways. The Lord is an exalted King like no other, and he is a just King in that he determines what is right. The emphasis on his holiness in both parts of the psalm (vv. 3, 5, 9) sets him apart from his creation. "*Holy* is a word to emphasize the distance between God and man: not only morally, as between the pure and the polluted, but in the realm of being, between the eternal and the creaturely."[22] Additionally, "The repeated cry, *Holy is he!* forbids us to take it casually."[23] The Lord is *above* his creation.

Equally, the Lord is *with* his creation. He is a relational King, as evident with Moses, Aaron, and Samuel. Even in God being enthroned in Zion—references to the temple in Jerusalem—the idea of the Lord residing in the midst of his people is present. The tabernacle and temple, especially the Holy of Holies, was a constant reminder that the Lord dwelt with his people. The Lord is *with* his people.

The concepts of *above* and *with* leave creation with no reasonable or possible response but to praise, worship, and exalt the Creator. Humble adoration is the posture of people before the Lord.

What Is the Significance of the Psalm for Preaching and Teaching?

The application of Psalm 99 for today is clear. We worship the same Lord, who is both above and with us. He is transcendent, wholly other than any aspect of creation, but he is also immanent, very near to us and actively seeking relationship with us. He does not use his supremacy against us, but rather to act for our good. He invites us to know him and to be in relationship with him. He pours out compassion on us. We can rest in him. The only reasonable and possible response is to worship his greatness. "The majesty is undiminished, but the last word is now given to intimacy. He is holy; He is also, against all our deserving, not ashamed to be called ours. Well may we worship."[24]

This psalm yields numerous implications for preaching and teaching. As we focus on the Lord and consider his person, both his greatness and his goodness, the result in our lives should be resounding praise and worship. It is an emotional experience to worship the living God. We may fall down in utter silence, feeling overwhelmed by God's majesty and compassion. We may rise up with praises on our lips as high as the volume will go. Ultimately, this God is the focus of theological inquiry. We must seek him, and we must seek him above all things, for we were made for worship. Reading the psalm, meditating on it, studying it, preaching it, and hearing it preached should lead everyone to an experience of praise and worship that is unmatched by anything this world can offer. The flow of thought is straightforward:

1. The Lord is transcendent, an exalted King (vv. 1–5)
2. The Lord is immanent, an ever-present King (vv. 6–9).

No matter how these points are expressed, it is imperative that two distinct, yet powerful concepts be clearly articulated for our hearers. The psalm intends us to understand the simplicity and profundity of the Lord's majesty and the Lord's presence. These points must not be missed in the teaching of this psalm. Sub-points for the two main parts of the psalm include:

A. Instruction about the Lord
B. Personal response: the psalmist personally ascribes praise to the Lord
C. Corporate response: the psalmist calls to the congregation to corporately praise the Lord

The movement is from doctrinal instruction to personal response to corporate response. As one praises, he/she is to point others to the powerful truth and invite them to join in shouting forth praises to the Lord. The echoes carry throughout the world as the people of the Lord celebrate his person, both his greatness and his goodness. We also see in this psalm an example of transformation. Hearing the truth leads to an overflow of praise to the Lord and culminates in the mission of pointing others to the Lord so that they will praise. The preaching of this psalm and the worship service surrounding it should pursue a similar transformation in the congregation.

Our people must grasp that nothing compares to the Lord. He is to evoke a sense of awe as we ponder his person. Systematic theology books devoted to his person are only able to provide beginning thoughts in describing him. Through all of life our growing understanding of his person will always remain limited. For all of eternity, we will be left in amazement by his grandeur, and we will never fully understand who he is. We will have only one response: a bowed knee in his presence as we exalt his greatness. We will worship. One of the saddest depictions of humanity is offered in Genesis 6:5 (NASB95): "every intent of the thoughts of his heart was only evil continually." In heaven, these words will be replaced with "every intent of the thoughts of his heart was only worship continually." Terms like *every*, *only*, and *continually* are used to describe people engaged in worship. The psalmist seeks to make this future hope a present reality.

Equally powerful is the teaching that the Lord is *our* God. This also evokes awe in us. How can it be that such a great God can be personal to us? How can it be that one who is so *above* all things can come so near as to be *with* us and communicate and answer us when we cry out? This truth is so utterly amazing that one will never comprehend it. Coming before the Lord's table always brings a sense of wonder that he is our God. He has made relationship with him possible. As we celebrate the birth of our Savior, it leaves us breathless as we ponder the implications of the concept "God with us."

These truths must overwhelm us. We must set these truths before the people of God. The church must see and experience the greatness of the Lord. He must never be minimized or marginalized. In the words of A. W. Tozer:

> The heaviest obligation on the Christian Church today is to purify and elevate her concept of God until it is once more worthy of Him–and of her. In all her prayers and labors this should have first place. We do the greatest service to the next generations of Christians by passing on to them undimmed and undiminished that noble concept of God which we received from our Hebrew and Christian fathers of generations past.[25]

In the words of the Lord, "I am the LORD, that is my name; / I will not give My glory to another, / Nor My praise to graven images" (Isa. 42:8, NASB95). Our finiteness cannot fathom, through even the most complex reasoning, the teachings of this psalm. We are simply left to hold them in faith and to respond in worship. This alone is true worship. May God grant us a growing sense of adoration for his greatness and depth of appreciation that, even though he is God almighty, he can still be our God.

The following may be used as a responsive reading to intensify the effect of the psalm in a worship service.

Narrator/Teacher   Verses 1–2
"The LORD reigns, the peoples tremble!
He sits enthroned on the cherubim, the earth quakes!
The LORD is great in Zion; he is exalted over all the peoples!" (AT)

Worship Leader   Verse 3a
"Let them praise your great and awesome name!
Yes, let them praise! Shout forth praise!"

Congregation Verse 3b
"Holy is he! Holy is he! Holy is he! Holy is he!"

PAUSE

(Have the congregation offer up spontaneous prayers of praise for the Lord's greatness)

Narrator/Teacher Verse 4a
"And let them praise the strength of a king, one who loves justice."

Worship Leader Verse 4b, c
"You have established equity!
You have executed justice and righteousness in Jacob!
You are to be praised! Shout forth praise!"

Congregation Verse 5
"Exalt the LORD, our God!
Worship at his footstool!
Holy is he! Holy is he! Holy is he! Holy is he!"

PAUSE

(Have the congregation offer up prayers of praise for the Lord's justice)

Narrator/Teacher Verses 6–7
"Moses and Aaron were among his priests,
Samuel also was among those who called on his name.
They called to the LORD, and he answered them!
In the pillar of cloud he spoke to them!
They kept his testimonies and the statute that he gave them."

Worship Leader Verse 8
"O LORD, our God!
You answered them!
You were a forgiving God to them, and an avenger of deeds.
You are to be praised! Shout forth praise!"

Congregation Verse 9
"Exalt the LORD, our God!
Worship at his holy mountain!
For Holy is the LORD, our God! Holy is the LORD, our God!
Holy is the LORD, our God! Holy is the LORD, our God!"

PAUSE

(Have the congregation offer up prayers of praise for the Lord's graciousness)

CHAPTER 11

Psalms 103 and 104

Hymns of Redemption and Creation

Richard E. Averbeck

Visiting the Grand Canyon is an awe-inspiring experience. Who can understand its depths, length, and history? As someone commented in a classic understatement, "something happened here." It can be surreal, trying to imagine that such a simple thing as running water could carve such a chasm through stratum upon stratum of rock. Scientists could spend days explaining the details of how that is possible, but that would miss the point. It would be more exciting to ride a donkey down into the canyon, or to go whitewater rafting through the canyon, or to watch an artist paint the hues of a Grand Canyon sunset, or to listen to an orchestra performing the "Grand Canyon Suite" of Ferde Grofé. We may even wish we could write a poem or compose a song or sketch a picture to express our depths of feeling and amazement about the grandeur of the Grand Canyon.

Many of the psalms take us to a scenic overlook or to the base of a mountain and invite us to stand in awe of God's creation. Look around at the works of God's hands and try to understand his creative powers. Look up at God and try to understand his majesty. Look at the depth and length of his grace and try to understand his love. Psalms 103 and 104 stand out in the Psalter as a duet of praise, bound together by the common refrain at the beginning and end of both: "Praise the LORD, O my soul!" The two psalms call us to explore the works of the Lord and to raise our voices in worship, thanking him from the depths of our souls for the wonders of redemption and creation. "In the galaxy of the Psalter these are twin stars of the first magnitude."[1]

Whether Psalms 103 and 104 were originally composed as a pair or were even written by the same author is irrelevant. Sometime in the history of the canon, a compiler (or compilers) determined that these psalms should be read in tandem; the first emphasizing redemption, the second creation. Psalm 103 recounts the Lord's redemptive benefits and, in its final lines, puts life in eternal perspective. Yahweh the redeemer is the God of all, enthroned in the heavens, and is to be praised. Even the hosts of heaven and earth are summoned to worship. Psalm 104 picks up where 103 leaves off, expounding on God's glory in the overwhelming wonders of creation. The end of Psalm 104 once again puts life in eternal perspective, but in a jarring manner. At first the Psalmist stands in awe, praising and celebrating the God of creation; but then he turns abruptly to call for the end of the wicked. When one gazes so directly at all the goodness and glory of God, the profound abomination of wickedness becomes all the more reprehensible.

Redemption and creation are arguably the two primary themes of biblical theology. On the one hand, God's creation provides perspective on the world in which we live—the sustaining structure within which we function. On the other hand, God's gracious benefits to us as vulnerable and sinful people provide us with purposeful direction.[2] Understanding how we dwell in the nexus between these two poles of biblical truth is essential for godly living.

Why Did the Author(s) Compose These Psalms?

We have three major ancient witnesses to the Old Testament text—the ancient Hebrew called the Masoretic Text, the earliest Greek manuscripts called the Septuagint translation, and the quite fragmentary Dead Sea Scrolls found at Qumran. At many places, particularly in the case of the titles opening individual psalms and chapter numbers, these three witnesses to the original text disagree.

This is exemplified in Psalms 103 and 104. Psalm 103 has the title "by David" as a superscript in verse 1 in the Hebrew text. The earliest Greek translation—the Septuagint—and some of the Qumran Dead Sea Psalms scrolls[3] have the same title also for Psalm 104. Note that the Greek Septuagint numbers the chapters in this section of Psalms one number lower than the numbering in the Masoretic Hebrew Text. Thus Psalms 103 and 104 in the Hebrew text are 102 and 103 in the Greek Septuagint. This is true also for other psalms in Book IV: the LXX has Davidic titles for Psalms 91–99 (numbered 90–98 in the LXX) where there are no such titles in the Hebrew text. See the table below. Yet neither language nor content of either Psalm 103 or 104 proves or disproves Davidic authorship.[4]

Masoretic (Hebrew) Number	Masoretic Title	Greek translation (LXX) number	LXX title	Qumran (Dead Sea Scrolls) Hebrew title
91	No	90	Praise song to David	?
92	A psalm song for the Sabbath	91	Praise song to the day of the Sabbath	No
93	No	92	Into the day before the Sabbath day when the earth was established; song of praise to David	No; precedes 141
94	No	93	Psalm of David; for the fourth day of the week	No
95	No	94	A praise song of David	Vv missing
96	No	95	When the house was being rebuilt after the captivity. A song of David	No title
97	No	96	To David when his land was being put down	Missing
98	A Psalm	97	A psalm of David	Missing
99		98	A Psalm of David	Yes
100	A Psalm of Thanksgiving	99	A Song for Thanksgiving	A Psalm for giving thanks {?}
101	Of David a Psalm	100	Of David a Psalm	Apparently yes
102	A prayer of the poor when faint and before Yahweh complaining	101	A prayer of the poor when he is weary and pouts out a petition before Yahweh	Prayer of one afflicted
103	To David	102	To David	yes; followed in different scrolls by 104, 109, 112
104	None	103	None	Yes, has of David;

2 scrolls after 118; one scroll after 147.				
105	None	104	None	After 147; no title
106		105		Before 107; v1 missing

The original author of either or both of these psalms, therefore, could be David; but this is by no means certain and has no discernible effect on their meaning, in any case. The author does not explicitly present himself as royalty or, for that matter, anyone of position. As noted earlier, whoever he may be, these songs incite the author himself to praise the Lord for what he has done in redemption and creation, respectively. The last verses of Psalm 103 include a plural exhortation to all creation that it should praise the Lord (vv. 20–22b), but the song then returns to the singular self-incitement in the final refrain (v. 22c). Psalm 104 repeats the self-incitement in its first line and in the second line from the last (vv. 1a, 35c), but then appends the well-know plural imperative "Praise the LORD!" (Hebrew, *halleluyah*; v. 35d). The LXX, however, attaches this final word to the beginning of Psalm 105. If we follow the LXX at this juncture, then both Psalms 105 and 106 would have *halleluyah* as their refrain at their beginning and ending.[5] Moreover, removing it from the end of Psalm 104 would highlight further the tandem self-incitement framework of Psalms 103 and 104.

The frame of these two psalms, therefore, presents them as individual hymns of thanksgiving and praise, in which the main purpose of the author was to incite his own soul to praise the Lord for all his redemptive and creative works.[6] The imperative verb translated as "praise" used in the surrounding self-incitement refrain, however, is not the well-known *halleluyah* ("praise the LORD"; root verb *hll* plus the shortened form of the divine name *Yah[weh]*), but the one normally translated "bless" (root word *brk*). Some highly regarded English versions retain that rendering, "Bless the LORD, O my soul" (see, e.g., NASB and NRSV). But what does it mean to "bless" the Lord, and how does this relate to "praise" in the more common expression? Some commentators ignore the difference and simply treat them as variants. Although the semantic fields of these terms may overlap, it is unlikely that they do so totally.

According to one of the major Hebrew lexicons, to "bless" means "to endue someone with special power," and for us to bless God means "to declare God to be the source of the special power."[7] The first occurrences of the verb "bless" in the Bible are when the Lord blessed the sea creatures and the birds in Genesis 1:22, and the man and woman in verse 28. In doing so God pronounced that the animals should multiply and that the man and woman should multiply and take dominion over the animals as God's image and likeness in the world, the crown of his creation. When God blesses he pronounces good things (cf. Gen. 12:3a, "I will bless those who bless you"; for Israel as God's covenant people, see Deut. 28:1–14). The opposite parallel is when God curses and so pronounces bad things (cf. Gen. 12:3b [NET]), "but the one who treats you lightly I must curse"; for Israel, see Deut. 28:15–68).

The approximately twenty-five Old Testament passages referring to people blessing the Lord indicate that to bless the Lord means to praise him with a special focus on God's powerful acts and/or wondrous provisions in our lives. The first instance of this occurs when the Lord leads Abraham's servant directly to Rebekah, Isaac's future wife, without the servant even having to search for her. He blessed the Lord (Gen. 24:48). Psalm 34:1–2 uses the two praise verbs together: "I will praise ['bless' *brk*] the LORD at all times;... I [lit. 'my soul'] will boast ['praise' *hll*] in the LORD..." In the next verse we read, "Let's praise [lit. 'raise high, exalt'; Hebrew *rmm*] his name together!" To bless his "name" is to extol him for his reputation gained through his deeds. It is to boast in what the Lord has done. Psalms 103 and 104 present one of the best examples of blessing the Lord in the Bible. They focus intensely on God's provision and power in redemption and in creation. They make much of the Lord's reputation, his holy name (Ps. 103:1b; cf. 96:2; 104:4c; see also the close association between the name of the Lord and the verb to bless in Pss. 63:4; 145:2).

We are called to be worshipers first of all and above all. Blessing is not only the most suitable response to our God, but it is also the most spiritually transforming activity we can engage in. Of course genuine worship of God is in spirit and truth (Jn. 4:23–24).[8] These two psalms emphasize worship of the Lord that gushes forth from within (Ps. 103:1b; i.e., worship "in spirit"), extolling God for all our Lord's overflowing redemptive and creative works (i.e., worship "in truth"). Worship puts everything else we do in proper perspective, whether in our personal life, our relationships in the community of faith, or our engagement with the world. These two psalms are individual praise hymns meant to be sung not only by the individual alone, but also by individuals as they make up the congregation.

Psalm 103 transitions from the purely individual address ("my soul") to plural but still first person ("all the oppressed," v. 6; "the Israelites," v. 7; "our sins," v. 10; etc.), then to plural "praise" imperatives addressed to the heavenly hosts and all of God's works (vv. 20–22b). In the end, however, it comes back to self-address to the psalmist's soul, "Praise the LORD, O my soul!" (v. 22c). Psalm 104 focuses the same personal soul praise on all God's works of creation, including the heavenly hosts. As it stands in the Hebrew text, this psalm never breaks with personal self-address, but has "my soul" reflecting on the wonders of the whole creation until the final plural exhortation to all at the very end, "praise the LORD!" (v. 35d). I, you, we, and all of creation with us can engage in the singing, praying, contemplating, and living out of the effects of what is so eloquently expressed here.[9] This is why the author wrote these Psalms.

How Did the Author Express His Ideas in Psalm 103?

As noted above, Psalm 103 begins with imperatives addressed to the author's own soul (the Hebrew word is feminine, matching the feminine imperative verbs translated "bless" and "do not forget"; vv. 1–2). The term "soul" is notoriously difficult to translate, but in this context it is defined by the parallel expression "all that is within me" (v. 1a; literally, "my inward parts"). Thus the psalm calls for the kind of worship that bursts forth from within our inner person as we are overcome by the Lord's kindness.

The end of the second verse comes directly to the point: "Do not forget all his kind deeds!" Verses 3–5a then list five "kind deeds" the Lord has performed in the author's life (or at least made available to him). For these the psalmist exhorts his soul (vv. 1–2) to extol the Lord (vv. 3–5a, a series of five parallel participles): the Lord is the one who forgives sins, heals diseases, delivers from death, adorns with loyalty and compassion, and satisfies with good things. The result of all this is that his soul's "youth is renewed like an eagle's" (v. 5b). The latter recalls the well-known exhortation in Isaiah 40:27–31 about the Lord who never wearies, so if we are willing to wait for the Lord's help we will find renewed strength, we will rise up as if we have eagles' wings. Such people of faith "run without growing weary, they walk without getting tired" (v. 31).

The first kind deed listed in verses 3–5 becomes the main topic in the remainder of the psalm: the Lord forgives sins.[10] The Lord deals in righteousness; he hands out justice to the oppressed (v. 6). The greatest example of God's care for the oppressed in Old Testament biblical history is that which took place when he "revealed his faithful acts to Moses, his deeds to the Israelites" (v. 7). The Lord delivered them from slavery. From here one expects the praise to take off in the direction of the exodus, but the psalmist turns unexpectedly to something that happened after the exodus had been accomplished, after they had already arrived at Sinai. Yes, God delivered them from the oppression in Egypt, but the point that gets developed further is that he also maintained his commitment to them even in their rebellion during the golden calf incident (Ex. 32–34).

This is the point of the quotation from Exodus 34:6 in Psalm 103:8, "The LORD is compassionate and merciful; he is patient and demonstrates great loyal love." These are the qualities that allowed the Lord to forgive and renew his covenant commitment to the Israelites in spite of their not showing covenant loyalty to him in making and worshiping the golden calf in Exodus 32. Moses prayed, and the Lord relented from destroying them totally at Sinai (Ex. 32:9–14). Moses was angry with Aaron and the people (vv. 15–29), but still Moses interceded for the people (32:30–35). The Lord insisted on bringing serious consequences on the rebellious people in spite of Moses' intercession. The Lord even threatened to send them on their way without his personal presence going with them, lest he break out and destroy them all in some other instance along the way (33:1–6). Moses argued successfully for the Lord's ongoing presence (vv. 12–23), and the Lord renewed the covenant on that basis (Ex. 34), even issuing orders for a new set of tablets (vv. 1, 4, 27–29).

One of the main features of this restoration of the covenant was the Lord's proclamation of his own name (= his divine character) in terms that met the needs of the occasion:

> The LORD passed by before him and proclaimed: "The LORD, the LORD, the compassionate and gracious God, slow to anger, and abounding in loyal love and faithfulness, keeping loyal love for thousands, forgiving iniquity and transgression and sin. But he by no means leaves the guilty unpunished, responding to the transgression of fathers by dealing with children and children's children, to the third and fourth generation." (Ex. 34:6–7)

This is God's character from God's lips. Psalm 103 calls us to bow in worship before God precisely because of these elements of his character, as Moses did immediately after hearing this proclamation (Ex. 34:8–9). The Lord proclaimed his own divine name in a way that based his remaking of the covenant with Israel in his own loyalty to them in spite of their rebellion, even while calling them to show loyalty to him in return by worshiping the Lord alone (see vv. 10–26).

We cannot unpack all of Exodus 34 here, or even all of verses 6–7 cited above. The important point for understanding Psalm 103 is that the psalmist cites the Lord's proclamation in Exodus 34:6 nearly word for word, except for the last two words ("and faithfulness," lit. "truth"), which were probably left off to keep this line in poetic balance with those surrounding it. In fact, this line is quoted numerous times throughout the

Old Testament, especially in contexts where the Lord's character as a forgiving God is the main point of concern (see most explicitly, e.g., Num. 14:18; Neh. 9:17; Pss. 86:15; 145:8; Joel 2:13; Jon. 4:2). First John 1:9 is one of the passages that Christians would turn to if asked about God's forgiveness, "…if we confess our sins, he is faithful and righteous, forgiving us our sins and cleansing us from all unrighteousness." Essentially, Exodus 34:6 is the Old Testament 1 John 1:9. This is the passage that most naturally came to mind when the writers and people of the Old Testament needed to bank on God's willingness to forgive.

The remainder of this psalm develops the implications of the quotation in light of forgiveness being one of the most important kind deeds of the Lord toward his people (vv. 2b–3a, see above). The overall structure of the psalm is essentially chiastic:

A–Bless the LORD O my soul, vv. 1–2

    B–Forgiveness and fear of the LORD, vv. 3–13

        C–Forgiveness and dust, v. 14

    B'–Faithfulness and fear of the LORD, vv. 15–19

A'–Bless the LORD all his works, vv. 20–22

Verses 9–10 repeat the particle "not" (Hebrew *lo*) four times, at the beginning of each clause (see English "does not" in each half-line of the English translation). Verse 9 emphasizes that the Lord does not keep grudges against us for our sins. Verse 10 says that, because of his forgiving character, he is not willing to deal with us according to our sinfulness. He just does not handle us that way. According to the last half-line of verse 10, "he does not repay us as our misdeeds deserve." The verb in the expression "does not repay us" is the root verb for the last word in verse 2, rendered "(kind) deeds" in the NET translation. The word actually refers to the way God deals with his people. He deals with us kindly, not according to what we deserve. The point is that, like the ancient Israelites (see, e.g., in the golden calf incident), we do not deserve good things from the Lord, but because of his personal character the Lord grants them anyway.

Why does he not give us what we deserve? Is it just a matter of his character (v. 8), or does it have something to do with us too? The next three verses explain further (vv. 11–13). You can see the structure in the English text based on "for" (= "because") at the beginning of verse 11 followed by three "as" clauses beginning verses 11–13, and "so" in the second lines of each. These are classic comparisons: as high as the skies are above the earth, as far as the east is from the west, and as a father has compassion on his children. All of them illustrate how good our God is to us: his love towers over us like the skies, he removes our guilt from us, and he has compassion on "his faithful followers" (vv. 11 and 13).

The phrase "his faithful followers" in the NET Bible is literally, "those who fear him." Here we can learn what to fear God means. Fearing God is based in the image of a good father and a rebellious child. The rebel has a kind of fear toward a compassionate father (v. 13a). It is real fear, but it is born out of knowing that a loving father simply does not allow his child to go in dangerously wrong directions in life without serious consequences. God disciplines us because he loves us (Prov. 3:11–12 and Heb. 12:4–11). He will not let us go our own rebellious way. Knowing elicits a certain fear of him. Such is a healthy fear that a child needs because it actually protects her or him from self-destruction. The same expression occurs later in the Psalm where the point is that the Lord is eternally faithful to "his faithful followers" (v. 17), who are defined further in verse 18 as those "who keep his covenant, who are careful to obey his commands." The father and child metaphor is not used as in verse 13, but the effect is the same. One who fears the Lord is careful to obey him faithfully. After all, our Lord "has established his throne in heaven; his kingdom extends over everything" (v. 19). He is no one to mess with!

The pivot point of Psalm 103 is verse 14, "For [or 'because'] he knows what we are made of [lit. 'knows our shape']; he realizes we are made of clay." On the one hand, this verse connects back to the previous verses to tell us why God is so gracious and forgiving to those who fear him (see the discussion of vv. 10–13 above). Our divine father himself (in v. 14 the pronoun "himself" is actually expressed in Hebrew) truly does know how we are shaped and what we are made of–clay. After all, he made us. God knows that we are just piles of dust, just lumps of clay that he, the universal potter, made into vessels (cf. Job 10:8–9; 33:6; 2 Cor. 4:7; and the same image used in a different way in Job 4:19–20; Jer. 18:1–12; Lam. 4:2; Rom. 9:19–23; 2 Tim. 2:20–21). The terminology here recalls Genesis 2:7a, "The LORD God formed [the verbal form for 'shape' in Ps. 103:14] the man from the soil of the ground…" ('soil' is translated from the same word as 'clay' in Ps. 103:14). This is the shape and substance out of which we are made. It is only the "breath of life" (Hebrew *neshamat hayyim*) from God himself that makes us "living being[s]" (Gen. 2:7b). Since our life derives from God, it belongs to God, whether we know it or not and whether we like it or not.

Another side of verse 14 reaches forward to the following verses. Genesis puts it this way: "…you are dust, and to dust you will return" (Gen. 3:19, an obvious reference back to 2:7). Psalm 103:15–16 makes the same point, but with the image of grass and flowers (cf. also Isa. 40:6–8 and the many other parallels). We are just like the grass that springs up and the flower that blooms. They last for only a brief time. When the hot summer wind blows through, they disappear. They are gone, and the place where they were provides no evidence they were there. The particular term translated as "person" at the beginning of verse 15 may imply the feeble constitution of humankind (cf. the verb form used in 2 Sam. 12:15 for when a child "became ill").

The poet contrasts feeble man with the Lord. The flower-frail human stands over against eternal God. We know God endures forever through his actions. As the psalmist points out in verse 17, God "continually [lit. 'from everlasting to everlasting,' or 'from age to age'] shows loyal love to his faithful followers" (lit. 'those who fear him'; i.e., those who are faithfully obedient to the covenant, v. 18). Divine love and righteousness is not limited to one generation. Such love continues into the lives of "their descendants" (lit. children's children or grandchildren, v. 17). The lives of the Lord's faithful followers are only temporary, but he is permanent. His commitment goes beyond our time to his faithful followers and their progeny in the following generations. We need to take this generational feature of the Old Testament seriously. The expression in Exodus 34:7a (cited above), "keeping loyal love for thousands, forgiving iniquity and transgression" probably refers not to numbers of people but to numbers of generations. It reflects on the second commandment, in which God is said to be a jealous God, "responding to the transgression of fathers by dealing with children to the third and fourth generations of those who reject me, and showing covenant faithfulness to a thousand generations of those who love me and keep my commandments" (Exod. 20:5-6, NET) (cf. Deut. 5:9-10 and esp. 7:9-10). According to the author, sin has generational effects to the third and fourth generations, but being a faithful follower of God draws on the Lord's grace for a thousand generations. We do not live just unto ourselves, one way or the other.

How Did the Author Express His Ideas in Psalm 104?

Limitations of space prohibit me from doing as much with Psalm 104 as I would like, but it is important to treat Psalms 103 and 104 together. As noted earlier, Psalms 103 and 104 are framed and bound together by the self-exhortation "Praise the LORD, O my soul!" Moreover, Psalm 104 picks up where Psalm 103 leaves off, expanding on God's works in the creation introduced in the final verses of Psalm 103. A second person address to the Lord, confessing how great and radiant God is (Ps. 104:1bc), leads immediately to a full-fledged extended focus on the Lord's works in creating and sustaining the world, following virtually the same basic order as Genesis 1 (see more on this below). At the end, the individual praise hymn nature of the psalm comes emphatically into focus once again: "I will..." (or "Let me..."; twice in v. 33), "my thoughts" (v. 34a), and "I will rejoice" (v. 34b; literally, "I myself will rejoice," an emphatic "I"). The psalm then repeats "Praise (*brk*) the LORD, O my soul!" (v. 35c).

The plural imperative *halleluyah* at the very end of Psalm 104 matches the plural imperatives near the end of Psalm 103. At the end of Psalm 104 the plural suggests a turn to the listeners (joint worshipers), calling them to praise the Lord along with the author. One could perhaps argue that this plural does triple service as a final conclusion to Psalms 103–104 combined, a conclusion to Psalm 104, as well as an introduction to Psalm 105 (see *halleluyah* at the end of Ps. 105 and surrounding Ps. 106). In the latter instance, it would bind Psalm (103–)104 to the historical Psalms 105–106, which conclude this fourth book of Psalms (Pss. 90–106).[11]

The psalmist is praising the Lord for his creation based on meditation over the fundamental cosmological structure of all things. The similarity to Genesis 1 is uncanny. They both have poetic features, but Genesis 1 is more of a highly structured narrative account, whereas Psalm 104 is more definitively poetic. Genesis 1 is a cosmology as much as a cosmogony, and so is Psalm 104. The body of the psalm follows the sequence of the six days in Genesis 1 in general, but in an extended overlapping manner. Essentially, the psalm body here consists of "thoughts"[12] (v. 34, perhaps a meditation or musing) about the Lord God's creation of the universe. As it relates to Genesis 1, Psalm 104 breaks down in the following way:

Day 1–vv. 1b–2a, light

Day 2–vv. 2b–4, the sky with its clouds, winds, and lightning

Day 3–vv. 5–18, dry land and vegetation

Day 3 expands into three parts:

> 1– The recession of the waters so dry land appears, vv. 5–9 (cf. the first "God said" in Gen. 1:9–10)
>
> 2– The flowing springs and streams that water the *animals*, vv. 10–13
>
> 3– The growth of vegetation as food and habitat for the *animals*, and as crops for *humans* to cultivate their own food, vv. 14–18 (cf. the second "God said" in Gen. 1:11–13)

Day 4–vv. 19–23, moon and sun, with *Day 4* expanding into two parts:

> 1– The night for *animals* to prowl, vv. 19–21
>
> 2– The day for *humans* to do their work, vv. 22–23

Day 5–vv. 24–26, sea and sea animals, including leviathan (NET "whale")[13]

Day 6–vv. 27–30, land animals and humankind

Day six does not appear in the form we find it in Genesis 1:24–28. Instead of the creation of land animals and humankind on day six, land animals and human beings are fit into the larger framework of the cosmos (see the outline above). Humans cultivate the crops of day three (vv. 14b–15) during the daylight hours of day four (vv. 22–23). We fit into the physical world with the plants and animals. The focus of attention through verse 26 is the wonders of the created environment within which we live, our "nest" so to speak. God has graciously and wondrously provided a nurturing environment within which we live and grow and make our living. One of the main differences between Genesis 1 and Psalm 104 is that in the former people were created to have dominion over nature (Gen. 1:26, 28), whereas in Psalm 104 the emphasis is on how people are integrated into creation as part of it.[14]

None of the problems of creation in its current condition appear until verses 29–30, and finally verse 35. Verses 27–30 form a unit that corresponds to the sixth day in Genesis 1, but in a manner that recalls Genesis 2:7 and 3:19 (cf. the remarks on Ps. 103:14 above), not the account in Genesis 1. All creatures wait (third person plural "they") for the Lord (second person singular "you") to provide their food when they need it (vv. 27–28). Death comes if the Lord turns away from them and takes away their life's breath (Hebrew *ruah*) so that they return to the dust (v. 29; cf. Gen. 3:19). Life is created when the Lord sends forth his life-giving breath (again, *ruah*) and renews or replenishes the surface of the ground (*adamah*) (v. 30). According to Genesis 2:7, the Lord formed the man from the soil (lit. "dust") of the ground (*adamah*) and then breathed into the man's nostrils the breath of life (Hebrew *nišmat ḥayyim*).[15]

The final unit of Psalm 104 (31–35b) comes before the call to praise in 35c and d. This final unit shifts to a different kind of grammar–from declarative praise to exhortation. It begins with a call: "May the splendor of the LORD endure! May the LORD find pleasure in the living things he has made!" (v. 31). The splendor here is the shining light of the Lord's "glory" (Hebrew *kavod*; cf. Ex. 13:21–22; 14:19–20; 24:15–18; 40:34–38; Lev. 9:23; 16:2; Num. 9:15–23; 10:11, 34; 1 Kings 8:10–11, etc., and note Ps. 105:39). It corresponds to the beginning of the psalm, where the creation sequence starts with light: "You are robed in splendor and majesty. He covers himself with light as if it were a garment" (Ps. 104:1c–2a; day one in Genesis 1). This is the beginning of all the works in which the Lord should find pleasure (v. 31b). In his glory, the Lord appeared at Sinai, the mountain of God, such that it shook and smoldered (v. 32; cf. Ex. 19:18, etc.).

The final verses return to the self-exhortation to praise the Lord in song, but with one element that stands out in contrast to the psalm as a whole: "May sinners disappear from the earth, and the wicked vanish!" (v. 35a and b). In the light of the glory of the wondrous creative deeds of the Lord celebrated in this psalm, sin and wickedness strike the psalmist as abominations that desperately need to be eradicated from the picture. Seeing God for who he really is and what he is truly like enables us to perceive the stark horror of sinfulness in the human heart and life, including our own (see, e.g., Isa. 6).

What Are the Important Interpretive Issues?

As discussed above, Psalm 104 clearly manifests a close relationship to Genesis 1, but is also distinctive and includes allusions to Genesis 2–3. This suggests that neither depends directly on the other, but that Genesis 1 and Psalm 104 independently present some of the same features of biblical cosmogony and/or cosmology. Of course, neither was written with our modern scientific perspective in view. The biblical view common to both Genesis 1 and Psalm 104 has similarities to the ancient Near Eastern conceptions of cosmogony and cosmology, but also features substantial differences.[16]

This brings us to one particular feature of Psalm 104 that requires further attention: the similarities between Psalm 104 and the Egyptian Great Hymn to the Aten.[17] This hymn articulates the short-lived doctrine of one god in Egypt during the days of Amenhotep IV (Akhenaten; fourteenth century B.C.E.). Compare and contrast, for example, Psalm 104 with the following excerpts from the hymn (in sequence, but not including all lines):

When you set in western lightland, (Ps. 104:20–21)
Earth is in darkness as if in death;
One sleeps in chambers, heads covered,
One eye does not see another.
       ...
Every lion comes from its den,
All the serpents bite;
Darkness hovers, earth is silent,
As their maker rests in lightland.
       ...
Earth brightens when you dawn in lightland, (Ps. 104:22)
When you shine as Aten of daytime;
As you dispel the dark,
As you cast your rays,
       ...
The entire land sets out to work, (Ps. 104:23)
All beasts browse on their herbs,

Trees, herbs are sprouting,
Birds fly from their nests,
Their wings greeting your *ka*. (Ps. 104:12)
All flocks frisk on their feet,
All that fly up and alight,
They live when you dawn for them.
Ships fare north, fare south as well, (Ps. 104:25–26)
Roads lie open when you rise;
The fish in the river dart before you,
Your rays are the midst of the sea.

...

How many are your deeds? (Ps. 104:24)

...

Good comparisons can certainly be made here. Note especially the similar sequence. The contrasts stand out just as much, perhaps even more. It is probably best to see this as primarily common reflections on patterns in nature that could be observed by people in various places in the ancient Near East. Literary traditions held in common throughout the ancient Near East may peak through. We know that the entire ancient Near East was connected through trade and various other means from the early days, even before Abraham.

Another interpretive issue is the canonical arrangement of Psalms 101–106, the last unit in Book IV of the Psalter (Pss. 90–106). The previous unit seems to end with Psalm 100.[18] Essentially, Psalms 101 and 102 reflect on the personal life of the psalmist(s)—a proclamation of personal integrity and a "cry for help" lament, respectively. Many of the motifs in these two psalms surface also in Psalm 103 and, to a lesser degree, in Psalm 104. Psalm 101 refers to "loyalty and justice" as the introduction to the author's personal integrity before the Lord (cf. 103:6–8) and ends with destruction of the wicked (cf. 104:35). Among other things, Psalm 102 twice uses the motif of the author's life withering like grass (vv. 4 and 11; cf. 103:15–16) and holds it in contrast to the Lord's permanence (vv. 12 and 23–28; cf. 103:17–18). It also refers to the "dust" of Zion and the Lord's care for her (v. 14; cf. 103:14), the continuing concern that the Lord has for the descendants of his followers (vv. 18 and 28; cf. 103:17–18), and the Lord as the creator and ruler of all (v. 25; cf. 103:19–22 leading into Ps. 104).

As discussed earlier, Psalms 103 and 104 are in tandem. Psalm 104 picks up from the end of Psalm 103 to expand on the Lord as the creator and ruler of all. So we move progressively from the Lord's acts in redemption in Psalm 103 to his acts in creation in Psalm 104. Psalms 105 and 106 are songs of historical narrative. Psalm 105 picks up from creation in Psalm 104 to expound on the Lord's gracious acts of covenantal loyalty in the history of Israel from the patriarchs (vv. 1–24) to the days and ministries of Moses and Aaron (vv. 25–43) and finally the conquest of the land (vv. 44–45). Psalm 106 is a confession of the sin of the covenant people from the exodus from Egypt through the period of the judges and eventually to the exile in Babylon, ending with a call to the Lord to remember his covenant commitment to his people according to his loyal love, so that they might return from exile to thank and praise him (vv. 44–48). Psalms 103 and 104 are the praise songs that make the shift from the personal life songs of Psalms 101–102 to the historical songs of Psalms 105–106.

What Is the Significance of These Psalms for Preaching and Teaching?

Worship is about seeing God: who he is and what he has done. It is about seeing God while looking life squarely in the face. It is not a means of escape from life, but a presentation of our life to God, whether personal or communal. When we present our life to him in worship, we actually have a chance to put life in perspective—divine perspective. Like Isaiah in the throne room of heaven, when we truly see him we will most certainly get impressed (Isa. 6). The apostle Paul writes about the eyes of the heart being enlightened (Eph. 1:18). We see with the heart too, not just with our eyes. Psalms 103 and 104 are about getting the heart, the soul, engaged in seeing God in such a way that everything else looks different too.

One of our main problems is that all too often we are impressed with the wrong things. The deepest kind of transformation takes place in us when we become so deeply impressed with God and his purposes in and through our lives that we are motivated to engage in the process of change and growth. When what we are impressed with changes, what we desire changes with it. The self-incitement of Psalms 103 and 104 is all about this very thing. When it comes down to reality, we are just piles of dust (Ps. 103:14). Sitting here writing this essay, I am just one pile of dust hoping to write something helpful for other piles of dust. As Martin Luther put it in his last written words: "We are beggars. That is true."[19] We are valuable to God nevertheless. Yes, we are merely dust, but God has made us in his image and likeness, and he is the kind of God who makes all things well (Ps. 104). Moreover, he takes care of what he makes (Pss. 103 and 104 combined).

Genesis 1–11 is in the Bible to level the ground of our human experience. It introduces who we are, how we got here, why we are here, and how we have gotten ourselves into such a mess. The rest of the Bible continues to develop this theme, but beginning with Genesis 12 it also narrates what God has done in history to provide a way of redemption and restoration right in the middle of the mess. Creation and corruption are like the two poles (positive and negative) of a coil producing more energy with increased circulation around the poles. The more intense the engagement between creation/corruption and redemption/restoration, the more energy is created for biblical theology and for life and godliness. Psalms 103 and 104, rightly understood and taken together, engage the two poles directly and intensely. Preaching and teaching them in tandem transmits a jolt of spiritually transforming energy straight from the pulpit or the lectern to the lives of those who have ears to hear.

Including the connection between these two psalms in preaching would be important, but they are best preached in two sermons, not one. They simply provide too much spiritual food for one sermon, and the two related topics of creation/corruption and redemption/restoration are both certainly worthy of serious treatment. The basic structure of both psalms is outlined above. As is well-known, one of the most important elements in preaching poetry in general, and the psalms in particular, is the unpacking of the pervasive figures of speech. In a sense, the psalms contain their own built-in sermon illustrations. The teacher or preacher can exercise all his or her creative capacities in painting the word pictures that are so prominent.

For example, one should make much of such expressions as: "your youth is renewed like an eagle's" (Ps. 103:5). Although some have suggested that this image refers to the molting that leads to an eagle growing new feathers, it more likely recalls the strength and majesty of the eagle as an image for the strength that the Lord provides through all his great benefits to us, which are listed in verses 3–5. Other images in Psalm 103 refer to the extremities of God's forgiveness toward those who take him seriously: "as the skies are high above the earth" (v. 11), "as far as the eastern horizon is from the west" (v. 12), and "as a father has compassion on his children" (v. 13). Our mortality is opposed to God's immortality, which retains importance for us even now. "A person's life is like grass. Like a flower in the field it flourishes, but when the hot wind blows by, it disappears, and one can no longer even spot the place where it once grew" (vv. 15–16). Compare this with "...the Lord continually shows loyal love to his faithful followers, and is faithful to their descendants" (v. 17). Even after we are gone from the earth, God stays faithful to us through our descendants. We are not permanent, but God is. So is his faithfulness to those who are faithful to him. We can bank on it eternally!

Psalm 104 likewise makes extensive use of figures of speech, but here they are all about God and his creation work. God's robe is light itself.

This image shows up at the beginning and end of this psalm: "You are robed in splendor and majesty. He covers himself with light as if it were a garment" (vv. 1c–2a), and, "May the splendor of the LORD endure!" (v. 31a). Nothing shines as bright as God. He truly is the light of our lives (cf. Jn. 1:1–14). As for his creative work: "He stretches out the skies like a tent curtain, and lays the beams of the upper rooms of his palace on the rain clouds. He makes the clouds his chariot, and travels along on the wings of the wind. He makes the winds his messengers, and the flaming fire his attendant. He established the earth on its foundations… The watery deep covered it like a garment" (vv. 2b–6a). God has made a tent for his creatures to dwell in—creation—and he occupies himself with it. He cares for it and the creatures he has placed here, including humankind. All creatures depend on his provision for sustenance and even for their very life breath (vv. 27–30). We are all here to praise him. That is our main purpose (vv. 31–35; cf. Ps. 103:19–22). The most important thing we can become is better worshipers! Praise the Lord, O my soul; Praise the Lord.

Book Five: Psalms 107–150

Book V of the Psalter is a grand climax to the episodic experiences of the Israelites. It celebrates the renewal of life with God in control. The story of the Israelites had come full circle. References to David, so common in Books I and II, had nearly dropped out of the psalms, but now he has reappeared. His dynasty would be restored as the people returned to the land of promise and to a life of faithfulness.

Although the heart of Book V is a torah psalm (Psalm 119) that highlights the central place the Torah would once again hold in the lives of God's people, praise psalms abound. Still following close behind are the individual and community lament psalms. (See "Classification of the Psalms by Category" at the end of the book.) Book V is the largest book of the Psalter, with forty-four chapters or psalms and yet has only one short doxological formula: "Let everything that has breath praise the LORD! Praise the LORD!" (Ps 150:6). Some people speak of the entire Psalm 150 as the closing doxology for Book V and for the entire Psalter.

Five psalms are featured in this chapter: a royal psalm, Psalm 110; a thanksgiving psalm, Psalm 116; a lament psalm, Psalm 130; and two praise psalms, Psalms 135 and 148.

CHAPTER 12

Psalm 110

A Royal Psalm of Assurance in the Midst of Change

Herbert W. Bateman IV

On a muggy day in August 1983, muggy even at ten in the morning, we were ready to leave Pennsauken, New Jersey, for Dallas, Texas, to study at Dallas Theological Seminary. We had spent the previous day loading our Ryder rental truck with all our earthly belongings—a sofa, an arm chair, and a coffee table I had built; a kitchen table with chairs and a half dozen boxes filled with dishes, pots, pans, etc.; an old oak desk I had refinished, three book cases, and twelve boxes of books. Naturally, our load included lamps, suitcases and boxes with our clothing, and five toolboxes filled with tools I had used for remodeling bathrooms and kitchens. Yet it did not take long to load everything. (How could it when you have two sets of parents and one set of grandparents helping?) We even took time to visit with some friends, who swung by for a final farewell.

After a good night's sleep and a good breakfast with the family, with our 1981 Ford Escort mounted securely on a tow dolly, we hugged and kissed our parents and grandparents, got into our truck, and drove off. I will never forget the framed reflection I saw in the side mirrors as we drove away: our family was standing in the middle of the street waving at us until we turned the corner and were out of sight. They knew that life was going to be different for them, as it would to be for us.

That day marked a huge transition in my life and in the life of my wife, Cindy. As we left our family standing in the middle of Oak Terrace, we naturally shared anxious feelings of the unknown. Neither of us had been to Texas. Neither of us had friends or family in Texas. Neither of us knew what studying at Dallas Seminary would be like. Still, exciting feelings of anticipation rose within us as we began to write a new chapter in our life as a young married couple, a chapter we spent twelve unexpected years writing while living in Dallas.

Life is full of transitions. Some are planned, and others surprise us. Some are welcomed, and others dreaded. Nevertheless, they happen. Children grow up and leave home. Adults make career changes. Families relocate. People graduate from degree programs, lose their jobs, find new ones, retire, and die. Psalm 110 is a psalm that can affirm us during those seemingly unsettling transitions of life. To understand how Psalm 110 can be a psalm of assurance and confidence during life's changes, we must first wrestle with why the psalm was written.

Why Did the Author Compose the Psalm?

Psalm 110 is a royal song, written to encourage both a group of people and a newly appointed Davidic king. More specifically, this royal psalm contains a public endorsement of a Davidic heir's divine appointment as Israel's new king–priest (1:1–2), and several promises for the newly appointed king concerning his military potential to dominate his enemies (1:3–7). Yet, to answer our question as to why the psalm was composed, we need to ask, who wrote the psalm? How do we know the psalm is a divine appointment to kingship? For whom was the psalm written, if not *only* for Jesus? (See the discussion below.) What might have been the social and historical circumstances behind the writing of Psalm 110?

The Psalmist

Despite the apparent absence of the author's name, the heading "a psalm of David" (*l'dawid*), coupled with New Testament claims (Mk. 12:36; Acts 2:34, 4:25), would appear to indicate authorship.[1] Thus, it seems reasonable to suggest that David authored the psalm. If so, how does David announce that a divine appointment of a king has taken place?

The Divine Appointment

David opens Psalm 110 with a decree from Yahweh ("the LORD says" NRSV), and proceeds to direct this divine decree to his lord ("to my) lord"). The Hebrew form for the psalmist's "lord," *'adon*, is obviously different from that used of the LORD God, *yhwh*. The two terms should not be blurred as though they were two divine references, because *'adon* is never a divine reference for Yahweh *anywhere* in the Old Testament.[2] David addresses his Lord (*'adon*) with a decree from the LORD (*yhwh*). David's "lord," then, would be a king to whom even David is subordinate because Yahweh has appointed a new king. Who then, might that be?

The Recipient

David's subordination to another king should not surprise us. The anointed king David often refers to king Saul as either "my lord" (1 Sam. 24:6, 8, 10; 26:18) or "my lord the king" (1 Sam. 24:8; 26:17, 19), and Achish of the Philistines as "my lord the king" (1 Sam. 29:8). However, neither of these men are candidates for being the recipient of Psalm 110–certainly not Achish, because he was a non-Israelite; and certainly not Saul because Zion, the city of David (Ps. 110: 2), had not been captured yet (2 Sam. 5:6–10). Furthermore, the promise of an heir and royal line was directed to David long after Saul's death (2 Sam. 7). The only other earthly king to whom David may have referred to as "my lord" is Solomon. In fact, Solomon is said *to sit on the* LORD's *throne* as a result of his coronation in 971 B.C.E. (1 Chr. 29:23).[3] So then, Psalm 110:1, 4 need not be *limited* to Jesus, but rather these verses could speak of a historical Davidic king.

Naturally, kings like David and Solomon exercised priestly prerogatives, which they initiated. For instance, David wore the priestly ephod, offered sacrifices, and pronounced a blessing over the people when the ark was moved to Ornan's threshing floor (2 Sam. 6:13–18; 1 Chr. 21:23–26, 22:7–19). David also interceded on behalf of his people and offered sacrifices to God (2 Sam. 24:10, 22). Solomon likewise offered sacrifices at Gibeon before God granted him wisdom (1 Kings 3:4–15; 2 Chr. 1:6). After Solomon had completed the temple and the ark of the covenant was moved into the temple, he offered sacrifices (2 Chr. 5:1–6). During the temple's dedication, Solomon again offered sacrifices (1 Kings 8:62; 2 Chr. 6:12–7:1, 5, 7, 8) and offered blessings on behalf of the people (2 Sam. 6:18; 1 Kings 8:14, 55). He also replaced high priests (1 Kings 2:27, 35). Thus both David and Solomon functioned as king-priests, though their role was predominantly that of king. Yet Davidites who exceeded their priestly privileges as king faced limitations and consequences. For example, Uzziah contracted leprosy for encroaching on those cultic rituals reserved for the Aaronic priesthood (2 Chr. 26:18). Nevertheless, though the Davidic king's function was predominantly to govern the nation, he executed priestly functions as well.

Therefore the unity involving both royalty and priesthood is understandable and helps explain why David recognizes Solomon's divine appointment as both king (v. 1) and priest (v. 4). This combination of royalty and priesthood, however, is not unique to David's royal court. The concept of a royal priesthood, ascribed to Solomon in Psalm 110:1 and 4, has its roots in Melchizedek and thereby resembles Melchizedek, who as Salem's priest-king blessed Abraham (then still known as Abram,

Gen. 14:17–20). What then may have been the social and historical situation for Psalm 110?

The Possible Circumstances

Solomon was appointed coregent and co-ruled with his father David beginning around 973 B.C.E. (1 Chr. 23:1). David may have written Psalm 110 to be sung at Solomon's ascension to the throne or coronation service as the divinely appointed king-priest. More pointedly, the psalm may have served as David's own personal endorsement of Solomon before the people of Israel in 971 B.C.E. (cf. 1 Kings 1:38–40).[4] But why? Why would Solomon ascend to David's throne before his father died?

Apparently the necessity for David's somewhat premature endorsement of Solomon as king-priest was due to Adonijah's self-promotion and attempt to usurp David's throne (1 Kings 1:5, 7, 9, 41–43, 49).[5] As a result, David acted immediately to enthrone Solomon. In fact, in 1 Kings 1:32–25, 43–45 and 1 Chronicles 28:1–8; 29:20–25, Solomon immediately takes action as king and is honored as king by Adonijah while David is still alive (1 Kings 1:49–53). Furthermore, David muses, "The LORD God of Israel is worthy of praise because today he has placed a successor on my throne and allowed me to see it" (1 Kings 1:48). Thus, David is portrayed in Scripture as honoring Solomon in 971 B.C.E. as his lord, the king over the nation of Israel.

Yet even if Psalm 110 is not by or for David but merely ascribed to him, "Today," says Hans-Joachim Kraus, "there is no longer doubt that Psalms 2; 20; 21; 45; 72; 89; 101; and 110 belong to the historical epoch of the time of the kings."[6] Naturally within these preexilic[7] royal psalms exists the portrayal of the Davidic ideal, an ideal ascribed to a real historic Davidite when he ascended to the throne of David. As indicated above, my presentation works from the assumption that David authored Psalm 110 and used it as a way to endorse Solomon as Israel's rightful king-priest at a coronation service sometime in 971 B.C.E.

How Did the Author Express His Ideas?

As mentioned earlier, this royal psalm contains a public endorsement of a Davidic heir's divine appointment to be Israel's new king-priest (1:1–2), as well as several promises for the newly appointed king concerning his military potential to dominate his enemies (1:3–7). In the process, David expresses two ancient Near Eastern concepts or themes: exaltation and holy war. Unfortunately, the New Testament's frequent mention of Psalm 110:1, which focuses on the psalm's exaltation theme mentioned only in verse 1, tends to overshadow the dominant holy war theme that pervades the psalm. Nevertheless, both themes are clearly expressed, and both are important to the psalm. How does David express the exaltation and holy war themes? He does so via the vivid use of symbols or figurative language.

Symbols for the Exaltation Theme

Exaltation and holy war themes entwine in verse 1. Using a classic symbol of the ancient Near East, the psalmist sings of Yahweh's invitation to his Lord: "Sit...at my right hand." In both Ugaritic poems and Egyptian iconography, sitting at the right hand of a god represented authority.[8] Moving beyond the anthropomorphism of God's hand, Solomon has been invited to a place of honor and authority via the symbolic act of sitting on God's right. The concrete symbol of sitting at the right hand of a divine figure illustrates an abstract concept: the idea of authority and honor (the technical term is a metonymy of subject). Here in Psalm 110:1, God's invitation epitomized Solomon's right to rule as Yahweh's vicegerent. Thus the pronounced invitation makes him God's man.

Yahweh's throne is in heaven (1 Kings 8:27–30; Pss. 2:4; 80:1–15; 89:5–18), while the king, as Yahweh's vicegerent still dependent on Yahweh, rules over Israel, (Pss. 80:17; 89:20–24). The symbolic picture is that Yahweh, "the Divine King" of Israel enthroned in heaven, gives the Davidic king, "the earthly king" of Israel, a special place of honor and authority to rule over Israel as his vice-regent. As noted above, Solomon presently "sits" (figuratively speaking) on "the throne of the LORD" (1 Chr. 29:23). Thus David speaks this divine oracle from Yahweh to the new vice-regent over Israel who is now his Lord, "*the* LORD's" anointed.

Symbols for the Holy War Theme

In the ancient Near East, war was linked with religion. Wars typically began with the approval of the gods, involved sacrifices to the gods, and were conducted with the help of the gods. Thus, all war in the ancient Near East might be construed as a "holy war."[9] Furthermore, the laws of holy war in the ancient Near East are without question crude. Aggressive nations, such as Assyria and Babylon, became known for their brutality and inhumane military tactics, which served as a means to persuade inhabitants of foreign cities to submit *without a fight.* Cities that chose to resist a foreign power were breached, dismantled, burnt, and reduced to rubble. People were deported, sold into slavery, tortured, or impaled on stakes.[10] Thus, the king's ability to succeed in battle via a god was essential to a nation's well-being.

As Solomon is invited to a place of honor by Yahweh and given authority to rule as Yahweh's vice-regent, Yahweh promises Solomon domination and rule, provision of an army, and divine protection. Naturally, such promises are important for anyone about to assume a position of kingship in the ancient Near East. In fact, it was not unusual for nations to rebel against Yahweh and Yahweh's anointed when a Davidite first takes the throne (Ps. 2:1–3). Thus a promise from Yahweh of military success builds confidence and assurance for both the people of Israel as well as the newly appointed king-priest, Solomon. Naturally, these promises are also communicated via the use of common everyday ancient Near Eastern symbols.

Promise of Domination and Rule

In verses 1 and 2, David again uses classic symbols of the ancient Near East to sing of the king's domination and rule over his enemies. In verse 1, the psalmist sings of Yahweh's promise to make the king's enemies "your footstool." In the ancient Near East, the footstool is an important part of the royal furnishings that parallel the supposed furnishings of God's throne room in heaven. David desires to build a temple for the ark of the covenant as a footstool for Yahweh (1 Chr. 28:2), and the psalmists speak of worshiping at God's footstool (Pss. 99:5, 132:7).[11] Naturally, God has no literal footstool. The concrete symbol of a footstool for one's feet serves as a picture for an abstract concept: the idea of subjection (once again a metonymy of subject). Here in Psalm 110:1, the footstool signifies complete subjection or domination over Solomon's enemies.

In a similar way, Egyptian reliefs show a Pharaoh wearing a crown of Upper Egypt and holding a mace in his right hand. He holds his enemy in subjection as with his left hand, fist clenched, he seizes his enemy by the locks of his hair. The captive awaits the deathblow from the king.[12] This is a clear picture of domination. When Joshua defeated the five kings at Beth-horon, Israelite leaders brought them from a cave, *put their feet on the necks of these kings,* and then struck them dead (Josh. 10:24; cf. Isa. 51:23). Thus, the author depicts domination. Here in Psalm 110:1, the reference is to the enemies on whom Solomon symbolically rests his feet, signifying Yahweh's promise of domination over Solomon's enemies (cp. 2 Sam. 7:9–11; Ps. 89:22–23).

The second common symbol occurs in verse 2. Here David employs a "scepter" (NRSV, NIV) or "rod" (KJV). Once again, a concrete symbol of a scepter communicates an abstract concept: the idea of rule (once again a metonymy of subject; see NET). In the ancient Near East, the scepter was a common symbol for a king's rule (Jer. 48:17; Isa. 14:5). Another Hebrew term used synonymously and also translated "scepter" represented the king's function as judge and administrator of his people (Ps. 45:7)[13] and conqueror of his enemies (Num. 24:17; Ps. 2:9). Here in

Psalm 110:2, the scepter signifies Solomon's rule over his enemies and may be rendered "rule in the midst of your enemies," (NET). Other royal psalms promise Davidic kings extensive authority as well (Pss. 2:8, 72:8–11). Thus, through the use of common everyday symbols of the ancient Near East, Solomon is first promised domination and rule over his enemies. Yahweh's second promise is equally relevant to a pristine king-priest.

Promise of an Army

Naturally, an army is essential to first achieve and then support domination and rule over one's enemies. Yahweh promises such an army to Solomon in verse 3. While declaring the willingness of the people to follow Solomon into battle[14] (see NET rendering), David avers, "from the womb of the morning, like dew, your youth will come to you" (NRSV). This statement strings together several figures of speech to describe the quality of Solomon's promised army. We begin with an attribute, "youth," which stands for the subject, young men (unlike the previous figures of metonymy, this is a metonymy of adjunct). Thus the author envisions and announces the presence of young men coming to serve in Solomon's army. They volunteer willingly to follow Solomon, the king-priest, into battle.

Then David presumes that his hearers will make a comparison between "your youth will come to you" and "*like* dew." David's declarative statement demands a comparison be made between "youth" and "dew" (the technical term is *hypocatastasis*). The notion of dew conveys the start of a new day before the rising sun's heat evaporates the early morning mist. Thus this army is a fresh army, one that is not battle weary and experiencing battle fatigue, but rather one that is energized and ready to make haste.

Finally, "dew from the womb of morning dawn" is a personification of dew's giving birth. The figure of speech signifies a pristine group of youth at its earliest stages. Together these three figures describe an army that is young, energized, and pristine. They need not be recruited. They will come voluntarily. Thus Yahweh promises an army that is not only willing but one whose volunteers are young and energized for battle. Yahweh's final promise is probably the most significant.

Promise of Divine Protection

David foresees Yahweh marching into battle with Solomon. The king, now the warrior, has by his side Yahweh as his protector (Pss. 16:8; 10:31; 121:5). Unlike verse 1 where at the "right hand" symbolizes authority and honor, here in verse 5 the concrete symbol "at your right hand" illustrates the abstract idea of protection (another metonymy of subject). Thus Yahweh will protect his anointed king as he proceeds to subdue his enemies in holy war. We might say that Solomon is promised (vv 5-6) divine empowerment "to crush" (Num. 24:8; Ps. 18:39 = 2 Sam. 22:39), "to judge," and "to heap up" (HCSB) his enemies. David expresses certitude at this point in the psalm (he uses what is called prophetic perfects) to indicate victory's certainty. Several graphic images are used to convey this certitude.

First is the promise that "he shatters their heads over the vast battlefield." The graphic image of shattered heads in verse 6 is yet another figure of speech where only the head is mentioned for the whole person (the technical term is *synecdoche*: a part for the whole). The Hebrew verb translated "to smash" or "to shatter" or "to crush" (*maḥaṣ*) in Psalm 110:5–6 appears in the ancient poetry in Judges 5:26 (Song of Deborah). There we read how the wife of Heber the Kenite hammered Sisera with a tent peg, "shattered his skull" and "smashed (*maḥᵃṣâ*) his head." A similar usage of the term occurs in Balaam's prophecy of King David ("a star"), who will "march forth out of Jacob" and "crush the skulls of Moab" (Num. 24: 17).[15] Thus the phrase "shatters their heads" is a graphic portrayal of death typical in battle.

Second, the king's conquest is "over a broad country" (NASB), of "the whole earth" (NIV; NLT), "far and wide" (JPS), "throughout the wide earth" (REB), "over the entire world" (HCSB), or "over the vast battlefield" (NET). Naturally, this is an exaggeration (a hyperbole) to describe the extent of the king's conquests: it is a great and extensive conquest. Thus the point is simply this: Solomon as king-priest will be victorious in an extensive conquest.

The final figure of speech occurs in verse 7, where we read, "Therefore he will lift up his head" (NRSV). The symbolic act of lifting up his head stands for the subject, "victory" (this is another metonymy of adjunct). Thus the act of a "raised head" could symbolize: (1) *restoration* to a former position of power, as in the cases of Pharaoh's chief cupbearer (Gen. 40:13) and David after Absalom's revolt (Ps. 3:3), (2) a proud attitude as a person anticipates an *unjust victory* over another (Ps. 140:9), or (3) a *just victory* and vindication over one's enemies (Ps. 27:6). Here in Psalm 110:7, "lift up his head" appears to stand for the promise of victory after being energized by a refreshing drink of water (cf. Judges 15:18–19; 1 Sam. 30:11–12). Thus David promises Solomon victory over all his enemies.

So then, how did David express his ideas of exaltation and holy war? How did he express God's promises to Solomon? He used vivid symbols or figures of speech to communicate Solomon's divine endorsement as

Israel's king and to make three promises. Through this divine oracle from Yahweh, David promises Solomon that he will have domination and rule, a fresh and pristine army ready and willing to fight, and divine protection and ultimate victory. Moving beyond these symbols, however, is yet another important issue to address.

What Are the Important Interpretive Issues?

According to one commentator, "No other psalm has in research evoked so many hypotheses and discussions as Psalm 110."[16] Some of these issues I have already addressed: author, recipient, situation, and symbolic language. Here, I will focus attention on yet another significant interpretive issue to ponder before you teach or preach this psalm.

In the past, commentators such as Luther, Perowne, and Delitzsch saw Psalm 110 as only prophetic and directly Messianic.[17] They felt the New Testament's use of this psalm demanded a directly prophetic interpretation. On the one hand, Psalm 110:1 was regarded as a direct prophecy about the exaltation of Jesus seated at the right hand of God and his victory over his enemies (Acts 2:34, 1 Cor. 15:25, Heb. 1:13, 10:13).[18] On the other hand, Psalm 110:4 was considered the clear demonstration of the abrogation of the Levitical priesthood (Heb. 5:6, 7:17, 21). Undoubtedly, the psalm's ultimate fulfillment occurs in Jesus and his exaltation as the Christ. Such views, however, overlooked the fact that Psalm 110 spoke of a historical figure such as David, or perhaps even one of his heirs.

Today, many believe Psalm 110 is a royal psalm similar to Psalms 2, 45, and 72, written by a poet or prophet addressing either David or some other Davidic king.[19] "The royal psalms, by their literary nature," avers Chisholm, "are not inherently prophetic and should not be understood as direct predictions of Jesus' messianic reign."[20] In fact, the royal psalms speak of a Davidic ideal, an ideal that was directed at many historical Davidic kings, particularly on the occasion of their accession to the throne.

In keeping with my social and historical evaluation of Psalm 110, it seems more than reasonable to suggest that *initially* Psalm 110 addressed someone other than Jesus and his future reign. Consequently, it seems extremely probable that Psalm 110 and other royal psalms were written for Solomon's ascension to the throne. Naturally, Solomon was the first Davidic heir to fulfill God's promise of 2 Samuel 7. Yet each successive Davidic king was a recipient of Yahweh's promise to David, and each took office assuming a special "father-son" relationship with Yahweh due to God's initial promise to David (2 Sam. 7:14; cf. Ps. 2:7). Needless to say, Jesus is the ultimate Davidic heir and recipient of the promise, the ultimate Lord of king David.

Therefore, it is important that the social and historical setting of Psalm 110 be considered to overcome our typical presuppositions about the psalm's final referent, Jesus. Helping people see beyond the New Testament's ultimate application of the psalm is an important interpretive issue to address because it provides people with a greater appreciation for how God progressively works his plan to restore his kingdom rule on earth and redeem a people to enter into that kingdom as history unfolds.

What Was the Author Seeking to Communicate?

David communicates both a practical and theological message in Psalm 110. On the one hand, the psalm's practical message is one of assurance and confidence not only for Israel's newly appointed king-priest, Solomon, but also for the nation of Israel as they listen to David's psalm, which may have been sung during Solomon's coronation. It begins with David's recognition of Solomon's divine appointment as king and with Yahweh's promise of future dominion over his enemies (vv. 1–2). Solomon is then promised a vibrant army and perpetual communion with Yahweh as priest (vv. 3–4). Finally, Solomon has unlimited divine protection and abilities to crush his foes and be ensured final victory (vv. 5–7).[21] Essentially, David, through a divine oracle from Yahweh, assured Solomon of his position as Yahweh's divinely appointed king-priest (110:1, 4) and provided confidence concerning Solomon's future domination over all of his enemies via Yahweh's intervention (110:1b, 3, 5–7).

On the other hand, we might say that the theological focus of this psalm about the Davidic king (i.e., the Lord) is an extension of Yahweh's (i.e., the LORD) sovereign rule. Yahweh is the sovereign ruler of the universe, who has established in Zion (or Jerusalem, v. 2) his earthly rule via a Davidic vice-regent. Yahweh's vice-regent and earthly representative (v. 1; cf. Pss. 2:6; 89:27) extends dominion and executes justice via holy war on behalf of Yahweh (vv. 2–3, 4, 6; cf. Pss. 2:9–11; 89:27).

The theological message of Psalm 110 may be simply stated in this manner: Yahweh has exalted and empowered the Davidic king (vv. 1–2); Yahweh has declared the Davidic king a priest, who as priest has perpetual access to Yahweh (vv. 3–4); and Yahweh will dominate and judge the nations through this divinely appointed Davidic king-priest (vv. 5–7). Thus Yahweh rules from Zion through his Davidic vice-regent, and promises to establish and extend his kingdom through holy war (which would be in keeping with 2 Sam. 7).

What Is the Significance of the Psalm for Preaching and Teaching?

Unfortunately, Psalm 110 is seldom taught in Sunday school classes. Nor is it preached very often from the pulpit on Sunday mornings.

Perhaps our vision is so blurred by the New Testament's application to an ultimate fulfillment in Jesus that we are unable to appreciate the psalmist's original social and historical context that precipitated the writing of the psalm. It seems to me, however, that Psalm 110 is a great psalm for assuring and providing confidence because it was written for a person about to transition from a Davidic heir to a Davidic king. Think about it! What could be more unsettling than accepting sole kingship over a kingdom? Solomon is about to experience a stupendous change or transition in his life. He is presented as one who is divinely appointed as king-priest of Israel and promised domination over his enemies (vv. 1–2). Yet God promises Solomon three things as he accepts this new platform as king-priest.

First, God promises to meet Solomon's *practical needs*. In this case, God promises an army to defeat his enemies (v. 3). This army is not just any army, but a fresh, energized, and pristine army. Second, God promises Solomon *perpetual access* to God. In this case, he is assured perpetual access to God as long as he lives as king-priest (v. 4). Finally, God promises Solomon *protection*. In this case, while battling holy war, God promises to stand by his man and intervene when necessary (vv. 5–7). Thus Solomon is provided assurance and confidence that as he transitions into a new phase of his life Yahweh will be with him each step of the way.

Is this psalm any less applicable to us today as we face changes or transitions in our lives? Granted, we are not kings. Nor does God rule through us. Yet as life unfolds, nothing happens by chance. God is sovereign, and we move through life and experience life as he directs. Will God not meet our *practical needs* in the process? Will God not provide *perpetual access* to him? Will God not provide *protection?* Granted, we may not be divinely appointed king-priests in need of a vibrant army to carry out a holy war, but as it was with Solomon, so it is with us. As we go through life's changes, God promises to provide for our practical needs (Mt. 6:25–34; 7:7–12), to provide perpetual access (Mt. 6:5–6), and provide protection (Mt. 6:8–13).

Or perhaps we might teach or preach this psalm with a christological thrust. Of all the psalms quoted or alluded to in the New Testament, no single psalm is mentioned more often than Psalm 110.[22] It is, without question, an important Old Testament text for the early development of Christianity. Jesus mentions it in his teachings about himself as the Son of David (Mk. 12:35–36, 14:62). Peter references the psalm in his sermons about Jesus as the exalted Christ (Acts 2:34–35). The author of Hebrews either alludes to or quotes it regularly in his homily to support his call to persevere in faith in Jesus as the divine king-priest (Heb. 1:13; 5:5–6; 7:17).[23]

Naturally, as followers of Jesus, Jesus is our king-priest. Yet unlike Solomon or any subsequent Davidite, Jesus is greater because Jesus is a divine Davidic king-priest (cf. Mt. 12:42 with Heb. 1:1–14).

In the letter to the Hebrews, Jesus is recognized as the appointed Davidic royal priest (1:2–3, 5:5–6; cf. 3:1–2, 7:28, 8:3), defined as the divine Davidic king (1:5–13), and seen as currently ruling from heaven (1:8–9, 12:28). As the appointed heir of all things (1:2; 7:28), Jesus' present kingdom and current rule will eventually be extended (cf. 2:5–9). The author of Hebrews recontextualizes Psalm 110:1b in Hebrews 1:13b to express the future expansion of the Son's kingdom. Psalm 110:1b is used to look toward the day when the Son's ruling authority will include the complete subjugation of his enemies (Ps. 8:4–6 in Heb. 2:5–9, 10:12–13; cf. Phil. 2:9–11, Rev. 5:8–10).[24]

God promises, through Jesus, to meet our practical needs, offer perpetual access, and provide protection. According to Hebrews, God through Jesus as our great king-priest provides for our *practical needs* through angelic beings (1:13–14) and through the believing communities that follow Jesus (10:24–25, 32–35). God through Jesus as our great king-priest provides *perpetual access* to God. Hebrews evidences this in numerous ways. Not only does Jesus as our great high priest–king understand our weaknesses (4:14–16), but Jesus also provides us perpetual access to God because of Jesus, our king-priest. He has passed through the heavens (4:14) and has entered, on our behalf, behind the heavenly curtain where God resides (6:19; 9:1–3). Thus we too can now enter behind that curtain into God's presence, where our king-priest presently intercedes for us (10:19–20). Finally, God through Jesus our great king-priest provides *protection* in that Jesus has experienced an initial victory, with victories yet to come. Hebrews recognizes that demonic forces (Heb. 2:14), death (Heb. 2:15), and earthly opponents (Heb. 10:26–31) still plague the Son's kingdom.[25] This is not to diminish the victory that the Son has achieved (Heb. 2:14–18; cf. 1 Cor. 15:54–57). It does, however, point to the fact that the Son's ruling authority over his kingdom is presently limited and thus not yet fully realized.

Regardless of what tack you take, Psalm 110 is a great psalm for assuring and providing confidence for people in the midst of transition and change because it was written initially for a person about to transition from a Davidic heir to a Davidic king. It is a psalm that expresses Yahweh's exaltation of a Davidic heir to be Israel's new king-priest, as well as Yahweh's overwhelming assurance of the king's successful reign over his enemies and vast domain.

CHAPTER 13

Psalm 116

Ordeal, Rescue, and Reaction

Martin G. Abegg Jr.

When my children were small, I encouraged them to say "thank you." Every time they received a kindness, a nearly automatic question posed on a regular basis was, "What do you say?" Generally the answer was just as automatic: "Thank you," often accompanied by the "grab and run" reflex before Dad made any further demands. For children *and* adults, we often fall into the trap of taking things for granted. We forget to give credit where credit is due. We mumble a word or two of thanks and move on to the next item on our agenda. That is not the case for our psalmist. Having been rescued from one or more of life's harrowing storms, the author of Psalm 116 erupts in a song of thanksgiving. His emotions at an all-time high, he could not do enough to express his gratitude. He created a verbal collage with various images of rescue, the language of praise, and promises to remain in faithful fellowship.

Ask any Christian to name the chief components of prayer, and giving thanks will almost certainly be one of the first mentioned. Like children, we may also relegate a "thank you" to the category of duty. Going through the effort to make praise a priority does not come naturally. Perhaps God sometimes feels like posing the question to us, "What do you say?" Here is where the psalmist shows us the way. He experienced no shortage of heartfelt thanks and praise.

A student in one of my first Hebrew classes inadvertently made an important point about expressing gratitude. Having left the weekly quiz at home on my desk, I announced that there would be no quiz that day and that a grade of 100 would be awarded simply on the basis of attendance. Turning to his neighbor, the immediate response of the student sitting front and center was to ask, "How do you say *hallelujah* in

Hebrew!?" We may need to remind ourselves that *hallelujah* is indeed a Hebrew word that means, "Praise the LORD!" Apart from revealing his need for the Hebrew class, this student also revealed a crucial point about the Hebrew language and culture. The response of the ancient Hebrews was, like this student, not thanks, but praise. We might go so far as to say that ancient Hebrew had no word for thanks, only for praise. As Claus Westermann has helpfully penned:

> [I]magine a world in which petition plays a thoroughly essential and noteworthy role, but where the opposite role of petition is not primarily thanks but praise. And this praise is a stronger, more lively, broader concept which includes our "thanks" in it. Thanking is here included entirely within praise.[1]

Psalm 116 offers important insights on worship and the proper response to what God does for us. How do we make sure that God is not inclined to ask us, "What do you say?" How do we make gratitude a priority? Are we to thank him or to praise him? And just what is the difference?

Why Did the Author Compose the Psalm?

Psalm 116 is untitled, one of thirty-four such psalms in the canon. Nevertheless, much about the psalm's setting, purpose, and even the author's situation can be determined from clues within the poem. With seventeen verbs in the first person singular–beginning with "I love the LORD"–the poem presents the personal praises of the author himself. These verbs provide the structure for the song (v. 1).

Regarding dating, based on studies of the Hebrew language and changes that occurred from the Bible's earliest compositions to the latest, it is relatively certain that the writer lived in the period following the return from Babylonian exile, known as the post-exilic period or Second Temple period. As to psalm type, Psalm 116 can be classified as a song of thanksgiving (more on this below). The psalmist extols God for hearing his prayer for rescue and for providing relief from what is described as a life-threatening situation ("the ropes of death tightened around me," v. 3). But the function of the psalm was not limited to private discourse with God. Based on wording within the psalm, it was composed to be sung in the temple ("in the courts of the LORD's temple," v. 19), in presence of the congregation ("before all his people," vv. 14, 18), and as an accompaniment to a thank offering ("I will present a thank offering to you," v. 17).

We can picture the psalmist living in or near Jerusalem 2500 years ago. Suffering from a life-threatening event, his faith (v. 10) brought him to his knees in prayer as he sought relief from his God. His knowledge of the Scriptures directed him to follow the example of Job (Job 22:27) as he offered a vow to bring a sacrifice and praise to God for answered prayer (vv. 14, 18). His painful situation had evidently brought a separation of fellowship, perhaps an evidence that—again as in the case of Job—his brethren had assessed his dire circumstances as a judgment from God and refused to aid him in his time of greatest need (v. 11). God, however, was merciful and answered his prayer. The psalmist responded by fulfilling his vow. He brought an offering to the temple. His offering—a cup of wine (v. 13)—gives evidence of the psalmist's joy (Eccl. 10:19) but perhaps also suggests his economic situation. He was unable to afford the more expensive cuts of meat that might have served as his offering. Finally, his fellowship with the congregation was restored. Instead of praising God in his closet, he joined God's people in the courtyard of the temple and made public his praise to the Lord who had answered his desperate prayer.

The psalmist's human situation, God's faithfulness, and the response were couched in words that struck a chord with other Israelites in similar need, leading to recognition that God's clear hand had not only been in the answered prayer but also in the literary response. This hymn of praise was eventually included in a group of psalms known as the Egyptian Hallel or Egyptian Praise psalms (Pss. 113–118). "Egyptian" refers to these six Psalms being reimagined as an expression of gratitude for God's rescue of the Hebrew people from Egyptian bondage ("when Israel left Egypt," Ps. 114:1). "Praise" refers to *hallelujah*, which forms a repeated refrain (Pss. 113:1, 9; 115:17–18; 116:19; 117:2). The *Mishnah* (written at the beginning of the third century C.E.) provides an ancient record that these six psalms were read yearly in the courtyard of the temple at the sacrifice of the Passover lamb and also following the Passover, where they were associated with the fourth cup of wine (Ps. 116:13) during the Passover meal.

These psalms occur together in the earliest psalm manuscripts found among the Dead Sea Scrolls. The oldest of these dates to the last decades of the first century B.C.E., giving evidence for the antiquity of the "Hallel" tradition.

How Did the Author Express His Ideas?

As is true throughout the Psalter, Psalm 116 is an example of ancient hymn writing at its most artful. Many thousands, if not millions, of hymns have been and continue to be written. A small percentage of these have sufficient staying power to be gathered and regathered into congregational hymnbooks and collections of praise music. That this hymn and the 149 other psalms have stood unchanged for well over 2,000 years is a tribute to the beauty of expression and the emotive force of Hebrew poetry. As poetry, that which makes for beauty in expression often results in difficulties of interpretation. The imagery and ambiguity that afford repeated readings also tie teachers and preachers into exegetical knots!

The flow of thought in Psalm 116 lends itself to a rather straightforward structure. The psalmist introduces the poem by making clear that the purpose of his hymn is to give praise to the Lord (vv. 1–2). In the main body of the psalm, the writer tells of his experience of tribulation and deliverance (vv. 3–9). The conclusion, in which the hymn writer becomes a congregant, gives thanks and praise to God in the temple (vv. 10–19).

A bit of reflection on modern writing brings us face to face with an interesting question. How much of what the psalm describes is based on the author's firsthand situation, and how much was the result of poetic imagination? Did the poet personally experience the tightening of "the ropes of death" or "the snares of Sheol" (v. 3)? Both of those expressions are almost certainly figures of speech, but do they reflect a near-death experience in the psalmist's life? Are the powerful images of death psychological or physical? Did the hymnist simply twist an ankle? Or did he suffer near death? On the one hand, a creative ancient Israelite seeking to compose a hymn that worshipers could identify with may have invented the experiences reflected here *whole cloth*. Certainly, some contemporary lyrics we sing were composed to reflect common experiences on this earth. On the other hand, when I think of some of my favorite hymns, for example, "It Is Well with My Soul" by Horatio Spafford, or "How Long, O Lord" by Brian Doerksen, which reflect the composers' real life experiences, I am drawn to the notion that the psalmist himself had walked through the "valley of death" and been rescued. The repetition and power of the imagery begs for the upper end of the scale—whether psychological or physical, we cannot say.

The psalm concludes with the imagery of the praise offering, the congregation of the faithful, and the Jerusalem temple. Were these weighty elements chosen for their emotive power to bring a tear to the eye or a lump in the throat? Or was the psalm written precisely to accompany a praise offering in the temple (an event, which if records were available, could be verified and dated)? Perhaps in the end some would say it matters little, but since the psalm was collected, safeguarded, and incorporated into the living liturgy of the community, I would prefer to opt for the reality of the events described in the psalm. In the absence of certainty we can be sure that the psalmist intended for the message of his hymn to ring true in the ears of the worshipers.

What Are the Important Interpretive Issues?

Given my own frustration with commentaries that leave the user stranded in time of greatest need, I will first discuss some interpretive issues that proved to be difficult to my own understanding. At the end of this section we will examine the two New Testament passages that reflect Psalm 116.

In verses 3, 4, 6, 10 we meet the most technical of our interpretive discussions. It concerns the tense of the Hebrew verb in verse 3 translated by the NET Bible as "I was confronted" ("I was overcome," NIV). To any student with even one year of Hebrew, the verbal form in question would appear to be a simple imperfect requiring a translation of "I shall be confronted," or at the very least, "I am confronted." However, this verb, as well as those translated as "I called" (v. 4), "he delivered" (v. 6), and "I said" (v. 10), are examples of the rare preterit form (that is, simple past tense).[2] It is rare when it is not found immediately following the conjunction "and" (the *waw* consecutive). Of all the English translations I checked, only the ASV disagrees with this assessment, and even then only at verse 10: "I will speak."

Regarding verses 4, 13, 17, we need to ask: What does it mean to "call on the name of the LORD?" I have asked this question in numerous Hebrew classes and have watched students tie themselves in knots trying to decode the syntax of the Hebrew. In Psalm 116 the matter is made clear. Two categories offer good examples for the pattern of usage elsewhere in the Old Testament. The clause, "I called on the name of the LORD, 'Please LORD, rescue my life!'" (v. 4) indicates that the point of calling is the simple prayer for deliverance that follows. So, in many cases, to "call on the name of the LORD" is simply to pray (1 Kings 18:24; Zech. 13:9). The clauses, "I will celebrate my deliverance, and call on the name of the LORD" (v. 13), and similarly, "I will present a thank offering to you, and call on the name of the LORD" (v. 17), are in the context of worship with God's people in the temple. Thus, "to call on the name of the LORD" refers on numerous occasions to worship (Gen. 4:26; 12:8; 13:4; 21:33; 26:25). The common factor of these two categories is conversation with God.

Verse 10 says, "I had faith when I said..." The Hebrew word (*kî*), translated here as the adverb "when," is—in most contexts—the equivalent of our English words *that* or *because.* Quite often, however, as certainly here, other meanings are to be preferred. The KJV and NIV offer "therefore," a meaning that is never found elsewhere for *kî* and appears to determine the sense of the Hebrew by relying on the Greek translation quoted at 2 Corinthians 4:13. The "when" of the NASB and NET is more true to the meaning of the Hebrew expression. This temporal sense—"When I said, 'I am severely oppressed,' I had faith."—is actually close to the preferred "concessive" rendering of the NRSV and HCSB ("though," "although," "even when"). Thus the sense of verses 10–11 would be a "true confession": in effect, the psalmist is simply saying, "in spite of complaining bitterly about my situation and jumping to the conclusion that all my friends were of no help whatsoever, I still held fast to my belief in God."

For verse 11, the NET translation –"I rashly declared, 'All men are liars'"–is more helpful than many modern translations. A comparison with the NIV–"And in my dismay I said, 'All men are liars'"–makes it clear that our problem is twofold. First, how are we to make sense of the Hebrew of the first clause? And, second, how are we to understand the second clause in the context of our psalm?

The expression found in the initial clause thankfully occurs elsewhere in the Old Testament, so we have some additional contexts to aid our understanding. At 2 Samuel 4:4, "in her haste" to flee from danger, Mephibosheth's nurse drops him and cripples him for life. At 2 Kings 7:15, "in their haste" to escape the supernatural powers that had attacked them at dusk, the Arameans left a trail of equipment and clothing as they headed for home. Even closer to the sense of our psalm is the occurrence in Psalm 31:22. The psalmist "in his haste" to figure out why God felt so far off concluded that "I am cut off from your presence." This false conclusion–though there is no doubt how he honestly felt at the time!–is corrected in the very next line: "But you heard my plea for mercy when I cried out to you for help." The NET Bible has found the perfect modern expression for this Hebrew phrase at 31:22: "I jumped to conclusions." Likewise, the author of Psalm 116 in the midst of his suffering "jumped" and "concluded," "all men are liars."

Now, second, how did the psalmist come to this conclusion? And what did he mean by it? It can hardly be–given the context of the false deduction arrived at by the "jump to conclusion"–that our psalmist intended to make a theological statement parallel to Romans 3:4: "Let God be proven true, and every human being shown up as a liar." It is more likely that in the midst of his suffering, which was beyond any human help (although his friends likely tried and failed), this was the way the world looked to him at the time. All of his friends' fine words and attempts to aid came to nothing more than "be warmed and filled" (Jas. 2:16, NRSV) in his eyes. Perhaps, if the suffering had gone on long enough, they would have avoided him altogether. After all, in the previous verse our psalmist admits that he did not suffer quietly!

For verse 13, the NET Bible translates the beginning of the verse, "I will celebrate my deliverance." Contrast this with the NIV: "I will lift up the cup of salvation." We must decide whether to take the expression "cup of salvation" literally or literarily. No doubt "cup" is quite frequently used metaphorically, as in the passages referring to the "cup of wrath" (Jer. 25:15–29; Lam. 4:21; Ezek. 23:31–33). The cup contains that which is one's punishment or reward. The "cup" in these passages is a mere figure of speech; wrath is the point. Likewise, in Psalm 116 our sufferer's prayer has been answered with God's salvation. Perhaps, as in the NET translation, the cup is mere imagery and salvation is the point. However, the context of 116:12–19 needs to be taken into careful consideration. When the psalmist at verse 12 asks how he might repay, he promises to fulfill his vows in verses 14 and 18, and in verse 17 he sacrifices his thank offering in the courts of the house of the Lord (v. 19). All of this strongly suggests a libation in the temple of a literal cup of wine, which does indeed celebrate our psalmist's deliverance.

Verses 14 and 17 speak of vows. Vowing seems to modern–and perhaps especially Protestant sensibilities–as in nearly the same category as a bribe. "God, if you answer my prayer I'll never skip a Sunday service again!" Vows were purely optional in Israelite religion. Not to vow was never a sin (Deut. 23:22). The vows recorded in the Old Testament are as a rule serious business about crucial issues: the end of barrenness and the birth of a child (1 Sam. 1:11), victory in battle (Ps. 76:11), and perhaps–as in our psalm–healing from illness or rescue from a life-threatening crisis (Job 22:27). Perhaps most importantly, the payment of the vow–and there were pointed warnings for not doing so (Deut. 23:21)–was to encourage continued fellowship in the congregation (Ps. 116:14, 18, 19) and the worship of God (vv. 13, 17, 19c).

In verse 15, we read, "Precious in the sight of the LORD is the death of his saints" (NIV). Many have found great comfort in this passage at the passing of a loved one. But translated in this manner, the verse fits the context of Psalm 116 only with great difficulty. The clear point, after all, is that our hymn writer has been *rescued from the clutches of death.* Another Psalm passage with nearly identical vocabulary may give some help for sorting out this mismatch. A literal translation of Psalm 72:14 reads: "From oppression and violence he will redeem their lives, in his eyes he will value their blood." As blood is frequently used in descriptions of death (Num. 35:27), and "to value" is simply the Hebrew verbal equivalent of the adjective "precious," this passage forms a near match to that of Psalm 116:15. In the case of Psalm 72 the parallel statement, "He will redeem their lives," makes the intent of "value their blood" unambiguous. In the case of Psalm 116, the context of the psalm–rescue from death–should be allowed to do the same. Thus the NET translation: "The LORD values the lives of his faithful followers," is to be preferred.

In verse 17 we read, "I will present a thank (*todah*) offering to you." At this juncture we are confronted with perhaps *the* key component of the hymn as we move toward considering how to apply this psalm in our twenty-first century context. The temple is no longer available to us, and the Old Testament form of Israelite religion passed with its destruction. So, just how does one–Jew or Gentile–offer a sacrifice of *todah* today?

First, we must examine the meaning of the word itself. *Todah* always refers either to the type of sacrifice commonly rendered "*thanksgiving* sacrifice"or "*thanks* offering," or the type of song sung on the occasion of such an offering (Jer. 30:19). This consistent and technical employment makes the determination of meaning somewhat difficult and circular and demands that we turn elsewhere for help.

Todah is a noun form from the Hebrew verb *yadah*. This verb is quite common in the Old Testament and is used in two contexts. First, the verb is employed occasionally in the praise of people (Gen. 49:8), but most frequently in praise of God (Gen. 29:35). So comparing these two Genesis passages we can appreciate the play on words surrounding the name "Judah" (also from the root *yadah*). Leah names her son Judah and says, "This time I will praise the LORD" (Gen. 29:35). On his death bed, Judah's father, Jacob, blesses him using what we might term a "pun." "Judah, your brothers will praise you" (Gen. 49:8).

Second, on occasion the verb used is in confession: "When I refused to confess my sin, my whole body wasted away" (Ps. 32:3). Thus, I might suggest that the essence of the verbal sense is to "confess in praise."

Claus Westermann, whose valuable studies on the psalms have influenced so much current thinking, examined in detail what I have outlined briefly above and concluded that the word *todah* does not mean "thanks" but rather–in keeping with the verbal use–"praise," and that the first and more limited concept is assumed in the latter. So again I refer to the quote at the introduction of this article, "…praise is a stronger, more lively, broader concept which includes our 'thanks' in it. Thanking is here included entirely within praise."[3] So our hymn writer brought an "offering of praise"(v. 13, lit.; "the cup of salvation," NIV) to God in payment of his vow, and authored a "praise song" (Ps. 116) to accompany it.

As mentioned above, verse 19 might raise objections to our accepting a liturgical setting of the psalm–that is, that the hymn was composed and used in an actual temple service. Although it cannot be denied that the imagery of congregation (vv. 14b, 17b) and offerings for the payment of vows (vv. 13a, 17a) in the context of the Jerusalem temple (v. 19) might be nothing more than an extended metaphor, their emphasis, in my view, appears rather to highlight the reality.

Psalm 116 is quoted directly in the New Testament in one instance (2 Cor. 4:13) and very likely alluded to in another (Mt. 26:27, 30; Mk. 14:23, 26; Lk. 22:20). In his second letter to the Corinthians, Paul includes an extended discussion on his apostolic ministry (2 Cor. 2:14–7:16). In the heart of this discourse he reflects on the amazing power that has been granted to mortal man in the form of the good news of salvation in Jesus the Christ (2 Cor. 4:7a). Far from bringing ease, the gospel brought tribulation and death in communion with Jesus' own sufferings (4:8–12). In this, Paul found comfort and fellowship in the near-death experience of our psalmist and his words as quoted from the Greek translation of the hymn: "I believed, therefore I spoke." Those who believe will share in Jesus' triumph over death (4:14), while those who do not believe will perish (4:3–4). Paul had believed and must speak.

As detailed in the discussion above concerning the use of Psalm 116 in Judaism, the *Mishnah* reflects the ancient practice of reciting the psalm and those in the Psalter immediately surrounding it (Pss. 113–118) during the Passover celebration. The gospel writers give evidence that they were also aware of this practice. After supper Jesus took the cup and commanded: "Drink from it, all of you, for this is my blood, the blood of the covenant, that is poured out for many for the forgiveness of sins" (Mt. 26:27b–28). This is an appropriate reflection on the "cup of salvation" (Ps. 116:13). The meal was concluded with the singing of "the hymn" (Mt. 26:30; Mk. 14:26), which according to Jewish tradition would have been the recitation of the "Egyptian Hallel" psalms (Pss. 113–118).

What Was the Author Seeking to Communicate?

Psalm 116 is a highly emotional hymn as befits the near-death experience of its author. Nevertheless, it follows a logical pattern of development. In the introduction, verses 1–2, the author makes it clear that his purpose is to praise the Lord. The psalmist unabashedly expressed his love for God (not all that common in the Old Testament) because when he called out, God heard and rescued him. The psalmist learned from his experience and vowed in the future to call out to God in times of need.

Verses 3–4 are given to a description of the trouble and the call for rescue. The clear expression of the agony the psalmist was experiencing is couched in terms of confinement and various images of death–"the ropes of death *tightened* around me, the *snares* of Sheol confronted me" (emphasis added here and below)–to be revisited in the concluding thoughts of verse 16: "You have freed me from my *chains* [of death]" (NIV). The claustrophobia of our sufferer's experience is made palpable, but the ambiguity as to the exact type of danger is what has given the psalm its timelessness. Any victim of life's calamities can relate and find solace with this fellow sufferer who has given voice to any number of hopeless situations.

The experience of rescue is expressed in verses 5–8. The psalmist began by giving evidence of a sound knowledge of theology. His call for rescue was not simply cast to the wind; indeed he witnesses in verse 5 that he directed his call to a God famous for mercy, justice, and compassion (Pss. 103:6–8; 111:3–4; 145:7–9; and Ex. 34:6). But his knowledge became experience and it was holistic. His soul was at rest (v. 7), his eyes no longer wept, his feet no longer stumbled (v. 8). The constrictions of death had been replaced by the broad places of life, and he once again walked in the "land of the living" (v. 9).

We come face to face with the humanity of the psalmist in verses 10–11. He freely acknowledges that the reactions to his sufferings were not always perfectly righteous. Although he held fast to his belief in the Lord, he admits that he complained about his tribulations (v. 10b). Perhaps the result was that he eventually ostracized himself from the community of believers and then ironically and rashly concluded, "All men are liars." They had promised their help, but all it came to in the veiled eyes of the sufferer was "be warmed and be filled"(Jas. 2:16, NRSV).

Verses 12–19 detail the psalmist's response to God's salvation from imminent death. He first acknowledges that he is bankrupt and could never repay his great debt to God (v. 12). Nevertheless he brought his humble offering, a cup of wine (vv. 13a [see NRSV, NIV], 17a), offered his heartfelt praise (vv. 13b, 17b, 19b), and devoted himself to serve his God (v. 16). Note our psalmist's clear emphasis on the location of this praise and worship: "before all his people" (vv. 14, 18), "in the courts of the LORD's temple" (v. 19). He has been rescued from death and reinstated to the fellowship of God's people. "*Hallelujah!*"

What Is the Significance of the Psalm for Preaching and Teaching?

The approach to teaching this psalm will depend on whether it becomes series of messages (assuming a multi-year tour through the psalms!) or is taken in one bite. To capture the power of the piece, I would prefer to base my exposition on the entire psalm and entitle my sermon: "Ordeal, Rescue, and Reaction." In my estimation this captures the essence of the psalmist's message *and* sets the stage to correct a bit of common "misthink" that I encountered in myself during my study of Psalm 116.

We cannot doubt the first two points of the equation. The psalmist was in deep trouble. Far too many of us have "been there." In perhaps the most central of biblical lessons, he called out to God and was rescued.

God desires for us to call to him in time of need because, after all, he is a God of "mercy, justice, and compassion." He is a God who values the life (not the death!) of his own.

As to the third point and our psalmist's reaction, does he thank God or praise God? And what is the difference? According to my brief review of the Hebrew word *todah* and its cognates, and leaning on the more in-depth studies of others, I am persuaded that praise is the point. On reflection it occurs to me at least three important lessons are to be learned from this observation.

First, the objects of our admiration—whether God, our spouses, our children, or our friends—are elevated by our praise, whereas in thanks their position remains the same. When my daughter does a brilliant job of mowing and trimming the lawns and I thank her, this takes care of my responsibility to respond kindly, but it does little to change her status in the family circle. Praise, on the other hand, raises her in recognition, at the same time bringing attention to her good work. All family members become aware of how I feel, and additional comments of appreciation from the rest of the family are the common result.

This naturally leads to the second lesson. Thanks quite often takes place more or less one-to-one, whereas praise by its very nature more often takes place in a group setting. This is clearly an important point made by the writer of Psalm 116. Three times the psalmist mentions that his heartfelt appreciation took place among the congregation (vv. 14, 18), and in the courtyard of the temple (v. 19). As my daughter's grounds-keeping efforts are additionally lauded by the family in response to my own praise, praise of God in the congregation brings opportunity for others to join in, perhaps remembering their own experiences with God that are called to mind by the testimony of the initial worshiper.

Third, praise also has the character of spontaneity and is driven by a heartfelt appreciation, whereas thanks can often carry the sense of duty. Thanks may need to be commanded, but praise commands itself. Of course this is not to say that praise is right and thanks is wrong, but rather that praise goes several steps higher. Again as Westermann has written, "...praise is a stronger, more lively, broader concept which includes our 'thanks' in it. Thanking is here included entirely within praise."[4]

The ancient songwriter challenged us to praise God in response to our own answered prayers. Rather than making this a private affair, it is best to take advantage of a congregational setting to give witness to God's provision. I am reminded of the common prayer accompanying the eucharist: "It is right to give our thanks and praise!"[5]

CHAPTER 14

Psalm 130

A Plea for Grace

William D. Barrick

Shortly after enrolling in the Doctor of Theology program at Grace Theological Seminary, I broke my back. During the initial days of severe pain, I was unable to sleep and spent many nighttime hours reading the book of Psalms. As a result, Psalm 130 came to be one of my favorites. In the dark of night and pain, I identified with the watchmen waiting for the morning. When the rosy slivers of dawn lightened the dark sky and the stars disappeared one by one, my hopes rekindled; and the pain seemed to ease. The thought that God had indeed redeemed and forgiven me brought comfort. He was in control of my pain and my sleepless nights. Since he had so graciously and compassionately forgiven my sins, I knew that I could trust him completely even in matters that were physical.

While waiting for God to bring about the time of my physical relief, I joined a long line of believers whom this psalm has impacted. It affected some, such as John Wesley, primarily by its message of forgiveness. On the afternoon of May 1738 Wesley had listened to and had been moved by the singing of Psalm 130 at the vespers in St. Paul's Cathedral in London. That very evening he attended a reading of Martin Luther's preface to Romans in a meetinghouse at Aldersgate. Unable to continue his resistance against divine revelation, Wesley believed the gospel of Jesus Christ and was wonderfully converted. Prior to Wesley, Luther had classified Psalm 130 among what he called the "Pauline Psalms," because of their emphasis on forgiveness of sins through God's grace.[1]

Psalm 130 provides an especially powerful text for ministering to needy people. The opening words, "out of the depths," (NRSV, NIV) point to the valleys of life that sooner or later we all pass through, perhaps because of our sinful behavior. The psalmist felt pressed down, afflicted, oppressed. His circumstances were demoralizing and debilitating. He was on the borders of life, far from the safe haven of comfort and rest. The paradox is that no matter how lonely and empty the psalmist felt, he knew that God was not far away, because he had already experienced his mercy and forgiveness in the past. These kinds of experiences often mean that we trudge on, waiting in hope for God to forgive us again. It can sometimes be like whiling away the endless hours of a long night, ever hoping for the darkness to end and the sun of healing to arise. Actually, the waiting might be for days on end, even months. Solutions for the messes our sinful behavior causes are rarely quick and easy. When we give ourselves into God's keeping, he will bring about our deliverance in his perfect timing. He is a forgiving and merciful God.

Many Christians expect confession of sin to be painless and forgiveness instantaneous. They seem not to realize that sin may have lasting natural consequences. Indeed, they tend to forget that sin can be so offensive that the offended party needs to hear more than a few words of confession. Consider a child who disobeys his father and throws a ball in the house, only to shatter the front picture window or break an antique lamp. "Hey, Dad, I'm sorry," probably will not be sufficient to appease the judge in this family court.

In Psalm 130 two themes run side by side: waiting and forgiveness. The psalmist's point is worthy of thoughtful consideration. How and under what circumstances does God forgive? Might he delay forgiveness while we learn the lesson of our sinfulness? Does he desire more from us than mere words of confession? This is not to suggest, however, that all the valleys of life are a result of sin. But in this psalm, the two are linked together.

Why Did the Author Compose the Psalm?

Although one-third of the psalms of ascent include a reference to authorship in their headings (David in 122; 124; 131; and 133; and Solomon in 127), Psalm 130 offers no such heading and no sure means of identifying its author. Both Psalms 130 and 131 conclude with the same exhortation, instructing Israel to "hope in the LORD" (Pss. 130:7; 131:3).[2] Both psalms also use the same poetic style in repeating their main imagery, thereby creating a greater emphasis on the main themes. It may also provide a potential connection between the two in terms of their arrangement within the Psalms (cf. 130:6, "more than watchmen do for the morning" [NET, twice] and 131:2, "like a young child" [NET, twice]). Relationships of this nature could indicate a common Davidic authorship, but they are not adequate evidence by themselves.

Commentators have difficulty reconstructing the psalmist's circumstances that led him to pen the song. The psalm heading ("A song of
ascents") provides, at minimum, a glimpse of the ultimate use to which
Israelite worship appointed the psalm. In Jewish tradition Levites sang
the fifteen songs of ascent on the fifteen steps leading from the temple's
court of the women to the court of the Israelites. Although pilgrims may
have employed these psalms while ascending to the temple, some of the
psalms obviously were not composed specifically for that purpose. Within
Psalms 120–134 some scholars identify a poetic steplike parallelism
wherein a term in one line is echoed in the following line. They associate
the psalms' heading ("A song of ascents") with that phenomenon. Other
interpreters associate these psalms with the exiles' return to Judah.[3] Most
commentators, however, are of the opinion that pilgrims to the annual
festivals in Jerusalem sang these psalms as they ascended to Jerusalem
and the temple (cf. 2 Kings 23:2; Neh. 12:37; Ps. 42:4).[4] Michael Wilcock
observes that the Feast of Tabernacles in 445 B.C.E., presided over by
Ezra and Nehemiah, might provide an event significant to the psalms
of ascent:

> The incident of Nehemiah 13:15–22 could date from the three
> or four Sabbaths between the setting up of Jerusalem's new gates
> (7:1–3; 13:19) and the beginning of Tabernacles. Both the people
> and their leaders were responsible for the Sabbath-breaking
> that it describes. The whole community needed cleansing.
> *Full redemption* covers the unrighteousness of all, repeated
> backsliding, and every sin.[5]

Leon Liebreich parallels these fifteen psalms with the fifteen Hebrew
words of the Aaronic benediction in Numbers 6:24–26. He takes the
psalms of ascent as an elaboration of the benediction's key terms.[6]
Wilcock, on the other hand, believes that the songs form five sets of three
psalms, each set focusing on a theme of distress in the first psalm, power
in the second, and security in the third.[7] In this fashion, in the fourth set
of three (Pss. 129–131) he identifies Psalm 129 with the theme of distress,
Psalm 130 with power, and Psalm 131 with security. Such a structure
echoes the overall arrangement of the collection, which commences
with a prayer of distress (Ps. 120) and concludes with a call to praise
(Ps. 134). However, Wilcock's identification of power as a theme in this
psalm appears to be in conflict with the theme of hope, which is evident
from the repetition of terms for hope. Likewise, verse 6 might indicate
"that the petitioner sang the song at night" while "waiting for Yahweh's
intervention, which...occurs mostly in the early morning."[8]

Depending on how one interprets the verbs, this psalm is either an individual prayer of thanksgiving (taking the verbs as past in time) or a personal lament (taking the verbs as present in time). This ambiguity results from the timing of the Hebrew verbs being a function of context rather than form. This is especially so in Hebrew poetry. Defining the genre is difficult–perhaps it consists of both an individual (vv. 1–6) and a community complaint (vv. 7–8).[9] At the start, the psalmist reveals his petition:

> O sovereign Master, listen to me!
> Pay attention to my plea for mercy! (v. 2).

Verses 3 and 4 focus primarily on the problem of sin, while verses 3–8 overall proclaim the psalmist's trust in the Lord to resolve this serious spiritual issue. The Lord's solution includes forgiveness of sins (vv. 3–4) and the granting of mercy (vv. 7–8; cf. v. 2).

How Did the Author Express His Ideas?

A rich repertoire of poetic devices appears in this brief psalm. Repetition of key words is characteristic of Psalm 130. Such repetitions behave as "links in a chain" within the psalm.[10] Hebrew poets appear to have employed repetition for a number of purposes. One purpose is to highlight a concept. At the ends of the two lines of verse 2 the repetition of "voice" might indicate that the psalmist verbalized his pleading, rather than praying silently. Verse 2a ends with "to me" (lit., "to my voice") and 2b ends with "my plea for mercy" (lit., "the voice of my supplications"). Likewise, both occurrences of "deliver" in verses 7 and 8 are from the same root (lit., "redeem"), highlighting the concept of deliverance.

Another purpose of repetition is to establish the boundaries of a section of a psalm. In verses 3 and 8 the repetition of "sins" brackets verses 3–8 in a way that provides cohesion for that section of the psalm. Yet another purpose of repetition is to indicate a theme. This usage of repetition is involved in the two occurrences of "I rely" (actually placed back-to-back in the Hebrew text) in verse 5a-b. "Wait" (v. 5c) and "hope" (v. 7a) are from another Hebrew root that is virtually synonymous with the term translated "rely." Therefore, these words provide a fourfold emphasis on the concept of hope or expectation, making "wait" or "hope" a theme in the psalm.

Yet another purpose for repetition is to provide a unifying element with which the psalmist might highlight a climax by a sudden change in the repetitive pattern. In Psalm 130 the psalmist employs three pairs of the divine names "LORD" (*Yahweh*) and "sovereign Master" (*Adonai*). Each of the three pairs are in the same order (vv. 1b, 2a, 3, 5a, 6a). Following these three pairs, verse 7 closes the psalm's patterned usage of divine names by repeating "LORD" twice, signaling the psalm's climax. Finally, repetition can be used to display unity within a psalm. This appears to be the reason that "watchmen...for the morning" occurs twice (v. 6)—to echo the first use of the same Hebrew root word translated as "keep track of" in verse 3. Such a use helps unify the psalm for the original audience and perhaps provides an aid for remembering the psalm's wording. Verses 1b–2a contain two parallel lines that mirror each other in inverse order:

A. From the deep water
  B. I cry out to you,
    C. O LORD.
    C'. O sovereign Master,
  B'. listen
A'. to me.

In this kind of mirror structure focus is on the central elements. Thus a God-centered theme is apparent (C and C'). Two divine titles draw attention to the twin facts that God has a covenant relationship to his people ("LORD") and that he is master of his creation ("sovereign Master").

What Are the Important Interpretive Issues?

Psalm 130's key interpretive issue involves the understanding of "deliver" (lit. "redeem" in vv. 7 and 8). Are the psalmist's statements merely references to divine rescue from earthly troubles,[11] or does the psalmist intend that his readers understand them as indications of spiritual salvation—forgiveness of sins? The Hebrew term "deliver" has a commercial background (namely, making a ransom payment or providing a redemption price). A synonym (from which the concept of "kinsman redeemer" is derived) occurs in other Old Testament passages. It indicates a family setting or relationship. In this psalm, however, "deliver" implies deliverance by means of a payment. The psalm includes no identification of the form of payment, who paid it, or to whom it was paid.

NET Bible's notes explain that the phrase, "is more than willing to deliver," represents what others have translated as "full redemption"[12] or even "plenteous redemption."[13] The Hebrew noun is somewhat rare in Scripture, occurring only here, Psalm 111:9; Exodus 8:19; and Isaiah 50:2. The double occurrence of "deliver" (or "redeem") brings the psalm to a close with a focus on the deliverance "from all his iniquities" (lit. translation). This prepositional phrase makes it clear that the psalmist does not intend that his readers think only of deliverance from physical circumstances and conditions. This can be a spiritual matter involving all of Israel's iniquities or guilt. Such a focus is the basis for the synagogue's selection of Psalm 130 as a reading for the Day of Atonement.[14]

In addition to the nature of the redemption, we must also consider the matter of its timing. Is the declaration historical ("he has redeemed"), prophetic ("he will *soon* redeem"), or eschatological ("he will *ultimately* redeem")? The historical viewpoint might point to the people of Israel coming to the temple to praise the Lord for their deliverance from the Babylonian captivity. The prophetic interpretation might represent Israel as performing an annual pilgrimage. At that time, they would be hoping for deliverance to come from some unidentified enemy or catastrophe (such as a locust plague or famine).[15]

The eschatological view would best apply to a distant expectation that God will ultimately fulfill all of his covenant promises for a permanent state of peace and righteousness. Such a state could only come about under the benevolent and just reign of King Messiah. As James Mays observes, "The declaration has an eschatological reach unusual in the Old Testament. Psalm 25:22 prays for the Lord 'to redeem Israel from all its troubles,' a prayer that in its similarity with the declaration reminds us that redemption includes liberation not only from guilt but also from the whole imprisoning network of sin's effects on life."[16] Psalm 130 might look to more than one reference or setting. First, the psalmist speaks of his immediate distress (unspecified circumstances) that is the consequence of his sinful behavior. Second, the psalmist might speak of Israel's eventual deliverance from the Babylonian exile. Lastly, such deliverances might be the springboard to consider an eschatological deliverance in the distant future.

What Was the Author Seeking to Communicate?

Psalm 130's structure offers some clues regarding its author's intended message. The psalmist reveals a problem with sin (vv. 3–4), which he confesses following his petition for mercy (v. 2). His petition is literally for "grace" ("plea for mercy" is literally a "plea for grace"–the root word in Hebrew is the source for the English name "Hannah"). Ultimately, divine forgiveness is the solution to the psalmist's problem (vv. 7–8).[17]

The Psalmist's Petition (vv. 1–2)

Verse 1 in the NET translation depicts the psalmist as floundering in deep water (cf. Ps. 69:1–2, 14–15). Terror and despair grip his heart as he anticipates a death that he can only associate with death by drowning.[18] His circumstances are serious, but their identity remains unspecified. Over his head in trouble, he cries out to the Lord and pleads for grace

(v. 2). Since God is sovereign over all circumstances, he is able to answer the psalmist's petition for unmerited divine favor.

The Psalmist's Peril (vv. 3–4)

Assurance of deliverance or forgiveness is not part of the psalmist's thinking at this point in the progress of the psalm.[19] He believes that God sees all and knows all and that God will not overlook sins the psalmist has committed. God will hold him accountable; his sin will not go unpunished. "You are willing to forgive" (v. 4a) might be translated literally as "with you there is forgiveness." This is the only occurrence in the psalms of the Hebrew noun translated as "forgiveness," the rare noun occurring only here and in Daniel 9:9 and Nehemiah 9:17. The corresponding Hebrew verb ("forgive") is used in Psalms 25:11; 86:5; and 103:3, along with forty-six other occurrences. On the human side of things, forgiveness is the ultimate goal for which the psalmist hopes and waits. On the divine side, however, the ultimate aim is that God might be feared (v. 4b).

Psalm 130's author focuses primarily on the concept of forgiveness, because it is the basis on which even physical deliverance occurs. A temporary deliverance from present danger is of no lasting value if the individual has no established spiritual relationship lasting beyond this world's circumstances. According to Leviticus 26:39–45, God promised to fulfill his covenants with the Israelites if they confessed their sins and humbled their hearts before him. Divine retribution (including Israel's time of exile) has as its ultimate goal the repentance of the Lord's covenant people. Fear of the Lord and repentance (turning from wickedness) are paired in Proverbs 3:7 ("fear the LORD and turn away from evil"). When Israel repents, God reinstates or reactivates the Abrahamic covenant's blessings. The Lord remains loyal to his covenant—even when his covenant people are disloyal (cf. a similar concept in 2 Tim. 2:13).

The Psalmist's Proclamation (vv. 5–6)

Because he has not yet experienced either the Lord's forgiveness for the sin(s) that resulted in his current distress or deliverance from it, the psalmist waits expectantly for any word from God that might indicate an answer to prayer (v. 5; cf. 40:1). His night of waiting seems unending, but he knows that morning will come (v. 6). Watchmen stand guard for a certain portion of the night. They are aware of the passing of time; citizens might even ask them the hour (cf. Isa. 21:11–12). When the light of dawn finally comes, the watchman realizes that the time of real danger has passed and that another will come to replace him. Anyone who has stood guard in the last hours of the night knows the sweet relief that morning light brings. The psalmist awaits deliverance with the same expectant hope.

The Psalmist's Paranesis and Prophecy (vv. 7–8)

Israel must wait for the Lord, because he exercises "loyal love" toward his people (v. 7a-b). God has not abandoned them, nor will he neglect to fulfill his covenant with them. Indeed, the Lord will deliver Israel by means of full (or abundant) redemption (v. 7c). In other words, he will deliver Israel completely from their sins (v. 8). Just as he will deliver the psalmist from his physical distress, the covenant Lord will deliver his people from their greater spiritual distress. (For a fuller discussion of this redemptive interpretation, see above under "What Are the Important Interpretive Issues?")

What Is the Significance of the Psalm for Preaching and Teaching?

Expositors must grasp the significance of forgiveness as the ultimate theological theme of Psalm 130. Without a right relationship with God, we have no promise of deliverance from even the temporal trials of life. The psalmist waits for his own deliverance with great expectation. His despair and terror are compounded by the thought that his current circumstances might permanently separate him from the Lord and his loyal love. Therefore, he confesses his sinful condition and petitions for grace (unmerited divine favor). Having done so, he awaits evidence of divine forgiveness. Confession alone is inadequate to bring about complete restoration. First, our sins bring natural consequences. Drug addiction might leave permanent damage to a person's brain that will never be healed. Abuse of a spouse's trust can lead to years of distrust and suspicion. Failure to be consistent in living one's faith can produce multiplied faithlessness in one's children and grandchildren lasting for generations. One must wait for the healing of such effects from sin. Waiting is part of the process of recovery, for even spiritual wounds take time to heal.

As the psalmist concludes the psalm, he turns to the community as a whole and exhorts them to also wait for the Lord. He has worked through his problem, understood the divine solution (which includes waiting), and exhorts Israel to follow his example. Redemption (deliverance) from sins is not for the psalmist alone—it is what God can and will accomplish for the nation. However, they, too, must be willing to wait patiently until their circumstances turn for the better. The wilderness wanderings lasted for two generations. The exile in Babylon lasted for seventy years. Many Israelites never saw the time of inheritance or the time of restoration. Confession of sin did not bring about immediate possession of the land nor restoration to the land. Complete deliverance is yet to come. Meanwhile, the believer must focus on his or her Deliverer–rely on him (v. 5), wait for him (v. 5), yearn for him (v. 6), and hope in him (v. 7).

Modern Christians can identify with the need for confession of sin to renew fellowship with God, rather than to walk in the deathlike darkness of broken fellowship (cf. 1 Jn. 1:8–2:2). Restoring that fellowship begins with focusing intently on him alone. That hope for renewed fellowship is but one application of the truths revealed in Psalm 130. Like Israel, New Testament believers have an eschatological hope (Rom. 8:23–39) that includes redemption, forgiveness, security, and final glorification. We, too, await our full salvation (1 Pet. 1:4–9). Like watchmen waiting for the morning, we ought to cry out, "Come, Lord Jesus!" (Rev. 22:20). He is Israel's "sun of vindication [who] will rise with healing wings" (Mal. 4:2). He is also the hope of the Church.

CHAPTER 15

Psalm 135

Expectations of a Servant

Richard D. Patterson

They were known as "Orphan Trains." They could have been called "Rags-to-Riches Trains." In the late 1800s, New York City was beset with a problem of epic proportions. Thousands of homeless and hopeless children roamed the streets of New York. The conditions were squalid. Disease was rampant. Education was nonexistent. The future was dark. But trains took them to homes across America in the hope that there they would receive new life.

Imagine the difference. Imagine the awe as child after child walked into the house they could now call home, as they sat down to home-cooked meals, as they learned to know their new brothers and sisters, and as they looked up at their new parents and blessed them.

The human race is much like those New York City orphans. Our parents, Adam and Eve, left us estranged from God and without hope. Left to our own devices, we meander the back alleys of life seeking to satisfy our cravings on our own terms. But all the streets are dead ends. The only hope is divine intervention. For the Israelites, the words of Psalm 135 were a Freedom Train departing from the station of hopeless despair: "Indeed, the LORD has chosen Jacob for himself, Israel to be his special possession" (135:4). The great benefactor had chosen the Hebrew nation to be adopted as his own family.

Psalm 135 overflows with a wealth of praise. The psalm is rich in its glowing exaltation of God, praising him for his goodness and greatness as creator and honoring him for being Israel's personal redeemer and sovereign, covenant Lord. The psalm is rich in words and images found throughout Scripture, giving readers the joy of being carried along by God's Spirit to familiar passages.[1] The psalm is rich in its rewards, written especially for those who serve as the Lord's ministers, while all who place their trust in him will be encouraged. Teachers and preachers who reap in this spiritual harvest field and embrace the psalmist's message will join the psalmist in praise and reverential trust. This psalm is a thrill to teach and preach. It can be classified as a hallelujah psalm.

Why Did the Author Compose the Psalm?

Since neither the author nor the historical setting is given in the psalm, dates before and after the exile have been proposed for its composition.[2] If the plethora of preexilic scriptural parallels cited is indicative of date (see footnote 1), the psalmist may be reminding his fellow worshipers that despite the imminent threat of exile, God is to be praised. He has been Israel's redeemer in the past and has shown himself repeatedly to be the true God. The psalm's emphasis on the spiritual presence of the Lord among his people also favors a date just before the exile. For, according to the prophet Ezekiel's vision, God's glory departed from the temple and from Jerusalem at the time of the exile (Ezek. 10:18–19; 11:22–25), not to return until the future reign of the messiah among a redeemed and regathered people (cf. Joel 3:17–21). Moreover, the psalmist is certain of God's future vindication of his people (v. 14). On the other hand, if the psalm is to be understood as written after the exile, these latter emphases would be singularly important for a people that had come back to the land of their fathers and could worship in a newly reestablished temple.

The psalm was designed for use in Israel's liturgy. This is suggested by the mention of those who serve in the temple and those who gather there for worship (vv. 1–2, 19–21). It is reinforced by the nature of the psalm as a hallelujah psalm. Such psalms were typically utilized in formal worship services and often feature an opening ascription of praise to Yahweh. They focus on God's praise as well as on the importance of his name (e.g., Pss. 106:1–3, 8, 12, 47, 48; 113:1–3, 9; 148:1–5, 7, 13–14; 149:1, 3, 9). Psalm 135 likewise underscores the importance of praising God (vv. 1–3, 13, 19–21).

The parallels noted above, echoing similar themes in other psalms, confirm that Psalm 135 was written for corporate worship. We may infer that the author drew from previously written texts to compose a hymnic anthology with a familiar ring in the ears of the worshipers. He may have written it for one of the three annual high feast days in the Hebrew liturgical calendar.[3]

In any event, the psalmist wishes to assure his hearers/readers that he is aware of things that they should know too. The Lord is sovereign over all things, whether in the natural or political worlds (vv. 6–12). God had elected Israel to be his very own people (v. 4). The Lord delivered Israel out of Egypt and subsequently brought them into the land of promise. All of this stands as historical reality. None of the so-called gods of the nations could do such things and so cannot be compared with the Lord (vv. 5, 15–18). Accordingly, the psalmist wishes all Israel to join him in heartfelt praise to the Lord (vv. 1, 19–21) as one whose name and reputation will last forever (vv. 13–14).

The psalmist is particularly concerned that those who lead in public worship are themselves not only conscious of the Lord's supreme worth but are well aware of their position as God's servants. This realization should inspire them to praise the Lord and to remember that it is their responsibility to lead the people in worship. All of this hints at the psalmist's own place within the priestly order. As a fellow priest, his concern was first and foremost the Lord's exaltation. Yet, as we have seen, the psalm's opening and closing emphases suggest the psalmist's added concern that his fellow ministers possess a sense of their privileged high calling.

How Did the Author Express His Ideas?

The poet's concerns and goals are expressed with great literary artistry, through the abundant use of imagery, figures, themes, and motifs resonating throughout his phraseology. They are as follows.

God's name (v. 1). By the psalmist's time the Lord's *name* came to indicate his established character and reputation.[4] The psalmist reminds his hearers that based on who God is and what he does, standing before him in service should be a pleasant task (vv. 3, 13).

God's ministers as servants (vv. 1–2, 14). Despite their high calling, the psalmist reminds leaders that they have a master–the Lord himself. Thus, they are his servants.[5] As such, they are expected to seek God's will and to be obedient, trustworthy, and faithful (cf. Mt. 10:24; 24:45; 25:21). The psalmist, therefore, is concerned at the outset that those who render service and praise to God be conscious of his role as master and of their role as servants.

God's goodness in considering Israel his special possession (v. 4). The force of the psalmist's words would be familiar to those trained in the Scriptures, reminding the people how they came to enjoy the special privilege of being God's chosen people.[6] Indeed, the metaphor here is a strong one involving a unique meaning derived both from the Hebrew word and from the interaction of the terms: God and Israel as God's special possession. God is portrayed as an owner/possessor and Israel as that which is possessed. More than that, Israel is declared to be God's unique, special possession. Much as man was created to be unique among God's creation (Gen. 1:26–27), a believing Israel, as his chosen and redeemed people (cf. vv. 8–12), is unique and special to God. Therefore, Israel should be reminded that they were to reflect the nature of the Redeemer to whom they belong.

God in his graciousness had purchased Israel, redeeming her out of bondage in Egypt, not because of her goodness, but simply because he loved her and because he would be faithful to the promise made to the Patriarchs (Deut. 7:6–11). He entered into a covenant with his people, asking only that they should love him and be faithful, just as he had been toward them (Ex. 19:5). This meant that they should reflect his holy standards in their lives (Deut. 14:1–2) and be assured of seeing good success (Deut. 26:16–19). They were to be to God "a kingdom of priests and a holy nation" (Ex. 19:6).[7] If this is true of the nation, it is especially true of those who serve as priests to God. As God's special ministers, they will care well for the master's special possession.

The psalmist uses the name Jacob rather than Israel. Although Jacob is often used to designate the Northern Kingdom and occurs in parallel with the name Israel (e.g., Nah. 2:2), the nature of Jacob's personal early character is usually not lost when it appears in later texts. Jacob the trickster had no claim on God's goodness (cf. Hos. 12:2–6). He achieved his greatness only when confronted with the supremacy and Lordship of the God who kindly conferred his blessings on him.[8] All Israel is blest only in the goodness of God and his choice of them to be his own.

The greatness of God. Using several figures, the psalmist underscores the greatness of the God whom he and his fellow servants served. By employing heaven, earth, and sea as figures to represent the whole created world, the poet calls attention to Yahweh as both the creator and controller of the natural world (v. 6; cf. Gen. 1:1–9; Ex. 20:4). He also likens God to a person who has vast storehouses where he keeps the various forces of nature (v. 7). Like a mighty ruler and great warrior, he may bring them out as his weapons or instruments to do his bidding whenever and wherever he chooses.

By implication, therefore, the Lord's greatness is seen not just in his control of nature but in the fact that he is nature's creator. The so-called gods of the nations, which were widely celebrated as being in charge of certain aspects of nature, are therefore inferior to Yahweh, in as much as he who creates things is the owner and master rather than being one who merely uses that which is at his disposal.

The exodus. The psalmist proceeds to an event that became a standard motif in ancient Israel–the exodus event (vv. 8–12; cf. Ex. 15:1–18; Judg. 5:4–5; Pss. 18:7–15; 68:7–8; 77:14–20; 144:5–6; Hab. 3:3–15). He provides a summary not only of that fateful night in which Egypt's firstborn died but also of the whole exodus movement from Egypt to Canaan (vv.

8–9; cf. Pss. 78:51; 105:36; 136:10). This included many victories over opposing nations along the way and Israel's eventual settlement in the promised land (vv. 10–12). The psalmist's portrayal of the acquisition of Canaan as Israel's inheritance serves as a reminder of the inviolability of God's promises, first to Abraham (Gen. 13: 14–15; 17:1–8) and then to Israel (Ex. 12:24–25; 15:13–18). These would later be channeled through the line of David (2 Sam. 7:11–26; Ps. 89:20–29, 35–37) and reach their culmination in a prophesied new covenant centered in the messiah (Jer. 31:31–34; Ezek. 34:20–30; 37:18–28). The New Testament would later reveal that the new covenant became enacted in Christ's finished word (Mt. 26:27–29; 2 Cor. 3:6; Heb. 8). In all of this the psalmist finds cause to celebrate God's greatness.[9]

The rehearsal of the exodus event stirs the psalmist to once again celebrate the force of the name of Yahweh and to bring to mind the image of God as judge (vv. 13–14; cf. Deut. 32:36). The psalmist presents God as the one who vindicates and judges on behalf of his people. This occasions the psalmist's further praise of God for his compassion on his chosen people (vv. 13–14). Here the psalmist plays on words whose sounds and letters resemble his statement in the earlier part of the psalm. God's compassion in vindicating his people thus recalls the effect of the pleasing nature of praising God's name (v. 4). Indeed God's goodness and compassion toward Israel in making them his own–and liberating them from Egypt and bringing them into the land of promise–has established Yahweh's name as pleasant and to be praised throughout all future generations.

Idols of the nations. The psalmist returns to considering the theme of the idols of the nations. The conquest of the various nations had demonstrated that their gods are powerless before the true God of the universe (vv. 15–18; cf. v. 5). Here the psalmist employs a literary genre known as satire. As with most satirical pieces, the psalmist has (1) a clear object of attack–the idols; (2) a satirical vehicle for expressing the attack–the fine poetry he has composed; (3) a satirical tone–a biting satire bordering on sarcasm; and (4) a satirical norm by which the object of attack is judged and criticized–the reality of the true God, Yahweh (cf. Ps. 115:2–8; Isa. 44:12–20).

The priesthood. A further source of imagery is seen in the psalmist's depiction of the priesthood as a house (NET, "family," vv. 19–20), and Jerusalem as God's dwelling (v. 21). The first image emphasizes the unity and solidarity of the priesthood, while the second speaks of the unity of God with his people. Here the psalmist's mind may well have carried him to God's past dwelling (or "tabernacling") among his people through the exodus journey. He would remember that God's dwelling with Israel is the result, not of Israel's merit, but of God's unmerited favor (Deut. 7:7–8; 9:1–6). Clearly, God's presence demanded what Israel did not always display–a holy life lived out in his people's consciousness as they lived in the presence of God (cf. Lev. 20:7–8; Deut. 26:16–19; 1 Kings 8:27–29; Pss. 116:8–9; 119:1–3; Isa. 2:1–3).

Structure of the psalm. The psalmist's literary artistry is displayed in his structuring of the whole psalm. The opening and closing hallelujahs make it clear that the psalmist has composed a praise psalm. Like other such psalms, this psalm has an opening call to praise the Lord (vv. 1–2), followed by a catalog of details that present motives for doing so (vv. 3–18), and concluding with a final invitation to join him in praising the Lord (vv. 19–21).

A distinctive feature of the psalmist's literary ability is his arranging of the central catalog in bi-fid (or two part) structure, each section nicely answering the other. The whole psalm may thus be outlined as follows:

Opening call to praise the LORD (vv. 1–2)	
Catalog of motives for praising the LORD (vv. 3–18)	
A. In his great goodness	B. His unchanging nature guarantees
God has chosen Israel to be his people (vv. 3–12)	**His vindication of and compassion for his people (vv. 13–18)**
1. Ascription of praise for God's goodness to his chosen people (vv. 3–4)	1. Declaration of God's fame and unchanging compassion (vv. 13–14)

2. Reminder of God's greatness (vv. 5–12)
  a. over all gods (v. 5)
  b. over nature (vv. 6–7)
  c. over Egypt (vv. 8–9)
  d. over the nations (vv. 10–12)
	2. Rehearsal of God's greatness as compared with other gods and their idols (vv. 15–18)

Concluding call to praise the LORD who dwells in Zion (vv. 19–21)	

Moreover, the individual parts of the whole psalm are arranged with consummate skill. The entire psalm is bracketed by the need for praise and the emphasis on ministers/priests (vv. 1–2, 19–21). Likewise, the psalmist has linked each section together by means of key words or themes. For example, verses 3–12 and 13–18 are linked together via the phrase "his people" (vv. 12, 14) and "his name" (vv. 3, 13), as well as by the importance of the exodus event as evidence of God's relationship with his people as a special possession (vv. 8–12, 13–14). Both portions of the central bi-fid structure contain an emphasis on God's goodness/ compassion (vv. 3–4, 13–14) and on his greatness (vv. 5–12, 15–18), particularly in comparison with the so-called gods of the nations (vv.

5, 15). Thus, the psalm displays at every turn the artistry of the poet in designing a carefully crafted piece of literature designed for use in the worship service and for ease of memorization.

What Are the Important Interpretive Issues?

Though the book of Psalms may appear to be a random collection of poems, closer inspection demonstrates that the psalms were intentionally placed in groups, often by material held in common, such as authorship or subject matter. Individual psalms usually contain some theme or catchword that links them to surrounding psalms.[10] While Psalm 135 is anonymous and cannot be linked on the basis of authorship, it is no surprise to discover that the previous psalm is also a hallelujah psalm, which begins in similar fashion with a call to those who minister in the Lord's service (Pss. 134:1; 135:1-2). Furthermore, both psalms end on a note of blessing/praise (Pss. 134:3; 135:19-21). Note that the word translated "praise" in Psalm 135:19-21 is the same Hebrew word meaning "bless." Psalm 134 invokes God's blessing on the ministers; in Psalm 135 the priests are to render back to God praises for the LORD's blessing on his people. Psalm 135 also has thematic associations with Psalm 136. Both psalms praise the Lord for his goodness and greatness (Pss. 135:3, 5; 136:1, 4).[11]

Unlike other psalms, Psalm 135 reads in straightforward fashion. The few interpretive difficulties are duly noted in the NET footnotes. Among these, however, a few are worthy of special attention. In verse 3 the NET Bible understands God's name to be pleasant; other translations stress the pleasantness of the act of praising God. Both are doubtless true, although the force of the context favors the reading in the NET footnote. In verses 4-5, as opposed to traditional translations, the NET has correctly rendered the introductory Hebrew particle *ki* as an emphatic particle meaning "indeed," or "yes." The NET translation has the advantage of underscoring the psalmist's stress on the certainty of his knowledge and convictions. Both verses could have been translated "surely," or "truly." In verse 9 the traditional "signs and wonders" of the Hebrew text is interpreted in the NET as "awesome deeds and acts of judgments." The main difficulty here is the loss of standard phraseology in a familiar motif dealing with God's activity.[12] The same phrase occurs in Exodus 7:3, which the NET duly translates "signs and wonders."[13]

What Was the Author Seeking to Communicate?

In the opening ascription of praise (vv. 1-2) the psalmist follows the traditional format of hallelujah psalms by praising the Lord and his name.[14] These beginning verses make it obvious that the psalmist is especially concerned that those who serve the Lord as his ministers/

priests share the same consciousness of the primacy of the Lord. They stand before God (v. 8) and not anyone else. They minister in his presence, serving the one whose name, character, and reputation have been fully demonstrated.

As though this were insufficient, the psalmist goes on to assign specific reasons for praise: God's goodness in choosing Israel as his very own special possession and his greatness as evidenced in his creation and control of nature–things that none of the false gods of the nations could do. The psalmist therefore wishes to emphasize both Yahweh's superiority to the so-called gods and their powerless idols, *and* Yahweh's love for his own. The psalmist reinforces the latter by reminding his readers of God's love for Israel during the exodus event.

All of this should serve as a motivation that challenges those who have been especially selected to minister for the Lord–the families of Aaron and Levi. In addition, they should realize that they minister as servants of their heavenly master, not as those who lord it over the ones to whom they minister. Theirs was a solemn responsibility to represent God to Israel, which was not limited to special times of worship. Their lives, therefore, should exemplify the one whom they represent. The psalmist is concerned not only for the priests. He wishes all Israelites to appreciate the great privilege they have as God's chosen ones.

Although this Psalm was designed to be used in Israel's liturgy, nevertheless the worshipers would have heard it orally. To be understood properly, the reader of the Psalm should "enter the world of the spoken word, a word that can be fully understood only by the exercise of the whole person. The reader must be attentive to the effect of the message not only on mind and eye but also on ear and heart."[15] As we read this Psalm, therefore, having utilized our basic interpretive tools (grammar, history/culture, literary and theological data), we should as much as possible imagine ourselves in the place of the original hearers. Can we perceive and appropriate what the psalmist was endeavoring to communicate and, having heard and understood, can we react properly?[16] If so, we should feel the psalmist's genuine love for God and his concern for God's reputation as well as the people's conscious response in admiration of the one who dwells in their midst. How good and great he is! Accordingly, ministers and priests alike should so live as to render back to the Lord praise for all the many blessings the Lord has bestowed on his people.

What Is the Significance of the Psalm for Preaching and Teaching?

Given its compelling message for God's people and for those who minister to them, this psalm is very appropriate for the pulpit and the Sunday school classroom. It is a timeless message, just as significant for those who are called to minister today as in the days of the psalmist.[17] Pastors should be reminded that they are empowered with a special place of leadership with awesome responsibilities similar to the Israelite priests. Yet they are no less servants of the same heavenly master as their parishioners (cf. Hab. 3:5; 2 Tim. 2:15, 21). For, like their Savior, Jesus Christ, they have been called not "to be served but to serve" (Mk. 10:45). In their service they are to be faithful in all things (Col. 1:7; 1 Tim. 1:12; Titus 1:7) as those who must give an account of their stewardship (Heb. 13:17; cf. Lk. 12:42–48).

Although the psalmist especially speaks to those who had special places of ministry as Israel's priests, he reminds all Israelites that they are to praise the Lord and live praiseworthy lives. Like Israel of old, Christians today have experienced God's goodness and greatness in being elected into God's family through faith in Christ Jesus (Rom. 8:28–30; Eph. 1:3–14; 2:4–10; 1 Thess. 2:13–14). As such, the New Testament believer likewise partakes of the promise of the patriarchs through faith in Christ (Gal. 3:6–9, 15–18, 26–29) and is counted as God's special possession (Titus 2:14). Christians, like Israel of old, are part of "a royal priesthood, a holy nation," serving God and reflecting God's holy standards (1 Pet. 2:9–12).

Made part of God's family through the grace of God and faith in Christ, the Christian may not only experience the abundant life that Jesus promised (Jn. 10:10) but may also be assured of God's loving regard as his "special possession," his peculiar treasure. With such a realization, the believer ought to live so as to produce a treasure-filled life (1 Cor. 3:12–13; 2 Cor. 4:1–7).

As believers live out their lives in a faithful walk and work for the Lord, they must never forget God's goodness and greatness. Much as Israel was redeemed out of Egypt and brought into the land of promise, Christians have been redeemed from slavery to sin (Eph. 1:7) so that they may proclaim the virtues of the one who called them "out of darkness into his marvelous light" (1 Pet. 2:9). No less than Israel (Ezek. 37:24–27) as heirs of the Abrahamic Covenant (Gal. 3:26–29), they look forward to a "promised land." Theirs will be a glorious future (Col. 1:27) when Christ shall reign on a refreshed and glorified earth and dwell among a believing mankind (Rev. 21:3).

The psalmist's final words concerning God's dwelling among his people take on a special significance. We are reminded that before that great day, Christ's first "dwelling" was also a glorious taking up of residence among men. When Christ became flesh, it was no less than a visitation of the *shekinah* glory.[18] It was the promised Immanuel–God with us! Nor was he less glorious when he hung on the cross for man's salvation and rose triumphant from the grave (Jn. 12:12–28: 17:1–4).

Paul reminds believers that with Jesus' incarnation mission accomplished at Calvary and in the resurrection, the ascended Lord has taken the believer into union with himself (Eph. 2:19–22). Therefore, the Christian has not only a sure hope of a glorious future (Col. 1:27) but an ever-present source of strength in the spiritual service (2 Cor. 12:9) of revealing that One to others (Gal. 1:16).

The psalmist's message, thus, has practical ramifications for all believers. Mindful of their high calling and God's goodness and greatness toward them, believers can and should proudly bear the name of God in Christ and live so as not to bring reproach on it (Acts 5:41; 3 Jn. 7). They who have been so blessed should live in his presence (cf. Gen. 17:1) so as to be a blessing to others (Gen. 12:2).

Unlike the children of Israel who were too often led astray into idolatry, today's believers need to guard themselves against idolizing the things of this world (1 Jn. 5:21). Like Jesus, they should submit their personal desires to the Lord's will (Jn. 5:30) "as good stewards of the varied grace of God" (1 Pet. 4:10).

In preaching and teaching Psalm 135 one should keep in mind the riches of this psalm. Paul reminds believers of the riches of God's grace all along the pilgrim journey: from the riches of his kindness that led to our repentance (Rom. 2:4), to the riches of God's forgiveness and redemption (Eph. 1:7) and saving work in Christ (Eph. 2:7), and on to the riches of his glory, by which he has fashioned believers for glorious living in his presence both now and forever (Rom. 9:23; Eph. 1:18). Paul summed it all up by stating, "Oh, the depth of the riches and wisdom and knowledge of God! How unsearchable are his judgments and how fathomless his ways!" (Rom. 11:33).

CHAPTER 16

Psalm 148

The Surprising Score of a Cosmic Anthem

Andrew J. Schmutzer

Reading the book of Psalms can be like listening to a symphony. Some movements may be in a minor key, with the emotion of a slow, plodding funeral procession. In the book of Psalms, laments are in a minor key, reflecting the psalmist's struggle with the "valley of the shadow of death." In other movements of a symphony, a composer may create a feeling of exhilaration. The music sparkles, the tempo is *allegro*, and the conductor calls on every instrument in the orchestra to offer the fullest sound possible. Among the psalms, hymns of praise uniquely sparkle, evoking the peak of lively emotions, as God's name is lifted up and all his creation praises him. The closing flourish of psalms (146–150) functions as the Psalter's *grand finale*. Within this grand finale, Psalm 148 stands out at several levels. Not only does creation receive startling attention, the very genre of a praise hymn is used in surprising ways. However, the simplicity of its movement from heavens (v. 1) to earth (v. 6) conceals a literary skill we must passionately read, not passively recite.

The power of Psalm 148 also comes from its placement within the *final doxology* of the Psalter (Pss. 146–150).[1] Understanding the canonical placement of Psalm 148 helps us not only appreciate other elements of praise, it also gives valuable clues to the historical and liturgical function of the psalm. Slowing down long enough to reflect on its location, literary contour, and theological message is essential to achieve a "thicker" reading. According to K. Vanhoozer, a reading "is sufficiently thick when it allows us to appreciate everything the author is doing in a text."[2] More than a chorus of praise, Psalm 148 envelops the reader in a cosmic anthem.

Why Did the Author Compose the Psalm?

Like many psalms, the purpose of Psalm 148 does not simply drop in one's lap; the communicator (pastor/teacher) must be willing to look further. A greater awareness of the Psalter's structure always contributes to the study and presentation of any given psalm. In the case of Psalm 148, not only are *internal* clues, such as place names, lacking, but the traditional *superscription* (title information) containing personal names, liturgical instructions, or genre designations is also absent.[3] The name of a Levite or even David might help clarify the psalm's aim, but the last Davidic unit, for example, comprises Psalms 138–145.

A psalm's lack of historical incidences or stated authorship may be intentional to facilitate its broader use in worship.[4] This certainly is the effect for 148. Nevertheless, to zero in on its purpose, we must examine the literary genre, textual environment, and socio-religious context surrounding 148. At several levels, Psalms 146–150 form a single literary unit, a doxological composite as the Psalter's *grand finale*.

The Political Setting

Psalm 148 reflects a political setting more than an author's occasion. The best argument for the setting of 148 is the post-exilic context.[5] Observing this exilic theme in the grand sweep of the Psalter seems to confirm this. Psalms 42 and 43 instruct the community how to face exile–"I was once walking along with the great throng to the Temple of God... Wait for God!" (42:4,11; *Book II*). Psalm 89 articulates the crisis of exile–"You have allowed his [David's] adversaries to be victorious" (v. 42; *Book III*).[6] Psalm 106 is a historical review, concluding with national exile and the people's plea for God to "gather us from among the nations!" (v. 47; *Book IV*).

Compiled in the post-exilic setting, *Book V* is in large measure dedicated to the dual reality of the nation's exile (Ps. 107:2–3) coupled with God's loyal love (Ps. 144).[7] The governorship of Nehemiah is a likely part of this socio-religious occasion. For Psalm 148 the Greek translation of the Old Testament (abbreviated LXX) adds the superscription: "of Haggai and Zachariah" (LXX Pss. 145:1; 146:1; 147:1; 148:1), two names directly associated with the post-exilic rebuilding of the temple (cf. Ezra 5:1; 6:14).

Given the common reference to the psalmist's "enemies," a remnant disillusioned by further exile in their own land is not surprising, especially following a new exodus (Ps. 135) and journey (Pss. 120–134).[8] Certain psalmic collections were likely exilic in composition but post-exilic in compilation. Use of the term *diaspora* (LXX Ps. 146:2) certainly confirms an exilic context.[9] In particular, Psalms 135–137 contain pointed reflection on the pain of the Hebrews' exile and God's imminent payback of their enemies–"How can we sing a song to the LORD in a foreign land?"–"O daughter Babylon, soon to be devastated!" (137:4, 8; *Book V*).

The Final Doxology

The literary environment of Psalm 148 has its own unique character. Holding a pivotal role, Psalm 145 not only closes out the final Davidic unit (Pss. 138–145), but it also serves to transition into the final doxology (Pss. 146–150). The note of divine kingship that begins Psalm 145, "I will extol you, my God, O king!" (v. 1), is developed as a theological theme in the cosmic praise of the final doxology. Psalm 145 is also distinguished as the last *alphabetical acrostic* in the Psalter, with its final exhortation–"Let all who live praise his holy name forever!" (v. 21). It is precisely this theme that is illustrated in the following final doxology, culminating in the Psalter's last verse and exhortation–"Let everything that has breath praise the LORD!" (150:6).

Psalms 2 and 149 as "Theological Bookends"

While the ensuing doxology has its own literary profile, numerous terms used in Psalm 145 anticipate their development in the final doxology. For example, the word translated "loyal followers" (145:10; Hebrew *ḥăsîdîm*) bridges 145 to the doxology. Not only does the term close Psalm 148, but it also occurs in the beginning, middle, and end of 149 (148:14; cf. 149:1, 5, 9).[10] More arresting, however, is how Psalm 149:6–9 reveals a *retrospective* advance, a finale of praise that defines the larger final doxology. The "nations," "people," and "kings" of Psalm 2:1–2 reappear as the same cast of characters in Psalm 149:4–8, defining a significant boundary of the Psalter (e.g., Psalms 2 ⇒ 149).

Two important observations emerge from these literary and theological "bookends." First, in the theology of the final doxology, God also judges Israel's enemies. Judgment is cleansing, and cleansing is part of praise. Israel's protection also disciplines the nations.

> May they praise God
> > while they hold a two-edged sword in their hand,
> in order to take revenge on the nations
> > and punish foreigners.
> They bind their kings in chains,
> > and their nobles in iron shackles,
> and execute the judgment to which their enemies have been
> > sentenced.
> All his *loyal followers* will be vindicated.
> Praise the LORD! (149:6–9; emphasis added)

Book V, then, uses a *new-exodus* theme as a theological precedent for post-exilic hopes. Second, Psalm 149 reassigns the task of implementing God's reign in the world to the "loyal followers" (Hebrew *ḥăsîdîm*), not the Davidic king as in Psalm 2. "God's reign is proclaimed as a *present realty,* but it is always experienced by the faithful amid opposition."[11]

From this alone, three implications can be noted. First, the final doxology completes a major theme by transferring promises formerly attached to the Davidic monarchy to the righteous remnant on a cosmic stage, transcending the particularity of ethnic boundaries. Second, Psalm 148, as we shall see, places *praise* and *judgment* on the same cosmic stage as servants of the universal King. Third, lexical and thematic concepts such as these boldly illustrate how literary relationships must be taken seriously in the wider literary context of theological interpretation in the Psalter.[12] Biblical communication must respect literary structure; communicative competence is built on literary competence.

The Role of Psalm 148 in the Final Doxology

In the final doxology, praise is summoned from key sources for specific reasons. Straddling the five closing praise hymns, Psalm 148 draws on the surrounding themes of nature and history (Pss. 146; 147) and the Zion-politic (Pss. 146:10; 147:12; 149:2) that alternate throughout the final doxology. Placed in the middle, Psalm 148 functions as the literary hinge. The cosmic temple of Psalm 148 unites these themes around creation in praise. On either side of the Zion-politic (i.e., Psalm 149), Psalms 148 and 150 employ imperatival hymns of praise ("praise him..."). In Psalm 148 the returned exiles are swept up in universal praise as part of the cosmic temple that no nation can destroy. This is the grandest temple for post-exilic Israel. In Psalm 148 the doxological worship extols the Lord's ultimate reign in the cosmos, dispelling any competing international powers (cf. Pss. 102:12–17; 123:1–4). Yet theirs is also an anticipatory praise, since "everything that has breath" hardly matches the exiles' experience.[13] Because of its sheer scope, Psalm 148 rises in the middle as the heavens and earth exhale in cosmic worship (vv. 1, 7).

King/Temple
148 Cosmic Praise
King (= Zion-politic) Land ⬆   Land (= Zion-politic) Temple
146—Zion 147—Zion   ➤149—Zion 150—Refrain

As the illustration shows, the final doxology is a doxological mosaic connected by a progression of royal themes: king, land, and temple. Psalm 146 illustrates the Lord's kingly ethics broached in 145:1, 11–13 (cf. 149:2). Compared to the Lord, human dignitaries prove inadequate

(146:3), incapable of "vindicat[ing] the oppressed" (v. 7a) or healing "the blind" (v. 8a); these are now rich metaphors of exile (cf. Isa. 61:1; Zech. 9:12).[14] Because "the LORD protects those residing outside their native land" (146:9a), his kingly mission also actively "rebuilds Jerusalem, and gathers the exiles of Israel" (147:2; cf. 149:4b). Unimpressed by the strength of horse or warrior, the Lord instead "takes delight in his faithful followers" (147:10–11). To Israel alone he has given "statutes" (147:19), a privilege unknown by "any other nation" (147:20; cf. 149:7).

The Lord's "loyal love" (*ḥesed*, 147:11) fosters "loyal followers" (*ḥăsîdîm*, 148:14). Kingly oversight requires cosmic protection. Even the "hailstones" he throws (147:17) are subsequently included in his royal arsenal of "fire," "hail," "snow," and "stormy wind" (148:8): the defense for his people (148:14). The "loyal followers" (*ḥăsîdîm*) closing Psalm 148 (v. 14) now comprise the "assembly of the godly" (*ḥăsîdîm*) that begins Psalm 149. The closing call for earthly praise (148:7–14) becomes the audible expressions of earthly "song," "dancing," and instrumental "accompaniment" ("tambourine and harp," 149:3). The "victorious" (148:14) now rejoice in their "vindication" (149:5). The "kings of the earth" (148:11) must themselves praise the divine "king" (149:2). Praise "from the heavens" (148:1) now echoes in his (heavenly) "sanctuary" (150:1). Psalm 150 intensifies the reality of worship by adding "horn," "lyre," "flute," and "cymbals" (150:3–5) to instruments already summoned for praise (i.e., "tambourine and harp," 149:3). The cosmos makes for a sizeable choir (Psalm 148), for everything owes the Divine King praise (150:6)!

How Did the Author Express His Ideas?

Here we can generally consider the genre of the praise hymn. In particular, we will investigate the broad literary shape of Psalm 148 and how the praise genre is expressed through specific devices. The unique doxological character of Psalm 148 deserves another look.

The Contribution of the Praise Hymn

In hymnic praise we find the equivalent of Israel's "statement of faith." Here the true worshipers of the Lord extol what they believe about their Creator and King (Ps. 149:2).[15] In the praise hymn, the Lord is the exclusive subject and the people are the awed and grateful chorus. The Hebrew expression of praise moves beyond the *specific acts* of God to his *characteristic acts*, so participles are common: "The LORD releases…gives sight… lifts up…loves…protects…opposes" (Ps. 146:7c–9). In Israel's liturgy, these characteristic acts became the *cherished attributes* of God's character: "The LORD is merciful… compassionate…patient…good" (Ps. 145:8–9).[16]

In the hymn, God is praised for several key reasons. These can focus on God as Creator and Ruler (Pss. 117; 147), Creator of Israel (Pss. 111; 114), or Creator of the world, his cosmic temple (Pss. 8; 104; 148). Generally speaking, the praise hymn uses a threefold structure:

> *Call to Praise* (= introduction/the opening summons)
> *Cause for Praise* (= the body with reason to praise using "for" [*kî*])
> *Renewed Call to Praise* (= conclusion/an echo of the beginning)

In this arrangement the cause for praise refers to some action of God benefiting the one praising. In effect, however, this praise is highly *theo-*centric. In the praise hymn, emotional commitment matches cognitive substance about God as celebratory voices break beyond narrative testimony to lyrical self-abandonment (cf. Rom 11:33).[17]

The Doxology of Poetry: The Anthem's Literary Score

The literary logic of Psalm 148 can be scanned as six units of bi-cola (vv. 1–2, 3–4, etc.), culminating with tri-cola (vv. 13–14). As an *imperatival hymn*, the psalm begins with the usual *call to praise,* but the detail that follows is hardly usual. The following chart illustrates how the author uses a profile of terms and syntactical techniques to shape the contour of Psalm 148. Each half (i.e., panel) contains a *domain, catalogue, exhortation,* and *reason.* Here is the literary "skeleton" of Psalm 148.

"LORD" w/ domain indicator ("from the heavens," v. 1a)   Panel A
    = "Praise him," catalogue of the called: imperative (vv. 2a-4b)
       + "LORD" exhortation ("Let them praise," v. 5a)
         "For," reason: 5b in verbal portrait (vv. 5b-6b)

"LORD" w/ domain indicator ("from the earth," v. 7a)   Panel B
    = "sea creatures," catalogue of the called: vocatives (vv. 7b-12b)
       + "LORD" exhortation ("Let them praise," v. 13a)
         "For," reason: 13b in nominal portrait (vv. 13b-14c)

"Praise the LORD" not only forms an *inclusion* (vv. 1a, 14c), it also elevates the central theme of doxological praise in Psalm 148 (twelve times) and the entire final doxology (thirty-two times). "Praise the LORD" is the superscription for each psalm in the final doxology. The "LORD" is not only the exclusive object of praise, its four occurrences in Psalm 148 set off the psalm's four core stanzas (vv. 1a–4b; 5a–6b; 7a–12b; 13a–14c; see above).

The First "Catalogue of the Called": The Heavens Resound in Chorus (2a–4b)

As a praise hymn, Psalm 148 begins in standard fashion (i.e., imperative). What is highly unique, however, is the extensive *call* that quickly becomes a catalogue in each half (vv. 2a–4b; 7b–12b). So prominent is each catalogue that the *cause for praise* appears almost as an afterthought (cf. Ps. 147:12–20). Nevertheless, the psalm's grand movement is not lost; instead, its cosmic emphasis is highlighted. Heaven initiates the cosmic downbeat (first panel) to which the earth must respond (second panel). The moral beings noted at the outset of the first catalogue are matched by the moral agents that close the second catalogue–from "angels" to "children" (vv. 2a; 12b). As the praise cascades down, the "kings of the earth" (v. 11a) form the counterpart to the "heavenly assembly" (v. 2b), the envoys of his divine court (cf. Ps. 89:6–9).

From angelic beings to heavenly bodies, inanimate objects of the skies are also summoned to cosmic worship (vv. 3–4). To the seven occurrences of "praise" in the heavenly domain (vv. 1b–4a) are now added seven corresponding entities (vv. 1b–4b). This use of the number of completeness helps awaken the reader's mind from the lethargy of the familiar as rhythms of nature are exquisitely captured in the rhythm of poetic lines.[18]

The "sun-moon-stars" is a special triad (cf. Ps. 136:7–9). As the angels order the unseen heavens, so the heavenly bodies ably witness to God's splendor and order the light of day (cf. Ps. 8:3). Psalm 148 uniquely personifies this triad as obedient agents in the Creator's praise. Through this triad Psalm 148 finally exclaims what the fourth day of creation could not–their *names*! ("sun and moon," Gen. 1:16). Only the necessity of cosmic praise could make divine heralds from nameless objects. The first catalogue ends with the superlative "highest heaven" (v. 4a; cf. Deut. 10:14). Thematically, the author closes the catalogue with "water," transforming the Creator's most mythological nemesis. Ironically, the very next element (second catalogue) plunges the reader into the watery world of "denizens and all deep regions" (v. 7b), in counterpoint to the spatial realm of the "heavens" (v. 1a). This dual reference to "heaven" (vv. 1, 4) forms a poignant symmetry in the first catalogue with chiastic effect.[19]

> *A.* "from [*min*] the sky" (v. 1a)
>   *B.* "in the heavens" (v. 1b)
>   *B'.* "highest heaven" (v. 4a)
> *A'.* "above [*mēʿal*] the sky" (v. 4b)

To the catalogue of who is summoned for praise is now added the motivation of why–the *cause for praise*. The first reason (vv. 5–6) employs six terms in a *verbal* portrait of the Creator's skill, dominance, and sustaining might. By contrast, the earthly domain will mount a more elaborate *cause for praise* that spans five cola (vv. 13b–14c). In contrast to the verbs of heavenly domain, nouns predominate in the lower realm, boasting six divine possessives. Whereas creation drives the initial reason

(vv. 5–6), historical acts define the second reason (vv. 13–14). Doxological liturgy merges these points. Israel's historical post-exilic *re*-gathering amounts to a national *re*-creation. History has become the "theatre of worship" that emulates the Creator's crafting power in skillful praise.

The irresistible object of praise is now specified as the Lord's name (v. 5, cf. v. 13). Earlier a temple was built for the same name, awing the temple with his name (1 Kings 5:17; 8:16; 9:7). His name was a radical gift of self-revelation that enabled an intimate relationship with his creation.[20] Heavenly bodies must speak in praise precisely because the Lord already spoke in creation (vv. 1a–5b). Therefore, creation will last (v. 6). The longevity of the heavenly bodies is intended to foster hope in the Creator-Redeemer (i.e., "name of the LORD," v. 5a). Those who live with an uncertain history on earth must model their lives on heaven's created order (vv. 7a–12b). History and creation share an interplay that provides an eschatological hope.

The Second "Catalogue of the Called": The Earth Joins the Heavenly Chorus (7a–12b)

The second catalogue is a colorful riot of voices. With only one verbal form ("carries out," 8b), nouns dominate the second catalogue. As a type of acrostic writing, this catalogue boasts twenty-two entities, the number of the Hebrew alphabet.[21] In other words, wholeness is emphasized through a cosmic pictograph of typological numbers, further evidence of the author's conscious writing.

The second catalogue is actually a listing device, a potent form of parallel expression that advances the poetic effect.[22] With so many verbless cola, this listing formula succeeds in parading the universe before the reader. "Psalm 148 profiles the nonhuman world as 'models of praise' for the human world to emulate. At the psalmist's behest, the natural order and the human world are placed on equal footing."[23] Thematically, however, nature finds the loftiest promotion in Psalm 148, not humankind. This helps explain the significance of precipitation (v. 8a) preceding "princes" (v. 11b), as the entire "earth" (v. 7a) now takes up the chorus of heaven–antiphonal choirs are poised for praise. The cosmos is unified, extolling the Cosmic King.

The greatest show of praise comes from nature itself, a carnival of creatures that breathe doxological delights. Scanning this catalogue, the might of praise moves like an army, conscripting the entire cosmos and drowning out the dissonance of hostile threats. Here is a wonderful illustration of a writer's poetic craft. Emphasizing variety in wholeness, the author employs numerous literary devices. For example, the second catalogue thematically closes with "earth" in both cola of verse 11–the very domain indicator of that catalogue (v. 7a). This is also what we find in the first catalogue with a dual use of "heaven" (NRSV) in verse 4–a strategic reiteration of the first domain (v. 1b). So each domain rhetorically uses three occurrences of its defining spatial term to open and close each respective catalogue. The culminating thematic unit (vv. 13–14 NRSV) appropriately employs both earth and heaven (v. 13c) as a merism (two words expressing a single whole). It identifies the entire organized universe in an echo of creation (cf. Gen. 2:1, 4).

Mimicking the topical rhythm of created life in Genesis 1 (i.e., *aquatic* → *aerial* → *animal/ humankind*), the second catalogue presents an inclusiveness verging on an article of faith. Every realm must give due homage to the Lord, so it is no mistake that the second thematic half of Psalm 148 begins with its lowest realms–from which it is able to build a mighty crescendo, culminating ultimately with the "name of the LORD"–again! (v. 13a; cf. v. 5a). "Praise *in* the world is united with praise *above* the world so that the name of the Lord is declared as the truth about all reality."[24]

Moving from general to specific, creatures of the sea (v. 7b) give way to such powerfully destructive elements as fire and hail (v. 8a; cf. Ex. 9:23). Elements of un-creation give way to the majestic topography and fertility with mountains and fruit trees (v. 9). Active animal life is divided into domestic ("cattle," v. 10a) and wild creatures ("birds," v. 10b). Dynamic human life rounds out the list with ruling classes ("kings," v. 11a) and domestic groups ("elderly," "children," v. 12b).

Through praise, the virtue and vitality of Eden becomes apparent once more, restored in physical representation and audible testimony. Praise not only joins heaven and earth, it also enjoins all creation. Doxological praise unites extremities connected in no other way.

What Are the Important Interpretive Issues?

Two key issues deserve further attention: the cosmology represented in Psalm 148 and the nature of the victory (literally, "horn," 14a).

Cosmology of Psalm 148

The strong divisions of Psalm 148 into heaven (vv. 1–6) and earth (vv. 7–14) reflect a *bipartite* ("heaven-earth") outlook of the organized universe.[25] The entities listed in verses 2–4 merge well with the separation phases of creation–but creation as it *emerged*, not as it began. In other words, it is not surprising that Psalm 148 has no "dark quarters" (Gen. 1:2a), "aimless waters" (1:2b), "uninhabited" spaces (1:10), or "unnamed" luminaries (1:16). Rather, in Psalm 148 we find that every element is alive, named, effervescent, and primed for praise!

Several reasons indicate why doxological praise in Psalm 148 requires a bipartite cosmology rather than a tripartite ("heaven-earth-sea"). First, the tripartite structure necessarily includes the underworld or sea as the third realm, usually for reasons of negative prohibition (Deut. 5:8) or as expression of God's sheer autonomy (Ps. 135:6). "It is no accident that the element omitted in the shorter form is precisely the sea (respectively, the world of the dead)...a far less necessary, independent, and positive element than the other two."[26] In other words, the cosmological ligaments connecting "sea" of the third-tier to the underworld breaks open a series of descriptors for *Sheol* itself: water imagery (Ps. 88:3–7), restrictions (Jonah 2:7; Ps. 107:8, 10), darkness (Pss. 82:5; 74:20; 88:12), silence (Pss. 101:5, 8; 115:17), and a strong association with wickedness (Pss. 18:40; 101:5, 8).

In the end, these core notions of Sheol are incongruous to the themes of light, vigor, righteous, and especially praise that pervade Psalm 148. Silence, detention, and devastation are utterly incompatible with the language, thrust, and theology of cosmic doxology—*praise is devoid of Sheol!*

The second fundamental reason Psalm 148 is construed bipartitely concerns the legal-ideological import of heaven and earth (i.e., merism). In the literary logic of Psalm 148, this key word pair is pressed into service as divine witness. Psalm 148 employs the pair in light of their covenantal backdrop (Ps. 145), but does so as metaphorical witnesses and enduring markers in the doxological hymn of 148 (cf. Pss. 50:4, 6; 78:69). "We encounter the bipartite division of the universe especially in texts describing creation or the greatness of the creator God."[27]

The Meaning of "Horn" in 148:14

The largest concentration of the Hebrew word for "horn" is found in the Psalter (fourteen times). While a literal horn is clear on many occasions (Gen. 22:13; cf. Ex. 27:2), the next key category is figurative (Deut. 33:17). Here it is common to take the figurative as a symbol of strength and power (Pss. 75:4–5, 10; 92:10; 112:9).[28]

While "horn" is vague in 148:14, with no obvious meaning,[29] a figurative sense is most likely (i.e., symbol of strength) rather than a Davidic king, which does occur elsewhere (Pss. 89:17; 132:17). Representing the literal view, the NIV reads: "He has raised up for his people a horn," explaining that it symbolizes a king (text note). The LXX (and Syriac) seem to concur with this view, but use the future tense ("will raise") as a reference for an expected Davidic king. This departs from the Hebrew MT and may represent the translator's own eschatological interpretation, just as the prophetic books in the Greek Old Testament are subsequently placed at the *close* of the canon, in contrast to the MT.

Taking a figurative interpretation, some translations read: "He has made his people strong" (NLT). Leslie Allen develops this, stating, "the imagery [is] of the wild ox triumphantly tossing its horn as a symbol of power," explaining that "the sense of the verse is that Yahweh's historical intervention on Israel's behalf has raised its stock in the world."[30] An idiom appears to be in use when the verb "to raise" (Heb *rum*) occurs with "horn" (= "to raise a horn"), meaning "to strengthen."[31] Israel as the faith community (*ḥăsîdîm*, 148:14b) gained new strength following their exile.

In this international theater of Israel's reestablishment (Jer. 33:7–9), "horn" also includes the *political* aspect of God's royal protective power for his people. His oversight flows from his creative power to establish people (148:11–12). This is often realized in divinely sanctioned military victory, so that those who draw near (148:14c) are given the protections granted by the Cosmic King.[32] "Horn" as international honor requires God's "protection," fostering hope in a realized Zion (Ps. 149:7–9). For this reason, the people cherished (148:14c) are "the people of Zion" rejoicing "in their king!" (149:2b). So against a post-exilic setting, "raising a horn" describes both the judgment of Israel's enemies and Israel's own restored reputation on an international scale. When the Lord procures Israel's socio-religious restoration, his people praise him for "raising a horn." Psalm 148 reaches its climax with verse 14, the intervention of God that animates praise of cosmic proportion. This is not mere history; it is hymnic confession!

What Was the Author Seeking to Communicate?

The author of Psalm 148 was seeking to comfort his post-exilic community. The psalm was written as cosmic praise to the eternal king when Israel had no earthly king. Because the Creator is able to sustain his vast creation, even with its elements of disaster (v. 8), he will sustain the exilic remnant as well. The "boundaries" of the Lord's kingdom are cosmic, with doxological praise being the functional language uniting them, vital truths for the displaced and discouraged.

In the Psalter, exile is more than national displacement; it is profound theological disillusion (cf. Ps. 89:38–51). Even after their return home, the post-exilic community applied Israel's Babylonian exile to the reality of their socio-religious struggle in their own land. From the time of the Judean deportation to Babylon in 597 B.C.E. (2 Kings 24:13–17) and the destruction of the temple in 586 B.C.E. (2 Kings 25:1–22), to the decree of Cyrus in 539 allowing the exiles to return (see Ezra 1–2), the ideals and institutions of a nation were turned upside down. Beyond geography, their defeat and exile convulsed Israel's core theological assumptions of temple, land, and king.[33] Under the leadership of Zerubbabel, the Jews rebuilt their temple in Jerusalem, but the later temple of 515 B.C.E. was a mere shadow of its predecessor. While only some Jews returned to Palestine, their national autonomy did not return at all. As for the monarchy, it had represented the very embodiment of God's presence on earth through the "adopted son" (Ps. 2:7; cf. 72), but it was never reestablished.[34]

This loss of temple, land, and king prompted a theological crisis for the nation's identity.[35] As the prophets had warned, here was God's abandonment of Jerusalem and judgment on a disobedient people.[36] Theological disillusionment lived on in the diaspora. Within the final post-exilic unit of the Psalter (i.e., Pss. 146–150), Psalm 148 was probably not written until the second century B.C.E. (*ca.* 150).[37] "We could therefore read the psalms as reassertions of these historic beliefs in the face of present experience."[38] Preceding the *final doxology*, the final Davidic unit (Pss. 138–145) "could easily achieve relevance for this community when placed on the new grid of history and prayed through the experience of the exiles. As Israel waited for the Lord to bring judgment on the nations, *David prayed on their behalf:* 'May all the kings of the earth praise you, O LORD…/Though the LORD is on high, he looks on the lowly, / but the proud he knows from afar' (Ps. 138:4a, 6)…[David] sends out this cantata of adoration to this humiliated and downcast community, *a community on which the praise of God could work its transforming power.*"[39]

Times of crisis prompt reflection, then and now. The closing shape of the Psalter, particularly in *Book V,* can be understood as an intentional response to the exile. In Psalm 148 the author was showing Israel her renewed status in the theodrama of God. A restoration of eschatological proportion (148:14) prompts an eschatological praise (149:6; 150:6). The Cosmic King had not forgotten his people!

What Is the Significance of the Psalm for Preaching and Teaching?

Practically, several points should be noted. First, creation and redemption should not be separated. The Old Testament does not consider the notion of redemption apart from earthly restoration, and, indeed, the earth "groans" for that redemptive day (Rom. 8:19). The very heart of biblical theology is arguably creation, since the cross enables a broken world to return to paradise, to our Creator-Redeemer.

Second, praise must take on a more robust sense of the collective and cosmic. An unfortunate product of *individual* salvation is an almost narcissistic bent toward *individual* worship. Psalm 148 is obviously a corrective to this, especially when the standard elements of destruction ("fire, hail," etc.) are also summoned for divine praise. One could say that doxology without judgment neglects the role of God as Cosmic King. When the minions of devastation are made to serve in the Cosmic Anthem of praise, paradise has arrived where it is most needed. The opposite of war is not peace but worship. Inasmuch as doxology does not obliterate its enemies, it redeems them to a constructive calling. This is the "every-knee-shall-bow" concept (Phil. 2:6–11). The earth's harshest voices may be heaven's sweetest heralds. In Psalm 148 lies the psalmic version of "turning spears into pruning hooks." We must make room in our definition of worship for the confession of sin and inclusion of our broken pieces, our destructive parts.

Doxological praise like Psalm 148 is not safe praise; it calls out every participant beyond him or herself toward a more vertical orientation to the Cosmic King. It recalibrates life to God, who deserves such praise, and away from *self*-orientation and our postmodern shift to "I."[40] It challenges our preoccupation with comfortable worship by reasserting a cosmic worship. In the challenge of Walter Brueggemann:

> Such doxology is a crucial resource in the life of the church, for it is a lyrical, communal counter to the power of technique—in all kinds of electric control—that wants to thin, flatten, and isolate life so that nothing is left of life but "us." Against such a temptation that empties the world of everything of God, hymns are a crucial counter-assertion that the world is to be received in awed gratitude for the mystery of God that is present in and presides over the world.[41]

PART 3

Applying
the
Psalms

CHAPTER 17

Applying the Psalms in the Christian Life

Julius W. L. Sing

A transaction is an exchange of goods. Ten dollars worth of bait leaves the buyer with worms and the seller with money. In transformational exchanges more than money and goods are involved. Something is transformed, changed forever. A part of oneself, a special connecting moment forever changes the relationship and possibly the network of relationships involved. The psalms, properly applied, engage their participants in a transformational way. In this essay we shall alert readers to ways to engage the psalms transformationally.

What if we felt our way into the discussion of the storyline of the psalms? In the exegetical process, application normally or ideally occurs after interpretation. When all or most of the details of a text are in place then some thought is given to making it live among today's audience and in the interpreter's life. The psalms demand such a sequence and more. But applying the psalms can also be a contemporaneous activity with interpreting the psalms.

This synchronous, mediated discussion board, the psalms, calls for participation. We are moving beyond exchange when the psalms ask us to make noises (e.g., the use of verbs of utterance such as "shout for joy" in Ps. 33:1, *rānan,* make a n-n-n-n-noise)[1], and when they ask that we adjust our body posture (e.g., the use of *verbs of motion,* "worship [*ḥwh,* bow down] before his footstool!" in Ps. 99:5). The psalms exchange information, extract our feelings, and entice us to action by inducing us into rhythms. Like one's involuntary tapping of the foot at a good beat (one-two-three, one-two-three, one-two-three) the use of parallelism in the psalms engages us rhythmically, stanza after stanza. Our world of feeling and the associated frames of how we think the world works are aroused and forced to expression on this discussion board by reframing familiar images. For example, "The LORD is my shepherd, I lack nothing" (Ps. 23:1) first frames the shepherd picture within an Ancient Near Eastern understanding of shepherd-king, a world far from us today. It rouses constructive emotive responses only to be dashed by a later posting reversing the image: "You [the same LORD] handed us over like sheep to be eaten" (Ps. 44:11).

These, and other coaxings by the psalms, invite interpreters to participate, to apply on the go. Performed correctly, the psalms make the reader respond immediately–like a patient frantically signaling to the dentist working beyond the active period of anesthesia! The normally wide hermeneutical cycle, from the left, to the center (interpretation), to the right, to the "here" (application) and back again is more like a fast-moving, tightly twirling twister.[2] Short-cycled movements shift between "saying the text" and "doing the text," where "saying" actually is "doing." The interpreter is singing the text while the text is writing a song in the interpreter even before the end of the psalm is reached. Dialogue, two-way interaction, is at the center of applying the psalms. Sing. Listen. Talk. Silence. Pray. Talk. Listen. Sing. Argue. Listen. Pray. Agree. Dance. Question. Admire. Sing.

If this short-cycled applicational approach is correct, it will require a different interpretive and applicational stand from what is normally practiced in other scriptural texts. Not all, not even most, of the details of a text will line up before feelings are engaged. One will experience the text before, or while, and after understanding the details of the text. Experiencing the text is applying the text. The psalms therefore change the pace and rhythm of our life beat. Because we are riding the psalms, the speed controls of the exercise machine are out of our reach and unpredictable. To be transformed by the psalms, one has to be willing to be engaged in a relational dialogue, phrase-by-phrase, image-by-image, stanza-by-stanza, book-by-book, and beyond. No wonder that unlike literature merely telling us to "do this" or "do that," and thus placing a distance between us and the text, the psalms become a twirling dance anyone may join.

The free-for-all invitation to participate in the psalms has created many portals into the psalms. Figure 1 sketches four main gates by which psalms' users today approach the psalms for contextualization into their world.

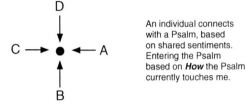

Entering the Psalms based on a big picture idea of **What** was communicated by its compilation into five books. Is there a story to the Psalms? If so what is it?

What was the imaginative and circumstantial thought-world of the Psalm writer? Entering the Psalms based on **How** the Psalms communicated (past tense).

An individual connects with a Psalm, based on shared sentiments. Entering the Psalm based on **How** the Psalm currently touches me.

Community asks how the Psalms should shape community life today. Entering the Psalms based on the need for modern day connections affecting the Liturgical calendar, etc.

Figure 1: How the Psalms are approached today for application

Approaches to the Psalms

Approach A

Approach A is evident in presentations such as, "When you have sinned, read Psalm 51." These are the "when, then" approaches. They become more complex when a whole Psalm is recontextualized. For example, Psalm 91: "though a thousand may fall beside you, and a multitude on your right side, it will not reach you" (v. 7) becomes the "Soldier's Psalm." The dark side of approach A, and sadly so common among some countries, uses psalms as spells or lucky mantras. For example, to relieve severe headache or backache, pray Psalm 3. "Let him pray this Psalm [...] over a small quantity of olive oil, [and] anoint the head or back while in prayer. This will afford immediate relief. (Psalm 3 contains the line, 'Thou, O LORD, art a shield for me; my glory, and the lifter of mine head.')"[3] Whatever brighter and darker sides, approach A is characterized by a rootedness in reality, often a painful one, and has an immediate, solution-oriented pragmatic approach to life. Who, especially those of us in pain, would not want to reach for a clearly and accurately labeled medicine chest?

Approach B

Approach B can be illustrated by the response of a Greek Orthodox representative to the question of the place of the psalms in liturgy. "Remembering that we Orthodox belong to the Judaeo-Christian tradition, it should come as no surprise that the liturgical cycles of the Orthodox Church are permeated by psalms. Vespers begin with an evocation of creation in Psalm 103 of the Septuagint, and then the illustration of mankind's helplessness after the fall of Adam and Eve from

Paradise in Psalms such as 140 and 129."[4] Approach B is characterized by ongoing revisions and/or preservations of the Psalter to adjust it to the realities of changing societies. Modern Bible translations of the psalms would fit here.

Approach C

Approach C could be characterized as an attempt to reproduce the form and content of the psalms for today. The former quality mainly distinguishes it from approach A. The psalms can by applied by doing them. The psalm practitioner is recognized if she, for example, sings the psalms. Figure 2 charts the range of actions commonly associated, as found on the Web, with performances associated with the psalms.

To self/God	To others/God	With others/God
Singing, Praying, Chanting, Reciting, Meditating, Intoning, Memorizing, Versifying, Picturing, Seeing, Analyzing, Studying, Interpreting, Decoding, Understanding, Engaging, Grouping.	Singing, Praying, Reciting, Preaching, Teaching, Incarnating, Quoting.	Singing, Praying, Chanting, Reciting.

Figure 2: Verbs commonly associated with approaching the psalms

Approach D

Approach D wrestles with the canonical placement and development of the psalms and asks how the narrative, the story of the combined psalms, adds up to a grid informing the application of individual psalms.[5] The most obvious practical output of this approach is that for some it lays the groundwork for Messianic fulfillment in Jesus, the ultimate expectation in the line of Davidic kings. The practical aspect of this line of thought is therefore apologetic ("See, it said so and now it happened, therefore take courage, be confident," etc.). Approach D moves the applicational possibilities forward to the New Testament and conditions how individual psalms function, even when read as if one lived 1,000 years before the New Testament.

Quest for a Storyline

The assumption of this essay is that the psalms are best heard together as a choir. Vertical performance strategies within an individual psalm focus on what has gone on in the verses before and the verses after, keeping in mind the required effect of the dynamics of the movements. Horizontal performance strategies pay attention to what is going on from left (Pss. 1, 2) to right (Pss. 146–150) and from right to left. The psalms do not sing solos. They are at least performing as duets, trios, quartets, but mostly as chorales.

The quest for the storyline, or even *a* storyline, best accounting for the arrangement and sequence of each of the psalms is a much-debated venture, as can be imagined. The issues are mainly methodological. Even after outlining refined controls on the history of endeavors to account for the seemingly meticulous arrangements of the psalms, Gerald Wilson, whose dissertation in 1985 prominently placed him as a voice in this discussion, remarks that the whole quest is "perhaps with never complete certainty."[6] David Howard is hopeful for significant breakthroughs, at least on the level of grammatical and syntactical connections between clusters of psalms because of morphologically and syntactically tagged Hebrew Bibles. "Now the studies at the lowest levels of analysis should be able to give much more precise correlation to the studies at the higher levels."[7] Each elemental component points to the big picture of the psalms (see chart on page 218).[8]

Psalms 1 and 2 act as an advance organizer for the other 148 psalms.[9] Psalm 150, led into by Psalms 146–149, provides the landing point. Someone concerned with appropriating the psalms should be able, in the thick of any psalm, to keep in mind the true north on the compass provided by Psalms 1 and 2. In other words, dialoging with Torah allows one to live in this world and not be of it (the transplanted tree). Psalm 2 centralizes all spirituality around a choice person, the Davidic line of kings. The essence of that spirituality is expressed in Psalms 1 and 2. These psalms are the trans-oceanic flight seatbelt signs coming on regularly, no matter which psalm one is taking off from, orienting the performer of the psalm, arriving at the ultimate landing point, which is the unitive praise of all creation to the Lord of the Davidic line. The landing point is not reached beyond this world (the dead do not praise you), but in this world. The psalm's performer must have high hopes for this current generation, this current society, this urbanizing world. All these systems can be called to exalt only one subject: Yahweh.

With multiple entrances, experiences, and exits for the psalms, what would be first-order postures, attitudes setting us up to experience and contribute to the possible melody line of the psalms? The following questions would help assure the incremental transformation toward the big picture. The questions are in first person yet assume that we are embedded as community and thus ultimately plurals. The "I" is therefore a "we." For the sake of even more contextualization, the "I" is assumed to be a leader among peers. How does a transformational leader know he or she is swept by the current called psalms? These questions function like buoys.

The Buoys of Psalm Interpretation

Buoy One: Am I Moving from "High-Definition" toward "Ultimate-Definition" of the Invisible King?

While participating in a psalm, I have to become aware of shifts in my picture of the one addressing me and whom I am addressing. My decentralized notions of Yahweh are slowly yet persistently mopped up into one bucket. I am moving from addressing and hearing "gods" to one "god" to "God" to Yahweh. The methods by which I am moved include everything possible: words, descriptions, silence, his concrete deeds, metaphors, etc. The question I need to ask here is whether I limited Yahweh in the ways he would like to get me to dialogue with him.

Occurrence of a word or phrase does not mean one knows how the phrase or word is used. Yet the number of times a term occurs is a general, very general, orientation beacon to ask if one is on the right track in implementing the term *Yahweh*. The frequency check provides a most obvious, although dimly flashing, buoy in an otherwise wide-open ocean of emotions, moves, sounds, and pictures.

The highest occurring nouns are two names of God, *Yahweh* (695 times) and *Elohim* (255 times).[10] Without entering into the complexities of the distribution and usage, especially the uniquely disproportional distribution of Elohim in Psalms 42–83 compared to the rest of the Psalter, it should be obvious to the practitioner of the psalms that the expressed person doing the action or receiving the action is not a general anonymous God but a specific, singular one. So, whether we are exuberant in praise, passionately petitioning, or loudly lamenting, we have to ask whether we are gradually envisioning a clearer audience of one. If so, the seas of emotions and associations, no matter what they are, have a chance to be more than therapeutic; they can be repeatedly redemptive.

One of the beauties of the psalms is permission—or is it a lure?—for a psalm-user to begin with vagueness about God. Yet the psalms are insistent on moving the user toward not mere high-definition of God but ultimate-definition of, and being defined by, Yahweh—the God of Israel. The permission is granted, reluctantly so, when the user enters the Psalter other than through the front portal (Pss. 1, 2). The sound of the word "LORD" in "the LORD is my shepherd, I lack nothing" (Ps. 23:1) does not convey to the listener today the divine name Yahweh and can quickly degenerate to the point that *any* understanding of deity is good enough. Applying the psalms one sound-bite at a time misses the symphony created at the entry portal, the red carpet (Pss. 1, 2) and grand exit (Ps. 150). "Success" (Ps. 1:3) in life is directly related to finding pleasure in obeying "the LORD's commands (v. 2)."

Let the viewer pay attention to the small caps![11] Let the hearer recognize his unique name Yahweh and raise the jubilant shout, "Yahweh rules." This LORD speaks (Ps. 1:2 AT)"Torah of the LORD," distinguishes, and acts on that distinction between righteous and wicked ("guards the way of the godly," v. 6), laughs and taunts those who rebel against his appointed, Zion-based Davidic ruler (Ps. 2:4, 6). The conclusions to the first four books–41:13; 72:18-19; 89:52; 106:48–are hints of how to respond to the contents of the psalms. They culminate with one grand doxology in Psalm 150:6: "Let everything that has breath praise the LORD! Praise the LORD!" *Hallel-u-yah,* the last word of the Psalms, is exactly that: raise the jubilant shout "Yahweh"!

Buoy Two: Navigating the Application of the Psalms

The second orienting buoy, navigating the application of the psalms, directly counters a use of the psalms by just anyone. The psalms may begin as public domain prayers and praise, but read as a unit they will steadily move one toward addressing and interacting with the one and only God. Not only will you find absence of vagueness of who this Lord is, but you will also discover increasing clarity, and increasing tension, of his person through his deeds. Psalm 19:14, for example, through imagery drawn from nature, "O LORD, my sheltering rock" and from his actual deeds in history, "my redeemer," demonstrates how the Psalm practitioner changes ordinary days into transplanted-living experiences.[12]

When the book of Psalms is approached from a big picture perspective and the distribution of "Yahweh" per words in a chapter is observed, Psalm 29 and Psalm 134 stick out for high frequencies. Psalm 134 concludes the songs of ascent with the major purpose of pilgrimage to Zion to receive the Lord's blessing. Psalm 29 uses the name of Yahweh four times in the introduction as well as in the conclusion. Psalm 29 captures God's communication of himself, not only from the east to the west as the sun imagery in Psalm 19 recalled, but also in the storm that moves from the west to the east. Psalm 29 evokes sounds: the phrase, "the LORD's shout," is used seven times, and the name of Yahweh, "LORD," another ten times. Why? The psalm resists attributing or associating thunderstorms to Baal, and invites the practitioner to synthesize all of experienced reality under one Lord, the God of Israel. The Lord's shout that shakes the northern wilderness (29:8) belongs to the same Lord who gives strength to his people (29:11).

Practices of the psalms that therefore use the psalms as self-talk, while they may be therapeutic, will fall short of the desired response envisioned by the psalm practitioner. The one who ends up reacting, "Reading the psalm made me feel better," is a world separated from the one who can also join in responding to the Lord: "everyone in his temple says, 'Majestic!'" (Ps. 29: 9).

The big picture of the psalms is dimly marked by its high frequency terminology. A discussion of the verbs and metaphors would bring the psalms into much greater clarity. So would a detailed exposition of every psalm, but the purpose here is much more modest. If the practitioner of the psalms asks this question first, they will have some assurance that there is validity to their experience of the psalms: Am I growing in my feelings, thinking, and actions about the one and only God, the LORD, Yahweh? The answer is yes if you can identify his qualities in the objects of nature around you, and if you can see continuity between his historical deeds on behalf of his people then and his people now.

If the major picture of Yahweh in the psalms is an interlocking between Yahweh as Refuge and Yahweh as King,[13] I need to ask myself two further questions. Does performing the psalms make me increasingly aware of the implications of Yahweh's rule? Am I becoming more and more aware of my substitutes for protection? Although neither question can be developed at this point, a broad "net casting" will have to suffice at this moment to keep us oriented.

Yahweh's introduction in the psalms is a sound: he "laughs" in the face of another sound, "the raging" of the nations (Ps. 2:1,3 NLT). His Zion-based rule requires "ortho-empathy": "give sincere homage" (Ps. 2:12; see NET Bible note on "kiss the son"), envisioning leadership of the nations flat before Yahweh, sincerely kissing his feet. All these sounds from Yahweh, taunting and laughing in the face of rebellion, are quieted at Psalm 150 and reversed, drowned out by the repetition of "Praise Yahweh" by everything and everyone. The psalms assume that God's rule will be experienced top down, through leaders. We who want to see society transformed have to assume that Yahweh wants to engage current leadership. Am I becoming increasingly aware of the implications of Yahweh's rule?[14] Am I becoming increasingly aware of Yahweh as protector? Asking that question assumes that I experience the need for shelter–that is, that I am vulnerable. This brings us to the third orienting buoy in the current called Psalms.

Buoy Three: Am I Moving from Merely "Between-the-Ears" Responses to "Engaging the Whole Body"?

The psalms invite us to join a conversation, not just listen to their talk. If your vocal cords or their equivalent are not vibrating, you are not applying yet. We may be accustomed to passive reading approaches, where the words of the text enter our consciousness through our eyeballs and dwell between our ears as thoughts. This intake approach fosters inaudible mental content existing only for us and only for a short while. The psalms are not only talking to us, speaking to us, addressing us, so that we have to take in, but they also invite us to participate in the communicative acts made up of bodily posture, audible expressions, and assisted instrumentation. "Oh come, let us sing to the LORD" (Ps. 95:1 NRSV) expects a response that the community and world outside of us will experience.

We may not be accustomed to being moved to action so quickly. Biblical texts need digesting first, comprehension first, conquering of the details first before we would know what to do. How can I join the performing choir if I do not know the music? But the psalms do not ask you to understand before performing. They ask for performance concurrent with the development of understanding. Already performing the psalms, praying them, singing them, crying them, etc....does it not open one up for all kinds of unpredictable emotions?

What lowers the threshold of joining the singing choir, or any of the psalms, is that God has already sanctioned these 150 psalms and their performance. They are Scriptures. We believe all of them to be useful at some point in the process of God revealing himself. This foundational belief may cause us to whisper some psalms and shout out others, but it will give us the posture that allows us to experiment with words, phrases, sentences, images, and methods of addressing God that may have been foreign or taboo to us. Physical activities awaken and make us aware of desires.

One way that C. S. Lewis' statement, "The most valuable thing the psalms do for me is to express the same delight in God which made David dance,"[15] can be read is, "The major thing the psalms do for me is to generate delight." Lewis, when read in context, is not addressing an ultimate dance, however. The right way for understanding Lewis is to see that he is highlighting the God-ward oriented affective domain, and he transfers David's dancing up the ladder of abstraction to delight in God. But certainly the psalms offer more to experience than delight in God.

Is there a way to map the emotions in the Psalms? The following is a functional proposal[16] for leaders who are asking the question: How do I know if I am poised to move from mere in-between-the-ears responses to full-body and environment involvement? The larger context of the question is the reality of Yahweh as shelter (protection) and my awareness of his sufficiency for my condition. How can I be led to the rock that is higher than I if I do not know where I am?

To apply the psalms we have to be like the glider initially towed by the motorized plane (all the emotions of the psalms) to be let loose at the appropriate height. Our minds will resist the unknown, but our mouths and bodies should engage with the process of being towed. The mind and its reasoning will be stimulated into a discussion about the flight. The psalms are being applied.

Music prompts. Reading or listening to a psalm accompanied by music may help process emotions on a deeper level. "Thus, music can rapidly and powerfully set moods and do so in a way not as easily attained by other means. Even if adequate to the task, the written word cannot do so as quickly and, when used, often must convey a particular setting, content, and visual imagery that itself interferes with or shifts thoughts."[17] The psalms with musical annotations ("according to the *gittith* style," Pss. 8, 81, 84 (NET); "according to the *al-tashcheth* style,'" Pss. 57, 58, 59 and 75; "according to the tune, 'Morning Doe,'" Ps. 22; "according to the tune 'Lilies,'" Pss. 45, 69; "according to the *shushan-eduth* style," Pss. 60, 80; "according to the *yonath-elem-rechovim* style," Ps. 56) beg the question why (assuming that these are musical annotations) these psalms have them and others do not. Rather than pondering the mystery to the point of paralysis, we should take the opportunity to explore connotative dimensions of a psalm that is enhanced by music. The connotations will provide opportunity for checking the dimensions within the larger picture of orthopraxy, orthodoxy, and ortho-empathy.[18]

What portion or psalm or cluster of psalms gave me an experience I would best describe as:

1. frustrated
2. bluesy, melancholy
3. longing, pathetic
4. cheerful, gay, happy
5. dark, depressing
6. delicate, graceful
7. dramatic, emphatic
8. dreamy, leisurely
9. agitated, exciting, enthusiastic
10. fanciful, light
11. mysterious, spooky
12. passionate
13. sacred, spiritual

Figure 3: Classification of Emotions in Music

Recreating the essence of the historical title is another way of increasing the range of possible associations. Some do not pay attention to the information in these titles because they may not have originated at the composition of the psalm but have been added later. Even so, something here may be redeemable. Psalm 3, for example, has as its title "A psalm of David, written when he fled from his son Absalom." Although in this case 2 Samuel 15:13–31 provides the background for the event and can be profitably read as drama, the suggestion for associations proposed here is simpler. It asks us to experience Psalm 3 when actually in a fleeing mode. The performer of the psalm is actually running or on the run. The words of the psalm are then either read by the performer or heard (recordings). In other words, a reenactment of the proposed setting may create profitable associations for our bodies and mind. For example, the title of Psalm 142 says "A Maskil of David. When he was in the cave. A prayer." We might create the associations of a cave by either reading the psalm in a cave or recreating a cavelike environment. Raymond Battegay, chief physician of the University Psychiatric Outpatient Department and professor and chairman of psychiatry at the University of Basel, reviewed J. L. Moreno's work in "New Perspectives in Acting Out." Battegay observes, "Moreno's psychodrama (1946, 1959) has taught psychotherapists that, in addition to verbal expressions, there are expressive, nonverbal manifestations of an individual that should be taken into consideration in the same way as words, both as material for therapeutic influence and for creative change.[19]

Because emotional stuff is messy, these open-ended free association exercises will not be welcomed by all. This method of doing evangelical theology takes getting used to. It is counter-systematizing and pro-recontextualization. It involves the whole body in the process of application, something counter-intuitive if only the brain has been addressed before. Being on the run and hiding in a cave does not make sense if one approaches the text as an individual. It takes a community to be on the run. Creating correlations by means of music and reenactment loosens otherwise calcified associations, which in turn can become points of further, passionate for sure, discussions.

Prayers and songs go somewhere. We may only know that our longings and aspirations amount to birth pangs that have given birth and will give birth.

Am I Dialoguing with YHWH?

Merely getting exegeted personally by a psalm is not the full movement within the big story of the psalms. The healthy posture demonstrating engagement in the psalms is necessary if one is to dialogue with God. Psalms celebrate dialogue with Yahweh, not monologue or self-talk. For example, Psalm 119 is the longest sustained dialogue in the Scriptures.

Poetry is orgasmic words. The first recorded speech of man in Genesis is poetry: "This one at last is bone of my bones / and flesh of my flesh" (Gen. 2:23a). Poetry invites relational interaction, participation. The psalms are accomplishing their purpose if they make you talk–talk to Yahweh, not to self, not to just any god. A major technique of the poetry of the psalms is to employ an image of reality that makes one question current practice. Entering into the discussion of the meaning of the metaphor is already application. The metaphor made you sense something deeply enough to provoke communication with God.

Walter Brueggemann has suggested that the dialogue with God consists of two moves: from orientation to disorientation, and from disorientation to new orientation. See Figure 4 at right.

Before all possible associations of an image are explored and the better one chosen, the psalms invite us to join the dialogue. The spirituality portrayed in the psalms is one of staying in motion. Fear of wrong interpretation (Is this the right product?) should be important, but it is in the back seat compared to the question, Am I taking the opportunity to be in dialogue with God? Now the question is, Is this the right process? Linearity is out the door; chaos theory finds application.

Psalms of Orientation	Psalms of Disorientation	Psalms of New Orientation
All is well, a peaceable kingdom, the system works. Everything is ordered and reliable, in heaven and on earth. This is a "no surprise world." This is how things are and always are. Creation faith: God's faithfulness and goodness are experienced as generosity, continuity and regularity. No Chaos. Canopy of certainty.	Raw reality. Loss of control. Experience the world as it really is and not in some pretend way. Bring all feelings to speech, and all speech must address God. A grievance observed and properly addressed. Relationships are amiss. Loss. Existence run amok.	Surprising turn. New inexplicable possibility emerged. Could not have been predicted or explained or programmed. This is not "natural outcome," but "transformation" made possible by God.
Songs of Creation [8, 33, 104, 145]	Personal Complaint Songs [13, 35, 86]	Personal Thanksgiving songs [30, 34, 40, 138]
Songs of Torah [1, 15, 19, 24, 119]	Communal Complaint Songs [74, 79, 137]	Thanksgiving Songs of the Community [65, 66, 124, 129]
Move of Faith 1		Move of Faith 2
"out of a settled orientation into a season of disorientation" [loss, dismantling the old causes, negativities, rage, resentment, guilt, shame, isolation, despair, hatred, hostility]		"from a context of disorientation to a new orientation." [surprise!, just when we thought all was lost, delight, amazement, wonder, awe, gratitude, thanksgiving, genuine newness]
Walter Brueggemann, *Spirituality of the Psalms*, Augsburg Fortress, 2002.		

Figure 4: Movement in the Psalms

Application in the psalms revolves around an encounter with a person. All paths—pain and pleasure—call for a response addressed to God. Whether alone (individual) or together (communal), the subject of the verbs is mostly God. Who else is addressed? The enemy, that person or group who threatens his quality and quantity of life here on earth. For the king of Israel, continuity was also at stake: his posterity.

Misapplication of the psalms is therefore not so much plumbing the depths of an emotion but ignoring that emotion in an orientation to the living God who speaks through the Davidic line.[20] The goal of the psalms is transformational exchanges by which participants are forever changed.

Figure 5: Big Picture of the Psalms

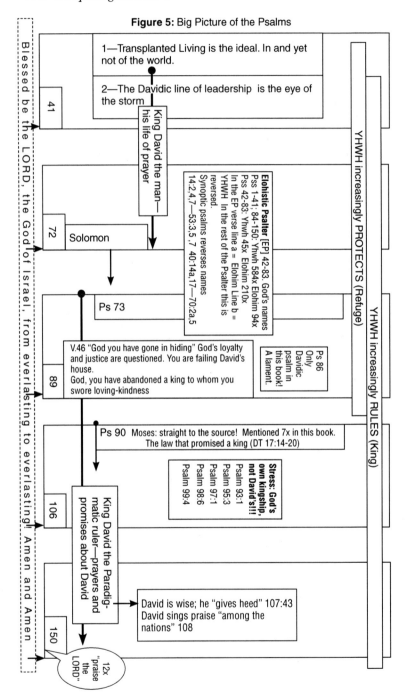

CHAPTER 18

The Psalms outside the Pulpit

Applications of the Psalms by Women of the Nineteenth Century

Marion Ann Taylor

The book of Psalms has always played a prominent role in the church. It is not only the oldest hymnbook, but it continues to have a central place in worship as it is read, recited, and sung. The psalms also have a life beyond the minister's study and the walls of the church. Individuals of all ages and situations have been drawn to read, pray, and meditate on the psalms, finding them to be a mirror of the human soul. As Rowland Prothero states:

> [The psalms] express in exquisite words the kinship which every thoughtful human heart craves to find with a supreme, unchanging, loving God, who will be to him a protector, guardian, and friend. They utter the ordinary experiences, the familiar thoughts of men; but they give to these a width of range, an intensity, a depth, and an elevation which transcend that capacity of the most gifted. They translate into speech the spiritual passion of the loftiest genius; they also utter, with the beauty born of truth and simplicity, and with exact agreement between the feeling and the expression, the inarticulate and humble longings of the unlettered peasant.[1]

While men have authored most of the published writings on the psalms, women have had a significant role in proclaiming the truths of the psalms too. Mothers teaching the psalms to their children, for example, have left an indelible mark on their lives. Women have gone beyond family life in their study and writings about the psalms. This chapter calls attention to various ways that nineteenth-century women have interpreted the psalms and been instrumental in helping people understand and appreciate their power. We will all learn from these women.

Psalms in the Lives of Children
Imprinting the Psalms on the Soul

Those responsible for the religious education of children in the nineteenth century often introduced the children under their care to the psalms at a very young age.[2] The nurse who looked after Lord Byron (1788–1824), for example, taught him to love the psalms. Even as a child, Byron found that the language of the lament psalms expressed his own despair.[3] The Scottish writer, James Hogg (1770–1830), memorized Psalm 122 before he knew the alphabet and memorized most of the psalms as he grew older.[4] The mother of author and critic John Ruskin (1819–1900) made him memorize many psalms, including Psalm 119. Afterward, Ruskin wrote about his experience of trying to memorize the longest psalm: "It is strange that of all pieces of the Bible which my mother thus taught me, that which cost me most to learn, and which was, to my child's mind, chiefly repulsive–the 119th Psalm–has now become of all the most precious to me in its overflowing and glorious passion of love for the law of God."[5] Ruskin argued that psalms contained "a compendium of human life…a complete system of personal, economical, and political prudence."[6]

Parents, who had committed the psalms to memory and who drew on them in good times and bad, taught their children the value of the psalms by example. The mother of the Scottish doctor who discovered chloroform, Sir James Simpson (1811–1870), modeled the devotional use of the psalms for her son when she repeated the Scottish paraphrase of Psalm 20 during times of trouble in the family bakeshop:

Jehovah hear thee in the day when trouble He doth send,
And let the name of Jacob's God thee from all ill defend.
O let Him help send from above, out of His sanctuary;
From Sion, His own holy hill, let Him give strength to thee.[7]

Like many children schooled in the Psalms, Simpson went on to use them as a spiritual resource for life.

Children's Books on the Psalms

A number of women involved in teaching children published books related to the psalms. Charlotte Yonge's catechism on the psalms is directed to older children, as she expected them to learn not only such things as the divisions of the Psalter into five books and the content of individual psalms, but also a helpful threefold method of interpretation that includes interpreting each psalm in light of its original context, the life of Christ, and the Christian reader.[8] Yonge begins her examination of Psalm 3 with questions about its historical setting and content. Sometimes she provides scriptural references as guides to readers:

1. When was this Psalm composed?
2. Who were drawn together to trouble David? (2 Sam. xv.13.)
3. How is his flight described? (Verse 30.)
4. When was he told there was not help for him in his God? (Chap xvi. 7, 8.) b) But where was his hope?...
16. What is meant by smiting the enemy on the cheek-bone? A[nswer]: Giving the most crushing and destroying of blows.

She then moves into her second level of interpretation by posing questions that assume a typological reading of David as Jesus:

27. When did He [Jesus] lay down to His Sleep?
28. How did he show that it was by His own Will that he thus lay in the grave? (St. John x. 17, 18–29.) What, then was His rising again?...
30. Who were the ten thousands that were at Him?
31. Who is the enemy, above all, whom He has smitten on the cheek-bone?

Yonge eventually moves into a third level and asks questions that lead to personal application:

35. What blessing has He left with us?
36. Which verse of this Psalm may we use for our own morning thanksgiving?
37. How does it show us that we need never to fear for any trouble or danger?
38. When we use prayers out of the Psalms, with whom are we praying? A[nswer]: With our Lord Himself.
39. Why can we feel this? A[nswer]: Because each Psalm is spoken prophetically in our Lord's Person.[9]

Yonge was a sophisticated and learned reader of the psalms; she expected children to attain a high level of understanding. She recommends: "Every little child should learn the 23rd, 8th, 121st, 148th, 104th, and 103rd Psalms and never be allowed to forget them, and when these are thoroughly its own, the 1st, 51st, 19th, 15th, and 107th should follow."[10] She also advises Anglican educators to teach the psalms in association with special occasions in the church year. Thus she recommends teaching Psalms 2 and 118, for example, on Easter, and Psalm 24 in preparation for Ascension.[11]

In *Talks with the Children or Questions and Answers for Family Use or First-Day Schools,* published in 1827, Jane Johnson, an American Quaker, includes a lesson based on Psalm 29, which focuses on the power of God in nature and calls all to respond in worship.[12] Johnson uses a question-and-answer format, beginning with questions related to the meaning of the psalm but quickly moving to moral and theological lessons. Thus, to the question, "Can any of you tell me what David meant, when he used that language?" Johnson provides the answer: "He meant that a holy life was acceptable worship."[13] Johnson then teaches children that God's voice (Ps. 29:2–6) is now experienced through impressions gained from experiencing God's power in nature. She provides a science lesson from the "general order of creation" about how animals adapt to variations in climate, noting how "animals which live in a frigid zone have a much thicker covering than those found in a torrid zone."[14] Following this excursus, Johnson brings the lesson back to the theme of the spiritual life, suggesting that David's positive experiences of divine power "show us the blessed results of coming under the divine influence."[15] Johnson's lesson based on Psalm 29 shows that she uses Scripture as a platform for teaching doctrine, theology, morals, and even science.

A less obvious way of teaching the psalms to children is seen in the novel entitled *Harry Beaufoy; or, The Pupil of Nature,* written by the British Quaker Maria Hack (1777–1844).[16] Hack uses the Sunday evening devotional reading of Psalm 19 as her entry point into a lesson on nature and natural theology. Similarly, Charlotte Maria Tucker (1821–1893), under the pseudonym "A.L.O.E." (A Lady of England) writes a novel entitled *The Wanderer in Africa. A Tale Illustrating the Thirty-Second Psalm* that fleshes out the meaning of Psalm 32.[17]

This brief survey of psalms in the life of nineteenth-century children suggests that those involved in the religious education of children, the majority of whom were women, placed a high value on the psalms. They taught the psalms to children under their care, encouraging them to "hear them, read, mark, learn, and inwardly digest them."[18] They wanted children to be familiar with the literal sense of the various psalms as well as their theological, educational, practical, and spiritual values. Some educators expected young readers to develop the ability to read the psalms on multiple levels—namely, historical/literal, christological, and personal. They used a wide variety of literary genres to teach the psalms. Nineteenth-century educators challenge parents and Christian educators today to give the psalms a more important place in their teaching.

Psalms and the Spiritual Life
Women's Private and Public Devotional Writings

Religious educators placed great value on the psalms because they experienced in them a rich source of inspiration. Not surprisingly, a significant body of women's writings on the psalms falls into the category of devotional literature. Some devotional writings on the psalms were never intended for the public eye. Florence Nightingale's (1820–1910) annotated Bible, for example, contains her personal study notes and reflections on the psalms. Her notes show that she used such scholarly resources as Johann Gottfried Herder's famous treatise on the psalms, *The Spirit of Hebrew Poetry* (1782–83), and various translations to enhance her understanding of the psalms.[19] Her comments demonstrate how she read the psalms through the lens of her life experiences: the psalmist's words were her words; and his suffering described her experiences of suffering. On the blank page opposite the published text of Psalm 42:4–8, Nightingale writes: "All thy waves and thy billows are gone over me; *les eaux d'une violente mortification* [the waters of a violent mortification] 27 October 1861, 15 October 1867, 3 January 1873, 22 February 1874." These dates relate especially to dark times in Nightingale's life.[20] Similarly, Jane Welsh Carlyle (1801– 1866), the wife of essayist Thomas Carlyle and a notable letter writer herself, uses the words of Psalm 6:2–4 to narrate her own experience of crying out for help on "one cold, rasping, savage March Day" in 1856:

> Have mercy on me, O Lord, for I am weak; O Lord, heal me, for my bones are vexed. My soul is also sore vexed; but Thou, O Lord, how long? Return, O Lord, deliver my soul; O save me for Thy mercies sake.[21]

The personal reflections of Nightingale and Carlyle demonstrate how readers can experience the psalms as a mirror of human experience, allowing them to give voice to their own fears, doubts, and prayers to the one who can hear, understand, and act on their behalf.

Other great saints from the nineteenth century reflecting on the psalms found that images and ideas in the psalms resonated with other texts in Scripture. Of note is the work of Susan Allibone (1813–1854), an American Episcopalian, who studied the Scriptures extensively during the many years she suffered ill-health. Allibone compiled an impressive inter-textual commentary on Psalm 119 without the use of a concordance or study Bible. She used Psalm 111:10 and Proverbs 16:1, for instance, to illuminate the meaning of Psalm 119:27, associating the notion of precepts in Psalm 119:27 with the commandments and wisdom in Psalm 111:10 and the notion of talking with the tongue in Proverbs 16:1.

27 Make me to understand the way of thy precepts: so shall I talk of thy wondrous works.

The fear of the Lord is the beginning of wisdom: a good understanding have all they who do his commandments: his praise endureth forever. Psalm cxi. 10.

The preparations of the heart in man, and the answer of the tongue, is from the Lord. Prov. xvi.1.[22]

Those who felt others would benefit from her devotional reflections on Psalm 119 published Allibone's work after her death.

Paraphrases, Poetry, and Hymns Based on the Psalms

Some women who meditated on the Psalms found it helpful to translate the psalms either closely or loosely into verse. Catherine Foster and Elizabeth Colling, for example, in 1838 published a *New Metrical Version of the Psalms of David.*[23] Sometimes more than one rhymed version of a Psalm is included in the volume. Compare, for example, the opening three stanzas of two metrical versions of Psalm 137; even the ordering of the stanzas is altered:

By the waters of Babel we sat down and wept,	Where Babylon's streams roll their billows
When we thought, our lost Zion, on thee!	There we sat down and wept;
Our harps, where the mute voice of melody slept,	There we hanged our harps on the willows,
We hung on each wave-mirrored tree.	And a sad silence kept!
For our tyrants, in mock'ry, required at our hand,	O Zion! The land of our love,
Once more their wild music to wake;	When we remembered thee,
Shall we sing the Lord's song in an enemy's land?	And they that led us captive, strove
Ask ye mirth of the hearts that ye break?	To wake thy melody,
O Salem! Lost Salem! If thee I forget,	Saying, to us that wept thy wrongs,
Let my right hand be reft of her skill;	And groaned beneath their chain;
On my tongue let a silence eternal be set,	Come! Sing us one of Zion's songs,
If it mourn not thy memory still!	To wake they melody.[24]

Other writers paraphrased the psalms, creating poems and hymns. The English poet Elizabeth Barrett Browning (1806–1861), for

example, wove the language and theology of the psalms into her poetry.
In her poem "The Sleep," based on Psalm 127:2 ("He giveth his beloved
sleep"), she writes:

Of all the thoughts of God that are
Borne inward unto souls afar,
Along the Psalmist's music deep,
Now tell me if that any is,
For gift or grace, surpassing this:
"He giveth His belovèd–sleep"?[25]

Browning's mediations of Psalm 80:5 ("Thou feedest them with the
bread of tears, and givest them plenteousness of tears to drink") inspired
the following lines:

Shall we, then, who have issued from the dust,
And there return–shall we, who toil for dust,
And wrap our winnings in this dusty life,
Say, "No more tears, Lord, God!
The measure runneth o'er"?[26]

Inspired by Psalm 139:17–18 ("How precious also are thy thoughts
unto me, O God!… When I awake, I am still with thee"), author Harriet
Beecher Stowe (1812–1896) wrote the following hymn:

Still, still with Thee, when purple morning breaketh,
When the bird waketh, and the shadows flee;
Fairer than morning, lovelier than daylight,
Dawns the sweet consciousness, I am with Thee.
Alone with Thee, amid the mystic shadows,
The solemn hush of nature newly born;
Alone with Thee in breathless adoration,
In the calm dew and freshness of the morn.
As in the dawning o'er the waveless ocean
The image of the morning star doth rest,
So in the stillness Thou beholdest only
Thine image in the waters of my breast.
Still, still with Thee, as to each newborn morning,
A fresh and solemn splendor still is given,
So does this blessèd consciousness, awaking,
Breathe each day nearness unto Thee and Heaven.
When sinks the soul, subdued by toil, to slumber,
Its closing eye looks up to Thee in prayer;
Sweet the repose beneath the wings o'ershading,
But sweeter still to wake and find Thee there.

So shall it be at last, in that bright morning,
When the soul waketh and life's shadows flee;
O in that hour, fairer than daylight dawning,
Shall rise the glorious thought, I am with Thee.[27]

Stowe's hymn and many others from the nineteenth century based on the psalms are still sung in churches today.

Translating the Psalms

Women trained in biblical languages felt it helpful to translate the psalms from Hebrew. In 1873, Joana Julia Greswell published a grammatical analysis of the Psalter to help others translate, read, and understand the Hebrew Psalter.[28] In 1876, Julia Evelina Smith (1792–1886)[29] published her translation of the psalms at her own expense in what is considered to be the first translation of the entire Bible by a woman.[30] Helen Spurrell published her translation of a Hebrew version of the Old Testament in 1885.[31]

Interpreting the Psalms

Like all thoughtful readers of the Psalter, women reflected on the question of how to read and interpret the psalms. In her book *The Scripture Reader's Guide to the Devotional Use of the Holy Scriptures,* British writer Caroline Fry (1787–1846) included two chapters on how to read the psalms. Fry begins her essay on the psalms with a reflection on why the book of Psalms is "so inestimable a treasure to the believer, so constant a favourite to the Scripture reader."[32] She reasons that it has to do with how the reader responds sympathetically with the "utterance of the bosom's secrecy" found in the psalms.[33] In the psalms, she avers, we find "the secret breathings of the heart within itself–the silent communications of the spirit with God, and his with it–the perpetual soliloquy, as it were, of the soul, holding close communion with itself through every circumstance of its passage through time into eternity; clothed at once in all the simplicity of truth, and all the exaltation of poetry."[34] Fry suggests, however, that those who read the psalms unfeelingly out of duty and those who are very young in the Christian faith will not experience reading the Psalms as a life-giving experience. She even goes so far as to say that "those who make a duty of reading every morning the psalms appointed for the day, yet never feel, never stop to consider whether they feel or not, a single sentiment those psalms express" may experience in their reading "the savour" of "death unto death" rather than "life unto life."[35]

Fry's sympathetic approach to reading is centered primarily on the associations the reader makes with the text. The psalms, she writes, "contain the finished portrait of the believer, as he appears before God–not

of one, but of every one–of Jesus first, and of every one after him, who
follows in his footsteps... [T]hey become thus a picture from which to
copy, an exemplar by which to try ourselves, to prove whether we are,
and what we want of being, what it is necessary that before God we
become."[36] When a believer reads Psalms 1:2 ("But his delight is in the
law of the LORD; and in his law doth he meditate day and night") (KJV)
for example, she is to ask herself if she measures up to the description
of the righteous person:

> Is the subject [God's law] so near my heart, that it comes into
> it the first in the morning?–so dear, that it will not go from it
> till the last at night; and if aroused at midnight, will come back
> again?–and this, not as a loathed spectre haunts the conscience
> to distract it–but because the presence and the thought of God
> are my consolation and my joy?[37]

Fry acknowledges that the psalms can be read in light of their
historical context, but she also regards David as both a type of a believer
and a type of Jesus. She suggests cautiously that the psalms be read in
light of the human experiences of Jesus.

> If the tears were the Saviour's tears, the vows the Saviour's
> vows, and the deep-wrought expression of human feelings and
> desires the prophetic language of the Saviour's humanity, their
> value to the pious mind is increased above all price. This does
> not, as some have thought, rob us of the personal application
> of the Psalms: rather it makes them doubly ours. What we
> are, he was–what he is we are to be... Sin he had not, it is
> true–but he had it to bear, to mourn, and to conquer...and the
> language which discloses the feelings of his humanity is the
> appropriate language of every devout believer who follows in
> his footsteps.[38]

Fry admits that reading the psalms in light of the humanity of Jesus
is controversial, unnecessary, but nevertheless is delightful.[39]

Fry illustrates her approach to reading the psalms with examples
of different types of psalms. She even addresses the thorny problems of
the enemies in the psalms and the imprecatory psalms. She suggests that
the enemies be understood as "the evil spirit that watches to destroy–the
temptations that every where surround us–our infirmities, our sins."[40] On
the issue of the cursing psalms, Fry offers a number of options, including
understanding the texts as prophetic rather than imperative and as relating
to Christ, who, "divine and innocent, had a right to invoke vengeance on
his oppressors," but she favors acknowledging that God's servants "may

and do desire the destruction of the wicked and must eventually rejoice in it."[41] This being the case, Fry suggests Christians can even read the imprecatory psalms sympathetically.

Fry's sympathetic approach to reading the psalms devotionally focuses primarily on the reader's response to text. Her primary interest lies not in the literal/historical sense of an individual psalm, but in the transforming process itself as the reader engages the text spiritually and is changed.

Fry's contemporary, Mary Anne SchimmelPenninck (1778–1856), also wrote a long essay on the interpretation of the psalms in 1821. It [42] was republished in 1825 as part of a book on the psalms, which establishes the historical setting of each psalm as the basis for determining its literal sense.[43] Like Fry, SchimmelPenninck is interested in hermeneutical questions related to the interpretation of the psalms. Her methods of interpretation are more sophisticated than Fry's, however. She places more rational controls on interpretation; she stresses the importance of establishing the literal sense as the basis for developing the spiritual senses. She is also critical of subjective spiritual applications, which are "the effusions of some pious mind, awakened by the subject at hand."[44] Undoubtedly, SchimmelPenninck would judge Fry's sympathetic approach to be too subjective, leading to "edifying and pleasing" though perhaps unsound interpretations.[45]

Unlike Fry, SchimmelPenninck places considerable weight on the text of the psalms and Hebrew and Greek superscriptions and uses these as clues to provide links to the historical books of the Old Testament, which provide data to flesh out the proposed historical context of each psalm. After establishing the authorship and historical setting, SchimmelPenninck develops the spiritual meaning of the psalm using a christological hermeneutic. She moves, for example, from a literal/historical reading of David as author, whose name she suggests means "Beloved," to Christ, the Beloved of God. Schimmelpenninck also associates individual psalms and groups of Psalms with events in Christ's life. For example, she suggests that Psalm 38 describes Christ's suffering in the garden of Gethsemane and, like Fry, she avers that the psalmist reveals Christ's "inmost heart, describing his internal conflicts and anguish."[46] She goes further, though, to read the pictures of Christ in the Psalms as portraits of the church, "his inseparably united bride."[47] This interpretive move allows SchimmelPenninck to come to terms with the human face in the psalms. Thus she writes:

> [W]e must unlock the passage by this key: That *Christ Jesus is of God made to us righteousness, sanctification, and redemption*; and thus may the church appropriate to herself all the triumphant

passages; because, *whilst glorying, she glories in her Lord.* By this means every passage applies both to Christ and to the church. To Christ literally the passages of triumph; and by imputation the humiliating ones: and to his bride, the converse.[48]

Like Fry, SchimmelPenninck reads the psalms in the light of Christ. However, her christological hermeneutic is distinctive. Fry stresses the humanity of Jesus, whereas SchimmelPenninck focuses on the risen Christ and the church as his very human bride. Furthermore, Fry stresses the spiritual benefit of a reader's sympathetic identification with the psalmist, an approach that Schimmpenninck would think was too subjective.

Commenting on the Psalms

Building on the work of those who translated and analyzed the psalms grammatically and who reflected on the complex hermeneutical issues related to the psalms are the women who actually wrote commentaries on the entire Psalter. The commentaries on the book of Psalms by Sarah Trimmer (1805) and Mary Cornwallis (1817) are part of their larger works on the entire Bible.[49] And Mrs. Thompson's two-volume work on the psalms published in 1826 deserves special attention.

Little is known about the prolific English commentary writer Mrs. Thompson. Her commentary on the psalms was known to Charles Spurgeon (1834–1892), who includes excerpts from it in his *Treasury of David*.[50] Like Fry, Thompson regards the psalms as a "sacred treasury" providing "words and sentiments" for those sunk in distress, or torn with conscious guilt; when harassed with the assaults of spiritual or earthly enemies; when mourning under the hidings of God's face; when longing to approach the throne of grace, for mercy or consolation, for strength or direction; when cheered with a sense of divine favour and deliverance; when penetrated with admiring views of the holiness, goodness, and glory of our God; and when all that is within us, burns with desire to bless his holy name.[51]

Thompson's two-volume work follows the standard commentary format. She comments on each psalm, verse by verse, and weaves together exposition and application. She draws on the writings of seventeenth- and eighteenth-century Anglican and nonconformist expositors Bishop Horne, Matthew Poole, Matthew Henry, and Thomas Scott. In contrast to SchimmelPenninck, Thompson does not regard the superscriptions as a primary interpretive tool. Nevertheless, she begins each exposition with her own superscription, which focuses on historical setting and often introduces key interpretive issues. Thus, introducing Psalm 2, she writes:

This Psalm was written by David (Acts iv.25)...as the forgoing [Psalm 1] was moral, and shewed us our duty; so this is evangelical, and shews us our Saviour. Here under the type of the kingdom, over which he was divinely appointed, and which prevailed at last over all the opposition made against it, the establishment of the Messiah's kingdom is predicted and celebrated.[52]

Like SchimmelPenninck, Fry, and Yonge, Thompson works with a complex interpretive model that allows her to read the psalms on multiple levels, including the literal/historical, typological, moral, prophetic, evangelical, and spiritual.

Following her introductory comments, Thompson moves into exposition and application, weaving them together seamlessly while focusing primarily, but certainly not exclusively, on the meaning of the text for her readers. Where appropriate, Thompson interprets a psalm in light of the proposed historical setting in the life of David. However, her penchant for application pushes her to explore a psalm's fuller meaning arguing as she does in her discussion of Psalm 9 that the psalm is "equally calculated for the use of the Christian church, and was doubtless intended by the Holy Spirit, to be thus appropriated."[53] Similarly, Thompson broadens the identity of the enemies in Psalm 5:9, for example, from David's "immediate enemies" to embrace "the whole world of the ungodly, and to the enemies of all righteousness, as manifested in the person of Christ, and in his church."[54] Thompson then speaks pastorally to readers facing troubles:

The Lord will prove a refuge for the protection and comfort of such as are oppressed or persecuted for his sake, by worldly and ungodly men, or by the frequent assaults of the wicked one; yea, be they ever so distressed, they will find the Redeemer will renew their strength by fresh supplies of grace, arm them with faith and patience, and animate them with the hope of never-fading glory, and eternal rest in heaven![55]

Thompson, believing that the psalms continue to speak to readers, suggests ways to appropriate their message.

Although Thompson often moves beyond a literal/historical interpretation using a number of different reading strategies, her readings are not arbitrary. In her introduction to Psalm 14, for example, she suggests that the historical setting of the psalm is not certain, though it is often associated with Absalom's rebellion. Against such a reading, Thompson argues that the expressions in the psalm are so general as to point beyond what she calls "private interpretation."[56] She continues:

"[T]herefore we may consider it as descriptive of the awful depravity of mankind in general, and of David's enemies in particular."[57] Similarly, Thompson clearly justifies a prophetic rather than typological reading of Psalm 45:

> This Psalm is allowed, by Jewish and Christian interpreters, to be an illustrious prophecy of the Messiah, the Prince. It describes the mutual love which subsides between him and his church; and, in many respects, resembles the Song of Solomon. Some have supposed it was written on occasion of Solomon's marriage with Pharaoh's daughter; but it is much more probable, that it is wholly a prophecy of Christ, being quoted as such, by the apostle in the 1st chapter of Hebrews.[58]

Thompson then places careful controls on interpretation; she looks for clues in the psalm or in the larger canonical context to support readings that go beyond the literal/historical sense. Thompson's comments are also practical and didactic. Commenting on Psalm 1:3, for example, Thompson suggests that by meditating on Scripture daily, a person "as naturally improves and advances in holiness, as 'a tree' thrives and flourishes in a good and well-watered soil."[59] She is a confident expositor, directing the reader with such imperatives as "Mark the difference of the opposite character [the ungodly in Psalm 1:4]."[60]

Thompson is not afraid to admit difficulties in interpreting and applying the psalms. She struggles to determine the relevance of particular verses for readers. Commenting on Psalm 1:5, she writes: "[H]owever difficult it may now be to distinguish the righteous from the wicked, (for at present, like wheat and chaff, they lie on the same floor,) a day is coming when the divine Husbandman shall appear with his 'fan in his hand.'"[61] At that time, he shall "thoroughly purge his floor," infallibly separating, "the ungodly from the congregation of the righteous."[62] In this case, Thompson uses Matthew 3:12, which mentions the burning of the chaff in unquenchable fire, as an intertext to suggest an eschatological reading of this verse.

Moreover, Thompson is willing to address moral problems in the text. For readers bothered by David's confession "against thee only have I sinned" (Psalm 51:4), when he obviously had sinned against many, she suggests:

> [T]he chief malignity of his conduct consisted in this; that it was a complication of most daring rebellions against the great and glorious Governor of the world; contempt of his majesty, excellency, and righteous laws; a most ungrateful return for immense obligations; and a falling from God through idolatrous

love of worldly pleasure...and thus seeing [his guilt], his mind was overwhelmed to such a degree, as to make every other consideration seem comparatively as nothing.[63]

Thompson also wrestles with the classic problem of the imprecatory psalms. She advises readers that curses against the evildoers, such as those in Psalm 5:10, be applied not to "private and personal enemies, but to the opposers of God and his Anointed; nor to any even among these, but such as are irreclaimable, and finally impenitent."[64] To justify this reading, she advocates reading the verb tenses of the future rather than imperative or optative, a method discouraged by Fry.

Thompson's contemporary, Charles Spurgeon, evaluated Thompson's commentary, saying it was a book, "consisting of comments which might occur to any motherly person."[65] Given that mothers were highly valued in the nineteenth century for their spiritual sensitivities, Spurgeon's remarks highlight the practical and spiritually edifying nature of Thompson's commentary. Indeed, Thompson's commentary has a timeless quality and continues to have value for those open to exploring practical and spiritual readings of the psalms.

Conclusion

An examination of the literature produced by nineteenth-century women is particularly informative. They placed a high value on the psalms. They made the psalms their own and drew on them as spiritual resources in good times and bad. They studied them using all the scholarly tools available, wrestling with issues of interpretation and translation. They wrote about the psalms for themselves and for fellow travelers of all ages. They used creative and innovative ways of teaching the psalms. These nineteenth-century women serve as models for the faithful today. They challenge us to reconsider our own commitment to teaching the psalms and to hearing them, not only as God's encounter with the authors and saints throughout the ages, but also with us.

CHAPTER 19

The Psalms and Their Influence on Christian Worship

David S. Dockery

The psalmist proclaims that God is enthroned on the praises of his people (Ps. 22:3). It is clear that God revels in the atmosphere of praise. Throughout church history, believers have recognized that praise is the instrument to bring us into the presence and power of God. The psalmist himself issues the invitation, "Enter his gates with thanksgiving, and his courts with praise" (Ps. 100:4). Other chapters in this book have focused on analysis and interpretation of the psalms. What about the practical use of the psalms in the history of Christian worship?

What do the psalms mean by "to offer praise to God"? The starting point is to recognize that the praise and worship of God is at the heart of the Psalter. Moreover, the psalms have been central to the formation of Christian worship for the past two thousand years.[1]

Words of praise are found to an astonishing degree, more so than any other book in the Bible, and such praise characterizes the psalms.[2] For example, we read:

For the LORD is great and certainly worthy of praise;
　he is more awesome than all gods. (Ps. 96:4)

Praise the LORD, for the LORD is good;
　Sing praises to his name, for it is pleasant. (Ps. 135:3)[3]

I will praise the LORD at all times;
　my mouth will continually praise him. (Ps. 34:1)

Because experiencing your loyal love is better than life itself, my
　lips will praise you.

For this reason I will praise you while I live; in your name I will lift up my hands. (Ps. 63:3–4)

Attention! Praise the LORD, all you servants of the LORD, who serve in the LORD's temple during the night.
Lift up your hands toward the sanctuary and praise the LORD! (Ps. 134:1–2)

Let everything that has breath praise the LORD! Praise the LORD! (Ps. 150:6)

The purpose of this chapter is to look at the influence of the psalms on Christian worship. However, before doing so, we need to see the role of the psalms in the worship of ancient Israel.

The Psalms in the Worship of Ancient Israel

The psalms are an invaluable source for understanding the worship of ancient Israel, providing a window into the various devotional practices of the Israelites. They express and typify the worship experience of those who brought tribute or praise, as well as prayers and songs, in response to the covenant love of God. The psalms not only expressed the responses of those who officiated in the sacrificial rites, including the Levitical singers, the musicians, and the leaders and representatives of the covenant community, but also reflected the responses of all who brought their praise to God.[4]

The psalms were used in the worship practices of the Israelite sanctuary in Jerusalem. Many of the psalms, which were presented as an offering to God alongside the sacrifices, probably originated in the tabernacle worship. When the temple of Solomon was built in Jerusalem, the psalms became increasingly important, taking their place alongside the recitations of the Pentateuch and the Prophets. Under the leadership of both David and Solomon, the forms of worship were duly ordered, which included the prominence of the ark of the covenant, sacrifices, dancing, and the singing of psalms. When we look at the wide-ranging influence of the psalms in the worship of Israel we can make several observations:

1. Worship as pictured in the psalms was God-centered, not human-centered;
2. Worship as portrayed in the psalms was active, not passive;
3. Worship as revealed in the psalms called for participation, not merely observation of a performance;
4. Worship as reflected in the psalms entailed a range of emotional responses to life's blessings, challenges, and disappointments; and
5. Worship as seen in the Psalms provided the framework for ongoing spiritual formation.[5]

The Kingdom of Israel was divided about 930 B.C.E. Jerusalem continued with its temple worship, Davidic kings, and singing of psalms until 586 B.C.E. Then the Babylonians destroyed the temple and the city of Jerusalem, carrying the Southern Kingdom into captivity. Guilds of psalm-singers sat mourning by the waters of Babylon (Ps. 137). For years a kind of lamenting worship continued: "How long, how long, O God?" cried the singers (Ps. 74).[6] The Jews carefully preserved the text of the psalms, even with musical rubrics that were no longer understood, up through the time of Jesus and the New Testament church.[7]

Psalms and Hymns in New Testament Worship

Geoffrey Wainwright has wisely observed: "Singing is the most genuinely popular element in Christian worship. Familiar words and music, whether it be repeated in response to biddings in a litany or the well-known phrases of a hymn, unite the whole assembly."[8]

The New Testament patterns and exhortations for singing can be traced to the practices found in the psalms. The New Testament invites Christ-followers to worship God, to ascribe to him supreme worth, for he alone is worthy to be praised (Heb. 13:15–16). This teaching has its roots in the psalms:

> For the LORD is great and certainly worthy of praise Ascribe to the
> Lord the splenor he deserves…
> Worship the LORD in holy attire. (Ps. 96:4, 8, 9)

Describing God's greatness and goodness and excellencies is a challenging responsibility. The gift of song and poetry help make worship possible. In his *Reflections on the Psalms*, C. S. Lewis wrote, "What must be said…is that the Psalms are poems, and poems intended to be sung; not doctrinal treatises, nor even sermons," which means we cannot separate the value of the psalms as Scripture from the psalms as songs to be sung.[9] Lewis helpfully points us to the importance of praise and singing, which has been centrally significant for Christian worship for two millennia.

The psalmist, in inviting us to praise God, is ultimately helping us to see God's incomparable worth. Lewis again observes, "I think we delight to praise what we enjoy because the praise not merely expresses but completes the enjoyment; it is its appointed consummation."[10] The New Testament worship patterns, following the Psalms, exhort us to offer God our devotion, praise, and prayer (Rom. 12:1–2; 1 Cor. 14:26; Eph. 5:19; Col. 3:16). This thought is to be uppermost in our minds and hearts: God alone, as he has revealed himself in Jesus Christ, is worshipful. We ascribe to him all that is in keeping with his nature and revealed person.[11] The claim is laid on all classes of people to praise the name of the Lord (1 Tim. 2:8), for his name alone is exalted; his splendor is above the earth and the heavens (Ps. 148:11–13).[12] The use of the Psalter was important as Christians, instinctively following the example of Jesus (Lk. 23:46; 24:44), turned to the psalms of David for language to express their deepest emotions in singing, in praise, and in prayer.[13]

In the way that the Old Testament worship characteristically celebrated the Sinai-event, New Testament worship focused on the entrance of Christ into the world for the purpose of redeeming his people from bondage to sin.[14] Early New Testament hymnody focused on the praise of God in the fulfillment of Old Testament prophecies (Lk. 1:45–55, 68–79; 2:14, 29–32). This theme is so pervasive throughout the New Testament that some scholars have suggested that portions of the New Testament reflect the developing patterns of early Christian worship.[15] It is possible that New Testament hymns are extensions of the patterns and practices found in the Old Testament psalms (cf: Phil. 2:6–11; Col. 1:15–20; Rev. 4:8, 11; 7:12; 11:17–18; 15:3–4).

The important aspect of continuing to tell the story of Jesus Christ in psalms and hymns and spiritual songs gave witness to the New Testament churches of their faith in the one true and triune God who has acted in history for the salvation of his people. The use of the psalms in the worship of the early churches had the impact of helping these believers proclaim God as King and Lord over all of life (Pss. 93; 96; 97; 99). Singing the psalms enabled believers to express their adoration, their praise, and their confession.[16]

Worship in the History of the Church

By the end of the second century, the worship services of the church included readings from the Law, the Prophets, Epistles, Acts, and Gospels, with psalms sung by cantors between the readings.[17] The people responded to the readings by singing psalms. Abundant evidence points to the use of the psalms in the early centuries of the church. Eusebius (260–340), who wrote *Ecclesiastical History* and served as the Bishop of Caesarea, observed, "The command to sing psalms in the name of the Lord was obeyed by everyone in every place: for this command to sing is in force in all the churches which exist among the nations."[18] Tertullian (*circa* 160–220) spoke of the use of psalms at household prayer and exhorted married Christians to emulate each other in psalm singing.[19]

By the time of the fourth century, monks, nuns, and members of the clergy committed the entire Psalter to memory. Jerome (347–420) supposedly went so far as to warn the nuns at Jerusalem that no sister might remain if she did not know the Psalms.[20] The early and medieval church agreed with Athanasius (296–373), who referred to the Psalms as a book that included "the whole life of man, all conditions of the mind, and all movements of thought."[21]

The Reformers, especially John Calvin (1509–1564), advocated the increased use of psalms in worship. Many similarities joined the various groups of Reformers, but their reform of worship was not uniform. Some groups radically broke with existing practices while others looked for continuity. In general, the Lutheran and Anglican movements retained many practices of the early and medieval churches. The Zwinglian and Anabaptist churches made a radical break with the past, while John Calvin and John Knox expressed a middle position.[22]

Martin Luther (1483–1546), who loved music, also loved the psalms, maintaining that the Psalter is "a Bible in miniature, in which all things which are set forth more at length in the rest of the Scriptures are collected into a beautiful manual of wonderful and attractive brevity."[23] Luther emphasized the importance of singing the psalms, but also encouraged the singing of other Christian hymns. Luther, himself, wrote many hymns. His best known, "A Mighty Fortress Is Our God" is based on Psalm 46.[24]

The best-prepared musician among the Reformers was Ulrich Zwingli (1484–1531). Yet, the radical Zwingli disallowed instruments in worship, including the organ. He not only rejected the singing of other hymns, but the psalms as well, in favor of a service focused only on the Word. The Reformation in Geneva, led by John Calvin, rejected the Lutheran pattern of singing additional Christian hymns, but did not go as far as Zwingli. Calvin called for Christians to sing only the psalms in their times of gathered worship.[25] Many Baptists and Presbyterians over the last four hundred years have maintained the regulative principle adoped by Calvin that only inspired and inscripturated psalms can rightly be sung during worship,[26] a pattern rejected by Benjamin Keach (1640–1704)[27] and Isaac Watts (1674–1748), the greatest hymn writer in the church's history.[28] Though Watts encouraged the use of hymns other than the psalms, like Luther, many of his hymns found their source in the Psalms.

Watts was a great innovator and was not afraid to rewrite the concepts and words of the Bible in what he thought to be more understandable ways. In many ways, Watts saw himself as a reviser of the psalms, giving them new life and providing new meaning for the church he served. Watts wanted to transpose the sacrificial language of the Old Testament psalms into the clear message of the love of God in Christ. Watts intended to redeem the psalmody of Israel with a focus on the work of grace in Jesus Christ.

Contemporary praise and worship services often blend the singing of psalms with modern choruses based on the psalms. Perhaps in God's providence, this Christ-centered and God-honoring worship can be the beginning point to bring renewal to the twenty-first–century church, similar to the ways that the singing of the Psalms did for ancient Israel and the early church.[29]

Toward Renewal in Evangelical Worship

The variety of worship practices in contemporary Evangelicalism provides a growing challenge to churches of various traditions.[30] The variety in today's worship practices has created an uneasiness for many. We can begin by recognizing that almost every tradition in every time period of Christian history has employed the singing of the psalms, with the Zwinglian and Quaker traditions being obvious exceptions. Grounding our praise and worship in the best of church history–in the praise of the psalms and in the pattern of the New Testament–will be a good beginning step toward genuine renewal. While we are hesitant to acknowledge one form of worship to be inherently better than another, we should always seek to ground our worship in the teaching of Holy Scripture. In doing so, we will see the importance of employing psalms, hymns, and spiritual songs (Eph. 5:19).

Perhaps taking our cue from the early church model in Acts 2, we should expect variety, including formal celebration in line with the temple worship and informal gatherings similar to synagogue and house worship. We need not only to sing the psalms, but to preach and teach them as a guide for all of life.

Worship in contemporary Evangelicalism needs renewal because our services tend to be human-centered. A pattern of worship in line with the psalms calls ultimately for the praise of God as we recognize his glory and exalt his name.

A restoration of the important place of the psalms will prioritize spiritual formation and congregational participation in praise, prayer, singing, and confession. We need to move away from an entertainment mentality in which church leaders and members come to church expecting to be entertained. We likewise need to balance the strong cerebral emphasis in some quarters where Bible teaching turns corporate worship into an extended classroom. Bringing the psalms alive for today will begin to re-ignite our churches toward praise.[31] The general trend toward secularization and adaptation of postmodern trends in our culture has diminished the difference between the Christian community and the world. Following C. S. Lewis, we can use the psalms as a guide to recognize that the highest calling in life is to enjoy and praise the triune God.[32]

The psalms call us to renewal in our praise of God. In our praise, we will learn that worship is not passive, but active. We thus gather on the Lord's Day not so much to receive, but to offer sacrifices of praise (Heb. 13:15–16). We acknowledge what God has done for us and is doing for us. Thus we bless him, sing hymns to him, and offer our gifts to him, as well as our praise and adoration. A recognition of the role the psalms have played in history is instructive. We need not adopt the regulative principle of the Calvin tradition to appreciate this significant role. In doing so, we will learn to see worship as active participation. Such recognition will surely help us overcome our misconception that times of praise, singing, Scripture reading, and the giving of offerings are merely the preliminaries before the preaching.

Turning afresh to the psalms opens the door to rediscover the wealth of resources available to us in the experiences of believers who have gone before us. Much that is often easily dismissed as merely tradition can be rebaptized by the Holy Spirit to reshape Evangelical worship. In doing so, we can gain a fresh glimpse of the importance of all things being done for the glory of God (1 Cor. 10:31).

Let us together begin to take steps away from our secularly influenced and human-centered emphases to concentrate on the praise of God in all of life. A renewed pattern of worship will call for full and active congregational participation enlivened by God's Spirit. When genuine worship takes place, not only is the entire body enhanced and built up, but the mission and outreach of the church can be strengthened. It is out of a recognition of God's greatness that we are led to see ourselves and God's world aright. The adoration of God will lend not only to confession and repentance, but also to a renewed desire to serve together on mission with God in the world.

The people of God who have worshiped their God and who have been mutually strengthened will be prepared to enter the world to touch lives, meet needs, counsel hurts, speak to injustices, and by life and witness proclaim the saving message of the Gospel. Reaching people and exalting God are hardly in conflict. As a matter of fact, real outreach, missions, and evangelism are prefaced on genuine worship (see Isa. 6:1–8; Mt. 28:16–20; Jn. 4; Acts 13).

Let us pray together for the renewing work of God's Spirit in our worship, even in the midst of our various styles and traditions. May we learn from the writers of the psalms, from the New Testament church, from Eusebius, Athanasius, Jerome, Luther, Calvin, Keach, and Watts. The psalms teach us that the worship and praise of God is an amazing privilege. God invites us to praise him. In worship we adore God and experience unrivaled pleasure. We enjoy him who is eternally enjoyable, and he enjoys being exalted in our enjoyment.[33] With the psalmist of old, we sing together:

> Praise the LORD!
> Praise God in his sanctuary!
> Praise him in the sky, which testifies to his strength!
> Praise him for his mighty acts!
> Praise him for his surpassing greatness!
> Praise him with the blast of the horn!
> Praise him with the lyre and the harp!
> Praise him with the tambourine and with dancing!
> Praise him with stringed instruments and the flute!
> Praise him with loud cymbals!
> Praise him with clanging cymbals!
> Let everything that has breath praise the LORD!
> Praise the LORD!
> (Psalm 150)

CHAPTER 20

The Psalms in the Hands of Teachers and Preachers

D. Brent Sandy and Kenneth Bickel

Interpreting the Psalms for Teaching and Preaching has explored two basic questions: how do we enter into the psalms and experience the meaning as the original authors and hearers did? And how do we bring the psalms to life in the experiences of contemporary hearers? Cicero, the first-century Roman orator and author, commented, "Study and knowledge...would somehow be lame and defective were no practical results to follow." For those of us who teach and preach God's word, the overarching goal is to gain "training in righteousness so that everyone who belongs to God may be proficient, equipped for every good work," which is the intent of all of Scripture (2 Tim. 3:16–17 NRSV). Thus we recognize that the Psalms, like all of Scripture, are meant to transform us.

The Transforming Power of the Psalms

If we did not have the psalms, would we sense we were missing something? Could we make it through the lonesome valleys of life without them? Similar questions can be asked about the spirituals of American culture. If the enslaved did not have their soulful songs, could they have kept on picking cotton under a blazing hot sun? If they were unable to join in singing the plaintive cries of their comrades, how would they have managed their circumstances of despair? The answer is clear: like the spirituals—yet much more than the spirituals—the psalms enrich our lives in significant ways. They speak to our hearts through unique and textured channels. We are hard pressed to imagine the Scriptures without the psalms. Life includes a kaleidoscope of experiences, pressures, and

241

releases that render our days anything but sane. They speak to our hearts through unique and textured channels. It is no surprise, then, that we love the psalms so much and return to them so often.

For Caroline Fry, a woman of the nineteenth century, the psalms are the "utterance of the bosom's secrecy." She refers to them as "the secret breathings of the heart within itself–the silent communications of the spirit with God, and his with it–the perpetual soliloquy, as it were, of the soul…clothed at once in all the simplicity of truth, and all the exaltation of poetry."[1] She was right. While the psalms generally record what humans said to God rather than God to humans, at the same time they offer divinely inspired insight into the human condition. They lead hearers to real solutions for the twists and turns of life. The psalms are bluntly honest: life is often not a bed of roses. The sting of thorns replaces the fragrance of flowers. Yet the psalms remind us that we must not run from God, but to him. He listens patiently. He is there in the valleys and on the mountaintops. The simple truth is this: a shepherd never leaves his sheep. We are in good hands when we are in God's hands.

Fry is also correct about the exaltation of poetry. The psalms speak a special language that coaxes us to come forward with our own feelings. They engage us with precisely what we're experiencing and with how we're responding, and they affirm the validity of both–troubles and despair, frustrations and complaints, needs and the supply of our needs. We may begin with a vague understanding of our own feelings, of our theology, of our needs. But when we listen to the psalms, before we know it, we are singing the same tune. With 150 psalms it is a symphony of themes and variations. The beauty of the psalms is encouragement to voice our laments, our hurt, our despair, but also our thanksgiving, our praise, our worship. The thoughts of the psalms become our thoughts, their words become our words, their prayers our prayers, their faith our faith. In essence, they transform us. This is particularly true when the psalms are placed in the hands of teachers and preachers who are able to help us enter into the psalms.

Entering into the Psalms

Those who have attempted to interpret a psalm and proclaim its meaning know the challenges. They face fundamental questions. What does God want us to grasp from the psalm? How can we bridge the distance in culture, language, literature, and time? Can we interpret an ancient Hebrew poem correctly and apply it biblically? Is it essential to study a psalm in depth and understand the original author's intent in composing the psalm? Or is it sufficient to read the psalm with an open heart and see how it speaks to contemporary needs?

Unfortunately, many examples of less-than-careful interpretations of the psalms lead us in the wrong direction and to much misunderstanding. Two close-to-home examples will suffice. The late Hobart Freeman, a Grace Theological Seminary professor for two years before changing his views, became concerned with humanistic tendencies in Christian subculture. He applied his concern to Christians calling on humans for help rather than on God. Thus, he claimed Psalm 103:3, describing God as the one who heals all our diseases, as the basis for declining any form of medical assistance. The church that he began, officially known as Faith Assembly, but informally known as the Glory Barn, grew rapidly and led to various church-plants, both locally and abroad. The movement became nationally notorious for the number of mothers and children lost in childbirth due to the lack of medical intervention.

Cheryl Sandy (Brent's wife) attended a well-known Christian college, where a professor taught that breaking a bone in your body was a sign of sin in your life. The basis for his conclusion was the psalms that state that the bones of the righteous shall not be broken (Ps. 34:20; 38:3).

The need for careful guidelines for interpreting the psalms is self-evident. Their uniqueness calls for specialized procedures. We cannot interpret them with normal methods that we might use for John's gospel or Paul's letters. The foregoing chapters have offered much guidance for interpreting the psalms, and they have made two primary emphasizes. One pertains to the poetry of the psalms and the other to the arrangement of the psalms as a book. As noted throughout the chapters, the overriding goal of interpretation is to grasp what God intended by inspiring the various authors to write about their experiences.

The most important characteristics of the poetry of the psalms are the ways Hebrew poems bring their messages to life. Picturesque language abounds throughout the psalms, especially in the form of figures of speech. For example, "Because you are my help, / I sing in the shadow of your wings (Ps. 63:7, NIV); "Rise up, LORD! Deliver me, my God! Yes, you will strike all my enemies on the jaw; you will break the teeth of the wicked" (Ps. 3:7, NET). Metaphors, similes, and hyperbole are especially frequent (e.g., Ps. 139:8–10). The preponderance of figures of speech are not simply ornamental flourishes of architectural design. The picturesque language is used because the psalms were written from hearts full of emotion and were designed to evoke similar emotions in hearers. The more figures of speech, the more emotional our feelings. For example, among American slaves a frequent topic of conversation concerned slipping away and escaping the oppressive slavery. In that light certain lyrics took on special meaning: "Steal away, steal away, steal away to Jesus! Steal away, steal away home, I ain't got long to stay here."

While emotional statements may be expressed without figures of speech, the pattern is that the stronger the emotion, the greater the likelihood that metaphors and hyperboles will be used to get a point across. David wrote about his near-death experiences when Saul sought to kill him: "The waves of death swirled about me; / the torrents of destruction overwhelmed me. / The cords of the grave coiled around me; / the snares of death confronted me" (2 Sam. 22:5–6 = Ps. 18:4–5, NIV).

Hebrew poetry is also characterized by repetition. To emphasize the message, concepts are restated with variation in wording. This is generally referred to as parallelism. The inclination to be expansive entails a piling on of figures of speech. In one line of poetry a thought is expressed. In a second line the thought of the first line is reiterated and advanced, often with another figure of speech to heighten the impact the poet was seeking to make (cf. Ps. 19:1–2; 139:13–16). The poet's creativity to revisit the same point line after line must be carefully considered when interpreting a psalm. Very often the psalmist is not making different points but the same point, though expressing it in different ways. For example, to say that the bones of the righteous will not be broken is a poetic way of continuing the thought of the preceding verses: God protects his own. It is not a separate proposition about the relationship of broken bones and righteous living.

With these two aspects of Hebrew poetry in mind, we turn to the arrangement of the psalms as a book. Many psalms were composed across hundreds of years of Israelite history and liturgy. The book of Psalms is a wonderful collection of 150 of those psalms. Unfortunately, the person(s) who made the selections and put them together as a single book is unknown. Contrary to how it may appear on the surface, the collection is not a random arrangement. Intentional placement and ordering of the psalms created the present canon of psalms. This canon is not a single book, but five books, each one reflecting a different emphasis. An underlying and fitting theme throughout the psalms is the Mosaic Law (e.g., see Pss. 1; 19; and 119). If God's chosen people were to have a proper relationship with God, it would depend on their maintaining the covenant relationship set forth in the Law. Since five books comprised the Law, the editors arranged the psalms in a fivefold structure also referred to as books. Different psalms played different roles in the concepts emphasized in the five books. For example, Psalms 1–2 are introductory to the whole collection. Psalm 89 brings to conclusion the first three books. Psalms 146–150 are the concluding doxology for all five books.

While we could look at other important guidelines modeled throughout the preceding chapters for interpreting the psalms, we turn now to the practical question of how to teach and preach the psalms to worshipers of the twenty-first century. This too has been an emphasis of this book.

Bringing the Psalms to Life for Contemporary Hearers

Some things in life are nice, but they are not necessities. That is not true about the psalms. They are more than nice; it is simply not enough to read them on occasion, or to teach or preach them once in a while. In the psalms we find anguished cries arising out of great personal pain; agitated calls for God to crush enemies who are on the attack; emotional complaints that sometimes find resolution in remembering the Lord, but not always; heartfelt shame for sin that was ignored too long; fervent encouragement to acknowledge the Lord and his ways as right; ecstatic praise for God in light of recent and miraculous deliverance; impassioned celebration of God for all his greatness and goodness. This kind of training in righteousness is indispensable for the community of believers. The psalms are a precious resource for teachers and preachers to use in communicating essential truths about life.

Plumbing the depths of the psalms, however, is challenging, as Walter Brueggemann admits: "The Psalms are a strange literature to study. They appear to be straightforward and obvious. They are not obscure, technical, or complicated. Yet when one leaves off study of them, one is aware that the unresolved fascination endures. Any comment on them is inevitably partial and provisional."[2]

Many teachers and preachers feel frustrated after speaking on one of the psalms. We want to be excited about sharing the message of a psalm; we want to capture its fullness and communicate not only the psalm's *logos* but also its *pathos*. Unfortunately, all too often we exit with a feeling of flatness. Standard sermon forms do not do justice. Common linear presentations—where emotions are referred to only in passing, if mentioned at all, and where cognitions comprise the majority of the focus—do not achieve all the psalms are intended to accomplish. Jeff Arthurs says it plainly: "You can see why some preachers avoid the psalms. Their intuition tells them that we murder when we dissect."[3]

The question is, can we discover forms that will help the preacher/teacher capture the richness of a psalm and aid in conveying that richness to listeners? Can a teacher or preacher set aside forms that work well for epistolary passages and instead employ forms more suited to poetry, and thereby not only help the listener to attend to all that is being said but to embrace cognitively *and* emotionally the richness of the psalm? We think so.

God has given no specified form(s) for lessons or sermons that can and should be used regardless of a passage's genre or content. As

Haddon Robinson declared: "I prefer to say that any form you can use that really communicates the idea and development of this text is perfectly legitimate."[4] Accordingly, we conclude that a variety of forms are appropriate for communicating the psalms, and those forms should largely be determined by the message of the psalm itself.

We believe that the pathway to a meaningful proclamation of the psalms is found in the word *experience*. Arthurs says: "Poetry makes the abstract concrete by embodying the universal in the particular. Like narrative, poetry incarnates its ideas so that knowledge is obtained vicariously through the author's experience. The subject matter of psalms is human experience, not propositions."[5]

Teachers and preachers should take intentional steps to help listeners experience a psalm to the greatest extent possible. As stated in the first chapter of this volume: "If this is the way poetry works, we must learn to see the psalms, hear them, and feel them. We must read with imagination and put ourselves into the psalmists' experiences." Listeners will gain the most when they experience a psalm. Here we are using the word "experience" to describe a situation in which hearers not only observe a speaking event, in which they not only hear words and ponder their intended meanings, in which they not only see movements and gestures, but in which they enter into a deeper encounter and interaction with stimuli suggested by a psalm.

However, lest we get ahead of ourselves, deciding on the form of presentation comes only after we have carefully studied a psalm. With the objective of helping listeners experience the communicative event in a psalm, we must take time to experience the psalm ourselves. These steps are essential for correct understanding of a psalm:

- Pray for Spirit-led imagination and Spirit-induced emotional responses as we meditate on a psalm.
- Explore key questions: What type of a psalm is it? What can we learn from the placement of the psalm in the collection as a whole? What can we discover about the author's original circumstances that led to his penning the psalm?
- Think about what the psalmist wanted the original hearers to grasp from the psalm. What was he seeking to communicate?
- Take account of the psalmist's mood and the emotional tone of the psalm, especially evident in the imagery, metaphors, and hyperboles.
- Note the movement that takes place within the psalm and the authenticity and vulnerability disclosed in the psalm.
- Ponder the subsequent meaning of the psalm in light of the New Testament and the redemptive work of Christ.

- Consider prayerfully the significance of the psalm for today's hearers.

These pursuits call for allowing the images presented in the psalm to stimulate our imaginations so that ideas and insights might expand and flow as the Spirit leads.[6] We need to open ourselves up to whatever feelings the psalm might evoke, so that we feel what the psalmist felt and feel what he wanted the original audience to feel.

Having spent time studying, meditating, praying, imagining, and emoting, the time comes to ponder how our experiencing of the psalm might be communicated to listeners. We may need to offer intensive stimuli, so that what hearers encounter could be described as compelling, captivating, or gripping. The goal is to evoke not only cognitive reactions within listeners but also emotional reactions. The more emotional the reaction, the more rich will be the experience. We may seek to create an experience for listeners that is multi-sensory, so that they will not only hear the words and the vocal variety and see the movements of the speaker, but that they might also smell, feel, and taste portions of the psalm (even if only in their imaginations.) Ralston might call this "persuasive preaching" (see page 33 in chapter 3).

Finally, we may include listener participation. We would suggest that anytime this process can occur as a result of a team effort, the richer will be the experience of preparing to teach or preach. Using a team composed of differently gifted but spiritually unified individuals can only expand the possibilities for how the impact of the psalm might be conveyed more meaningfully to contemporary audiences.

Ideas for Teaching and Preaching the Psalms with Power and Impact

To meet the goal of having "the same rhetorical effects in our sermons that the psalms produce: imagination, identification, concretizing,"[7] we offer the following suggestions for helping participants experience the psalms.[8]

Use Word Pictures

"Metaphor and simile offer many entries into the psyche, which is why they are considered the tools of the poets."[9] The psalms are filled with word pictures. If a lesson or sermon is going to approximate the effect of a psalm, it too should be filled with word pictures. "The Psalms are both models and permits. We stand under their discipline, and we are authorized by their freedom."[10] Therefore, do not be content with abstract explanations and applications. Use word pictures to put flesh on concepts and emotions. Use strong, interesting verbs rather than weak, insipid verbs. (For example, instead of "the man went down the street," describe "the grandfather who shuffled" or "the CEO who strutted.")[11]

Suppose your text is Psalm 139. Consider the word picture of an individual (known to most of those present) who had recently undergone the kind of MRI in which the entire body is exceedingly confined. Use mental pictures and vibrant language to convey what it is like to be hemmed in to the extreme, to be bombarded with the incessant pounding noises of the machine, and to be examined physically in intricate detail. Imagine, then, if such a procedure could be used to discern not merely the physical characteristics of one under scrutiny but to disclose fully the person's thoughts, intentions, preferences, and motives. Surely, anyone subjected to such an examination would be asking questions such as, "Where can I go from your Spirit? Where can I flee from your presence?"

You may also wish to describe mental (and emotional) journeys to towering mountains that lead perilously and gaspingly up into the heavens, as well as descents into deep and dark caverns under the earth that can squeeze the heart and lungs with terror. Pictures delivered via PowerPoint® might well add to the effect, as will concrete words that help participants feel the cold and hear the furious winds of the mountain peaks, and then smell the dank, stale air of the subterranean caverns.

Consider a dialogue (accompanied by appropriate pictures or diagrams) that describes vividly the complexity of the human body (or even one small part of the human body–the eye, for example) as a contemporary way to express the psalmist's point in verses 13 and following.

The discourse on Psalm 139 could be closed by returning to the image of an individual lying on the MRI table, but this time she is joyfully inviting–no, *requesting*–that God would examine her inward self with great scrutiny, so that appropriate life-changes might be made and that she might more fully pursue the path of eternal life.

Images as teaching tools were powerful in David's day; they are no less powerful today. J. Clinton McCann and James Howell assert, "You may trust that people sitting in the congregation are fascinated by images, given the explosion of symbolism in our media culture."[12] Since we have biblical precedent, since images connect well with cultural influences, and since the form of the psalm under consideration sets the example, it seems entirely appropriate to use a series of images suggested by the psalm to help participants experience the impact of the psalm.

Use Emotions

"[Psalms are] intended to appeal to the emotions, to evoke feelings rather than propositional thinking, and to stimulate a response on the part of the individual that goes beyond mere cognitive understanding of certain facts."[13] If we are to be true to the genre, it is entirely appropriate to display the emotion being conveyed in a psalm, or at least to describe it with sufficient vividness that listeners might not just hear about the emotion, but sense it themselves.

Think about Psalm 42. You could ask participants to do their very best to be brutally honest, and then to answer this question with full candor: Just how often in life do our souls really pant for the Lord the way a deer might pant for streams of water in a dry and arid land? You are not seeking to be cynical. You just want honesty. Even after singing the well-known chorus, or a more contemporary chorus expressing the same sentiment, can we authentically say that we deeply thirst for the Lord?

That kind of sincerity might lead to an honest encounter with Psalm 42 and thereby help participants to experience the context and passion of the psalm more fully. Verses 3, 5–6, and 9–11 declare that the psalmist is tearful, downcast, mournful, and distressed. Perhaps it is precisely in those realms of life that the believer is in the best position to thirst and pant after God. Since the experience of pain and discouragement is common to all, it might be profitable to seek to move listeners mentally (and hopefully emotionally) to recall such times in their lives. Or, better yet, perhaps Psalm 42 represents the kind of passage to use when a congregation is experiencing a shared tragedy.

We do not normally think of moving people into greater sadness or despondency, but is not that the point of a lament psalm? Many Christians will do their best not to let fellow believers see the evidence of their discouragement or despair, but then do they not miss one of the possible blessings that come from a season of life where pain is encountered? During those times, if we have a heart for God, we can actually experience what it means to pant and thirst for him.

We need to be clear about this desire to help participants experience the psalm through identifying with it. We are talking about more than simply asking them to ponder these thoughts. We are referring to giving hearers permission to hurt and grieve and weep and be miserable, but with a purpose. The purpose is to enable them to taste a bit of what it means to really need God to go on. Believers really do need God to live life to the fullest, but they do not always understand that until they hurt. Perhaps a sermon on Psalm 42 could help them understand.

Use Personal Testimony

Perhaps you would like to convey the message of Psalm 73. We should be grateful that the Holy Spirit led men of God to pen words of such bold authenticity. Could you genuinely describe internal dialogues you had as you pondered life's realities, as you struggled with the black doubts that begin this psalm? If you are uncomfortable being that vulnerable with your own struggles (which would be a pity), you may find people in the audience who would be willing to let you represent their thoughts (anonymously, of course). A parallel testimony alongside Psalm 73 would help listeners to appreciate the message of the psalm.

The use of personal testimony to communicate the messages of Psalms 32 and 51 would also work well. We would need to be very wise about disclosing the kind of sin that might precipitate such confessions and appeals for mercy, but given our age's desire for transparency, this approach might accomplish more than simply conveying the *logos* and the *pathos* of the psalm.

Psalm 88 may be presented as the testimony of a genuine God-follower who is gripped by depression, for whom no immediate resolution is evident (as is true in the psalm). It could be a very powerful time to allow listeners to spend a few minutes in group deliberations in which they could discuss their reactions to the psalm. Such methodology, though out of the ordinary for many Sunday worship services, would provide an opportunity to experience the psalm more personally (and more powerfully).

Follow the Movements in a Psalm

A meaningful approach to communicating a psalm is to "capture its inner dynamic,"[14] that is, the movements to be found in the psalm. In some psalms the movement is from one setting to another (e.g., Ps. 23). In some psalms the movement is from one addressee to another (e.g., Ps. 27). In some psalms the movement is from one mood to another (Ps. 52). A faithful communicator of a psalm will be sensitive to the importance of these movements and include in the sermon indications of when they are important and why.

Use an Entire Worship Service to Emphasize the Point of a Psalm[15]

Think about Psalm 2, where you may wish to point participants toward the reality that the Lord has all authority and is in control as framed in a coronation psalm for one of Israel's anointed kings. You may want to emphasize that efforts to deny his authority and to defy his will are foolish and will ultimately fail; he will have his way. It could be a powerful experience if you (and the others who plan worship) were to dedicate an entire service to repeated reminders of the message of Psalm 2, which would lead to a celebration of his kingship and to appropriate submission of his people. For example:

- Psalm 2 could be read at the outset of the service, perhaps by someone gifted in the dramatic reading of Scripture with expressed emotion.
- Hymns and contemporary worship songs that point to God as King of kings and Lord of lords could be sung. Verbal promptings that key people's thoughts toward his dominion could be offered at strategic times before, during, and after the songs. Music that conveys the message of a psalm is especially appropriate. "The psalmists used music; why shouldn't we?"[16] Music carries a unique ability to influence people emotionally (filmmakers certainly understand this and use that knowledge with great sophistication). Especially when a spiritual song captures both the content and the emotion of a psalm, it is strategic to sing it congregationally or to allow a gifted singer to perform it.
- An individual gifted in storytelling could speak of a modern context (parallel to the original setting of enemies plotting against God's plans) when a godless group (e.g., Nazis, Stalinists) was seeking to rise to power so that its malicious ideas and activities might prevail. The final chapter of the group's story proved that the movement failed utterly. The storyteller could then invite participants to ponder and affirm that God really was present during those dark days, that he really does exercise authority over the movements of history when he deems the time to be right, and that no one can defy him longer than he chooses to allow them to do so.
- At the normal time for the sermon, Psalm 2 could be read again, this time from a different version of the Bible, but with the words of the text being projected for all to see and follow.
- Excerpts from the early chapters of Exodus could be read (with some appropriate observations inserted) at the point when the text describes Pharaoh arrogantly resisting the Lord. Of course, in the end, Pharaoh lost all–his firstborn son, his army, and his life.
- An individual of the church body could describe how he or she fought against God's will for a season, but how, after running into many roadblocks, finally yielded to God and his way.
- Psalm 2 could be read again, this time by all the participants present.
- With some visual images being projected, the following passages could be read dramatically: Revelation 4; 5:11–14; 19:11–21.
- The "sermon time" could conclude with a brief challenge to recognize, remember, and embrace the certainty that the Lord is in control, which calls for fitting responses from his people.

- The service could close with a pastoral prayer focusing on the Lord and the help the participants need from the Lord to live day by day in light of the clear message of Psalm 2.

The uniqueness of an entire service dedicated to the message of a psalm would surely create a memorable event. However, the desire should go beyond that. Hopefully, structuring a service around the core truths of Psalm 2 and the implications for believers' lives would create an experience that could press onto participants the kind of impact intended by the genre.

Use as Many Participants as Possible

The kind of service proposed above involves participation by more than the average number of individuals. But there may be opportunities to encourage an even larger number of participants. Consider the following example.

The psalm you want to teach or preach is Psalm 1. Begin by reading verses 1–2. At that point, choose an individual to come forward with a Bible and sit on a stool. Ask four other people to come up, and give each one a piece of paper with a statement printed on it. The four statements are, "With money you can get whatever you want in life!" "The one who dies with the most stuff wins!" "Do unto others before they can do unto you!" "You only go around once, so do whatever feels good!" Position the four volunteers around the individual seated on the stool. While the person on the stool reads Psalm 1 aloud, have each of the others simultaneously read clearly and loudly the statements they are holding until the reading of Psalm 1 is finished. The leader can then ask members of the audience how the demonstration underscores the message of the psalm. Once the point has been recognized about the world shouting its beliefs at us—making it hard to meditate meaningfully on the truths of the Scriptures—then the leader could ask individuals in the audience to suggest ways the wicked actually do shout at us in real life. More questions and answers along this line could be raised as deemed appropriate.

Let it be clearly understood that the point of all this is not to entertain. The intent is to offer an experience that is dramatic enough so that the main teachings of the psalm are imprinted in the long-term memory of the participants. The Old Testament prophets understood the principle: powerful demonstrations allow those who are present to experience a point, and that creates impact! Creating impact is a main purpose of the poetic genre.

Conclusion

Poetry is a significant medium that seeks to influence human experience. For that reason, the preaching of the psalms should help listeners experience the intended message as fully as possible. The psalms, as with all Scripture, deserve to have teachers and preachers use their imaginations, gifts, and skills as dramatically as circumstances allow to impact listeners in line with the content and character of the psalm being proclaimed.

Classification of Psalms by Categories

Categories of Psalms	Book I Psalms 1–41	Book II Psalms 42–72	Book III Psalms 73–89	Book IV Psalms 90–106	Book V Psalms 107–50
Laments Individual Laments	3, 5, 6, 7, 9, 10, 13, 17, 22, 25, 26, 27, 28, 31, 35, 38, 39, 40	42, 43, 51, 52, 54, 55, 56, 57, 59, 61, 64, 69, 70, 71	77, 86, 88	102	108, 109, 120, 130, 140, 141, 142, 143
Communal Laments	12, 14	44, 53, 58, 60	74, 79, 80, 83, 85	90, 94, 106	123, 126, 137
Declarative Praise Individual Thanksgiving	23, 30, 32, 34, 41	63, 66		91, 92, 103	107, 116, 118, 121, 138, 139
Communal Thanksgiving		50, 48, 65, 67	75, 76		124
Descriptive Praise Hymns	8, 29, 33		81, 82	100, 104, 105	111, 113, 114, 117, 134, 135, 136, 145, 146, 147, 148, 149, 150
Songs of Zion		46, 48	84, 87	95	122
Enthronement God's Kingship	24	47, 68		93, 96, 97, 98, 99	132
Davidic Kingship: Royal Psalms	2, 18, 20, 21	45, 72	89	101	110, 144
Didactic Wisdom	1, 37	49	73, 78		112, 127, 128, 133
Torah	15, 19				119
Songs of Trust Trust of the Individual	4, 11, 16, 23	62			131
Trust of People					125, 129 (?)

This chart was prepared by Herbert W. Bateman IV from numerous sources, but a major influence was Allen P. Ross's "The Book of Psalms: Class Notes for the Exegesis of the Hebrew Psalter" (Dallas: n.p., 1986), Nancy L. deClaissé-Walford, *Introduction to the Psalms* (St. Louis: Chalice, 2004), the NET Bible, and the contributors of this book.

Classification of Psalms by Titles

Titles of Psalms	Book I Psalms 1–41	Book II Psalms 42–72	Book III Psalms 73–89	Book IV Psalms 90–106	Book V Psalms 107–50
For the choir director (55 psalms)	4, 5, 6, 8, 9, 11, 12, 13, 14, 18, 19, 20, 21, 22, 31, 36, 40, 41	42, 44, 45, 46, 47, 49, 51, 52, 53, 54, 55, 56, 57, 58, 59, 60, 61, 62, 64, 65, 66, 67, 68, 69, 70	75, 76, 77, 80, 81, 84, 85, 88		109, 139, 140
A Psalm of David (54 psalms) or Maskil / Mikhtam of David* (10 psalms)	3, 4, 5, 6, 8, 9, 11, 12, 13, 14, 15, 18, 19, 20, 21, 22, 23, 24, 25, 26, 27, 28, 29, 30, 31, 32, 34, 35, 36, 37, 38, 39, 40, 41 *16	51, 61, 62, 63, 64, 65, 68, 69, 70 *52, 53, 54, 55, 56, 57, 58, 59, 60		101, 103	108, 109, 110, 138, 139, 140, 141, 143, 144
A Psalm of Asaph		50	73, 75, 76, 77, 79, 80, 81, 82, 83		
A Psalm of the sons of Korah or A Maskil of the sons of Korah*		48 *42, 44, 45, 46, 47, 49	84, 85, 87, 88		
Other		66, 67	72	90, 92, 98, 100	

Notes

Chapter 1: Approaching the Psalms

[1]Phillip Yancey, *The Bible Jesus Read* (Grand Rapids: Zondervan, 1996), 10.

[2]Hans-Joachim Kraus, *Theology of the Psalms,* trans. Keith Crim (Minneapolis: Augsburg, 1979); Jerome F. D. Creach, *The Destiny of the Righteous in the Psalms* (St. Louis: Chalice, 2008); Nancy L. deClaissé-Walford, *Introduction to the Psalms: A Song from Ancient Israel* (St. Louis: Chalice, 2004).

[3]Some typical introductory material for the book of Psalms will be mentioned only in passing in this chapter, for two reasons: first, the intent here is to emphasize ideas that are most important and sometimes overlooked in studying the psalms; and second, standard introductory information is readily available in study Bibles, Bible dictionaries, and commentaries.

[4]G. B. Caird, *The Language and Imagery of the Bible,* 2d ed. (Grand Rapids: Eerdmans, 1997), 14.

[5]Some useful sources include John H. Walton, *Ancient Near Eastern Thought and the Old Testament: Introducing the Conceptual World of the Hebrew Bible* (Grand Rapids: Baker, 2006); Alfred J. Hoerth, Gerald L. Mattingly, and Edwin M. Yamauchi, eds., *Peoples of the Old Testament World* (Grand Rapids: Baker, 1994); Roland de Vaux, *Ancient Israel: Its Life and Institutions,* trans. John McHugh (Grand Rapids: Eerdmans, 1997; orig. pub. 1961); and Victor H. Matthews, *Manners and Customs in the Bible* (Peabody: Hendrickson, 1988). John H. Walton, Victor H. Matthews, and Mark W. Chavalas, *Bible Background Commentary* (Downers Grove, Ill.: InterVarsity, 2000) provide verse-by-verse insights for interpreters (note in particular the introductory comments on common concepts and metaphors in the Psalms, 511–18); John H. Walton, ed., *Zondervan Illustrated Bible Backgrounds Commentary, 5 Volume Set, : Old Testament* (Grand Rapids: Zondervan, 2009) is very helpful as well. Specific topics can be looked up in a Bible dictionary–for example, David Noel Freedman, et al. (eds.), *Eerdmans Dictionary of the Bible* (Grand Rapids: Eerdmans, 2000) or Trent C. Butler, Chad Brand, Charles Draper, and Archie England, eds., *Holman Illustrated Bible Dictionary,* (Nashville: Holman, 2003).

[6]*Quest Study Bible* (Grand Rapids: Zondervan, 1994), 729.

[7]Laurence Perrine, *Sound and Sense: An Introduction to Poetry,* 7th ed. (San Diego: Harcourt Brace Jovanovich, 1987).

[8]J. C. L. Gibson, *Language and Imagery in the Old Testament* (Peabody: Hendrickson, 1998), 8.

[9]Louis A. Markos, "Poetry-Phobic: Why Evangelicals Should Love Language That Is Slippery," *ChrT* (Oct 1, 2001): 66; cf. W. B. Stanford, *Enemies of Poetry* (London: Routledge and Kegan Paul, 1980).

[10]Spirituals, composed primarily from the 1600s until emancipation–though continuing into the twentieth century–number over 6,000; see Gwendolin Sims Warren, *Ev'ry Time I Feel the Spirit: 101 Best-Loved Psalms, Gospel Hymns, and Spiritual Songs of the African-American Church* (New York: Henry Holt, 1997); Jon Michael Spencer, *Protest and Praise: Sacred Music of Black Religion* (Minneapolis: Fortress, 1990); Christa K. Dixon, *Negro Spirituals: From Bible to Folk Song* (Philadelphia: Fortress, 1976); James Weldon Johnson and J. Rosemund Johnson, *The Books of American Negro Spirituals* (New York: Viking, 1925, 1926).

[11]William P. Brown, *Seeing the Psalms: A Theology of Metaphor* (Louisville: Westminster John Knox, 2002), 2.

[12]C. Hassell Bullock, *Encountering the Book of Psalms: A Literary and Theological Introduction* (Grand Rapids: Baker, 2001), 15–16.

[13]Susan E. Gillingham, *The Poems and Psalms of the Hebrew Bible* (Oxford University Press, 1994), 4, 188.

[14]Brown, *Seeing the Psalms*, x. Compare Dave Bland and David Fleer, eds., *Performing the Psalms* (St. Louis: Chalice Press, 2005).

[15]Luis Alonso Schökel, *A Manual of Hebrew Poetics* (Rome: Pontificio Istituto Biblico, 1988), 102, 104.

[16]See Nancy L. deClaissé-Walford, *Introduction to the Psalms: A Song from Ancient Israel* (St. Louis: Chalice Press, 2004), 31–44.

[17]For a complete listing of the psalms see "Classification of the Psalms by Titles" at the end of this book.

[18]See deClaissé-Walford, *Introduction to the Psalms*; Gerald H. Wilson, "The Structure of the Psalter," 229–46, in *Interpreting the Psalms: Issues and Approaches,* ed. David Firth and Philip S. Johnson (Downers Grove, Ill.: IVP Academic, 2005).

[19]See Jerome F. D. Creach, *The Destiny of the Righteous in the Psalms* (St. Louis: Chalice, 2008) for a reading of "righteousness" as the key to the entire Psalter.

[20]See deClaissé-Walford, *Introduction to the Psalms* for an alternative reading of the central themes of the five books of the Psalter.

[21]Bullock, *Encountering the Book of Psalms*, 15; cf. Michael E. Travers, *Encountering God in the Psalms* (Grand Rapids: Kregel, 2003), especially the appendix, "Major Attributes of God in the Psalms," 296–309.

[22]Kraus, *Theology of the Psalms*, 189.

[23]See, e.g., Richard Longenecker, *Biblical Exegesis in the Apostolic Period* (Grand Rapids: Eerdmans, 1975); and Darrell Bock, "Use of the Old Testament in the New," in *Foundations for Biblical Interpretation: A Complete Library of Tools and Resources,* ed. David S. Dockery, K. A. Matthews, and R. B. Sloan (Nashville: Broadman and Holman, 1994), 97–114.

[24]*Typology* is: "A way of setting forth the biblical history of salvation so that some of its earlier phases are seen as anticipations of later phases, or some later phase as the recapitulation or fulfillment of an earlier one" (J. D. Douglas and N. Hilyer, eds., *New Bible Dictionary,* rev. ed. [Wheaton, Ill.: Tyndale, 1962, 1982]), 1226.

[25]Douglas J. Moo, *The Old Testament in the Gospel Passion Narratives* (Sheffield: Almond, 1983), 31; cf. Walter C. Kaiser Jr., *The Uses of the Old Testament in the New* (Chicago: Moody, 1985).

[26]See, e.g., Craig A. Evans, ed., *From Prophecy to Testament: The Function of the Old Testament in the New* (Peabody: Hendrickson, 2004); S. Moyise and M. J. J. Menken, eds., *The Psalms in the New Testament* (NTSI; London: T. & T. Clark, 2004).

[27]Tremper Longman III, *How to Read the Psalms* (Downers Grove, Ill.: InterVarsity, 1988), 67–68.

[28]Bullock, *Encountering the Book of Psalms*, 15.

[29]John Calvin, *Commentary on the Book of Psalms,* trans. J. Anderson (Grand Rapids: Eerdmans, 1949), 1: vii.

Chapter 2: Interpreting the Psalms

[1]For a useful overview of the literary genres in the book of Psalms, see C. Hassell Bullock, *Encountering the Psalms: A Literary and Theological Introduction* (Grand Rapids: Baker, 2001), 119–238. For a more technical study of literary forms in the psalms, see Erhard S. Gerstenberger, *Psalms Part 1,* FOTL, XIV (Grand Rapids: Eerdmans, 1988), and *idem, Psalms, Part 2, and Lamentations,* FOTL, XV (Grand Rapids: Eerdmans, 2001).

[2]For a complete listing of the psalms see "Classification of the Psalms by Categories" at the end of this book.

[3]Major studies of Hebrew poetry include the following: Robert Alter, *The Art of Biblical Poetry* (New York: Basic Books, 1985); Adele Berlin, *The Dynamics of Biblical Parallelism* (Bloomington: Indiana University Press, 1985; rev. ed., Grand Rapids: Eerdmans, 2007); James Kugel, *The Idea of Biblical Poetry* (New Haven: Yale University Press, 1981); W. G. E. Watson, *Classical Hebrew Poetry,* JSOTSup, 26 (Sheffield: JSOT, 1984).

[4]For help in understanding biblical poetic imagery and metaphors see Leland Ryken, James C. Wilhoit, and Tremper Longman III, editors, *Dictionary of Biblical Imagery* (Downers Grove, Ill.: InterVarsity, 1998), as well as G. B. Caird, *The Language and Imagery of the Bible* (Philadelphia: Westminster, 1980).

[5]In the Hebrew text the wordplay is even more developed, for "shaking," used to describe the psalmist's bones in verse 2, translates this same Hebrew verb. While NET preserves the wordplay to some degree (it uses "terrified" in both vv. 3 and 10, but "shaking" in v. 2), NIV fails to reflect the word repetition of the original, opting for "are in agony" (v. 2), "is in anguish" (v. 3), and "dismayed" (v. 10). Notice HCSB: "are shaking" (v. 2), "is shaken with terror" (v. 3), and "shake with terror" (v. 10).

[6]For an introduction to the interpretive process as it informs exposition, see Robert B. Chisholm Jr., *From Exegesis to Exposition: A Practical Guide to Using Biblical Hebrew* (Grand Rapids: Baker, 1998). See as well Craig C. Broyles, ed., *Interpreting the Old Testament: A Guide for Exegesis* (Grand Rapids: Baker, 2001), Douglas Stuart, *Old Testament Exegesis*, 3rd ed. (Louisville: Westminster John Knox, 2001), and Mark D. Futato, *Interpreting the Psalms: An Exegetical Handbook* (Grand Rapids: Kregel, 2007).

[7]Major exegetical commentaries on the psalms include the following: Leslie C. Allen, *Psalms 101–150*, WBC 21 (Waco: Word, 1983; rev. ed. 2002); Peter C. Craigie, *Psalms 1–50*, WBC 19 (Waco: Word, 1983; rev. ed., 2004); Marvin Tate, *Psalms 51–100*, WBC 20 (Waco: Word, 1990); Frank-Lothar Hossfeld and Erich Zenger, *Psalms 2*, Hermeneia, trans. Linda M. Maloney (Minneapolis: Fortress, 2005); Hans J. Kraus, *Psalms: A Commentary*, trans. H. C. Oswald; 2 vols. (Minneapolis: Augsburg, 1988–89); Marvin E. Tate, *Psalms 51–100*, WBC 20 (Dallas: Word, 1990); Willem A. VanGemeren, "Psalms," in *The Expositor's Bible Commentary*, vol. 5, ed. Frank E. Gaebelein (Grand Rapids: Zondervan, 1991); Gerald H. Wilson, *The NIV Application Commentary*, vol. 1, Ps. 1–72 (Grand Rapids: Zondervan, 2002); James L. Mays, *Psalms*, Interpretation (Louisville: John Knox Press, 1994).

[8]Introductory works on Old Testament textual criticism include the following: Ellis R. Brotzman, *Old Testament Textual Criticism* (Grand Rapids: Baker, 1994); P. Kyle McCarter Jr., *Textual Criticism* (Philadelphia: Fortress, 1986); Ernst Würthwein, *The Text of the Old Testament*, trans. Erroll F. Rhodes, 2nd ed. (Grand Rapids: Eerdmans, 1995).

[9]See, for example, the text-critical note on Psalm 2:9 in the *New English Translation* (NET).

[10]In this regard interpreters may find the notes in the *New English Translation* (NET) helpful. These notes explain the translator's rationale for his decisions. While the notes are not an exhaustive commentary on the text, they do surface the major issues the interpreter must address. The notes do assume some acquaintance with Hebrew, yet they are written in a style that should be accessible to the nonspecialist as well.

[11]For help with Hebrew word studies, interpreters may consult the *TDOT*, in 15 vols. (Grand Rapids: Eerdmans, 1974–2006, orig. German 1970–1995); and Willem A. VanGemeren, ed., *NIDOTTE*, in 5 vols. (Grand Rapids: Zondervan, 1997).

[12]I am indebted to Eugene L. Lowry for this concept of sermonic plot structure and the attendant labels that introduce each of the main points. See his *The Homiletical Plot: The Sermon as Narrative Art Form* (Louisville: Westminster John Knox, 2000).

Chapter 3: Preaching the Psalms

[1]Teaching and preaching share the goal of persuasion (learning with a corresponding effect) and the characteristics of effective communication. They are distinguished, however, by the methods available to engage the listener in the act of persuasion. Teaching traditionally employs more activities by which a learner engages with the teacher in the process of persuasion. Preaching has fewer learner-centered activities, concentrating on the mental processes involved in persuasion—the arrangement of argument and the stimulation of the learner's imagination.

[2]Most of these ancient sermons deal with the prophetic/apologetic significance of these texts. In the east, see Basil of Caesarea (329–379; nine sermons), Chrysostom (347–407; fifty-nine sermons), and Methodius (d. 311; one sermon); and in the west see Jerome (c. 340–420; some homilies) and Hilary of Poiters (c. 300–368; three homilies). These sermons must be distinguished from the "dry" exegetical comments and commentaries by Ambrose of Milan (c. 340–397), Theodoret of Mopseusta (350–428) and Augustine of Hippo (354–430). Through the Middle Ages psalm sermons remain rare, with the notable exception of Bernard of Clairvaux's (1090–1151) seventeen Lenten sermons on Psalm 91.

[3]Peter Chrysologus (405–450) divided Christian preaching into epistles, gospels, and psalms, possibly reflecting the liturgical use of these texts. See Hughes Oliphant Old, *The Reading and Preaching of the Scriptures in the Worship of the Christian Church, Vol. 2: The Patristic Age* (Grand Rapids: Eerdmans, 1998), 420.

[4]By analogy, while English syntax is direct, German requires that the listener hold the entire sentence in suspension until the main verb is heard at the sentence conclusion. A German speaker intuitively knows how to do this, while an English speaker usually finds this a difficult exercise.

[5]A modernist listener accepts proof constructed from objective data and logical organization, while a postmodern listener, who values successful personal and community engagement, may prefer proof by example in contemporary experience. See Leonard Sweet, *Postmodern Pilgrims* (Nashville: Broadman and Holman, 2000), 45.

[6]This statement has been called the "central thought" (H. G. Davis, *Design for Preaching* [Philadelphia: Fortress, 1958], 20–21), "main idea" (H. Robinson, *Biblical Preaching* [Grand Rapids: Baker, 1980], 31–41), "big idea" (K. Willhite and S. Gibson, *The Big Idea of Biblical Preaching: Connecting the Bible to People* [Grand Rapids: Baker, 1998], *passim*), "central proposition" (T. S. Warren, "A Paradigm for Preaching," *BSac* 148 [1991]: 463–86, and in R. Richard, *Scripture Sculpture* [Grand Rapids: Baker, 1995], 67–78, 87–97, and also A. P. Ross, *Creation and Blessing: A Guide to the Study and Exposition of the Book of Genesis* [Grand Rapids: Baker, 1988], 45–46); "propositional statement" (R. Grant and J. Reed, *The Power Sermon: Countdown to Quality Messages for Maximum Impact* [Grand Rapids: Baker, 1993], 25–26), or "central idea" (D. M. McDougall, "Central Ideas, Outlines, and Titles," in *Rediscovering Expository Preaching*, ed. R. Mayhue [Dallas: Word, 1992], 225–41).

[7]By comparison, the exegetical main idea of the biblical passage is controlled by the biblical text and represents a single-sentence summary of the passage's meaning for its biblical audience: both the subject (what the biblical author is talking about) and the complement (what the biblical author is saying about the subject).

[8]Walter Brueggemann, *Praying the Psalms* (Winona, Minn.: St. Mary, 1989), 17.

[9]For example, the hymn "It Is Well with My Soul" is a Christian favorite for its story. In 1871 a Chicago lawyer and real estate investor, Horatio Spafford, and his wife, Anna, were still mourning the recent loss of their only son when the Great Chicago Fire (Oct. 8–10) destroyed everything they owned. Still recovering in 1873, business plans threatened to delay a family trip to Europe, so Spafford sent his wife and four daughters ahead on the steamship, *S.S. Ville Du Havre*. On November 21 a mid-atlantic collision sank the ship, taking 226 people to their deaths, including his four daughters. After rescue, Anna's telegram began, "Saved alone." Weeks later as he passed the spot of the wreck during his own Atlantic crossing, he committed his faith to paper in a poem, "It Is Well with My Soul." Philip P. Bliss later composed its tune under the ship's name, VILLE DU HAVRE. Its refrain opens with the tolling of a ship's bell marking the watch, perhaps the most poignant combinations of words and music in English hymnody.

[10]See F. G. Hibbard, *The Psalms* (New York: Carleton & Porter, 1856).

[11]Eugene L. Lowry, *The Homiletical Plot: The Sermon as Narrative Art Form* (Atlanta: John Knox, 1980), 6.

[12]Brueggemann, *Praying the Psalms*, 14–15.

[13]Speakers usually compensate for this loss of tension in deductively structured messages by the effective use of illustration that connects emotionally with the audience.

[14]For example, consider John Irvin's made-for-TV movie *Noah's Ark* (1999) which compressed and confused Genesis: God destroys Sodom and Gomorrah but saves Noah and his best friend, Lot; after Lot's wife dies, they part company; God sends a universal flood and saves Noah's family in the ark; in the post-apocalyptic world, Noah meets floating survivors (such as Methuselah) and eventually encounters Lot, now leader of a ruthless band of pirates. Almost all media representations of biblical events take liberties with the plots. Sadly, such distortions often color the recollection and associations of the modern listener and replace any previous knowledge and associations with the true biblical story.

[15]For a good discussion of translating images in interpersonal communication, see Gary Smalley and John T. Trent. *The Language of Love: How to Be Instantly Understood by Those You Love* (Wheaton, Ill.: Tyndale, 2006).

Chapter 4: Psalms 1 and 2

[1]The view that Psalm 1 was introductory was common among interpreters prior to the twentieth century. Examples include *Calvin's Commentary on the Psalms*, trans. James Anderson (Grand Rapids: Eerdmans, 1949); the editors of the Gutenberg Bible; and J. J. Stewart Perowne, *The Book of Psalms: A New Translation with Introductory Notes Explanatory and Critical*, 4th ed., 2 vols. in 1, reprint ed.(Grand Rapids: Zondervan, 1966 [orig. 1878]).

[2]I sometimes say, too simplistically, to my divinity students that whereas the Pentateuch is *prescriptively* God's law as it pertains to *behavior* and belief, the Psalms are *descriptively* God's law as it pertains to *experience* and belief.

[3]Sandy and Rata write (p. 9): "Psalms 1–2 introduce the whole Psalter, meditating on the path of obedience to the Law of the LORD, on God's sovereignty, and on God's appointed king." Book I continues with Psalms 3–41, which emphasize God's covenant with David. Compare Creach, "*The Destiny of the Righteous in the Psalms* (St. Louis: Chalice, 2008), 55–59 and Nancy L. deClaissé-Walford, *Introduction to the Psalms: A Song from Ancient Israel* (St. Louis: Chalice, 2004), 59–64.

[4]A few scholars, believing that Israel's hope in a human, messianic king is discontinued in Books IV and V–being completely replaced by an emphasis alone on God's kingship–have found it hard to reconcile the messianic theme of Psalm 2 with that psalm being an introduction to the whole book of Psalms. However, Psalms 110 and 132 attest to the continuation of the messianic theme throughout the book, thus obviating the problem. These scholars usually interpret Psalm 2 to affirm the sovereignty of God in general rather than his specific rule through the agency of the messiah.

[5]This is evident from some of the Qumran manuscripts, in which the sequential order of the psalms is still in flux beyond Psalm 89. See Martin Abegg, Jr., Peter Flint, and Eugene Ulrich, *The Dead Sea Scrolls Bible* (San Francisco: Harper San Francisco, 1999), 505–89.

[6]Compare deClaissé-Wolford, *Introduction to the Psalms*, 129–44. The progression was noted in traditional (older) scholarship as well. This progression is visually apparent in the "Classification of Psalms by Categories," which can be found at the end of this book.

[7]Psalm 73 begins Book III and relates how the psalmist was able to overcome a personal crisis of faith that arose from observing the apparent prosperity of unbelievers. He did this implicitly by recognizing that faithful believers ("those whose motives are pure," v. 1) are not exempted from pain and suffering. (I owe this observation to Clinton McCann.) The psalmist did this also, and more obviously, by having a moment of revelation. Visiting the sanctuary complex, he came to realize that the godless end life in terror, not knowing God. In contrast, the psalmist knew he was

blessed beyond imagination through daily experience of God's comfort, counsel, and "nearness." For more on Psalm 73, see, for example, Clinton McCann, "Psalm 73: A Microcosm of Old Testament Theology," in *The Listening Heart: Essays in Wisdom and the Psalms in Honor of Roland E. Murphy*, ed. Kenneth G. Hoglund, et al. (JSOTSup 58; Sheffield: Sheffield Academic Press, 1987), 247–57; Dave Bland, "The Goodness of God: Psalm 73," in *Performing the Psalms*, ed. Dave Bland and David Fleer (St. Louis: Chalice, 2005), 151–58; James Crenshaw, "Standing Near the Flame," in *The Psalms: An Introduction* (Grand Rapids: Eerdmans, 2001), 114; deClaissé-Wolford, *Introduction to the Psalms*, 86–90, 134–38.

[8]Gerald H. Wilson, *The Editing of the Hebrew Psalter* (SBL Dissertation Series 76; Chico, Calif.: Scholars Press, 1985), 13–138.

[9]Nowhere else in these books do two consecutive psalms occur without a superscription. Only four other psalms in the first three books omit a superscription (10, 33, 43, and 71), likely due to their connectedness to the preceding psalm.

[10]Compare Genesis 1:1–2:4a, which, preceding the passages with the framework of headings, "these are the generations of x" seems similarly to be an introduction to the book of Genesis, if not to the whole Pentateuch.

[11]A word in English that suffices in both contexts is "muse." The word conveys the notion of murmuring, either for the purpose of absorbing God's teaching (as in Psalm 1) (compare the imagery of the modern-day orthodox Jew wearing the *tephilim* on his forehead, moving his head back and forth, and murmuring devoutly as he reads the Torah), or grumbling (as in Psalm 2) (likely with a view to plot cunningly).

[12]Psalm 1:1 conveys mobility by referring to the wicked at one time "walking," at another "standing," and at still another "sitting." (see NASB95). No less mobile is the imagery of verse 4, which reads, literally: "Not so, [with] the wicked, but rather as the chaff that the wind blows away." (As the literary scholar Robert Alter has noted, the wicked are here not afforded the dignity of being even the subject of a verb!) Robert Alter, *The Art of Biblical Poetry* (New York: Basic, 1985), 114–17. All this stands in stark contrast to the imagery of the godly man being rooted like a tree. Psalm 2 has the wicked (kings) making a vain effort to (literally) "take a stand" against the LORD and his anointed (v. 2a): and the peoples devising a vain thing? The kings of the earth take their stand and the rulers take counsel together against the LORD and against His Anointed (NASB95; compare HCSB). Their desire to break free of servitude to Judah, expressed by "Let us break the cords of their yoke, shake off their ropes from us!" (JPS) similarly conveys a wayward disdain for that which provides security. This stands in stark contrast to the notion of fixedness conveyed by references to the One who "sits in heaven" and who himself "has installed my king": "He who sits in the heavens laughs, The Lord scoffs at them. Then He will speak to them in His anger and terrify them in His fury, saying, 'But as for Me, I have installed My King Upon Zion, My holy mountain." (2:4-6 NASB95).

[13]Jews in the first century C.E., likely including Jesus and the disciples, were familiar with a Greek translation of the Old Testament that renders the Hebrew word translated as "happy" in Psalms 1:1 and 2:13 as *makarios/makarioi* (singular and plural respectively). This is the same Greek word that Jesus used in the Beatitudes and which we know through the KJV as "blessed."

[14]For a lengthy assessment of the evidence both in favor and (ultimately) against seeing Psalms 1 and 2 as a single entity, see John T. Willis, "Psalm 1––An Entity," *ZAW* 91 (1979): 381–401.

[15]These prose traits are the definite article, the relative pronoun, and several particles such as "therefore" and "but rather." In the Hebrew text (compare HCSB), the definite article appears on man (v. 1), the wicked (v. 4), the judgment and the sinners (v. 5). The same Hebrew relative pronoun receives various English translations ("who, v. 1; that, vv. 3-4; whatever, v. 3). The two-word Hebrew particle (instead or but rather (vv. 2,4) appears along with the two words meaning "therefore" (v. 5). To be sure, many of these grammatical features (especially the definite article) are found elsewhere in the psalms. However, in no other psalm of similar or even greater

length are so many of these prosaic features found together. Further, nowhere else in the Psalms does the prose particle "but rather" appear, yet it occurs twice in Psalm 1 (vv. 2 and 4).

[16]I remember raising this interpretative question in my days as a student at Dallas Theological Seminary in the late 1970s. The issue came up in a similar discussion of Judges 4–5. Here is the problem: if the student of the Bible is to seek only the intended meaning of the original author, who's intended meaning is the student to follow? That of the original composer of Judges 5 who likely lived in the twelfth or eleventh century B.C.E.? Or that of the editor who, for his own purposes, later included Judges 5 into the narrative framework of the book of Judges?

[17]One further example is the Trinitarian allusion allegedly inherent in the words of Genesis 1:26: "Let us make humankind in our image." As comparison with the Ugaritic texts strongly suggests, the original human writer was likely thinking of God addressing what we today might call a parliamentary chamber of angels. However, throughout the centuries Christian interpreters such as Martin Luther have seen an obvious correspondence between the plurality of "us" and the plural (triune) nature of God. Martin Luther, Lectures on Genesis Chapters 1–5. Luther's Works, vol. 1, ed. Jaroslav Pelikan, trans. George V. Shick (St. Louis, Concordia, 1958), 57–59. The point is this: surely God, unbeknownst to the original human writer, is no less aware of the correspondence between the plural language of "us" and his being than were theologians like Calvin.

[18]Brevard S. Childs, *Introduction to the Old Testament as Scripture* (Philadelphia: Fortress, 1979), 513–14. In his later *Old Testament Theology in a Canonical Context* (Philadelphia: Fortress, 1985), Childs describes the Psalms as a guide to the obedient life and stresses the relation of the Psalms as an affirmation of life over the threat of death.

[19]W. H. Bellinger Jr., *Psalms: Reading and Studying the Book of Praises* (Peabody, Mass.: Hendrickson, 1990), 129–30.

[20]Creach, *The Destiny of the Righteous in the Psalms,* 58.

[21]deClaissé-Wolford, *Introduction to the Psalms,* 64.

[22]James L. Mays, *Psalms,* Interpretation: A Bible Commentary for Teaching and Preaching, ed. James L. Mays et al. (Louisville: John Knox, 1994), 40–41.

[23]Ibid., 44 (compare also p. 48).

[24]David C. Mitchell, *The Message of the Psalter: An Eschatological Programme in the Book of Psalms* JSOTSup 252 (Sheffield: Sheffield Academic Press, 1997), 245.

[25]Patrick D. Miller Jr., *Interpreting the Psalms* (Philadelphia: Fortress, 1986), 91.

[26]James Limburg, "Psalms, Book of," *ABD* V, 535.

[27]Gerald T. Sheppard, "Psalms: Or, 'How to Read a Book that Seems Intent on Reading You,'" *Theology: Notes & News* (October 1992): 17.

[28]Patrick D. Miller observed a similar connection: "Psalm 1 placed before Psalm 2, therefore, joins Deuteronomy in a kind of democratizing move… While Psalm 2 invites the reader to hear the voice of the LORD's anointed in the following psalms, Psalm 1 says that what we hear is the voice of *anyone* who lives by the Torah, which may and should include the king." Patrick D. Miller, "The Beginning of the Psalter," in *The Shape and Shaping of the Psalter,* ed. J. Clinton McCann; JSOTSup 159 (Sheffield: Sheffield Academic Press, 1993), 91.

[29]I confess to being less enthusiastic about this approach. The psalms are different enough in character to "want to be heard" less as one than separately.

[30]Perowne, *The Book of Psalms: A New Translation.*

[31]Ibid., 43–55 (esp. pp. 43, 49). Perowne writes (p. 49): "Now, the Psalms are typical. They are the words of holy men of old—of one especially, whose life was fashioned in many of its prominent features to be a type of Christ. But just as David's *whole* life was not typical of Christ, so neither were all his words. His suffering and humiliation first, and his glory afterwards, were faint and passing and evanescent images of the life of Him who was both Son of David and Son of God. But the sorrowful shadow of pollution which passed on David's life, *that* was not typical…"

Thus, typology is a form of biblical interpretation that deals with the correspondence between traditions concerning divinely appointed persons, events, and institutions within the framework of salvation history. S.v. "Typology," *ABD*, 6:682.

[32]For a previous discussion, see D. Brent Sandy and Tiberius Rata's earlier chapter in this volume, "Approaching the Psalms: Key Insights," 11–14.

[33]Bruce A. Cameron, "Preface," to *Psalms: With Introductions by Martin Luther* (St. Louis: Concordia, 1993), 4.

[34]I do not mean to imply that the book of Psalms is to be read *only* as messianic. Other ways, many based on the grammatical-historical approach modeled elsewhere in this book, abound to the benefit of the reader and are in keeping with how the book was edited.

[35]For an accurate and accessible translation of the Septuagint version of the Psalms, see *A New English Translation of the Septuagint and Other Greek Translations Traditionally Included under that Title: The Psalms,* trans. Albert Pietersma (Oxford/New York: Oxford University Press, 2000).

[36]See Abegg, Flint, and Ulrich, *The Dead Sea Scrolls Bible,* 507–510, 583–84.

[37]Although Christians take the three terms "Messiah," "Christ," and "Jesus" to be synonymous, Jews prior to the time of Jesus (and since) obviously did not. In other words, when I use the terms messianic and christological to describe a Jewish hope before the time of Jesus, those terms do not refer to Jesus but to a hoped-for messiah.

[38]Of course, anyone's pre-understanding of the Messiah (including my own) cannot help but affect his or her reading of the Psalter. For a similar attempt, see James L. Mays, *The LORD Reigns: A Theological Handbook to the Psalms* (Louisville: Westminster John Knox, 1994), 99–107.

[39]Luke 2:47 (NJKV).

[40]Compare Matthew 5:1–10 (TEV).

[41]Compare Matthew 7:28–29.

[42]I find it surprising that few scholars take these psalms as testimony of the suffering of the messiah. Many New Testament scholars judge from the absence of evidence for any *expectation* of a suffering messiah in Jesus' time that there was no Jewish *literature* regarding the suffering of the messiah. A radical, but not uncommon extension of this view is that the early Church, in desperation to explain the crucifixion, read the lament psalms back into the memory of the life of Jesus. But why are Jesus' followers allowed this innovation, but not the master rabbi who inspired them? This is all the more strange given that the earliest traditions are uniform in attributing the notion of a suffering messiah not to the church but to *Jesus.*

[43]John H. Eaton, *Kingship and the Psalms,* second ed.; The Biblical Seminar (Sheffield: JSOT Press, 1996), 133.

[44]In each of the synoptic gospels Moses meets with Jesus (in the transfiguration) in the pericope that follows Jesus' disclosure that the messiah must suffer (Mk. 8:31–9:13; Mt. 16:21–17:13; Lk. 9:22–36).

[45]See Mays, *The LORD Reigns,* 99.

Chapter 5: Psalm 19

[1]Speaking of the Psalms, Hyppolytus (170–236), elder in the church at Rome, tells us David "first gave to the Hebrews a new style of hymnody. Through it, he... introduces the new hymn and new style of jubilant praise in the worship of God." (Hippolytus, *Exposition of the Psalms,* ANF 5:170). Other statements about the Psalms' priority of place include Athanasius, "An epitome of the whole Scriptures"; Basil, "A compendium of all theology"; Martin Luther, "A little Bible, and the summary of the Old Testament"; Melancthon, "The most elegant work extant in the world"; James Anderson, "Introductory Notice," in *Calvin's Commentary on the Psalms,* trans. James Anderson (Grand Rapids: Eerdmans, 1949), v–xx.

[2]See "Classification of Psalms by Titles" at the end of this book.

³J. L. Mays, "The Place of the Torah-Psalms in the Psalter," *JBL* 106/1 (1987): 12. Additionally, Gerald Wilson argues that the psalm titles form a sub-categorization of genre groupings for which Psalm 19 introduces a section that ends with Psalm 24, based on the Hebrew term *mzmwr*. Gerald Henry Wilson, *The Editing of the Hebrew Psalter*, SBLDS 76 (Chico, Calif.: Scholars Press, 1985), 159. Wilson's larger thesis is that the Psalter has been edited to set forth David as an exemplar or model.

⁴J. G. Gammie, *Holiness in Israel* (Minneapolis: Fortress, 1989), 131. Poetic themes of victory leading to rule resident in this passage appear in an Ethiopic victory inscription of the early sixth century C.E. from southwest Arabia in which the emperor Axum cited from Psalm 19 (K. A. Kitchen, *On the Reliability of the Old Testament* [Grand Rapids: Eerdmans, 2003], 93). The *Torah* connection in Psalm 19 is critical: "Kingship is linked together with torah from the outset of the Psalter and, interestingly, the next explicitly royal psalms in the Psalter are Psalms 18, 20, and 21 which also revolve around a torah psalm (Ps. 19)." J. A. Grant, "The Psalms and the King," in *Interpreting the Psalms: Issues and Approaches,* ed. D. Firth and P. S. Johnston (Downers Grove, Ill.: InterVarsity, 2005), 115.

⁵J. L. Mays, *The LORD Reigns: A Theological Handbook to the Psalms* (Louisville: Westminster John Knox, 1994), 17.

⁶For a description of the realities in which the metaphor is rooted, see A. R. Millard, "Oral Proclamation and Written Record: Spreading and Preserving Information in Ancient Israel," in *Historical, Epigraphical and Biblical Studies in Honor of Prof. Michael Heltzer* ed. Yitzhak Avishur, Robert Deutsch, and Michael Heltzer (Tel Aviv-Jaffa: Archaeological Center Publications, 1999), 237–41. Additionally, M. Z. Brettler addresses the broader issue of God's messengers: "The officials of the royal court that are important for understanding God's kingship are…the 'messengers', who played an important role in conveying or making public the royal word (e.g. 1 Sam. 16:19; 2 Kgs 1:2; 14:8; cf. 19:9)." M. Z. Brettler, *God Is King: Understanding an Israelite Metaphor,* JSOTSup 76 (Sheffield: Sheffield Academic Press, 1989), 100.

⁷Messenger activity was a ready source of vivid imagery, even in the ancient world. One commercial letter from Mesopotamia likens it to "throwing stones from afar." See K. R. Veenhof, "'Dying tablets' and 'Hungry Silver': Elements of Figurative Language in Akkadian Commercial Terminology," in *Figurative Language in the Ancient Near East,* ed. M. Mindlin, M. J. Geller, and J. E. Wansbrough (London: School of Oriental and African Studies, University of London, 1987), 46.

⁸When the psalmist alludes to Genesis 1, he may also be drawing on its subtle message regarding God's incomparability. See D. C. Deuel, "Polemical Doxology: Genesis 1 as a Response to the Gods of the Nations and an Invitation to Worship," unpublished paper presented to the Evangelical Theological Society, 2002. Gordon Wenham says, "The author of Genesis 1 therefore shows that he was aware of other cosmologies, and that he wrote not in dependence on them so much as *in deliberate rejection of them* (emphasis added)." G. J. Wenham, Genesis 1–15, WBC 19 (Waco: Word, 1987), 9.

⁹See K. Lawson Younger Jr., "Black Obelisk," in *The Context of Scripture: Monumental Inscriptions from the Biblical World,* ed. W. H. Hallo with K. Lawson Younger Jr. (Leiden: Brill, 2000), 269–70; A. J. Hoerth, *Archaeology & the Old Testament* (Grand Rapids: Baker, 1998), 321–22; Clifford M. Jones, *Old Testament Illustrations,* The Cambridge Bible Commentary (Cambridge: University Press, 1971), 85–86.

¹⁰From James B. Pritchard, *The Ancient Near East in Pictures: Relating to the Old Testament* (Princeton, N. J.: Princeton University Press, 1954), 122. Printed with the permission of the British Museum. All rights reserved.

¹¹C. Zaccagnini, "Sacred and Human Components in Ancient Near Eastern Law," *History of Religions* 33 (1994): 265–86. For a discussion of the monumental use of writing, see K. A. Kitchen, "Now You See It, Now You Don't! The Monumental Use of and Non-Use of Writing in the Ancient Near East," in *Writing and Ancient Near Eastern Society: Papers in Honour of Alan R. Millard,* ed. P. Bienkowski, C. Mee, and E. Slater (New York: T & T Clark, 2005), 178.

[12]For example, K. Seybold cautiously proposes "some process of reworking which produced this very complicated text." K. Seybold, *Introducing the Psalms,* trans. R. G. Dunphy (Edinburgh: T & T Clark, 1990), 51. Compare E. S. Gerstenberger, *Psalms Part 1 with an Introduction to Cultic Poetry,* FOTL 4 (Grand Rapids: Eerdmans, 1988), 101. For the unity of the psalm, see J. Clinton McCann Jr., "Psalms," *New Interpreter's Bible* 4 (Nashville: Abingdon, 1996), 751.

[13]This study finds agreement with those who embrace a unified final text: McCann says, "To bisect Psalm 19, however, is to fail to appreciate a carefully constructed poem and to miss entirely its message about the *torah* of the LORD." J. C. McCann, *A Theological Introduction to the Book of Psalms: The Psalms as Torah* (Nashville: Abingdon, 1993), 28. See also Peter Craigie: "It is reasonably certain that the psalm in its present form is a unity..." Craigie and Tate, *Psalms 1–50,* 179. Finally, see the work of M. Fishbane in which he draws out the complex literary structure of Psalm 19, revealing a unified artistic design. M. Fishbane, "Psalm 19: Creation, Torah and Hope," in *Text and Texture* (New York: Schocken, 1979), 84–90.

[14]Speaking about thematic transitional devices, O. Keel says, "Ps 19 suggests an association between the sun and world order (law) when it celebrates the sun (vv. 4c–6), then moves abruptly to praise the law of Yahweh (vv. 7–10), which enlightens the eyes (v. 8)." O. Keel, *The Symbolism of the Biblical World: Ancient Near Eastern Iconography and the Book of Psalms,* trans. T. J. Hallett (Winona Lake: Eisenbrauns, 1997), 36–37. See also Seybold's discussion of the sun as emblematic of justice and law. Seybold, *Introducing the Psalms,* 194. Craigie adds, "Although the transition is sharp, it is entirely natural." Craigie and Tate, *Psalms 1–50,* 182.

[15]G. B. Caird, *The Language and Imagery of the Bible* (Philadelphia: Westminster, 1980), 76. "To praise means to give Yahweh the dwbk (*kabod,* 'glory') (Ps. 29:1)," that is, to acknowledge and submit to the effects of these truths regarding God's character and works. H. J. Kraus, *Theology of the Psalms,* trans. Keith Krim (Minneapolis: Augsburg, 1986), 13. The author elaborates specifically with respect to God's holiness and his kingship: "*Glory* (*kabod*) is the manifestation of Yahweh's holiness... Holiness connotes the will of Yahweh the king to attain sole authority and to overcome everything that stands in opposition to his will." H. J. Kraus, *Theology of the Psalms,* 42.

[16]T. N. D. Mettinger, "YAHWEH SABAOTH–The Heavenly King on the Cherubim Throne," in *Studies in the Period of David and Solomon and other Essays,* Papers Read at the International Symposium for Biblical Studies, Tokyo, 5–7 December, 1979; ed. T. Ishida (Winona Lake: Eisenbrauns, 1982), 129.

[17]See N. Sarna, "Psalm XIX and the Near Eastern Sun-God Literature," *Fourth World Congress of Jewish Studies, Papers I* (Jerusalem, 1967), 171–75. The Hebrew term for sun in this context is masculine, while its common use is feminine. *GKC* makes the observation that when functioning as natural forces or instruments the heavenly bodies are regarded as feminine, but when taken as names, they are masculine (*GKC,* 122). O. Perowne called the sun the "Chiefest herald of God's praise." J. J. Stewart Perowne, *The Book of Psalms* (Andover: Warren Draper, 1882), 197.

[18]R. J. Clifford, "The Hebrew Scriptures and the Theology of Creation," *TS* 46 (1985): 516. Mays concurs, noting that God's power and wisdom manifest regularity and order: "The torah of the LORD is just as certain and everlasting, just as much a part of the nature of reality, as the succession of day and night and the regular course of the sun." Mays, *The LORD Reigns,* 129. C. S. Lewis believed that the line, "there is none hidden from its heat," created a transition in the composition. C. S. Lewis, *Reflections on the Psalms* (London: Geoffrey Bles, 1958), 56.

[19]J. L. Crenshaw raises the question of the juxtaposition of the wisdom themes of instruction (vv. 7–11) versus concealment (v. 3). See J. L. Crenshaw, *Education in Ancient Israel: Across the Deadening Silence* (New York: Doubleday, 1998), 257. King Solomon's kingship was like God's in that he was also a teacher (Prov. 1:8).

[20]"The Hebrew poet liked to play with words; he liked to set them in various contexts so their various shades of meaning might be exposed." Nic. H. Ridderbos, "The Psalms: Style-Figures and Structure: Certain Considerations, with Special

Reference to Pss. XII, XXV, and XLV," in *Studies on the Psalms,* Oudtestamentische Studiën 13, ed. P. A. H. de Boer (Leiden: Brill, 1963), 48. The relationship between "law" *(torah)* and the subsequent five words is described by Mays as "companion terms for torah... The cluster of terms is not so much a list of synonyms that refer to one entity, but more a vocabulary that refers to a variety of writings that are regarded as having one function. The list is meant to include whatever serves as instruction about the way of the LORD and of his servants." Mays, *The LORD Reigns,* 129–30.

²¹D. J. A. Clines, "The Tree of Knowledge and the Law of Yahweh Psalm (XIX)," *VT* 24 (1974): 8–14. While this writer finds general agreement with Clines' insightful study, he disagrees with some of the author's observations about specific phrases in verses 8–11. Mays says of the Torah Psalms in general, "All are the works of poets who are bringing together the elements of vocabulary, style, and theology from various parts of the emerging Hebrew canon of scripture." Mays, "The Place of the Torah-Psalms in the Psalter," 4. Drawing on the wisdom connection, J. Barr interprets the phrase "the knowledge of good and evil" as "the power of rational and especially ethical discrimination..." J. Barr, *The Garden of Eden and the Hope of Immortality* (Minneapolis: Fortress, 1993), 62.

²²A. Berlin, *The Dynamics of Hebrew Parallelism* (Bloomington: Indiana University Press, 1985), 59.

²³His petition and thoughts about his propensity toward sin may be a reflection on the fall passage in Genesis 3. See A. Altmann, *"Homo Imago Dei* in Jewish and Christian Theology," *JR* 48 (1968): 235–59, especially 249, cited in D. J. A. Clines, "The Tree of Knowledge and the Law of Yahweh Psalm (XIX)," 12, n. 3. Charles A. and Emilie Grace Briggs saw a connection between Psalm 19 and Genesis 4: "Such transgressions overpower the man and reduce him to servitude. The phrase so greatly resembles that of Genesis 4:7 that it is probable the author had in mind the story of Cain, where sin like a wild beast couches at the door... [S]o here the presumptuous sins are personified." C. A. Briggs and E. G. Briggs, *A Critical and Exegetical Commentary on the Book of Psalms* (Edinburgh: T & T Clark, 1906–7), 170.

²⁴The center of human life, the heart, is the site of all thought, planning, reflection, explaining, and ambition, the place where the whole person suffers the full weight of joy, sorrow, anxiety, fear, bitterness and hope. H. J. Kraus, *Theology of the Psalms,* 145. H. W. Wolff's thorough discussion of the heart focuses on the reasoning process as it relates to volition, but not to the exclusion of feelings and wishes. H. W. Wolff, *Anthropology of the Old Testament,* trans. M. Kohl (Philadelphia: Fortress, 1974), 40–58.

²⁵Mays questions meditation-study: "How is it that the instructing word has been incorporated in the very structure of consciousness?" His answer is simply by a kind of study mentioned in the contexts of two of these quotations (Pss. 119:11; 37:30–31) and in all three of the torah psalms. It is a kind of study that proceeds orally; it rehearses and repeats. It searches the instruction of God by reciting in receptivity until the matter becomes part of the thinking and willing and doing. For this kind of discipline any text that has become scripture can become instruction, command, word, precept. Mays, "The Place of the Torah-Psalms in the Psalter," 9.

²⁶J. L. Mays, *Preaching and Teaching the Psalms* (Louisville: Westminster John Knox, 2006), 50.

²⁷F. F. Bruce, *The Defense of the Gospel in the New Testament* (Grand Rapids: Eerdmans, 1959), vii.

²⁸Origen, *Against Celsus* 5.13., in *The Early Church Fathers: Ante-Nicene Period.*

²⁹Cited in E. M. Yamauchi, *Persia and the Bible* (Grand Rapids: Baker, 1990), 520. I would be remiss if I failed to mention a hymn that Dr. John Davis sang with his students in seminary chapel during his years of dedicated instruction and administration.

"Sun moon and stars in their courses above
Join with all nature in manifold witness
To Thy great faithfulness, mercy and love."
    −T. O. Chisholm, "Great Is Thy Faithfulness," 1923

Chapter 6: Psalm 46

[1]The Wild Turkey simile reflects my past life experiences, and yet it aptly describes God's Spirit working in me at the time (cp. Eph. 5:18).

[2]Daniel Estes, however, considers the psalm to be an example of a song of trust because it is not composed in the standard form of a descriptive praise psalm. Daniel J. Estes, *Handbook on the Wisdom Books and Psalms* (Grand Rapids: Baker, 2005), 196. Regardless of how the psalm is classified, it is clear that the psalm reeks of confidence and trust in God.

[3]Hans Kraus is a little more elusive. He views Psalm 46 as a preexilic psalm of worship in Zion, concepts of which come from a pre-Israelite, ancient Canaanite area. Hans-Joachim Kraus, *Psalms 1–59* (Minneapolis: Fortress, 1993), 460–61. Whether the psalmist borrows concepts from a previous period of time or not is beyond the scope of our discussion. Yet what is important is that the psalm was written before the exile to Babylon in 586 B.C.E.

[4]For primary evidence about Tiglath-pileser, see 2 Kings 15:17–29; cp. *ANET* 194. For Shalmaneser V and Sargon II see 2 Kings 17:1–6; 18:9–12; cp. *ANET* 195–196. For king Hezekiah of Judah, cp. Isaiah 20:1–6 with 2 Kings 19:32–34; Isaiah 37:14–21, 33–37; see also *ANET* 199–200.

[5]John Hayes avers, "The tradition of Yahweh's election of Zion is, of course, based on the bringing of the ark to Jerusalem." John H. Hayes, "The Tradition of Zion's Inviolability," *JBL* 82 (1963): 419–26.

[6]For others who view this historical setting, see A. F. Kirkpatrick, *The Book of Psalms* (Cambridge: University Press, 1910), 253f; Lloyd Neve, "The Common Use of Traditions by the Author of Psalm 46 and Isaiah," *ExpTim* 86 (May 1975): 243–46; John Phillips, *Exploring the Psalms: An Expository Commentary,* JPCS (Grand Rapids: Kregel, 1988), 363–69.

[7]For similar comparisons, see Isaiah 51:15; Jeremiah 5:22; 6:23; 31:35; 51:42, 55. See also Sidney Kelly, "Psalm 46: A Study in Imagery," *JBL* 89 (1970): 305–12.

[8]F. Delitzsch, *Psalms,* Commentary on the Old Testament, 10 vol. (Grand Rapids: Eerdmans, 1982), 5:94. A. A. Anderson, *Psalms (1–72),* vol. 1, NCBC (Grand Rapids: Eerdmans, 1972), 1:357; Jerome F. D. Creach, *The Destiny of the Righteous in the Psalms* (St. Louis: Chalice, 2008), 116–17.

[9]Neve, "The Common Use of Traditions by the Author of Psalm 46 and Isaiah," 244. Some, however, may consider this to be a reference to Hezekiah's handcut tunnel through solid rock whereby the spring of Gihon, located below the steep eastern hill of Ophel in the Kidron Valley, was diverted through a conduit 1777 feet long. Phillips, *Exploring the Psalms,* 366.

[10]The term "Most High" reflects the idea of omnipotence, thus stressing the total supremacy of God (Gen. 14:18, 19; Num. 24:16; Deut. 32:8; Ps. 83:18; Lam. 3:35, 38; Isa. 14:14).

[11]Several elements of a holy war tradition exist throughout Psalm 46: "The nations are in an uproar" (v. 6 NRSV; cp. 2b–3), "God rescues at the break of day" (v. 5b NLT), Yahweh is the one who "commands armies" (v. 7a NET); "Witness the exploits of the LORD" (v. 8 NET), and "He brings wars to an end" (v. 9a CEV). For a discussion concerning a "holy war," see R. de Vaux, "The Holy War," in *Ancient Israel: Social Institutions,* trans. J. McHugh (New York: McGraw–Hill, 1961), 1:258–267; Rudolf Smend, *Yahweh War & Tribal Confederation,* trans. M. G. Rogers (Nashville: Abingdon Press, 1970); Peter C. Craigie, *The Problem of War in the Old Testament* (Grand Rapids: Eerdmans, 1978); Millard Lind, *Yahweh Is a Warrior: The Theology of Warfare in Ancient Israel* (Scottdale , Pa.: Herald Press, 1980); Gerhard von Rad, *Holy War in Ancient Israel,* trans. J. H. Yoder and M. J. Dawn (Grand Rapids: Eerdmans, 1996; German orig. 1958); Susan Niditch, *War in the Hebrew Bible: A Study in the Ethics of Violence* (New York: Oxford University Press, 1993). The Mesha Stele or Moabite Stone and the stele from Tell Dan both show elements of holy war theology practiced

by Israel's neighbors. K. Lawson Younger Jr., *Ancient Conquest Accounts: A Study in Ancient Near Eastern and Biblical History Writing,* JSOTSup 98 (Sheffield: Sheffield Academic Press, 1990), 258–60 suggests eliminating "Holy War" from our vocabulary in light of the widespread ideas and the difficulty in differentiating a holy war from a secular one, but holy war still indicates the understanding that God is deeply involved in Israel's warfare or that other nations see their god(s) so involved.

[12]A six-sided Assyrian Prism dated *circa* 691 B.C.E. contains the final edition of Sennacherib's annals. Included on it is this account of Sennacherib's third military campaign in the west and his siege of Jerusalem. The most that is said about his encounter with Hezekiah is that "I made Hezekiah a prisoner in Jerusalem, his royal residence, like a bird in a cage. I surrounded him with earthwork in order to molest those who were leaving his city's gate." Jerusalem, however, is never described as being vanquished. The translation is from James B. Pritchard, ed., *The Ancient Near East,* vol. 1 (Princeton: University Press, 1958), 199–200.

[13]Herbert B. Huffman, "The Treaty Background of Hebrew Yáda,'" *BASOR* 181 (February 1966): 31–37; Herbert B. Huffman and Simon B. Parker, "A Further Note on the Treaty Background of Hebrew 'Yáda,'" *BASOR* 184 (December 1966): 36–38.

[14]Kenneth Osbeck muses, "The single most powerful hymn of the Protestant Reformation Movement was Luther's 'A Mighty Fortress Is Our God,' based on Psalm 46. This hymn became the battle cry of the people, a great source of strength and inspiration even for those who were martyred for their convictions." Kenneth W. Osbeck, *101 Hymn Stories* (Grand Rapids: Kregel, 1982), 14.

[15]See *TJud* 24, 25; *TDan* 5:10–12; *Ezra* 13.1–11; 11Q13.

[16]Gerhard Delling, "*katargeō*," *TDNT* 1:453, cp. 2 Tim. 1:10).

Chapter 7: Psalm 63

[1]Augustine, Bishop of Hippo, *The Confessions of Saint Augustine,* 10 vols., ed. by Paul M. Bechtel (Chicago: Moody, 1981), 1.1.6.

[2]For a helpful discussion of psalm superscriptions in general, see C. Hassell Bullock, *Encountering the Book of Psalms* (Grand Rapids: Baker, 2001), 24–30, and J. H. Waltner, *Psalms,* Believers Church Bible Commentary (Scottdale, Pa.: Herald, 2006), 772–74. Franz Delitzsch views the title of Psalm 63 as an accurate portrayal of an actual historical event. Franz Delitzsch, *Biblical Commentary on the Psalms,* vol. 2, trans. Francis Bolton (Grand Rapids: Eerdmans, 1949), 213.

[3]Erhard S. Gerstenberger, *Psalms, Part 1, with an Introduction to Cultic Poetry,* FOTL 14 (Grand Rapids: Eerdmans, 1988), 30–34.

[4]Marvin E. Tate, *Psalms 51–100,* WBC 20 (Dallas: Word, 1990), 124.

[5]Bullock, *Encountering the Book of Psalms,* 144; Hans-Joachim Kraus, *Psalms 60–150,* trans. Hilton C. Oswald (Minneapolis: Fortress, 1993), 18; Leopold Sabourin, *The Psalms* (New York: Alba House, 1974), 251; Tate, *Psalms 51–100,* 125; Willem A. VanGemeren, *Psalms,* Expositor's Bible Commentary 5 (Grand Rapids: Zondervan, 1991), 435.

[6]Erhard S. Gerstenberger, *Psalms, Part 2, and Lamentations,* FOTL 15 (Grand Rapids: Eerdmans, 2001), 13–14.

[7]Walther Eichrodt, *Theology of the Old Testament,* vol. 1 (trans. J. A. Baker) (Philadelphia: Westminster, 1961), 186–92.

[8]Kraus, *Psalms 60–150,* on the other hand, states, "In the Elohistically edited part of the Psalter we should here probably read יהוה (yhwh) instead of אלהים ('elohim)" (p. 18).

[9]VanGemeren, *Psalms,* suggests, "In the Elohistic Psalter (Pss. 42–83), the emphatic 'O God' signifies essentially the same as Yahweh ('LORD'), the covenant-faithful God" (p. 425).

[10]Gerstenberger, *Psalms, Part 2, and Lamentations,* 14.

[11]Tate, *Psalms 51–100,* 125.

[12]Gerstenberger, *Psalms, Part 2, and Lamentations*, 15–16.

[13]For the role of "historical imagination" in recovering the past, see R. G. Collingwood, *The Idea of History* (Oxford: Clarendon Press, 1946), 231–40. For the idea of human commonality as a key to historical understanding, see Wilhelm Dilthey, *Pattern and Meaning in History* (New York: Harper & Row, 1961), 64–82.

[14]John N. Day, "The Imprecatory Psalms and Christian Ethics," *BSac* 159 (2002): 166–86.

[15]Delitzsch, *Biblical Commentary on the Psalms*, 212.

[16]Gerstenberger, *Psalms, Part 2, and Lamentations*, 12–13.

[17]Kraus, *Psalms 60–150*, 18.

[18]Tate, *Psalms 51–100*, 125.

[19]VanGemeren, *Psalms*, 425.

Chapter 8: Psalm 73

[1]Martyn Lloyd-Jones, *Faith on Trial* (Grand Rapids: Eerdmans, 1965), 11.

[2]E. Zenger, *Psalmen* in F. L. Hossfeld and E. Zenger, *Psalmen 51–100*, Hermenia, trans. Linda M. Maloney (Minneapolis: Fortress, 2000), 353–54. J. C. McCann calls Psalm 73 "a microcosm of OT theology," J. C. McCann, Jr. "Psalm 73: A Microcosm of Old Testament Theology," in *The Listening Heart*, ed. K. Hogland et al. (Sheffield: JSOT Press, 1987), 247–57.

[3]Most take the plural noun "sanctuaries of God" to be a metonymic allusion to the Jerusalem temple including all its precincts.

[4]Many base this judgment on the fact that already by the third century B.C.E., when the Greek Septuagint translation was made, many of the meanings of the terms used in the superscriptions of about half of the Psalms were already enigmatic and unknown to the translators.

[5]Included in the Asaph psalms are Psalms 50; 73; 74; 75; 76; 77; 78; 79; 80; 81; 82; 83. See the distribution of these psalms throughout the Psalter in the "Classification of the Psalms by Categories" at the end of this book.

[6]Hermann Gunkel and J. Begrich, *Einleitung in die Psalmen* (Göttingen: Vanderhoeck & Ruprecht, 1933), 388–89.

[7]Claus Westermann, *The Praise of God in the Psalms*, ET (Richmond, Va.: John Knox, 1965), 80.

[8]Sigmund Mowinckel, *The Psalms in Israel's Worship*, vol. 2 (Oxford: Blackwell, 1962), 114. An unusually different categorization of this psalm comes from J. A. Vos, *Theopoetry of the Psalms* (London: T & T Clark, 2005), 174, who puts the psalm in a wisdom class, but ends up saying it is a pastoral prayer monologue, which is also a confessional monologue. J. H. Waltner, *Psalms*, Believers Church Bible Commentary (Scottdale, Pa.: Herald Press, 2006), 356, calls Psalm 73 "one of the most remarkable and satisfying of all the psalms... In the end, the psalm becomes a reflective testimony, providing others in the community with guidance and insight regarding the problem of the disparity between faith and experience."

[9]The criteria for distinguishing wisdom psalms can be divided into two sets: (1) formal (literary style) and (2) thematic (content). Some of the formal criteria are: (1) alphabetic structure such as acrostic psalms, (2) numerical sayings such as "three, yea four," (3) blessed sayings [Hebrew '*ashre*], (4) "better" sayings, (5) comparisons or admonitions, (6) the address of father to son, (7) the use of wisdom vocabulary and turns of phrases, and (8) the employment of proverbs, similes, rhetorical questions, and metaphors. As for wisdom themes or content, we would list: (1) the problem of retribution, (2) the contrast of the wicked and righteous, (3) exhortations to trust personally in the Lord, (4) references to the "fear of the LORD," and (5) meditation on the written law of God. Typically, the following psalms are labeled wisdom psalms: Psalms 1; 19; 37; 49; 73; 111; 112; 127; 128; and 133. See the distribution of these Psalms throughout the Psalter in the "Classification of the Psalms by Categories" at the end of this book.

[10]See Leslie C. Allen, "Psalm 73: An Analysis," *TynBull* 33 (1982): 110, n 55. L. G. Perdue adds three more wisdom terms from this Psalm 73 to make twelve wisdom terms. Perdue, *Wisdom and Cult: A Critical Analysis of the View of Cult in the Wisdom Literatures of Israel and the Ancient Near East* (Missoula: Scholars Press, 1977), 287.

[11]Allen, "Psalm 73," 93–97. M. E. Tate noted that "no less than thirty-seven literary patterns have been proposed for Ps 73," in Tate, *Psalms 51–100,* WBC 21 (Dallas: Word, 1985), 232.

[12]Allen, "Psalm 73," 97–107.

[13]Zenger, *Psalmen,* 350–51.

[14]Brevard S. Childs, *Introduction to the Old Testament as Scripture* (Philadelphia: Fortress, 1979), 511–25.

[15]Mention can be made of J. C. McCann, ed., *The Shape and Shaping of the Psalter,* JSOTSup 159 (Sheffield, JSOT Press, 1993); G. H. Wilson, *The Editing of the Hebrew Psalter* (Chico, Calif.: Scholars Press, 1985); *idem.,* "The Shape of the Book of Psalms," *Int* 46 (1992): 129–42; Nancy L. deClaissé Walford, *Introduction to the Psalms: A Song from Ancient Israel* (St. Louis: Chalice, 2004), 85–90, and Jerome F. D. Creach, *The Destiny of the Righteous in the Psalms* (St. Louis: Chalice, 2008), 65–66.

[16]Walter Brueggemann and Patrick D. Miller, "Psalm 73 as Canonical Marker," *JSOT* 72 (1996): 45–56.

[17]Martin Buber, "The Heart Determines," reprinted in *Theodicy in the Old Testament,* ed. J. L. Crenshaw (Philadelphia: Fortress, 1983), 109–18.

[18]Christopher Seitz, "Royal Promises in the Canonical Books of Isaiah and the Psalms," in *Isaiah in Scripture and the Church* (unpublished manuscript, 1994) referred to in Brueggemann and Miller, "Psalm 73 as Canonical Marker," 51, n 17.

[19]Note also that the vocabulary of Psalm 73:18–28 is strikingly similar to that of Psalms 15–24, where in these royal psalms, as Patrick Miller argued, the center of Psalms 15–24 is found in Psalm 19, which also stresses obedience to torah. This argument for the role and placement of Psalm 73 is a very thoughtful and helpful analysis for getting at the theology and practical preaching values of this psalm. See Patrick D. Miller, "Kingship, Torah Obedience, and Prayer: The Theology of Psalms 15–24," in *Neue Wege der Psalmenforschung,* ed. K. Seybold and E. Zenger, HBS, 1 (Freiburg: Herder, 1994), 127–42.

[20]Martyn Lloyd-Jones, *Faith on Trial,* 11.

[21]J. Clinton McCann Jr. and James C. Howell, *Preaching the Psalms* (Nashville: Abingdon, 2001), 16.

[22]Ibid., 35.

[23]Ibid., 36 quoting Dietrich Bonhoeffer, *Psalms: The Prayerbook of the Bible,* trans. James H. Burtness (Minneapolis: Augsburg, 1970 [originally published in German, 1940]), 11.

[24]For a sample sermon on Psalm 73, see Dave Bland, "The Goodness of God: Psalm 73," in *Performing the Psalms,* ed. Dave Bland and David Fleer (St. Louis: Chalice, 2005), 152–58.

Chapter 9: Psalm 89

[1]For the designation of Psalm 89 as a communal lament/complaint, see C. Westermann, *The Psalms: Structure, Content and Message,* trans. by R. D. Gehrke (Minneapolis: Augsburg, 1980), 47; J. L. Mays, *Psalms* (Louisville: John Knox, 1994), 287; and Erhard S. Gerstenberger, *Psalms, Part 2 and Lamentations* FOTL, vol. 15 (Grand Rapids: Eerdmans, 2001), 154. Numerous scholars apply the label with more restriction to verses 38–51; see, for example, H. J. Kraus, *Psalms 60–150: A Commentary,* trans. H. C. Oswald (Minneapolis: Augsburg, 1989), 202. However, the characterization of the psalm as a lament of the community, in my opinion, is an apt description of the overall rhetorical flavor of the piece, and thus it may be considered to be a royal lament psalm. As Nancy L. deClaissé-Walford, *Introduction to the Psalms: A Song from Ancient Israel* (St. Louis: Chalice, 2004), 96, finds: "The tone of Psalm 89

changes dramatically in verse 38. Without explanation, without transition, the royal psalm becomes a lament."

[2]For a brief survey of the various proposals of an historical situation as the object of the lament in Psalm 89, see M. E. Tate, *Psalms 51–100*, WBC 20 (Dallas: Word, 1990), 416–17. The superscription offers little assistance. It describes the psalm as a *maskil*, a term implying the didactic quality of the work. The psalm is associated with Ethan, an Ezrahite. Nothing is known of this figure apart from an association with being wise (1 Kings 5:11) and having ability in music (1 Chr. 15:17, 19).

[3]Gerstenberger, *Psalms, Part 2 and Lamentations*, 154–55.

[4]The review of opinion on this issue here is not exhaustive. For greater detail in the discussion concerning the setting for the use of the psalm, see Tate, *Psalms 51–100*, 413–17.

[5]Gerstenberger, *Psalms, Part 2 and Lamentations*, 154–55.

[6]Westermann, *The Psalms*, 31–47. For a survey of the historical development of the genre, see, by the same author, *Praise and Lament in the Psalms*, trans. K. R. Crim and R. N. Soulen (Atlanta: John Knox, 1981), 165–213. The insights incorporated in the following discussion concerning the form of communal laments are drawn from the first work cited in this note.

[7]For a demonstration of this form with reference to Psalm 80, see Westermann, *The Psalms*, 33–36.

[8]deClaissé-Walford, *Introduction to the Psalms*, 97, observes that "the psalm ends with a plea to God to remember God's servant, and just as with Psalm 88, the lament portion of Psalm 89 has no *Expression of Trust* and no *Expression of Praise and Adoration*."

[9]This analysis follows the translation of the NET Bible, which is in agreement with MT (against LXX) in understanding the psalmist's quotation of divine speech to begin in verse 3.

[10]As regent on behalf of divinity, kings of many cultures in the ancient Near East were agents of protection from foreign invasion, keepers of justice, and conduits of blessing. See Psalm 72, in which Israel's monarch is expected to fulfill such functions. To the degree that kings represented the will of divinity, they were perceived to be "sons" of gods. For a brief survey of the ideas associated with the title in the ancient Near East and its christological associations in Christian interpretations of the Psalms, see J. L. Mays, *The Lord Reigns: A Theological Handbook of the Psalms* (Louisville: Westminster, 1994), 108–16.

[11]For a detailed list of the parallels between God's dominion and David's dominion in the psalm, see Tate, *Psalms 51–100*, 423. The qualitative similarities emphasize the continuity of divine dominion between heaven and earth. God's will is done on earth, just as it is in heaven.

[12]Gerstenberger, *Psalms, Part 2 and Lamentations*, 153, notes the similar prominence of the second-person pronoun (referring to God) in reading between verses 9–13 and 38–45. In the previous passage, the second-person pronouns emphasized the unique qualities and abilities of God. Here in the latter passage, the pronouns designate blame for the current state of affairs.

[13]With the conclusion of verse 48, it becomes evident that Westermann's observation of a focus on three parties (God, the enemies, and the one lamenting) in the lament holds true in the case of Psalm 89.

[14]B. S. Childs, *Introduction to the Old Testament as Scripture* (Philadelphia: Fortress, 1979), 515–17.

[15]G. H. Wilson, *The Editing of the Hebrew Psalter* (Chico: Scholars Press, 1985), 209–28. Compare deClaissé-Wolford, *Introduction to the Psalms*, 85–98, who concludes: "God can again be provider, protector, and sustainer; but the people must go back, must remember, and must learn from the past. With that knowledge, Israel will be able to survive as a distinct group of people within the vast empires which will conquer them time and again in the centuries following" (p. 98).

[16]For discussion of Psalms 103 and 104 see chapter 11 of this volume by Richard E. Averbeck, entitled "Psalms 103–104: Hymns of Redemption and Creation."

[17]Childs, *Introduction to the Old Testament as Scripture,* 515–17.

[18]See Ronald Cox, "The New Testament Preaches the Psalms: Problems and Possibilities," in *Performing the Psalms,* ed. Dave Bland and David Fleer (St. Louis: Chalice, 2005), 83–104.

[19]Walter Brueggemann, "The Costly Loss of Lament," in *The Psalms and the Life of Faith,* ed. P. D. Miller (Minneapolis: Fortress, 1995), 98–111; see esp. pages 103–4.

[20]Ibid., 107.

[21]Walter Brueggemann, "Covenanting as Human Vocation: The Relation of the Bible and Pastoral Care," in *The Psalms and the Life of Faith,* 150–66.

[22]See Walter Brueggemann, "The Psalms as Limit Expressions" in *Performing the Psalms,* 31–50.

[23]See John Mark Hicks, "Preaching Community Laments: Responding to Disillusionment with God and Injustice in the World," in *Performing the Psalms,* 67–82.

[24]See J. Clinton McCann Jr., "Greed, Grace, and Gratitutde: An Approach to Preaching the Psalms," in *Performing the Psalms,* 51–66, and Mark Love, "Going to Church in the Psalms: Psalm 89," 159–68 in the same volume.

Chapter 10: Psalm 99

[1]Marvin Tate observes, "The setting in worship for the kingship-of-Yahweh psalms eludes any certain conclusion and probably varied at different times in different communities." Marvin Tate, *Psalms 51–100,* WBC 20 (Dallas: Word, 1990), 507.

[2]Erhard Gerstenberger, *Psalms, Part 2, and Lamentations,* FOTL 15 (Grand Rapids: Eerdmans, 2001), 201.

[3]Tate, *Psalms 51–100,* 530.

[4]J. J. S. Perowne, *Commenting on the Psalms* (Grand Rapids: Kregel, 1989), 205.

[5]Cf. A. A. Anderson, *The Book of Psalms,* NCBC 2 (Greenwood: Attic, 1972), 693.

[6]Tate, *Psalms 51–100,* 507.

[7]Ibid., 508.

[8]R. N. Whybray, "'Their wrongdoings' in Psalm 99:8," *ZAW* 81:2 (1969): 237.

[9]Derek Kidner, *Psalms 73–150, A Commentary on Books III-V of the Psalms,* TOTC 14b (Downers Grove, Ill.: InterVarsity, 1975), 354; for another structure, see Tate, *Psalms 51–100,* 528–29: affirmation of Yahweh as King (vv. 1–5) and encouragement from salvation history (vv. 6–9).

[10]Willem VanGemeren, "Psalms," in *The Expositor's Bible Commentary,* vol. 5, ed. by Frank E. Gaebelein (Grand Rapids: Zondervan, 1991), 635; see also Frank-Lothar Hossfeld and Erich Zenger, *Psalms 2: A Commentary on Psalms 51–100,* Hermeneia, trans. Linda M. Maloney (Minneapolis: Fortress, 2005), 484.

[11]R. C. Sproul, *The Holiness of God* (Wheaton: Tyndale, 1985), 55; see all of chapter 3, pages 53–65, "The Fearful Mystery," for a helpful discussion of "holy."

[12]Ibid., 57.

[13]See Paul R. Raabe, *Psalm Structures: A Study of Psalms with Refrains,* JSOTSup 104 (Sheffield: JSOT, 1990), 202–3, for a similar approach.

[14]For a good discussion of these issues, see Frank-Lothar Hossfeld and Erich Zenger, *Psalms 2: A Commentary on Psalms 51–100,* 483–4.

[15]Other translations include: RSV: "Mighty King, lover of justice"; NEB: "He is holy, he is mighty, a king who loves justice"; REB: "The King in his might loves justice"; NJB: "holy is he and mighty! You are a king who loves justice"; NIV: "The King is mighty, he loves justice"; CEV: "You are our mighty King, a lover of fairness"; God's Word: "The king's strength is that he loves justice"; NAB: "O mighty king, lover of justice"; NKJV: "The King's strength also loves justice."

[16]See the extensive discussion of Tate, *Psalms 51–100,* 526.

[17]Other translations include: NASB: "and *yet* an avenger of their *evil* deeds"; RSV: "but an avenger of their wrongdoings"; HCSB: "but punished their misdeeds"; NLT: "but you punished them when they went wrong."

[18]C. F. Whitley, "Psalm 99:8," *ZAW* 85:2 (1974): 227.

[19]Ibid., 230.

[20]Whybray, "'Their wrongdoings' in Psalm 99:8," 238.

[21]Compare Jeremiah 32:16ff; Joel 2:13; Nahum 1:2–3; Jonah 4:2.

[22]Kidner, *Psalms 73–150,* 354.

[23]Ibid.

[24]Ibid., 355.

[25]A. W. Tozer, *The Knowledge of the Holy: The Attributes of God: Their Meaning in the Christian Life* (New York: Harper, 1961), 4.

Chapter 11: Psalms 103 and 104

[1]Derek Kidner, *Psalms 73–150: A Commentary on Books III–V of the Psalms,* TOTC (Downers Grove, Ill.: InterVarsity, 1975), 364.

[2]See, e.g., Albert M. Wolters, *Creation Regained: Biblical Basics for a Reformational Worldview,* 2nd edition (Grand Rapids: Eerdmans, 2005), 59, and the overall argument of the book.

[3]Peter W. Flint, "The '11QPs[a]–Psalter' in the Dead Sea Scrolls, Including the Preliminary Edition of 4QPs[e]," in *The Quest for Context and Meaning: Studies in Biblical Intertextuality in Honor of James A. Sanders,* ed. Craig A. Evans and Shemaryahu Talmon (Leiden: Brill, 1997), 182, 188; and Martin Abegg Jr., Peter Flint, and Eugene Ulrich, *The Dead Sea Scrolls Bible* (New York: HarperCollins, 1999), 551. In the various Qumran Psalms scrolls and fragments, Psalm 104 comes after Psalm 118 or 147, not Psalm 103 as in the MT and LXX.

[4]Arguments for the lateness of these psalms are not convincing, but dating them is precarious in any case. Scholarly opinion is quite mixed. Hans-Joachim Kraus, *Psalms 60–150: A Commentary,* trans. Hilton C. Oswald (Minneapolis: Augsburg, 1989), 290 and 298–99, argues that Psalm 103 is postexilic because of references made to "Second Isaiah" and supposed Aramaisms in the language, but that a preexilic date for Psalm 104 "is not out of the question." Erhard S. Gerstenberger, *Psalms Part 2 and Lamentations,* The Forms of Old Testament Literature, vol. 15 (Grand Rapids: Eerdmans, 2001), 227, argues that Psalm 104 is exilic-postexilic. Leslie C. Allen, *Psalms 101–150,* WBC, vol. 21 (Waco: Word, 1983), 20–21, agrees with Kraus on the postexilic dating of Psalm 103 and is inconclusive on Psalm 104. Kidner, *Psalms 73–150,* simply treats Psalm 103 as truly Davidic, which is the tendency of the present writer as well. The date of original authorship, however, does not exclude later editorial work and canonical placement of this psalm during the time of the second temple.

[5]See the very helpful analysis of the psalm superscripts (at the start) and postscripts (at the end) in Bruce K. Waltke, "Superscripts, Postscripts, or Both," *JBL* 110 (1991): 583–96, and specifically p. 593, on the issues of *Halleluiah* in Psalms 104–107. The situation is complicated. According to his analysis, not only does the Psalm 104:35 *Halleluiah* belong originally to the front of Psalm 105, but the one at the end of Psalm 106 belongs to the front of Psalm 107, so the framing effect before and after both Psalms 105 and 106 is lost anyway.

[6]Kraus, *Psalms 60–150,* 290, 297–98 crystallizes this point well.

[7]Ludwig Koehler and Walter Baumgartner, "Bless," in *The Hebrew and Aramaic Lexicon of the Old Testament,* trans. and ed. M. E. J. Richardson (Leiden: Brill, 1994), 1.160.

[8]For a rather extensive discussion of this combination, see Richard E. Averbeck, "Worshiping God in Spirit" and "Worshiping God in Truth," in *Authentic Worship:*

Scripture's Voice, Applying Its Truth, ed. Herbert W. Bateman IV (Grand Rapids: Kregel, 2002), 79–133.

[9]Individual psalms can be used communally. Kraus, *Psalms 60–150,* 290 and 297–98, recognizes the initially individual nature of Psalm 103, but also notes that it moves beyond just the communal directions with the move beyond just the psalmist's own personal experiences in vv. 6ff. He also emphasizes the individual nature of Psalm 104. Gerstenberger, *Psalms Part 2 and Lamentations,* 216, 219, 222, and 225 takes the individual focus of Psalms 103 and 104 to be distributive; that is, they refer to each individual worshiping in the communal context.

[10]For a discussion of sin and forgiveness in the Psalms, see the excursus in Willem A. VanGemeren, "Psalms," in *The Expositor's Bible Commentary,* ed. Frank E. Gaebelein, vol. 5 (Grand Rapids: Zondervan, 1991), 655–57.

[11]See the related remarks in footnote 4 above.

[12]The exact meaning of this term is hard to determine. It depends largely on the context in which it is used. See the unusually lengthy lexical discussion with references in Koehler and Baumgartner, *The Hebrew and Aramaic Lexicon of the Old Testament,* 3.1319–1321.

[13]In this context and Job 41, leviathan is a gigantic sea creature that God created to romp in the seas as a plaything (Kidner, *Psalms 73–150,* 372). The same animal inspires fear in humans because we cannot handle it. Here leviathan is not a sinister evil being, but a part of God's natural creation. He is God's plaything, his "rubber ducky," so to speak. (See William P. Brown, *Seeing the Psalms: A Theology of Metaphor* [Louisville: Westminster John Knox, 2002], 161.) In other contexts the term leviathan refers to the great serpentine evil monster that promotes evil on the earth and has background in the Ugaritic Baal myth that dates to around the time of Moses and has parallels in other ancient Near Eastern texts as well. For discussion of this leviathan as it has to do with the Bible, see Richard E. Averbeck, "Ancient Near Eastern Mythography as it relates to Historiography in the Hebrew Bible: Genesis 3 and the Cosmic Battle," in *The Future of Biblical Archaeology: Reassessing Methodologies and Assumptions,* ed. James K. Hoffmeier and Alan R. Millard, eds. (Grand Rapids: Eerdmans, 2004), 328–56.

[14]Brown, *Seeing the Psalms,* 160.

[15]Genesis 7:22 uses similar terminology (including *ruah* "spirit") for all the air-breathing animals: "Everything on dry land that had 'the breath of life' in its nostrils died" (Hebrew Hebrew *nišmat ruah hayyim,* literally "breathe of the spirit of life").

[16]See now the very good introduction to this discussion in John H. Walton, *Ancient Near Eastern Thought and the Old Testament: Introducing the Conceptual World of the Hebrew Bible* (Grand Rapids: Baker, 2006), 165–99. One of the methodological problems hampering this whole scholarly enterprise, in my opinion, is the lack of attention to the poetic effect of analogical thinking. Scholars often take poetic analogical metaphorical images used by the ancients as if they actually understood them to correspond to the physical nature of the universe in some direct sort of way, rather than as an analogy. This is true of our interpretations of ancient Near Eastern cosmogonic and cosmological texts overall, not just the Bible. A biblical example is Psalm 104:3a, where the text refers to the Lord laying "the beams of the upper rooms of his palace on the rain clouds." This does not mean that the psalmist thought there were beams in the sky, or that some kind of hard physical dome held up the waters above. The ancients were wonderful observers of nature. They knew, for example, that it did not rain unless there were clouds in the sky. Furthermore, they knew what clouds were because they knew what fog was, etc. etc. We cannot deal with this in detail here. See Averbeck, "Ancient Near Eastern Mythography," 328–37 and the literature cited there.

[17]See the very helpful summary of the data and its interpretations in Allen, *Psalms 101–150,* 28–31. For a good modern translation of the hymn with cross references to the Bible and notes, see Miriam Lichtheim, "The Great Hymn to the Aten," in *The*

Context of Scripture: Volume I, Canonical Compositions from the Biblical World, ed. William W. Hallo and K. Lawson Younger Jr. (Leiden: Brill, 1997), 44–46.

[18]See David M. Howard Jr., *The Structure of Psalms 93–100,* BJSUCSD, vol. 5 (Winona Lake: Eisenbrauns, 1997). Compare Nancy L., deClaissé-Walford, *Introduction to the Psalms: A Song from Ancient Israel* (St. Louis: Chalice Press, 2004), 99–111; Jerome F. D. Creach, *The Destiny of the Righteous in the Psalms* (St. Louis: Chalice Press, 2008), 70–79.

[19]Cited in Gordon Mursell, ed., *The Story of Christian Spirituality: Two Thousand Years, from East to West* (Minneapolis: Fortress, 2001), 173.

Chapter 12: Psalm 110

[1]The heading might also be rendered "for David" (* l'dawid*), and thereby indicate that a person wrote the psalm for David. See Eugene H. Merrill, "Royal Priesthood: An Old Testament Messianic Motif," *BSac* 150 (Jan–Mar 1993): 50–61. For a complete listing of the psalms see "Classification of the Psalms by Titles" at the end of this book.

[2]Herbert W. Bateman IV, "Psalm 110:1 and the New Testament," *BSac* 149 (Oct–Dec 1992): 489–53, specifically p. 448.

[3]Compare the parallel language of 1 Chronicles 29:23 with Psalm 110:1. See E. H. Merrill, "1 Chronicles," in *Bible Knowledge Commentary,* gen. ed. J. F. Walvoord, R. B. Zuck (Wheaton: Victor, 1985), 1:612–17. See also Bateman, "Psalm 110:1 and the New Testament," 489–53 for a detailed presentation of timeframe, speaker, and recipient of Psalm 110.

[4]For a very nice outline of the life of David and a summary of the last years of David's life, see E. H. Merrill, *Kingdom of Priests: A History of Old Testament Israel* (Grand Rapids: Baker, 1987), 248, 244.

[5]König and Gundry also appeal to 1 Kings to suggest that David wrote Psalm 110 to legitimize Solomon's kingship, which was in keeping with Nathan's oracle. E. König, *Die messianischen Weissagungen des Alten Testament* (Stuttgart: B. C. Belser, 1923), 149–50. R. H. Gundry, *The Use of the Old Testament in St. Matthew's Gospel: With Special Reference to the Messianic Hope* (Leiden: Brill, 1975), 228.

[6]Hans-Joachim Kraus, *Psalms 1–59* (Minneapolis: Fortress, 1993), 64.

[7]Pre-exilic refers to the period of time prior to Babylon's deportation of the inhabitants of Jerusalem, the dismantling of the Davidic dynasty, and the destruction of the temple in 586 B.C.E.

[8]A Canaanite example: Keret "was seated at the right hand of the mightiest Baal." See J. C. L. Gibson, *Canaanite Myths and Legends* (Edinburgh: T & T Clark, 1978), 61–62. An Egyptian example: Pharaoh Horemheb is seated at the right hand of his god, Horus. O. Keel, *The Symbolism of the Biblical World, Ancient Eastern Iconography and the Book of Psalms* (New York: Seabury, 1978), 262–63.

[9]For a discussion concerning the holy war, see R. de Vaux, "The Holy War," in *Ancient Israel: Social Institutions,* trans. J. McHugh (New York: McGraw-Hill, 1961), 1:258–267; Eugene H. Merrill, *Everlasting Dominion: A Theology of the Old Testament* (Nashville: B&H Academic, 2006), 415–17; Walter Brueggemann, *Reverberations of Faith: A Theological Handbook of Old Testament Themes* (Louisville: Westminster John Knox, 2002) 227–29; Susan Niditch, *War in the Hebrew Bible: A Study of the Ethics of Violence* (Oxford: Oxford University Press, 1995).

[10]See author's previous discussion about Assyrian warfare in chapter 6 of this volume, "Psalm 46: A Psalm of Confidence."

[11]In a similar way, the term for "footstool" is also employed for the Canaanite god "El" in Ugaritic (4 iv 29; 5 vi 12–13; 6 i 58). See Gibson, *Canaanite Myths and Legends,* xi.

[12]See Keel, *Symbolism of the Biblical World,* 293, illustration 397, cf. 403. Or see *Zondervan Illustrated Bible Backgrounds Commentary, Old Testament;* Grand Rapids: Zondervant, 2009, 4, 54. For a king using a defeated king as a footstool, see ibid, 4, 166.

[13]See J. P. J. Olivier, "The Scepter of Justice and Psalm 45:7b," *JNSL* 7 (1979): 45–54, esp. 47–49.

[14]The first phrase of this verse is difficult, as readily observed in the various English renderings. Difficulty surrounds one term, which literally means "voluntariness" and is rendered numerous ways: "will offer themselves willingly" (NRSV), "will volunteer freely" (NASB), "your people willingly follow you" (NET). Elsewhere in the Old Testament, the term is used in the context of war to describe a willingness to fight (Judg. 5:2, 9; Ex. 14:4; 15:4; 1 Sam. 17:20).

[15]For other smashing examples, see Deuteronomy 32:39 (Song of Moses); Deuteronomy 33:11 (Blessing of Moses); Psalms 18:39; 68:22, 24; Job 5:18; 26:2; and Habakkuk 3:13. For further reading see J. H. Patton, *Canaanite Parallels in the Book of Psalms* (Baltimore: John Hopkins Press, 1944), 30, 37, 41; H. H. Rowley, "Melchizedek and Zadok (Gen 14 and Ps 110)," in *Festschrift: Alfred Bertholet* (Tübingen, Germany: J. C. B. Mohr, 1950), 463–72; H. G. Jefferson, "Is Psalm 110 Canaanite?" *JBL* 73 (Sept. 1954): 152–56.

[16]Hans-Joachim Kraus, *Psalms 60–150* (Minneapolis: Augsburg, 1989), 3:345.

[17]Martin Luther, "Psalm 110," in *Luther's Works: Selected Psalms II*, vol. 13, trans. H. Richard Klann and ed. by Jaroslav Pelikan (St. Louis: Concordia, 1956), 225–348. J. J. Stewart Perowne, *The Book of Psalms: Psalms 1–72*, vol. 1 (Grand Rapids: Zondervan, 1966), 294–315. F. Delitzsch, *Psalms,* Commentary on the Old Testament, trans. James Martin (Grand Rapids: Eerdmans, reprint 1982), 10:183–85.

[18]Two proponents of this view are Elliott E. Johnson, "Hermeneutical Principles and Psalm 110," *BSac* 149 (Oct-Dec 1992): 428–37, and Walter C. Kaiser, *The Uses of the Old Testament in the New* (Chicago: Moody, 1985), 109, 131, 141.

[19]A. F. Kirkpatrick provides an early attempt to explain the psalm in this way. A. F. Kirkpatrick, *The Book of Psalms* (Cambridge: University Press, 1910), 660–65.

[20]Robert B. Chisholm Jr., "A Theology of the Psalms," in *A Biblical Theology of the Old Testament,* ed. R. B. Zuck (Chicago: Moody, 1991), 271.

[21]Like Kirkpatrick (*Psalms,* 665–71) and Delitzsch (*Psalms,* 188–96), I divide Psalm 110 into three parts. Whereas Kirkpatrick breaks his divisions as follows: vv. 1–3 (Yahweh's oracle), v. 4 (the king's priesthood), and vv. 5–7 (the battlefield), Delitzsch divides the psalm as I do above (vv. 1–2, 3–4, 5–7). Others, like Allen, divide the psalm into two sections. See Leslie C. Allen, *Psalms 101–150,* WBC 21 (Waco: Word, 1983), 79. For a fourfold structure (v. 1, promise; vv. 2–3, victory; v. 4, promise; vv. 5–7, victory) see Willem A. VanGemeren, "Psalm 110," in *Expositor's Bible Commentary,* vol. 5 (Grand Rapids: Zondervan, 1991), 696–700.

[22]D. M. Hay lists some thirty-two uses in the New Testament and some early church fathers' usage. D. M. Hay, *Glory at the Right Hand: Psalm 110 in Early Christianity,* SBLMS 18, ed. R. A. Kraft (Nashville: Abingdon, 1973), 45–47.

[23]George Buchanan argues that the first twelve chapters of Hebrews are a midrash on Psalm 110. George W. Buchanan, *To the Hebrews,* AB (Garden City: Doubleday, 1972), xxi–xxii.

[24]In Hebrews 2:5–9, the author is looking toward the Messianic world to come. See Donald R. Glenn, "Psalm 8 and Hebrews 2: A Case Study in Biblical Hermeneutics and Biblical Theology," in *Walvoord: A Tribute,* ed. Donald K. Cambell (Chicago: Moody, 1982), 39–51. While Saucy recognizes the existence of the Son's kingdom, he also recognizes a future consummation of the kingdom (Acts 1:6–8; 1 Cor. 6:9–10, 15:50; Gal. 5:21; Eph. 5:4; Col. 1:12–13). Mark Saucy, *The Kingdom of God in the Teaching of Jesus* (Nashville: W Publishing Group, 1997), 339–40. See also J. Lanier Burns, "The Future of Ethnic Israel in Romans 11," in *Dispensationalism, Israel and the Church* (ed. C. A. Blaising and D. L. Bock (Grand Rapids: Zondervan, 1992), 188–29.

[25]See also Revelation 20:10–15. First Corinthians also specifies death as an enemy, the last enemy, to be subjugated by the Son (15:26). First Corinthians, however, qualifies what "all things" does not include—i.e., God the Father is not subject to the Son (15:27–28; cf. 11:3). In addition, Clement, while commenting on much of Hebrews 1, mentions, "And again he says to him, 'Sit thou on my right hand

until I make your enemies a footstool for thy feet.' Who then are the enemies? Those who are wicked and oppose his will." *1 Clement*, 36:5–6. See also Harold W. Attridge, *Hebrews*, Hermeneia (Minneapolis: Fortress, 1989), 62.

Chapter 13: Psalm 116

[1]Claus Westermann, *Praise and Lament in the Psalms*, trans. K. Crim and R. Soulen (Atlanta: John Knox, 1981), 25.

[2]Leslie C. Allen, *Psalms 101–150*, WBC 21 (Waco: Word, 1983), 151.

[3]Westermann, *Praise and Lament*, 25.

[4]Ibid., 25.

[5]In writing this chapter in honor of John Davis, I am reminded of an incident that occurred within the first weeks at my very first teaching post: Grace Theological Seminary. In the hour before my morning Hebrew class I had been invited to the office of President Davis, that he might welcome me to the faculty. I had met Dr. Davis in passing only once before but had spent an entire semester with him in book form several years earlier during my seminary studies (*Paradise to Prison* and *Moses and the Gods of Egypt*). I was thus a bit anxious as I walked through the door of his office, imagining his numerous books would be prominently displayed along with pictures of Dr. Davis arm-in-arm with other prominent scholars. What I saw instead was ducks. Rather than the imagined books or pictures, colorful duck decoys lined the tops of his bookshelves. I learned that day that John Davis is a man as comfortable in a duck blind as in the library. Somehow I was relieved and comforted to find that he was so human.

Chapter 14: Psalm 130

[1]James Montgomery Boice, *Psalms*, 3 vols. (Grand Rapids: Baker, 1998), 3:1138.

[2]Ibid., 3:1145.

[3]Leslie C. Allen, *Psalms 101–150*, WBC 21 (Waco: Word, 1983), 219. However, some of the psalm headings themselves appear to discourage associating these songs solely with the return from Babylon (e.g., Pss. 122; 124; 127; 131; 133). According to Allen (p. 195), post-exilic dating depends on what ostensibly might be late language (two Hebrew words are found only in post-exilic contexts: that translated as "pay attention" in v. 2, cf. 1 Chr. 6:40; 7:15; and the word translated as "forgive" in v. 4, cf. Neh. 9:17; Dan. 9:9). Willem A. VanGemeren, "Psalms," in *Expositor's Bible Commentary*, ed. Frank E. Gaebelein (Grand Rapids: Zondervan, 1991), also indicates that he views "the greater awareness of sin and the need for forgiveness in the postexilic era" (5:799) as an argument for the post-exilic dating for the psalm.

[4]C. Hassell Bullock, *Encountering the Book of Psalms: A Literary and Theological Introduction* (Grand Rapids: Baker, 2001), 79. VanGemeren identifies the use of these psalms for the three annual festival processions ("Psalms," 5:769). See also, David G. Barker, "'The LORD Watches over You': A Pilgrimage Reading of Psalm 121," *BSac* 152/606 (April 1995): 164.

[5]Michael Wilcock, *The Message of Psalms 73–150: Songs for the People of God*, ed. J. A. Motyer, BST (Downers Grove, Ill.: InterVarsity, 2001), 239; see also 220.

[6]Leon J. Liebreich, "The Songs of Ascents and Priestly Blessing," *JBL* 74 (1955): 33–36.

[7]Wilcock, *The Message of Psalms 73–150*, 220.

[8]Hans-Joachim Kraus, *Psalms 60–150*, Continental Commentary, trans. Hilton C. Oswald (Minneapolis: Fortress, 1993), 465.

[9]Erhard S. Gerstenberger, *Psalms, Part 2 and Lamentations*, FOTL, vol. 15 (Grand Rapids: Eerdmans, 2001), 357. According to Allen, *Psalms 101–150*, 220, Psalm 130 is an individual complaint reused in a liturgical communal complaint.

[10]Konrad Schaefer, *Psalms*, Berit Olam Studies in Hebrew Narrative & Poetry (Collegeville, Minn.: Liturgical Press, 2001), 310.

[11]According to Allen, *Psalms 101–150,* 192, the reference is to deliverance rather than forgiveness of sins.

[12]"The expression 'full redemption' relates his favor to many different circumstances as well as the many objects of his grace" (VanGemeren, "Psalms," 5:802).

[13]"Coverdale's beautiful expression, *plenteous redemption,* adopted by AV, RV, has been happily retained in RSV; it shines very brightly against the darkness of the psalm's beginning"–Derek Kidner, *Psalms 73–150: A Commentary on Books III-V of the Psalms,* TOTC (London: InterVarsity, 1975), 447. Even the ancient Jewish Targum employs "plenteous redemption" as the translation.

[14]Bullock, *Encountering the Book of Psalms,* 93.

[15]"The psalm presupposes that the awaited positive response from God did come, as in Ps 22" (Allen, *Psalms 101–150,* 196).

[16]James Luther Mays, *Psalms,* Interpretation (Louisville: John Knox, 1994), 407.

[17]See Bullock, *Encountering the Book of Psalms,* 141–42. Cp. VanGemeren, "Psalms," 8:800. George Zemek, *Road Maps for the Psalms: Inductive Preaching Outlines Based on the Hebrew Text* (Valencia: Master's Academy International, 2006) applies vv. 1–6 to a personal and vv. 7–8 to a corporate wrestling with the realities of human sin.

[18]Kidner, *Psalms 73–150,* 446; cf. Robert Davidson, *The Vitality of Worship: A Commentary on the Book of Psalms* (Grand Rapids: Eerdmans, 1998), 424–25.

[19]Kidner, *Psalms 73–150,* 446.

Chapter 15: Psalm 135

[1]Compare v. 1 with Ps. 113:1; v. 2 with Ps. 134:1; v. 3 with Pss. 106:1; 118:1, 29; 147:1; Nah. 1:7; v. 4 with Deut. 7:6; 14:2; 26:18; Titus 2:14; 1 Pet. 2:9: v. 5 with Ex. 18:11; v. 6 with Ps. 115:3; v. 7 with Jer. 10:13; 51:16; vv. 8–12 with Ps. 136:10–22; v. 13 with Ex. 3:15; Ps. 102:12; v. 14 with Deut. 32:36; vv. 15–18 with Ps. 115:4–8; vv. 19–21 with Pss. 115:12–13; 118:2–4.

[2]For details, see Leslie C. Allen, *Psalms 101–150,* WBC 21 (Waco: Word, 1983), 225; Joseph A. Alexander, *Commentary on Psalms* (Grand Rapids: Kregel, reprint 1991), 537.

[3]These feast days included the Passover, the Feast of Weeks, and Tabernacles (Deut. 16:1–17). For regulations concerning these three festivals, see A. Cohen, *The Soncino Chumash* (London: Soncino, 1983), 1072; Alfred Edersheim, *The Temple* (Grand Rapids: Eerdmans, reprint 1972), 195–99, 208–28, 249–87.

[4]For the significance and use of "the Name" with regard to God, see Richard D. Patterson, "Joel," in *The Expositor's Bible Commentary,* ed. Frank E. Gaebelein (Grand Rapids: Zondervan, 1985), 7:255. In modern Hebrew it is still used as one of two terms to designate the Hebrew *tetragrammaton* and in expressions of wish, "If the Name is willing" (cf. Latin *Deo Volente,* "God willing").

[5]The Hebrew verb for "serve" (*'ābad*) is a common term for doing service or work. In its noun form (*'ebed*) it can refer to a servant or even a slave. In the Psalms the verb is customarily used for one who does religious service. Another term (Hebrew *shārēt*) is commonly used to depict the religious duties of the Levites and priests who served in the tabernacle and temple services (cf. Ex. 28:35, 43; 1 Chr. 16:4, 37). It often designated a person who did special secular service (Gen. 39:4; Ex. 24:13; Esther 2:2). Whether doing sacred or secular service, God's servants were to represent him well.

[6]Leland Ryken, *Words of Delight* (Grand Rapids: Baker, 1987), 168–69, observes, "Metaphor and simile are basic to poetry." Moreover, "metaphor and simile are not 'poetic devices'; they are a way of thinking and formulating reality." For the Hebrew word used here, see Richard D. Patterson, "*segullā*" in *TWOT,* ed. R. Laird Harris (Chicago: Moody, 1980), 616; Eugene Carpenter, "*segullā*" in *NIDOTTE,* ed. Willem A. VanGemeren (Grand Rapids: Zondervan, 1997), 3:224.

[7]Significantly, Peter cited Exodus 19:5–6 as being applicable likewise to those who serve Christ under the terms of the New Covenant (1 Pet. 2:9–10). As Israel was

a people whom God had redeemed out of Egypt (Ex. 19:3–4; 20:1–2), so today's believers have experienced spiritual redemption through the finished work of Christ (Eph. 1:4–8; Col. 1:14).

[8]On Jacob, the trickster, see Richard D. Patterson, "The Old Testament Use of an Archetype: The Trickster," *JETS* 42 (1999): 385–94.

[9]See further Richard D. Patterson, "The Song of Redemption," *WTJ* 57 (1995): 453–61; idem, "Victory at Sea: Prose and Poetry in Exodus 14–15," *BSac* 161 (2004): 42–54; Richard D. Patterson and Michael E. Travers, "Contours of the Exodus Motif in Jesus' Earthly Ministry," *WTJ* 66 (2004): 25–47.

[10]For thematic and verbal associations as a principle for linking scriptural passages and books together, see Umbrerto Cassuto, "The Sequence and Arrangement of the Biblical Sections," in *Biblical and Oriental Studies,* trans. Israel Abrahams (Jerusalem: Magnes Press, 1973), 1:1–6. Franz Delitzsch, *Biblical Commentary on the Psalms* (Grand Rapids: Eerdmans, 1955 [Ger. Orig., 1859–60; 2nd ed. 1867]), 1:21, cites the "principle of homogeneousness" as the means of arrangement in the Psalms: "The psalms follow one another according to their relationship as manifested by prominent external and internal marks."

[11]It is interesting in light of this standard ancient Near Eastern approach to ordering material that in the Psalms Scroll found at Qumran (11Q Psa) Psalm 135 follows Psalm 119. It also appears in other places in texts found in Cave 4. In one such text Psalm 135:12 is followed immediately by Psalm 136:23. Minor differences between the Psalms Scroll and the Masoretic Text also occur. For details, see Martin Abegg Jr., Peter Flint, and Eugene Ulrich, *The Dead Sea Scrolls Bible* (San Francisco: Harper, 1999), 567–68.

[12]This combination occurs more than two dozen times in the Scriptures: Deut. 4:34; 6:22; 7:19; 13:2–3; 26:8; 28:46; 29:3; 34:11; Neh. 9:10; Pss. 78:43; 105:27; Isa. 8:18; 20:3; Jer. 32:20-21; Dan. 4:2; 6:27; Mt. 24:24; Mk. 13:22; Jn. 4:48; Acts 4:30; 5:12; 14:3; 15:12; Rom. 15:19; 2 Cor. 12:12; Heb. 2:4.

[13]Note a still further difference in the NET handling of Nehemiah 9:10, which contains the same phraseology.

[14]Compare Psalms 106:1–3, 8, 12, 47, 48; 113:1–3, 9; 148:1–5, 7, 13–14; 149:1, 3, 9.

[15]Richard D. Patterson, "Old Testament Prophecy," in *A Complete Literary Guide to the Bible,* ed. Leland Ryken and Tremper Longman III (Grand Rapids: Zondervan, 1993), 298.

[16]Longman reminds us, "The Psalms appeal to the whole person; they demand a total response. The Psalms inform our intellect, arouse our emotions, direct our wills and stimulate our imaginations. When we read the Psalms with faith, we come away changed and not simply informed." Tremper Longman III, *How to Read the Psalms* (Downers Grove, Ill.: InterVarsity, 1988), 13.

[17]Psalm 135 is particularly apropos for a volume dedicated to John Davis, one who has lived his life serving well his institution, his students, his community, and above all his Lord.

[18]This text is a reminder that in the Old Testament the shekinah glory had descended on Mount Sinai (Ex. 24:16–17) and then had guided the Israelites all along the wilderness journey (Num. 9:15–17) to the promised land (Deut. 12:10–11). God's glory had filled both the tabernacle (Ex. 40:34–38) and the temple (1 Kings 6:11–13). Yet due to Israel's apostate heart, the shekinah left both the temple and Jerusalem (Ezek. 10:18–19; 11:22–25), not to return until the reign of the messiah among his repentant and redeemed people (Joel 3:17–21).

Chapter 16: Psalm 148

[1]J. H. Hutchison, "The Psalms and Praise," in *Interpreting the Psalms: Issues and Approaches,* ed. D. Firth and P. S. Johnson (Downers Grove, Ill.: InterVarsity, 2005), 96 n. 39; B. K. Waltke, "Psalms: Theology of," in *NIDOTTE,* 5 vols. (Grand Rapids: Zondervan, 1997), 4:1110.

²K. Vanhoozer, *Is There Meaning in This Text: The Bible, The Reader, and the Morality of Literary Knowledge* (Grand Rapids: Zondervan, 1998), 284.

³J. Clinton McCann Jr., "The Book of Psalms," in *The New Interpreter's Bible: Old Testament Survey* (Nashville: Abingdon, 2005), 205–6.

⁴Waltke, "Psalms: Theology," 4:1103.

⁵H. J. Kraus, *Psalms 60–150,* trans. H. C. Oswald (Minneapolis: Fortress, 1993), 561; McCann, "Book of Psalms," 209–10; J. Limburg, "Psalms, Book of," *ABD,* 5:526.

⁶For discussion about Psalm 89 see chapter 9 of this volume, "Psalm 89: A Community Lament," by Bernon P. Lee.

⁷C. H. Bullock, *Encountering the Book of Psalms: A Literary and Theological Introduction* (Grand Rapids: Baker, 2001), 69. As a term, "loyal love" (*hesed*) occurs 60 times in *Book V* alone. For a helpful discussion, see P. R. Bedford, "Postexilic Temple," in *Dictionary of the Old Testament Historical Books,* ed. B. T. Arnold and H. G. M. Williamson (Downers Grove, Ill.: InterVarsity, 2005), 802–6.

⁸Bullock, *Encountering the Book of Psalms.* For expressions of "wicked" and "enemies," see 138:7; 139:19–21; 140:1–5, 8–11; 141:4, 5b–10; 142:6; 143:3, 9, 12; 144:6–8, 11; 145:20; 146:9; 147:6, etc.

⁹Exilic dispersion is evident in all of its eleven other occurrences (cf. Deut. 28:25; 30:4; Neh. 1:9; Judith 5:19; 2 Macc. 1:27; Sol. 8:28; 9:2; Isa. 49:6; Jer. 15:7; 41:17; Dan. 12:2). For further discussion, see P. R. Trebilco and C. A. Evans, "Diaspora Judaism," in *Dictionary of New Testament Background,* ed. C. A. Evans and S. E. Porter (Downers Grove, Ill.: InterVarsity, 2000), 281–96. See G. H. Wilson, "The Structure of the Psalter," in *Interpreting the Psalms,* ed. Patrick Miller (Philadelphia: Fortress, 1986), 229–46, esp. 235–36.

¹⁰As a term, *hāsîd* ("godly, favored") occurs ten times in *Book V,* more than in any of the other four Books (cf. Pss. 116:15; 132:9, 16; 145:10, 13, 17; 148:14; 149:1, 5, 9); cf. *hesed* ("loyal love"), Psalms 145:8; 147:11.

¹¹McCann, "Book of Psalms," 212; emphasis added. God is addressed as the King throughout the Psalter (Pss. 5:2; 10:16; 24:7–10; 29:10; 44:4; 47:2, 7; 48:2; 68:24; 74:12; 84:3; 95:3; 98:6; 145:1; 149:2).

¹²McCann, "Book of Psalms," 208, 210.

¹³Hutchison, "The Psalms and Praise," 98.

¹⁴D. L. Smith-Christopher, *A Biblical Theology of Exile,* OBT (Minneapolis: Fortress, 2002), 72.

¹⁵J. L. Mays, *The Lord Reigns: A Theological Handbook to the Psalms* (Louisville: Westminster John Knox, 1994), 65.

¹⁶Walter Brueggemann, "The Hymn," in *Reverberations of the Faith: A Theological Handbook of Old Testament Themes* (Louisville: Westminster John Knox, 2002), 104.

¹⁷Ibid, 105.

¹⁸"Sun," in *Dictionary of Biblical Imagery,* ed. L. Ryken, J. C. Wilhoit, T. Longmann III (Downers Grove, Ill.: InterVarsity, 1998), 927.

¹⁹W. A. VanGemeren, "Psalms," in *The Expositor's Bible Commentary,* vol. 5, ed. F. E. Gabelein (Grand Rapids: Zondervan, 1991), 5:872.

²⁰G. H. Wilson, *Psalms,* NIVAC (Grand Rapids: Zondervan, 2002), 200.

²¹L. Alonso Schökel, *A Manual of Hebrew Poetics,* Subsidia Biblica 11 (Rome: Editrice Pontificio Istituto Biblico, 1988), 191. For other uses of 22-part structure, see Psalms 9–10; 25; 34; 37; 111; 112; 119; 145; Nahum 1; Proverbs 31:10–31.

²²D. L. Peterson and K. H. Richards, *Interpreting Hebrew Poetry,* ed. G. M. Tucker (Minneapolis: Fortress, 1992), 28.

²³W. P. Brown, *Seeing the Psalms: A Theology of Metaphor* (Louisville: Westminster John Knox Press, 2002), 164.

²⁴J. L. Mayes, "'Maker of Heaven and Earth': Creation in the Psalms," in *Essays in Honor of W. Sibley Towner,* ed. W. P. Brown, S. D. McBride Jr. (Grand Rapids: Eerdmans, 2000), 86.

²⁵M. A. Grisanti, s.v. "Sea," in *NIDOTTE,* 4:464; J. Bergman/M. Ottosson, s.v. "Earth," in *TDOT,* 1:389, 394, 397.

[26]O. Keel, *The Symbolism of the Biblical World: Ancient Near Eastern Iconography and the Book of Psalms,* tran. T. J. Hallett (Winona Lake: Eisenbrauns, 1997), 30; see E. C. Lucas, "Cosmology," in *Dictionary of the Old Testament: Pentateuch,* ed. T. Desmond Alexander, David W. Baker (Downers Grove, Ill.: InterVarsity, 2003), 137; J. A. Soggin, "Heaven," in *TLOT,* 3:1369; D. Rudman, "The Use of Water Imagery in the Descriptions of Sheol," *ZAW* 113 (2001): 240–44; T. J. Lewis, s.v. "Dead, Abode of the," *ABD,* 2:101–105.

[27]M. Ottosson, s.v. "Earth," in *TDOT,* 1:394.

[28]*HALOT,* 1145; see BDB 901–2; *HALOT,* 1145–46. For further discussion, see M. L. Süring, *The Horn-Motif in the Hebrew Bible and Related Ancient Near Eastern Literature and Iconography* (Berrien Springs: Andrews University Press, 1998).

[29]H. J. Kraus, *Psalms 60–150: A Commentary,* trans. H. C. Oswald (Minneapolis: Augsburg, 1989), 564. For the view of "horn" as the expected messiah in Psalm 148:14, see "Horn," in *Dictionary of Biblical Imagery,* 400.

[30]L. Allen, *Psalms 101–150,* WBC 21 (Nashville: Thomas Nelson, 2002), 394. HCSB translates the phrase literally, but takes a figurative view (p. 1059).

[31]*HALOT,* 1146; cf. BDB 927, s.v. Hiph. 1f; cf. Qal 2b. Dictionaries or lexicons list meanings in verbs according to these conjugations; qal-simple meaning; niphal is passive or reflexive; piel is intensive; pual is intensive passive; hiphil is causative; hophal is causative passive.

[32]For discussion about such a relationship between God and his people see chapter 6, "Psalm 46: A Psalm of Confidence," by Herbert W. Bateman IV.

[33]McCann, "Book of Psalms," 209.

[34]Ibid.

[35]R. W. Klein, *Israel in Exile: A Theological Interpretation* (Philadelphia: Fortress, 1979), 1–8.

[36]W. Brueggemann, "Exile," in *Reverberations of Faith,* 70.

[37]Waltke, in *NIDOTTE,* 4:1109; G. H. Wilson, "A First Century CE Date for the Closing of the Hebrew Psalter?" in *Haim M. I. Geraryahu Memorial Volume* (Jerusalem: World Jewish Bible Center, 1990), 136–43.

[38]G. Wenham, "Towards a Canonical Reading of the Psalms," in *Canon and Biblical Interpretation,* SHS, ed. C. G. Bartholomew and A. C. Thiselton (Grand Rapids: Zondervan, 2006), 348.

[39]Bullock, *Encountering the Psalms,* 69; emphasis added.

[40]Brueggemann, "Hymn," 105.

[41]Ibid. For further discussion, see T. E. Fretheim, "Nature's Praise of God," in *God and World in the Old Testament: A Relational Theology of Creation* (Nashville: Abingdon, 2005), 249–68.

Chapter 17: Applying the Psalms in the Christian Life

[1]John Goldingay, *Psalms,* vol. 1 of Baker Commentary on the Old Testament, ed. Tremper Longman III (Grand Rapids: Baker, 2006), 50. Other examples are cited that focus on worship and praise.

[2]See Dave Bland and David Fleer, eds., *Performing the Psalms* (St. Louis: Chalice Press, 2005), especially Walter Brueggemann, "Psalms in Narrative Performance," 9–29.

[3]"Secret of the Psalms," www.spellmaker.com/psalms.htm.

[4]From the Constantine Papas interview in "Music of the Psalms: Four Great Traditions," an episode of The Spirit of Things radio program of ABC Radio National, accessed in April 2010 at http://abc.net.au/rn/spiritofthings/stories/2006/1534298.htm.

[5]See Nancy deClaissé-Walford, *Introduction to the Psalms: A Song from Ancient Israel* (St. Louis: Chalice Press, 2004).

[6]Gerald H. Wilson, "Understanding the Purposeful Arrangement of Psalms in the Psalter: Pitfalls and Promise," in *The Shape and Shaping of the Psalter,* JSOTSup 159, ed, J. Clinton McCann (Sheffield: JSOT, 1993), 50.

[7]David M. Howard Jr. "Editorial Activity in the Psalter: A State-of-the-Field Survey," in *The Shape and Shaping of the Psalter,* 70. His comment appears as a postscript added in May 1991. Howard remained hopeful even after serious critical comments of Norman Whybray, who questioned and denied purposeful arrangements of the Psalms (Whybray, *Reading the Psalms as a Book* [Sheffield, Eng.: Sheffield Academic, 1996]). Howard concludes, "In sum, Whybray is to be credited with shining a critical light on this area of research and presenting some valid challenges, but his is by no means the last word." See Howard's review of Whybray, *Reading the Psalms* in *RBL* (April 15, 1998).

[8]Christopher Seitz, *Word Without End: The Old Testament as Abiding Theological Witness* (Grand Rapids: Eerdmans, 1998), 158–67. Bruce Waltke, "Psalms," in *New International Dictionary of Old Testament Theology and Exegesis,* ed. W. VanGemeren (Grand Rapids: Eerdmans, 1998), 1108–11.

[9]For a discussion of Psalms 1 and 2, see Glen Taylor's contribution to this volume: chapter 4, "Psalms 1 & 2: A Gateway into the Psalter and Messianic Images of Restoration for David's Dynasty."

[10]Theme Discovery using the NASB 95 edition reports two hundred fifty-five occurrences for *Elohim* and 308 for *Yahweh.* TLOT I, 116 reports 365 for *'elōhîm,* while TLOT 2, 523 notes 695 occurrences of YHWH in the Psalms.

[11]English Bible translations traditionally translate the divine name Yahweh by LORD with a regular capital letter L and small caps ORD. Lord without small caps translates the Hebrew word *'adōnai,* meaning lord.

[12]For a discussion of Psalm 19, see David C. Deuel's contribution to this volume: chapter 5, "Psalm 19: Proclaim the King's Glory, for His Law Is Perfect."

[13]The complex and convincing research is nicely summarized and illustrated by Mark. D. Futato, *Interpreting the Psalms: An Exegetical Handbook,* HOTE, ed. David M. Howard Jr. (Grand Rapids: Kregel, 2007). See especially the section "The Relationship between Refuge and Kingship," 101–3.

[14]Taking a cue from Satan's temptations of Jesus in Matthew 4 and observing Satan's (mis)use of Psalm 91 to test the sonship of Jesus, we have to leave the reigning of God open to temptation for someone to misunderstand it. Apart from the Deuteronomic controls (the SHEMA, where Jesus counteracts with Deuteronomy passages in context), the psalms could inaugurate God's full rule now. We know we are applying the Psalms on the edge if inauguration of Yahweh's rule looks like it is/should fully be now. Leave room for temptation and be ready for Zion-based, Yahweh-only focused presence and allegiance as the ultimate fulfillment of God's reign.

[15]C. S. Lewis, *Reflections on the Psalms* (Orlando: Harvest, reprint 1986), 45.

[16]Research in classifying emotions in music demonstrated the need for multi-labels. See *Some Issues on Detecting Emotions in Music* http://www.springerlink.com/content/4qyxvj5bkh9c53xp/ accessed November 16, 2007, and *Multi-label Classification of Emotion in Music* http://www.mir.uncc.edu/docs/papers/04_Multi-label%20classification%20of%20emotions%20in%20music.pdf accessed November 16, 2007. Developing a retrieval system for the abundance of music available motivated the researchers. Their ongoing research contains many caveats severely, but not completely, limiting a wholesale adoption for functionally classifying the psalms. The major limitation is that the classification is built by and for Western culture users. For the most promising cognitive-linguistics based semantic domains for the vocabulary of the Psalms see Reinier de Blois, *Lexicography and Cognitive Linguistics: Hebrew Metaphors from a Cognitive Perspective,* 2002 SBL paper, published in *DavarLogos* 3, no. 2 (2004): 97–116. Online at dialnet.unirioja.es/servlet/fichero_artic ulo?codigo=2313980&orden=84210 accessed April 2010.

[17]N. M. Weinberger, "'Elevator Music': More than It Seems," *MuSICA Research Notes,* 2.2 (Fall 1995); http://www.music.ucil.edu.

[18]The twenty resources mentioned at http://www.calvin.edu/worship/psalms/recordings.php would be a good place to begin. The selection includes jazz, chants, and contemporary music. The music of the Australian and New Zealand group "Sons

of Korah" is specifically designed and tastefully executed as "an impacting musical journey into the spirit and world of the psalms." See: http://www.sonsofkorah.com/.

[19]Raymond Battegay, "New Perspectives on Acting-out," *JGPPS 42*, no. 2 (1990).

[20]Wilson, "Understanding the Purposeful Arrangement of Psalms in the Psalter," 42–51.

Chapter 18: The Psalms outside the Pulpit

[1]Rowland E. Prothero, *The Psalms in Human Life* (2d ed. (New York: John Murray, 1905), 14.

[2]In two chapters on the influence of the psalms on the lives and writings of dozens of religious leaders, scientists, writers, philanthropists, missionaries, and 'ordinary folk' during the eighteenth and nineteenth centuries, Prothero calls special attention to a number of remarkable mothers and nurses. Ibid., 237–329.

[3]Ibid., 289.

[4]Ibid.

[5]Ibid., 293. David Livingston (1813–73) won a New Testament for memorizing Psalm 119 when he was nine years old (ibid., 312).

[6]Ibid.

[7]Ibid., 286.

[8]Charlotte M. Yonge, "The Heir of Redclyffe," in *Questions on the Psalms* (London: Walter Smith, 1881), 6.

[9]Ibid.,10–11.

[10]Ibid., 2.

[11]Ibid., 3

[12]Jane Johnson, *Talks with the Children or Questions and Answers for Family Use or First-Day Schools* (Philadelphia: Ellwood Zell, 1827).

[13]Ibid.

[14]Ibid.

[15]Ibid.

[16]Maria Hack, *Harry Beaufoy; or, The Pupil of Nature* (London: Harvey and Darton, 1821).

[17]A. L. O. E., *The Wanderer in Africa: A Tale Illustrating the Thirty-Second Psalm* (Edinburgh: Gall & Inglis, 1867).

[18]These words are taken from a prayer composed for the first Anglican Book of Common Prayer in 1549: "Blessed Lord, who caused all holy Scriptures to be written for our learning: grant us so to hear them, read, mark, learn, and inwardly digest them, that we may embrace and ever hold fast the blessed hope of everlasting life, which you have given us in our Savior Jesus Christ; who lives and reigns with you and the Holy Spirit, one God, for ever and ever. Amen."

[19]The largest number of quotations in her annotations are from Johann Gottfried Herder's *Vom Geist der hebräishen Poesie*, vol. 2, 1783. The next most used source was George Heinrich von Ewald's *Die Propheten des Alten Bundes*. See Florence Nightingale, *Florence Nightingale's Spiritual Journey: Biblical Annotations, Sermons and Journal Notes*, ed. Lynn McDonald, Collected Works of Florence Nightingale, vol. 2 (Waterloo: Wilfred Laurier, 2001), 34, 94.

[20]McDonald notes: "The first date corresponds with a particularly low period in Nightingale's life, after Sidney Herbert's death and with Clough's death expected soon; the third and fourth were periods with heavy preoccupation with her mother's care, the fourth notably soon after her father's death." Ibid., 144.

[21]Prothero, *The Psalms in Human Life*, 317.

[22]Susan Allibone, *Psalm CXIX. Amplified and Illustrated by Other Scriptures*, 2d ed. (Philadelphia: American Sunday-School Union, 1855), 22.

[23]C. F. & E. C. [Catherine Foster and Elizabeth Colling], *New Metrical Version of the Psalms of David* (London: Simpkim, Marshall, 1838).

[24]Ibid., 280–83. In the copy of the *New Metrical Version of the Psalms of David* housed in Harvard College Library, an unknown hand has attributed both versions of this poem to C. F. (Catherine Foster).

[25]Elizabeth Barrett Browning, "The Sleep," stanza one, as cited in Prothero, *The Psalms in Human Life*, 291.

[26]Browning, "The Measure," stanza two, as cited in Prothero, *The Psalms in Human Life*, 29.

[27]Harriet Beecher Stowe, "Resting of God," was published first in 1855 in a collection of hymns by her brother, Henry Ward Beecher, ed., *Plymouth Collection of Hymns and Tunes*, as cited in Kenneth W. Osbeck, *101 More Hymn Stories* (Grand Rapids: Kregel, 1985), 79.

[28]Joana Julia Greswell, *Grammatical Analysis of the Hebrew Psalter* (Oxford: J. Parker, 1873).

[29]For a full treatment of Julia Smith and her family, see Susan J. Shaw, *A Religious History of Julia Evelina Smith's 1876 Translation of the Holy Bible: Doing More Than Any Man Has Ever Done* (San Francisco: Mellon Research University Press, 1993).

[30]Julia Evelina Smith, *The Holy Bible: Containing the Old and New Testaments* (Hartford: American Publishing Company, 1876).

[31]Helen Spurrell, *The Old Testament Scripture. A Translation of the Old Testament Scriptures from the Original Hebrew* (London: James Nisbet, 1885).

[32]Caroline Fry, *The Scripture Reader's Guide to the Devotional Use of the Holy Scriptures* (London: James Nisbet, 1828), Section the Seventh.

[33]Ibid.

[34]Ibid.

[35]Ibid.

[36]Ibid.

[37]Ibid.

[38]Ibid.

[39]Ibid,

[40]Ibid., Section the Eighth.

[41]Ibid.

[42]Mary Anne SchimmelPenninck, *Biblical Fragments* (London: Ogle, Duncan, and Co., 1821).

[43]Mary Anne SchimmelPenninck, *Psalms According to the Authorized Version; With Prefatory Titles, and Tabular Index of Scriptural References, From the Port Royal Authors, Marking the Circumstances and Chronologic Order of Their Composition. To Which is Added, An Essay On the Psalms, and their Spiritual Application* (London: J. & A. Arch, 1825).

[44]SchummelPenninck, *Biblical Fragments*, 75.

[45]Ibid.

[46]Ibid.

[47]See Lissa M. Wray Beal's discussion of three of SchimmelPenninck's christological interpretive methods: prophetic-christological, canonical christological, and ecclesiological-christological in "Mary Anne SchimmelPenninck: A Nineteenth-Century Woman as Psalm-Reader," in *Recovering Nineteenth-Century Women Interpreters of the Bible*, SBL Symposium Series 38, ed. Christiana de Groot and Marion Ann Taylor (Atlanta: Society of Biblical Literature, 2007), 90.

[48]SchimmelPenninck, *Biblical Fragments*, 38.

[49]Sarah Trimmer, *A Help to the Unlearned in the Study of the Holy Scriptures: Being an attempt to explain the Bible in a familiar way* (London: F.C. & J. Rivington, 1805); Mary Cornwallis, *Observations, Critical, Explanatory, and Practical, on the Canonical Scriptures*, 4 vols. (London: Baldwin, Craddock, & Joy, 1820).

[50]Charles Spurgeon, *The Treasury of David: an Original Exposition of the Book of Psalms; a Collection of Illustrative Extracts from the Whole Range of Literature; a Series of Homiletical Hints on Almost Every Verse; and Lists of Writers on Each Psalm*, 7 vols. (London: Marshall Brothers, 1869–1885).

[51]Mrs. Thompson, *Family Commentary on the New Testament, A Practical Illustration of the Book of Psalms,* 2 vols (York: Thomas Wilson and Sons, 1826), vi.

[52]Thompson, vol. 1, 4.

[53]Ibid., 30.

[54]Ibid., 16.

[55]Ibid., 32.

[56]Ibid., 54.

[57]Ibid.

[58]Ibid., 206.

[59]Ibid., 2.

[60]Ibid., 3,

[61]Ibid.

[62]Ibid.

[63]Ibid., 238.

[64]Ibid. 16–17.

[65]Charles Spurgeon, *Commenting and Commentaries* (1876; reprint, Ada: Baker, 1981).

Chapter 19: The Psalms and Their Influence on Christian Worship

[1]See James F. White, *A Brief History of Christian Worship* (Nashville: Abingdon, 1993). Benedict of Nursia, in the sixth century, noted that "the whole psalter, of a hundred and fifty psalms, [should] be sung every week,... [O]ur holy fathers bravely recited the psalter in a single day; God grant that we, their degenerate sons, may do the like in seven." See "The Rule of Saint Benedict" in *Western Asceticism,* ed. Owen Chadwick (Philadelphia: Westminster, 1958), 309.

[2]See Claus Westermann, *Praise and Lament in the Psalms,* trans. Keith R. Crim and Richard N. Soulen (Atlanta: John Knox, 1981); also see Allen Ross, *Recalling the Hope of Glory: Biblical Worship from the Garden to the New Creation* (Grand Rapids: Kregel, 2006).

[3]For a discussion of Psalm 135, see Richard D. Patterson's contribution to this volume, chapter 15, entitled, "Psalm 135: Expectations of a Servant."

[4]See W. O. E. Oesterly, *A Fresh Approach to the Psalms* (New York: Scribners, 1937).

[5]I have particularly been helped by the insights of David P. Nelson, "Voicing God's Praise: The Use of Music in Worship," in *Authentic Worship: Hearing Scripture's Voice, Applying Its Truths,* ed. Herbert W. Bateman IV (Grand Rapids: Kregel, 2002), 145–70.

[6]See John Eaton, *The Psalms Come Alive: Capturing the Voice and Art of Israel's Songs* (Downers Grove, Ill.: InterVarsity, 1984), 1–9.

[7]See the very helpful essay by Richard C. Leonard, "Psalms in Biblical Worship," in *The Biblical Foundations of Christian Worship,* ed. Robert E. Webber (Nashville: Star Song, 1993); also see Paul R. House, *Old Testament Theology* (Downers Grove, Ill.: InterVarsity, 1998).

[8]Geoffrey Wainwright, *Doxology: The Praise of God in Worship, Doctrine, and Life* (New York: Oxford University Press, 1980), 200; see "Music and Singing in the Liturgy" in *The Study of Liturgy,* ed. Cheslyn Jones, Geoffrey Wainwright, and Edward Yarnold, (New York: Oxford, 1978), 440–65.

[9]C. S. Lewis, *Reflections on the Psalms* (Orlando: Harvest, reprint 1986), 2.

[10]Ibid., 90ff.

[11]See Ralph P. Martin, *Worship in the Early Church* (Grand Rapids: Eerdmans, 1964).

[12]For a discussion of Psalm 148, see Andrew J. Schmutzer's contribution to this volume, chapter 16, entitled, "Psalm 148: The Surprising Score of a Cosmic Anthem."

[13]See Patrick Henry Reardon, *Christ in the Psalms,* Ben Lomond (Calif.: Conciliar, 2000); G. W. H. Lampe, "The Evidence in the New Testament for Early Creeds, Catechisms and Liturgy," *Expository Times* 71 (1960): 359–63; and Martin Hengel, "Hymn and Christology," *StudBib* 3 (1978): 173–97.

[14]See Ferdinard Hahn, *The Worship of the Early Church* (Philadelphia: Fortress, 1973).

[15]C. F. D. Moule, *Worship in the New Testament* (Bramcote, Eng.: Grove Books, 1977).

[16]See William D. Maxwell, *An Outline of Christian Worship* (London: Oxford, 1939); Donald Coggen, *The Prayers of the New Testament* (New York: Harper, 1967); and Gregory Dix, *The Shape of Liturgy* (London: Dacre, 1945).

[17]See Maxwell, *Outline of Christian Worship,* 14; Cyril Richardson, *Early Christian Fathers* (Philadelphia: Westminster, 1953).

[18]Eusebius, cited by Mary Berry, "Psalmody," in *The New Westminster Dictionary of Liturgy and Worship,* ed. J. G. Davies (Philadelphia: Westminster, 1986), 450–51.

[19]Berry, "Psalmody," 451.

[20]Ibid.

[21]Athanasius, cited in Ibid.

[22]See Hughes Oliphant Old, *The Patristic Roots of Reformed Worship* (Zurich: Theologischer Verlag Zurich, 1925); Timothy George, *Theology of the Reformers* (Nashville: Broadman, 1988).

[23]Martin Luther, *The Works of Martin Luther* (St. Louis: Concordia, 1973), 3:356.

[24]For a discussion of Psalm 46, see Herbert W. Bateman's contribution to this volume, chapter 6, entitled, "Psalm 46: A Psalm of Confidence."

[25]See James Hastings Nichols, *Corporate Worship in the Reformed Tradition* (Philadelphia: Westminster, 1968).

[26]See Bruno Burki, "The Reformed Tradition in Continental Europe: Switzerland, France, and Germany," in *The Oxford Dictionary of Christian Worship,* ed. Geoffrey Wainwright and Karen B. Westerfield Tucker (Oxford: Oxford University Press, 2006), 436–62.

[27]Benjamin Keach, *The Breach Repaired in God's Worship* (London: Hancock, 1691).

[28]See N. A. Woychuk, *Singing Psalms with Isaac Watts* (Seattle: SMF, 2004).

[29]See Robert E. Webber, *Worship Old and New* (Grand Rapids: Zondervan, 1982).

[30]See Paul Basden, *Exploring the Worship Spectrum: Six Views* (Grand Rapids: Zondervan, 2004); D. A. Carson, *Becoming Conversant with the Emerging Church* (Grand Rapids: Zondervan, 2005); D. A. Carson, ed., *Worship by the Book* (Grand Rapids: Zondervan, 2002); Marva Dawn, *How Shall We Worship? Biblical Guidelines for the Worship Wars* (Carol Stream, Ill.: Tyndale, 2003); Donald Hustad, *Jubilate and Church Music in the Evangelical Traditions* (Carol Stream, Ill.: Hope, 1981); Elmer Towns, *Putting an End to Worship Wars* (Nashville: Broadman & Holman, 1997); and Robert E. Webber, *Planning Blended Worship* (Nashville: Abingdon, 1998).

[31]See Robert G. Rayburn, *O Come, Let Us Worship: Corporate Worship in the Evangelical Church* (Grand Rapids: Baker, 1980).

[32]Lewis, *Reflections on the Psalms,* 94–98.

[33]Ibid. These reflections greatly influenced Webber, Carson, Basden, Nelson, Dawn, Rayburn, and Hustad.

Chapter 20: The Psalms in the Hands of Preachers and Teachers

[1]Caroline Fry, *The Scripture Reader's Guide to the Devotional Use of the Holy Scriptures* (London: James Nisbet, 1828), Section the Seventh.

[2]Walter Brueggemann, *The Message of the Psalms: A Theological Commentary* (Minneapolis: Augsburg, 1984), 9.

³Jeffrey Arthurs, *Preaching with Variety: How to Re-create the Dynamics of Biblical Genres* (Grand Rapids: Kregel, 2007), 39.

⁴Haddon Robinson, "Set Free from the Cookie Cutter: How the Text Can Form the Sermon," in *The Art and Craft of Biblical Preaching,* ed. Haddon Robinson and Craig Brian Larson (Grand Rapids: Zondervan, 2005), 325.

⁵Jeffrey Arthurs, *Preaching with Variety,* 45. See also: Jeffrey Arthurs, "Creative Doorways into a Psalm and Sermon: It Takes Imagination, not Just Analysis, to Recreate the Impact of a Psalm," (Part One), http://preachingtoday.com/skills/article_print.html?id=16840.

⁶J. Clinton McCann Jr. and James C. Howell, *Preaching the Psalms* (Nashville: Abingdon, 2001), 51.

⁷Arthurs, "Creative Doorways into a Psalm and Sermon."

⁸In keeping with the design of developing an experience for those present for the sermonic event, listeners may be referred to as participants.

⁹Charles Denison, *The Artist's Way of Preaching* (Louisville: Westminster/John Knox, 2006), 52.

¹⁰Walter Brueggemann, as quoted in McCann and Howell, *Preaching the Psalms,* 51.

¹¹McCann and Howell, *Preaching the Psalms,* 51.

¹²Ibid., 53.

¹³Gordon D. Fee and Douglas Stuart, *How to Read the Bible for All It's Worth: A Guide to Understanding the Bible* (Grand Rapids: Zondervan, 2003), 207.

¹⁴McCann and Howell, *Preaching the Psalms,* 69.

¹⁵Greg Parsons, "Guidelines for Understanding and Proclaiming the Psalms," *BSac* 147 (1990): 185–86.

¹⁶Arthurs, "Creative Doorways into a Psalm and Sermon."

Selective Bibliography for Interpreting and Preaching the Psalms

Naturally, numerous works exist that are helpful for interpreting, teaching, and preaching the psalms, so our list below is a mere suggestion of some works that we feel are good sources for studying the Psalms.

Current Status of Research

Enns, Peter. *Poetry and Wisdom.* IBR Bibliographies 3. Grand Rapids: Baker, 1997.

Howard, David M., Jr. "The Psalms and Current Study." *Interpreting the Psalms: Issues and Approaches,* 23–40. Edited by David Firth and Philip S. Johnston. Downers Grove, Ill.: InterVarsity, 2005.

———. "Recent Trends in Psalms Study." *The Face of Old Testament Studies,* 329–68. Grand Rapids: Baker, 1999.

Kuntz, J. Kenneth. "Engaging the Psalms: Gains and Trends in Recent Research." *Currents in Research: Biblical Studies* 2 (1994): 77–106.

Introductions

Bullock, C. Hassell. *Encountering the Book of Psalms: A Literary and Theological Introduction.* Grand Rapids: Baker, 2001.

DeClaissé-Walford, Nancy L. *Introduction to the Psalms: A Song from Ancient Israel.* St. Louis: Chalice, 2004.

Estes, Daniel J. *Handbook on the Wisdom Books and Psalms.* Grand Rapids: Baker Academic, 2005.

Lucas, Ernest. *Exploring the Old Testament: A Guide to the Psalms and Wisdom Literature.* Downers Grove, Ill.: InterVarsity, 2004.

Interpreting the Psalms

Bellinger, W. H. *Psalms: Reading and Studying the Book of Praises.* Peabody: Hendrickson, 1990.

Bland, Dave and David Fleer, eds. *Performing the Psalms.* St. Louis: Chalice, 2005.

Brown, William P. *Seeing the Psalms: A Theology of Metaphor.* Louisville: Westminster John Knox, 2002.

Eaton, J. H. *The Psalms Come Alive: Capturing the Voice and Art of Israel's Songs.* Downers Grove, Ill.: InterVarsity, 1984.

Futato, Mark D. *Interpreting the Psalms: An Exegetical Handbook,* Handbooks for Old Testament Exegesis. Edited by David M. Howard. Grand Rapids: Kregel, 2007.

Gillingham, S. E. *The Poems and Psalms of the Hebrew Bible.* Oxford: Oxford University Press, 1994.

Lewis, C. S. *Reflections on the Psalms.* New York: Harcourt, Brace, Jovanovich, 1958.

Longman, Tremper. *How to Read the Psalms.* Downers Grove: InterVarsity, 1988.

McCann, J. Clinton, ed. *The Shape and Shaping of the Psalter.* JSOTSup 159. Sheffield, Eng.: Sheffield Academic, 1993.

Miller, Patrick D. *Interpreting the Psalms.* Philadelphia: Fortress, 1986.

Theology of the Psalms

Brueggemann, Walter. *The Message of the Psalms: A Theological Commentary.* Minneapolis: Augsburg, 1984.

Chisholm, Robert. "A Theology of the Psalms." *A Biblical Theology of the Old Testament,* 257–304. Edited by R. B. Zuck. Chicago: Moody, 1991.

Kraus, Hans-Joachim. *Theology of the Psalms.* Minneapolis: Augsburg, 1986.

Mays, James L. *The Lord Reigns: A Theological Handbook to the Psalms.* Louisville: Westminster/John Knox, 1994.

McCann, J. Clinton. *A Theological Introduction to the Book of Psalms: Psalms as Torah.* Nashville: Abingdon, 1993.

Travers, Michael. *Encountering God in the Psalms.* Grand Rapids: Kregel, 2003.

Teaching and Preaching the Psalms

Howell, James, and Clinton McCann. *Preaching the Psalms.* Nashville: Abingdon, 2001.

Mays, James L. *Teaching and Preaching the Psalms.* Edited by Patrick Millar and Gene Tucker. Louisville: Westminster John Knox, 2006.

Parsons, Greg. "Guidelines for Understanding and Proclaiming the Psalms." *BSac* 147 (1990): 169–87.

Commentaries

Blaising, Craig A. and Carmen S. Hardin, eds. *Psalms 1-50.* Old Testament Vol. 7. Ancient Christian Commentary on Scripture. Downers Grove, Ill.: InterVarsity, 2008.

Goldingay, John. *Psalms.* Vol. 1, 1-41; vol. 2, 42–89; vol. 3, 90–150. Baker Commentary on the Old Testament Wisdom and Psalms. Edited by Tremper Longman III. Grand Rapids: Baker Academic, 2006.

Hilber, John W. *Psalms.* Edited by John H. Walton. Vol. 5 of Zondervan Illustrated Bible Background Commentary. Grand Rapids: Zondervan, 2009.

Kidner, Derek. *Psalms 1-72* and *Psalms 73-150.* Tyndale Old Testament Commentary. Downers Grove, Ill.: InterVarsity, 1973, 1975.

Mays, James L. *Psalms.* Interpretation: A Bible Commentary for Teaching and Preaching. Louisville: John Knox, 1994.

McCann, J. Clinton. *The Book of Psalms: Introduction, Commentary, and Reflections.* New Interpreter's Bible 4. Nashville: Abingdon, 1996.

Ross, Allen P. "Psalms." *The Bible Knowledge Commentary: Old Testament,* 779–899. Edited by John F. Walvoord and Roy B. Zuck. Wheaton, Ill.: Victor Books, 1985.

VanGemeren, Willem. "Psalms." *Expositors Bible Commentary,* volume 5, 3–880. Edited by Frank E. Gaebelein. Grand Rapids: Zondervan, 1991.

Wesselschmidt, Quentin F. *Psalms 51-150.* Old Testament Vol. 8. Ancient Christian Commentary on Scripture. Downers Grove, Ill.: InterVarsity, 2007.

Wilcock, Michael. *The Message of the Psalms 1–72* and *The Message of the Psalms 73–150.* Bible Speaks Today. Downers Grove, Ill.: InterVarsity, 2001.

Wilson, Gerald H. *Psalms.* Vol. 1, NIV Application Commentary: From Biblical Text to Contemporary Life. Grand Rapids: Zondervan, 2002.

For other commentaries, see Tremper Longman III, *Old Testament Commentary Survey,* 4th ed. Grand Rapids: Baker, 2007.

Psalms Discussed

CPSIA information can be obtained at www.ICGtesting.com
Printed in the USA
BVOW011841170113

310927BV00012B/217/P